Essentials of

VISUAL BASIC® 6.0 PROGRAMMING

David I. Schneider
University of Maryland

An Alan R. Apt Book

Prentice Hall, Upper Saddle River, New Jersey 07458

Library of Congress Cataloging-in-Publication Data

Schneider, David I.
    Essentials of Visual Basic 6.0 Programming
        David I. Schneider
        p. cm.
    Includes index.
    ISBN: 0-13-012720-5
    1. BASIC (Computer program language). 2. Microsoft QuickBASIC.
    2. Microsoft Visual BASIC. I. Title

Publisher: *Alan Apt*
Acquisitions Editor: *Laura Steele*
Production Editor: *Rhodora Penaranda*
Editor-in-Chief: *Marcia Horton*
Assistant Vice President of Production and Manufacturing: *David W. Riccardi*
Managing Editor: *Eileen Clark*
Manufacturing Manager/Buyer: *Trudy Pisciotti*
Cover Director: *Heather Scott*
Cover Designer: *Tamara Newnam-Cavallo*
Editorial Assistant: *Kate Kaibni*
Interior Designer: *Judith Matz-Coniglio*
Compositor: *Rebecca Evans & Associates*

©1999 by Prentice-Hall, Inc.
Upper Saddle River, NJ 07458

The author and publisher of this book have used their best efforts in preparing this book.
These efforts include the development, research, and testing of the theories and programs
to determine their effectiveness. The author and publisher make no warranty of any kind,
expressed or implied, with regard to these programs or the documentation contained in
this book. The author and publisher shall not be liable in any event for incidental or consequential damages in connection with, or arising out of, the furnishing, performance, or
use of these programs.

TRADEMARK INFORMATION
IBM is a registered trademark of International Business Machines Corporation.
Hercules is a trademark of Hercules Computer Technology.
Microsoft is a registered trademark of Microsoft Corporation.

Printed in the United States of America.

10 9 8 7 6 5 4 3 2 1

ISBN 0-13-012720-5

Prentice-Hall International (UK) Limited, London
Prentice-Hall of Australia Pty. Limited, Sydney
Prentice-Hall Canada Inc., Toronto
Prentice-Hall Hispanoamericana, S.A., Mexico
Prentice-Hall of India Private Limited, New Delhi
Prentice-Hall of Japan, Inc., Tokyo
Simon & Schuster Asia Pte. Ltd., Singapore
Editora Prentice-Hall do Brasil, Ltda., Rio de Janeiro

PREFACE

This text presents the fundamentals of programming in Microsoft® Visual Basic® 6.0 on IBM PC compatible computers.

Due to its extraordinary combination of power and ease of use, Visual Basic has become the tool of choice for developing user-friendly Windows applications in the business world. In addition, Microsoft has made Visual Basic the language used to take full control of its best selling Windows applications such as Microsoft Word, Access, and Excel. Not only is Visual Basic the state of the art in Basic programming, but Visual Basic is fun! Learning Visual Basic was very exciting to me, and most students have similar reactions when they see how easy it is to build powerful visual interfaces using it.

My objectives when writing this text were as follows:

1. To develop focused chapters. Rather than covering many topics superficially, I concentrate on important subjects and cover them thoroughly.

2. To use examples and exercises with which students can relate, appreciate, and feel comfortable. I frequently use real data. Examples do not have so many embellishments that students are distracted from the programming techniques illustrated.

3. To produce compactly written text that students will find both readable and informative. The main points of each topic are discussed first and then the peripheral details are presented as comments.

4. To teach good programming practices that are in step with modern programming methodology. Problem solving techniques and structured programming are discussed early and used throughout the book.

5. To provide insights into the major applications of computers.

Unique and Distinguishing Features

Exercises for Most Sections. Each section that teaches programming has an exercise set. The exercises both reinforce the understanding of the key ideas of the section and challenge the student to explore applications. Most of the exercise sets require the student to trace programs, find errors, and write programs. The answers to most of the odd-numbered exercises are given at the end of the text.

Practice Problems. Practice problems are carefully selected exercises located at the end of a section, just before the exercise set. Complete solutions are given following the exercise set. The practice problems often focus on points that are potentially confusing or are best appreciated after the student has worked on them. The reader should seriously attempt the practice problems and study their solutions before moving on to the exercises.

Programming Projects. Beginning with Chapter 2, every chapter contains programming projects. The programming projects not only reflect the variety of ways that computers are used in the business community, but also present some games and general interest topics. The large number and range of difficulty of the programming projects provide the flexibility to adapt the course to the interests and abilities of the students.

Comments. Extensions and fine points of new topics are reserved for the "Comments" portion at the end of each section so that they will not interfere with the flow of the presentation.

Case Studies. The two case studies focus on important programming applications. The problems are analyzed and the programs are developed with top-down charts and pseudocode. The programs can be found in the Programs directory of the enclosed CD.

Chapter Summaries. In Chapters 2 through 5 the key results are stated and the important terms are highlighted.

Procedures. The early introduction of general procedures in Section 2.6 allows structured programming to be used in simple situations before being applied to complex problems.

Appendix on Debugging. Placing the discussion of Visual Basic's sophisticated debugger in an appendix allows the instructor flexibility in deciding when to cover this topic.

How to Appendix. This appendix provides a compact reference on how to carry out the standard tasks for using the Visual Basic environment.

Examples and Case Studies CD. Each book contains a CD holding all the examples and case studies from this text.

Visual Basic 6.0 Included. The Working Model Edition of Visual Basic 6.0 is packaged with every copy of the book. The Working Model is identical to the Learning Edition with the exceptions that it cannot compile to an exe file and it does not have on-line help. In particular, the Working Model contains the Data control and the FlexGrid control.

Instructors Diskette. Diskettes containing the solution to every exercise and programming project, and a test item file for each chapter is available for the instructor.

What's New in the Second Edition

1. The version of Visual Basic has been upgraded to Visual Basic 6.0. The VB 6.0 software packaged with the book now contains the Data control and the FlexGrid control.

2. Several functions that are new in Visual Basic 6.0 are introduced and used extensively. They include Round, FormatNumber, FormatCurrency, and FormatPercent

3. A section on databases has been added.

4. The section on general procedures appears earlier.

5. The keyword Let has been eliminated from assignment statements and the keyword Rem has been replaced by an apostrophe.

6. Boolean variables have been introduced and are used for flags.

7. The real-life data in the examples and exercises have been updated and revised.

8. Engineering Supplement: Contains additional examples, case studies, and exercises from engineering, mathematics, and the sciences.

9. Companion Web site for instructors and students: This Web site will provide an on-line study guide for students that includes additional exercises and Visual Basic learning resources. The instructors' portion will include, among other materials, PowerPoint.

ACKNOWLEDGMENTS

Many people are involved in the successful publication of a book. I wish to thank the people at Prentice Hall whose support and diligence made this textbook possible. Trudy Pisciotti, Rhodora Penaranda, and Bayani DeLeon did a fantastic job producing the book and keeping it on schedule. Heather Scott and Tammy Cavallo created the innovative covers for my Visual Basic series. Alan Apt, Marcia Horton, and Kate Kaibni provided the needed editorial support and assistance.

I also wish to thank Susanne Peterson, Janie Schwark, and Amy Stuhlberg at Microsoft for providing me with Visual Basic information and software to support the texts.

I extend special thanks to my editor Laura Steele and my typesetter Rebecca Evans. Laura's ideas and enthusiasm helped immensely with the preparation of the book. Rebecca's considerable skills and congenial manner made for an uncomplicated and pleasant production process.

David I. Schneider

CONTENTS

1 An Introduction to Computers and Visual Basic

1.1 AN INTRODUCTION TO COMPUTERS

Essentials of Visual Basic 6.0 Programming is a book about problem solving with computers. The programming language used is Visual Basic, but the principles taught apply to many modern programming languages. The examples and exercises present a sampling of the ways that computers are used in society.

Computers are so common today that you certainly have seen them in use and heard some of the terminology applied to them. Here are some of the questions that you might have about computers and programming.

Question: What is meant by a personal computer?

Answer: The word "personal" does not mean that the computer is intended for personal, as opposed to business, purposes. Rather, it indicates that the machine is operated by one person at a time instead of by many people.

Question: What are the main components of a personal computer?

Answer: The visible components are shown in Figure 1.1. Instructions are entered into the computer by typing them on the keyboard or by reading them from a diskette in a diskette drive or from a hard disk. Characters normally appear on the monitor as they are typed. Information processed by the computer can be displayed on the monitor, printed on the printer, or recorded on a diskette or hard drive. Hidden from view inside the system unit are the microprocessor and the memory of the computer. The microprocessor, which can be thought of as the brain of the computer, carries out all computations. The memory stores the instructions and data that are processed by the computer.

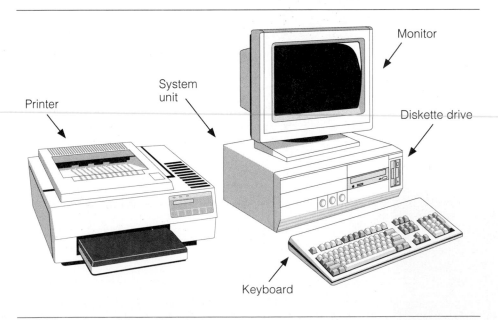

Figure 1.1 Components of a personal computer.

Question: | What are some uses of computers in our society?

Answer: | Whenever we make a phone call, a computer determines how to route the call and calculates the cost of the call. Banks store all customer transactions on computers and process these data to revise the balance for each customer. Airlines record all reservations into computers. This information, which is said to form a database, can be accessed to determine the status of any flight. NASA uses computers to calculate the trajectories of satellites. Business analysts use computers to create line and bar charts that give visual impact to data.

Question: | What are some topics covered in this text that students can use immediately?

Answer: | Computer files can be created to hold lists of names, addresses, and phone numbers, which can be alphabetized and printed in entirety or selectively. Line graphs or attractive tables can be created to enhance the data in a term paper. Mathematical computations can be carried out for science, business, and engineering courses. Personal financial transactions, such as bank deposits and loans, can be recorded, organized, and analyzed.

Question: | How do we communicate with the computer?

Answer: | Many languages are used to communicate with the computer. At the lowest level, there is machine language, which is understood directly by the microprocessor but is awkward for humans. Visual Basic is an example of a higher-level language. It consists of instructions to which people can relate, such as Print, Input, and Do. The Visual Basic software translates Visual Basic programs into machine-language programs.

Question: | How do we get computers to perform complicated tasks?

Answer: | Tasks are broken down into a sequence of instructions that can be expressed in a computer language. (This text uses the language Visual Basic.) The sequence of instructions is called a **program**. Programs range in size from two or three instructions to tens of thousands. Instructions are typed on the keyboard and stored in the computer's memory. (They also can be stored permanently on a diskette or hard disk.) The process of executing the instructions is called running the program.

Question: | Are there certain features that all programs have in common?

Answer: | Most programs do three things: take in data, manipulate them, and give desired information. These operations are referred to as input, processing, and output. The input data might be held in a portion of the program, reside on a diskette or hard drive, or be provided by the computer operator in response to requests made by the computer while the program is running. The processing of the input data occurs inside the computer and can take from a fraction of a second to many hours. The output data are either displayed on the screen, printed on the printer, or recorded onto a disk. As a simple example, consider a program that computes sales tax. An item of input data is the cost of the thing purchased. The processing consists of multiplying the cost by a certain percentage. An item of output data is the resulting product, the amount of sales tax to be paid.

Question: What are the meanings of the terms *hardware* and *software*?

Answer: The term **hardware** refers to the physical components of the computer, including all peripherals, central processing unit, disk drives, and all mechanical and electrical devices. Programs are referred to as **software**.

Question: What are the meanings of the terms *programmer* and *user*?

Answer: A **programmer** is a person who solves problems by writing programs on a computer. After analyzing the problem and developing a plan for solving it, he or she writes and tests the program that instructs the computer how to carry out the plan. The program might be run many times, either by the programmer or by others. A **user** is any person who uses a program. While working through this text, you will function both as a programmer and as a user.

Question: What is meant by *problem solving*?

Answer: Problems are solved by carefully reading them to determine what data are given and what outputs are requested. Then a step-by-step procedure is devised to process the given data and produce the requested output. This procedure is called an **algorithm**. Finally, a computer program is written to carry out the algorithm. Algorithms are discussed in Section 1.5.

Question: What types of problems are solved in this text?

Answer: Carrying out business computations, creating and maintaining records, alphabetizing lists, and drawing line graphs are some of the types of problems we will solve.

Question: What is the difference between standard BASIC and Visual Basic?

Answer: In the early 1960s, two mathematics professors at Dartmouth College developed BASIC to provide their students with an easily learned language that could tackle complicated programming projects. As the popularity of BASIC grew, refinements were introduced that permitted structured programming, which increases the reliability of programs. Visual Basic is a version of BASIC that was written by the Microsoft Corporation to incorporate object-oriented programming into BASIC and to allow easy development of Windows applications.

1.2   USING WINDOWS

Programs such as Visual Basic, which are designed for Microsoft Windows, are supposed to be easy to use—and they are once you learn a little jargon and a few basic techniques. This section explains the jargon, giving you enough of an understanding of Windows to get you started in Visual Basic. Although Windows may seem intimidating if you've never used it before, you need to learn only a few basic techniques, which are covered right here.

Mouse Pointers

When you use Windows, think of yourself as the conductor and Windows as the orchestra. The conductor in an orchestra points to various members, does something with his or her baton, and then the orchestra members respond in certain ways. For a Windows user, the baton is called the **pointing device**; most often it is a **mouse**. The idea is that as you move the mouse across your desk, a pointer moves along the screen in sync with your movements. Two basic types of mouse pointers you will see in Windows are an arrow and an hourglass.

The **arrow** is the ordinary mouse pointer you use to point at various Windows objects before activating them. You will usually be instructed to "Move the pointer to. . . ." This really means "Move the mouse around your desk until the mouse pointer is at. . . ."

The **hourglass** mouse pointer pops up whenever Windows is saying: "Wait a minute; I'm thinking." This pointer still moves around when you move the mouse, but you can't tell Windows to do anything until it finishes what it's doing, and the mouse pointer no longer resembles an hourglass.

Note: The mouse pointer can take on many other shapes, depending on which document you are using and what task you are performing. For instance, when entering text in a word processor or Visual Basic, the mouse pointer appears as a thin, large, uppercase I (referred to as an I-Beam).

Mouse Actions

After you move the (arrow) pointer to a place where you want something to happen, you need to do something with the mouse. There are four basic things you can do with a mouse—point, click, double-click, and drag.

Tip: You can pick the mouse up off your desk and replace it without moving the mouse pointer. This is useful, for example, when the mouse pointer is in the center of the screen but the mouse is about to fall off your desk!

Pointing means moving your mouse across your desk until the mouse pointer is over the desired object on the screen.

Clicking (sometimes people say single-clicking) means pressing and releasing the left mouse button once. Whenever a sentence begins "Click on . . . ," you need to

1. Move the mouse pointer until it is at the object you are supposed to click on.

2. Press and release the left mouse button.

An example of a sentence using this jargon might be "Click on the button marked Yes." You also will see sentences that begin "Click inside the. . . ." This means to move the mouse pointer until it is inside the boundaries of the object, and then click.

Double-clicking means clicking the left mouse button twice in quick succession (that is, pressing it, releasing it, pressing it, and releasing it again *quickly* so that Windows doesn't think you single-clicked twice). Whenever a sentence begins "Double-click on . . . ", you need to

1. Move the mouse pointer until it is at the object you are supposed to double-click on.

2. Press and release the left mouse button twice in quick succession.

For example, you might be instructed to "Double-click on the little box at the far left side of your screen."

Note: An important Windows convention is that clicking selects an object so you can give Windows or the document further directions about it, but double-clicking tells Windows (or the document) to do something.

Dragging usually moves a Windows object. If you see a sentence that begins "Drag the . . . ", you need to

1. Move the mouse pointer until it is at the object.

2. Press the left mouse button, and hold it down.

3. Now move the mouse pointer until the object moves to where you want it to be.

4. Finally, release the mouse button.

Sometimes this whole activity is called *drag and drop*.

Starting Windows

Windows starts automatically when you turn on your computer. After a little delay, you will first see the Windows logo and finally a screen looking something like Figure 1.2. The little pictures (with labels) are called **icons**. You double-click on the My Computer icon to see your computer's contents and manage your files. (Double-clicking on the icon that represents a program starts the program in Windows.) You click on the Start button (at the bottom left corner of the screen) to run programs such as Visual Basic, end Windows, and carry out several other tasks. (The Start menu also can be accessed with Ctrl+Esc.)

Figure 1.2 Windows desktop.

Windows and Its Little Windows

Windows gets its name from the way it organizes your screen into rectangular regions. When you run a program, the program runs inside a bordered rectangular box. Unfortunately Windows jargon calls all of these windows, so there's only a lowercase *w* to distinguish them from the program called Windows.

When Windows' attentions are focused on a specific window, the bar at the top of the window is highlighted and the window is said to be **active**. The active window is the only one that can be affected by your actions. An example of a sentence you might see is "Make the window active." This means that if the title bar of the window is not already highlighted, click inside the window. At this point, the (new) window will be responsive to your actions.

Using Notepad

We will explore the Windows application Notepad in detail to illustrate the Windows environment. The Notepad is used extensively in this text to create data files for programs. Most of the concepts learned here carry over to Visual Basic and other Windows applications.

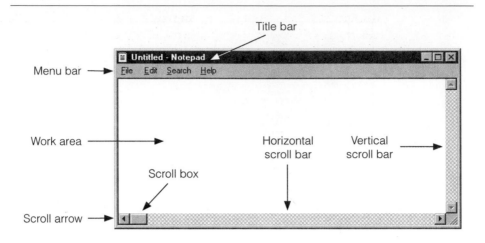

Figure 1.3 The Notepad window.

To invoke Notepad from Windows, click the Start button, point to Programs, point to Accessories, and click Notepad. As its name suggests, Notepad is an elementary word processor. You can type text into the Notepad window, edit the text, print the text on the printer, and save the text for later recall.

The blinking vertical line is called the **cursor**. Each letter you type will appear at the cursor. The Notepad window is divided into four parts. The part containing the cursor is called the **Work area**. It is the largest and most important part of the window because documents are typed into this window.

The **Title bar** at the top of the screen holds the name of the document currently being written. Until the document is given a name, the document is called "Untitled."

You can change the window to exactly suit your needs. To adjust the size

1. Move the mouse pointer until it is at the place on the boundary you want to adjust. The mouse pointer changes to a double-headed arrow.

2. Drag the border to the left or right or up or down to make it smaller or larger.

3. When you are satisfied with the new size of the window, release the left mouse button.

If the Work area contains more information than can fit on the screen, you need a way to move through this information so you can see it all. For example, you will certainly be writing instructions in Visual Basic that are longer than one screen. You can use the mouse to march through your instructions with small steps or giant steps. A **Vertical scroll bar** lets you move from the top to the bottom of the window; a **Horizontal scroll bar** lets you move within the left and right margins of the window. Use this Scroll bar when the contents of the window are too wide to fit on the screen. Figure 1.3 shows both Vertical and Horizontal scroll bars.

A scroll bar has two arrows at the end of a channel and sometimes contains a box (usually called the **Scroll box**). The Scroll box is the key to moving rapidly; the arrows are the key to moving in smaller increments. Dragging the Scroll box enables you to quickly move long distances to an approximate location in your document. For example, if you drag the Scroll box to the middle of the channel, you'll scroll to approximately the middle of your document.

The **Menu bar** just below the Title bar is used to call up menus, or lists of tasks. Several of these tasks are described in this section.

Documents are created from the keyboard in much the same way they would be written with a typewriter. In computerese, writing a document is referred to as editing the document; therefore, the Notepad is called a **text editor**. Before discussing editing, we must first examine the workings of the keyboard.

There are several different styles of keyboards. Figure 1.4 shows a typical one. The keyboard is divided into several parts. The largest portion looks and functions like an ordinary typewriter keyboard. Above this portion are twelve keys labeled F1 through F12, called the **function keys**. (On many keyboards the function keys are located on the left side.) Function keys are used to perform certain tasks with a single keystroke. For instance, pressing the function key F5 displays the time and date. The right portion of the keyboard, called the **numeric keypad**, is used either to move the cursor or to enter numbers. Press the **Num Lock** key a few times and notice the tiny light labeled NUM LOCK blink on and off. When the light is on, the numeric keypad produces numbers; otherwise, it moves the cursor. The Num Lock key is called a toggle key because it "toggles" between two states. When the numeric keypad is in the cursor-moving state, the four arrow keys each move the cursor around the existing document.

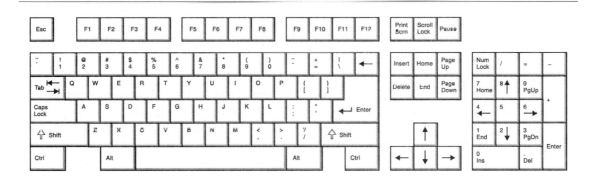

Figure 1.4 IBM PC keyboard.

Two very important keys may not have names printed on them. The **Enter** key is the key with the hooked arrow (and/or the word Enter). It corresponds to the carriage return on a typewriter, and is used to start a new line of a document. The **Backspace** key is the gray key with the left-pointing arrow located above the Enter key. It moves the cursor one space to the left and erases any character in that location.

After Notepad has been invoked, the following routine will introduce you to the keyboard.

1. Click on the Work area of the Notepad.

2. Type a few words into the Notepad.

3. Use the right and left cursor-moving keys on the numeric keypad to move the cursor.

4. Press the **Home** key to move the cursor back to the beginning of the line. In general, the Home key moves the cursor to the beginning of the line on which it currently is located.

5. Now press the **End** key (on the numeric keypad). The cursor will move to the end of the line.

6. Type some letters using the central typewriter portion of the keyboard. The two **Shift** keys are used to obtain uppercase letters or the upper character of keys showing two characters.

7. Press the **Caps Lock** key and then type some letters. The letters will appear in uppercase. We say the keyboard is in uppercase mode. To toggle back to lowercase mode, press the Caps Lock key again. Only alphabetic keys are affected by Caps Lock. *Note:* When the keyboard is in the uppercase state, the tiny light labeled CAPS LOCK on the keyboard is lit.

8. Type some letters and then press the Backspace key a few times. It will erase letters one at a time. Another method of deleting a letter is to move the cursor to that letter and press the **Del** key. (Del stands for "Delete.") The backspace key erases the character to the left of the cursor, and the Del key erases the character to the right of the cursor.

9. Hold down the **Ctrl** key (Ctrl stands for "Control"), and press the **Del** key. This combination erases the portion of the line to the right of the cursor. We describe this combination as **Ctrl + Del**. (The plus sign indicates that the Ctrl key is to be held down while pressing the Del key.) There are many useful key combinations like this.

10. Type a few letters and use the appropriate cursor-moving key to move the cursor in front of one of the letters. Now type any letter. Notice that it is inserted at the cursor position and that the letters following it move to the right. This is because the Notepad uses **insert mode**. Visual Basic has an additional mode, called **overwrite mode**, in which a typed letter overwrites the letter located at the cursor position. In Visual Basic, overwrite mode is invoked by pressing the **Ins** key. (Ins stands for "Insert.") Pressing this toggle key again reinstates insert mode. The cursor size indicates the active mode; a large cursor means overwrite mode.

11. The key to the left of the Q key is called the **Tab** key. It is marked with a pair of arrows, the upper one pointing to the left and the lower one pointing to the right. At the beginning of the line, pressing the Tab key indents the cursor several spaces.

12. Type more characters than can fit on one line of the screen. Notice that the leftmost characters scroll off the screen to make room for the new characters.

13. The Enter key is used to begin a new line on the screen.

14. The **Alt** key activates the Menu bar. Then, pressing one of the underlined letters, such as F, E, S, or H, selects a menu. (From the Menu bar, a menu can also be selected by pressing the right-arrow key to highlight the name

and then pressing the Enter key.) As shown in Figure 1.5, after a menu is opened, each option has one letter underlined. You can press an underlined letter to select an option. (Underlined letters are called **access keys**.) For instance, pressing A from the file menu selects the option "Save As". Selections also can be made with the cursor-moving keys and the Enter key. **Note 1:** You can select menus and options without the use of keys by clicking on them with the mouse. **Note 2:** You can close a menu, without making a selection, by clicking anywhere outside the menu, or pressing the Esc key twice.

Figure 1.5 A menu and its options.

15. The **Esc** key (Esc stands for "Escape") is used to return to the Work area.

16. Press and release Alt, then press and release F, and then press N. (This key combination is abbreviated Alt/File/New or Alt/F/N.) The dialog box in Figure 1.6 will appear and ask you if you want to save the current document. Decline by pressing N or clicking on the No button.

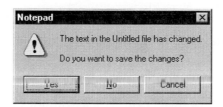

Figure 1.6 A "Do you want to save the changes?" dialog box.

17. Type the following information into the Notepad. (It gives the names of employees, their hourly wages, and the number of hours worked in the past week.) This document is used in Section 2.5. **Note:** We follow the convention of surrounding words with quotation marks to distinguish words from numbers, which are written without quotation marks.

"Mike Jones", 7.35, 35
"John Smith", 6.75, 33

18. Let's store the document as a file on a disk. To save the document, press Alt/<u>F</u>ile/Save <u>A</u>s. A dialog box appears to request a file name for the document (see Figure 1.7). The cursor is in a narrow rectangular box labeled "File <u>n</u>ame:".

Figure 1.7 Save As dialog box.

Type a drive letter, a colon, and a name, and then press the Enter key or click on Save. For instance, you might type A:Staff. The document will then be stored on drive A. This process is called **saving** the document. Notepad automatically adds a period and the extension txt to the name. Therefore, the complete file name is Staff.txt on the disk. **Note:** If you want to save the document in a specific folder (directory) of the disk, also type the folder (directory). For instance, you might type A:\Myfiles\Staff. See Section 1.3 for a discussion of folders. (**Note:** You can move around in any dialog box by repeatedly pressing the Tab key.)

19. Press the key combination Alt/<u>F</u>ile/<u>N</u>ew to clear Staff.txt from Notepad.

20. Restore Staff.txt as the document in the Notepad by pressing Alt/<u>F</u>ile/<u>O</u>pen, typing Staff (possibly preceded by a drive letter and a colon, such as A:, and a folder) at the cursor position, and then pressing the Enter key.

21. Move the cursor to the beginning of the document, and then press Alt/S/F to invoke the Find dialog box. This dialog box contains several objects that will be discussed in this book. The text to be found should be typed into the rectangle containing the cursor. Such a rectangle is called a text box. The phrase "Find what:", which identifies the type of information that should be placed into the text box, is referred to as the caption of a label.

22. Type "smith" into the text box and then click on the "Find Next" button. This button is an example of a command button. Clicking on it carries out a task. Text boxes, labels, and command buttons are discussed in Section 2.2.

23. The small square to the left of the words "Match case" is called a check box. Click on it to see it checked, and then click again to remove the check mark.

24. The object captioned "Direction" is called a frame. It contains a pair of objects called option buttons. Click on the "Up" option button to select it, and then click on the "Down" option button. Only one option button at a time can be selected. Check boxes, frames, and option buttons are discussed in Section 5.2.

25. Press Alt/File/Exit to exit Notepad.

Ending Windows

To close Windows, click the Start button and then click Shut Down. You are presented with a message box that looks like the window in Figure 1.8. Click Yes. (If you forgot to save changes to documents, Windows will prompt you to save changes.) A screen message might appear to let you know when you can safely turn off your computer.

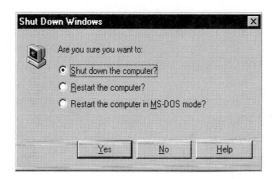

Figure 1.8 Dialog box for ending Windows.

Comments

1. The key sequences discussed in this section follow the format key1+key2 or key1/key2. The plus sign (+) instructs you to hold down key1 and then press key2. The slash symbol (/) tells you to release key1 before pressing key2. Some useful key combinations that we have not discussed yet are the following:

(a) Ctrl+Home: moves the cursor to the beginning of the document
(b) Ctrl+End: moves the cursor to the end of the document
(c) Alt/F/P/Enter: prints a copy of the current document on the printer

2. When the work area is completely filled with lines of text, the document scrolls upward to accommodate additional lines. The lines that have scrolled off the top can be viewed again by pressing the **PgUp** key. The **PgDn** key moves farther down the document.

3. There are several ways to clear the work area. You can either erase the lines one at a time with Ctrl+Del, select the entire document with Alt/E/A and then erase all lines simultaneously with Del, or begin a new document with Alt/F/N. With the last method, a dialog box may query you about saving the current document. In this case, use Tab to select the desired option and press the Enter key. The document name in the Title bar will change to Untitled.

4. Notepad can perform many of the tasks of word processors, such as search and block operations. However, these features needn't concern us presently. A discussion of them can be found in Appendix B, under "HOW TO: Use the Editor."

5. Txt is the default extension for files created with Notepad.

6. The title bar of the Notepad window, or of any window, contains buttons that can be used to maximize, minimize, or close the window. See Figure 1.9.

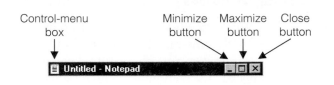

Figure 1.9 Title bar of the Notepad window.

You can click on the Maximize button to make the Notepad window fill the entire screen, click on the Minimize button to change the Notepad window into a button on the taskbar, or click on the Close button to exit Notepad. As long as a window isn't maximized or minimized, you can usually move it around the screen by dragging its title bar. (Recall that this means to move the mouse pointer until it is in the title bar, hold down the left mouse button, move the mouse until the window is where you want it to be, and then release the mouse button.) **Note 1:** If you have maximized a window, the Maximize button changes to a pair of rectangles called the **Restore button**. Click on this button to return the window to its previous size. **Note 2:** If the Notepad window has been minimized, it can be restored to its previous size by clicking on the button that was created on the task bar when the Minimize button was clicked.

7. You should end Windows by the procedures discussed in this section whenever possible. It is a bad idea to end Windows by just shutting off your machine.

 PRACTICE PROBLEMS 1.2

(Solutions to practice problems always follow the exercises.)
Assume you are using Windows' Notepad.

1. Give two ways to open the Edit menu.

2. Assume the Edit menu has been opened. Give three ways to pick a menu item.

EXERCISES 1.2

1. What does an hourglass icon mean?

2. Describe "clicking" in your own words.

3. Describe "double-clicking" in your own words.

4. Describe "dragging" in your own words.

5. What is the blinking vertical line in Notepad called, and what is its purpose?

6. How can you tell when a window is active?

7. What is the difference between "Windows" and "windows"?

8. What is the purpose of the vertical scroll bar in Notepad?

9. How do you open Notepad when the Notepad icon is visible?

10. By what name is a Notepad document known before it is named as part of being saved on disk?

11. What is a toggle key?

Figure 1.10 shows many of the special keys on the keyboard. In Exercises 12 to 36, select the key (or key combination) that performs the task in Windows' Notepad.

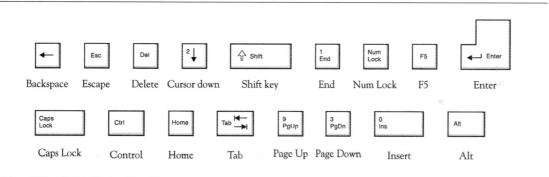

Figure 1.10 Some special keys.

12. Scroll the document to view a higher part.

13. Scroll the document to view a lower part.

14. Erase the line containing the cursor.

15. Erase the character to the left of the cursor.

16. Access the Start menu.

17. Toggle the numeric keypad between states.

18. Erase the character to the right of the cursor.

19. Toggle the case for alphabetic characters.

20. Move the cursor to the beginning of the line containing the cursor.

21. Move the cursor to the end of the line containing the cursor.

22. Display the time and date.

23. Cause the upper character of a double-character key to be displayed.

24. Move down to the next row of the screen.

25. Print a copy of the current document on the printer.

26. Exit Notepad.

27. Move the cursor to the beginning of the document.

28. Move the cursor to the end of the document.

29. Move from the Work area to the Menu bar.

30. Cancel a dialog box.

31. Move from the Menu bar to the Work area.

32. Move from one option rectangle of a dialog box to another rectangle.

33. Save the current document on a diskette.

34. Clear the current document from the Work area and start a new document.

35. Create a blank line in the middle of a document.

36. Remove a pull-down menu from the screen.

✔✔ **Solutions to Practice Problems 1.2**

1. Press Alt/Edit or click on the word Edit in the toolbar to display the Edit menu. The jargon says the menu is "dropped down" or "pulled down."

2. Press the Down arrow key to highlight the item and then press the Enter key, press the underlined letter in the name of the item, or click on the item.

1.3 DISKS AND FOLDERS

Modern computers have a hard disk, a diskette drive, and usually a CD drive. The hard disk is permanently housed inside the computer. You can read information from all three drives, but can only write information to the hard disk and to diskettes. Most diskette drives accommodate the type of diskette shown in Figure 1.11. This diskette has a plastic jacket and measures $3\frac{1}{2}''$ in width.

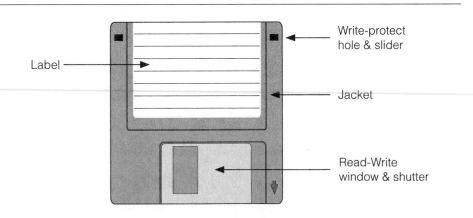

Figure 1.11 $3\frac{1}{2}''$ diskette.

When the diskette is inserted into a drive, the shutter slides to the right and exposes the read-write window. The diskette drive records and reads data through the read-write window. The write-protect hole is normally covered. When the write-protect hole is uncovered by sliding the slider on the back of the diskette, nothing can be erased from or recorded on the diskette. To insert a diskette, hold the diskette with the label facing up and the read/write window pointing toward the diskette drive. You insert the diskette by just pushing it into the drive until you hear a click. You remove it by pressing the button on the drive.

When handling a diskette, be careful not to touch the exposed surface in the read-write window. Also, do not remove a diskette from a diskette drive while the little light on the diskette drive is lit.

We use the word "disk" to refer to either the hard disk, a diskette, or a CD. Each drive is identified by a letter. Normally, the hard drive is identified by C, the diskette by A, and the CD drive by D or E.

Disk management is handled by the computer's operating system. VB 6.0 requires that your computer use a Windows 95, Windows 98, or Windows NT 4.0 (or later) operating system.

Disks hold not only programs but also collections of data stored in **data files**. The term *file* refers to either a data file or a program file. We created a data file in Section 1.2. Traditionally, each file has a name consisting of a base name followed by an optional extension consisting of a period and one or more characters. Letters, digits, spaces, periods, and a few other assorted characters (see Comment 1) can be used in file names. Extensions are normally used to identify the type of file. For example, spreadsheets created with Excel have the extension xls, documents created with Word have the extension doc, and files created with Notepad have the extension txt. Some examples of file names are "Annual Sales.xls," "Letter to Mom.doc," and "Phone.txt".

Because a disk is capable of holding thousands of files, locating a specific file can be quite time-consuming. Therefore, related files are grouped into collections that are stored in separate areas of the disk. For instance, one area might hold all your Visual Basic programs, and another the documents created with your word processor.

Think of a disk as a large folder, called the **root folder**, that contains several smaller folders, each with its own name. (The naming of folders follows the same rule as the naming of files.) Each of these smaller folders can contain yet other named folders. Each folder is identified by listing its name preceded by the names of the successively larger folders that contain it, with each folder name preceded by a backslash. Such a sequence is called a **path**. For instance, the path \Sales \Ny.98\July identifies the folder July, contained in the folder Ny.98, which in turn is contained in the folder Sales. Think of a file, along with its name, as written on a slip of paper that can be placed into either the root folder or one of the smaller folders. The combination of a drive letter followed by a colon, a path, and a file name is called a **filespec**, an abbreviation of "file specification." Some examples of filespecs are C:\Vb98\Vb6.exe and A:\Personal\Income98.txt.

In DOS and earlier versions of Windows, folders were called directories. Many Visual Basic objects and commands still refer to folders as directories. Windows contains two programs (My Computer and Windows Explorer) that help you view, organize, and manage the folders and files on your disks. We will carry out these tasks with My Computer. We will learn how to create, rename, copy, move, and delete folders and files.

Using My Computer

To invoke My Computer, double-click on the My Computer icon. Your initial window will show an icon for each drive (and a few other icons). If you double-click on one of the drive icons a second window containing the folders and files for that drive will appear. Figure 1.12 shows a possible pair of windows. A folder is identified by a folder icon, a file created with Notepad is identified by a small spiral notepad, and an executable file is identified by a rectangle (with a thin bar across its top) icon.

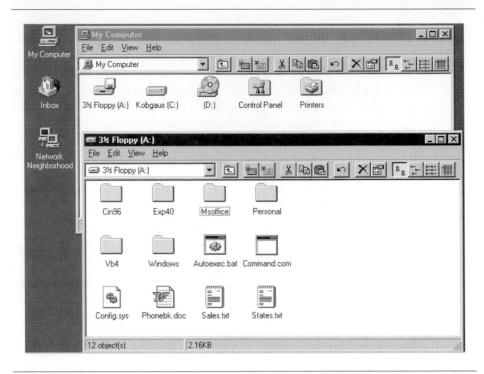

Figure 1.12 Windows created with My Computer.

To open a folder, double-click on that folder. A window with the folder's name in its title bar will appear. This window will contain an icon for each subfolder and file of the original folder. Figure 1.13 shows such a window.

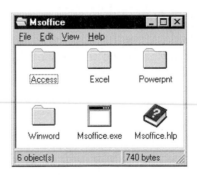

Figure 1.13 A window produced by opening a folder.

To create a new folder:

1. Open the folder that is to contain the new folder as a subfolder.

   Note: Initially, the root folder is open.

2. On the File menu, point to New, and then click Folder. (Or press Alt/File/New/Folder.)

   The new folder appears with a temporary name.

3. Type a name for the folder and then press the Enter key.

To rename a folder or file:

1. Click on the folder or file.

2. On the File menu, click Rename. (Or press Alt/File/Rename.)

The current name will appear highlighted inside a rectangle.

3. Type the new name and then press the Enter key.

To delete a folder or file:

1. Click on the folder or file.

2. On the File menu, click Delete. (Or press Alt/File/Delete or Del.)

A "Confirm File Delete" input box containing the name of the folder or file will appear.

3. Click on the Yes button.

To copy a folder or file:

1. Click on the folder or file to be copied.

2. On the Edit menu, click Copy. (Or press Alt/Edit/Copy.)

3. Open the folder or disk where the copy is to be placed.

4. On the Edit menu, click Paste. (Or press Alt/Edit/Paste.)

To move a folder or file:

1. Click on the folder or file to be moved.

2. On the Edit menu, click on Cut. (Or press Alt/Edit/Cut.)

3. Open the folder where the folder or file is to be placed.

4. On the Edit menu, click Paste. (Or press Alt/Edit/Paste.)

You also can carry out some of the preceding operations by "drag and drop." For details, see the Help Topics accessed through the My Computer Help menu. For instance, you can delete a folder or file by dragging it to the Recycle Bin and releasing the left mouse button.

Comments

1. File names can consist of digits, letters of the alphabet, spaces, and the characters & ! _ @ ' ' ~ ( ) { } – # % . + , ; = [ ] $.

2. File names can consist of up to 255 characters including spaces. However, a name cannot contain the following characters: \ / : ? * " > < |

3. Names of folders do not usually have an extension.

4. Neither Windows nor Visual Basic distinguishes between uppercase and lower-case letters in folders and file names. For instance, the names COSTS99.TXT, Costs99.Txt, and costs99.txt are equivalent.

5. Because you cannot write to a CD drive, you cannot rename or delete files or folders residing on a CD drive.

6. When you delete a folder directory containing other subfolders or files, you will be queried about the removal of these subfolders and files.

7. Most diskettes purchased these days are "preformatted." Formatting prepares the disk for use with your computer and deletes any previous information stored on it. If you have a diskette that has not been formatted, you must format it yourself before you can use it.

   To format a diskette

   (a) Insert the diskette in a drive, and select the drive in My Computer.
   (b) From the File menu, choose Format.
   (c) In the Format Disk dialog box, specify the various options. (Most likely, the default values will be appropriate.)
   (d) Click the Start button.

8. You can obtain further information about My Computer by selecting "Search for Help on" from its Help menu and then specifying a topic.

9. Refer to Step 18 in the Notepad walkthrough of Section 1.2, and suppose you typed A:\Myfiles\Staff into the "File name:" box. The disk drive and directory could have been specified with other parts of the dialog box.

   (a) Click on the arrow to the right of the "Save in:" box and click on "3 1/2 Floppy (A:)" to select the A: drive.
       The large box in the center of the "Save As" window shows the subfolder of the selected drive.
   (b) Open the desired folder by double-clicking on it.
       The folder will replace the drive in the "Save in:" box and its subfolders will appear in the large box. This process can be repeated as many times as required to locate the desired folder.
   (c) Return to the "File name:" box and type in Staff.
   (d) Press the Enter key or click on the Save button.

10. There are many uses of dialog boxes such as the one discussed in comment 9. For instance, they pop up to report errors in a Visual Basic document. In general, the Tab key is used to move around inside a dialog box and the Enter key makes a selection. Although dialog boxes often have a cancel button, the Esc key also can be used to remove the dialog box from the screen.

11. In DOS and early versions of Windows, file names were limited to no more than eight characters followed by an optional extension of at most 3 characters. This is referred to as the 8.3 format. In this text we use the 8.3 format so that folders also can be explored in DOS and with all utility programs.

12. Some books use the word "path" to mean what we call "filespec."

✔ **PRACTICE PROBLEMS 1.3**

1. Give two ways to remove all information from a diskette.

2. Suppose the filespec for a file is C:\Games\Board\Chess.exe. How many folders must you open in My Computer to reach the file?

➤ **EXERCISES 1.3**

1. Explain why "Who is there?" is not a valid file name.

2. Explain why "Four star hotel ****" is not a valid file name.

3. What is wrong with the filespec "C:/Sports/Tennis.doc"?

4. What is the maximum number of characters in a file name?

5. Suppose "C:\U.s.a\Maryland\Montgomery county\Silver spring.doc" is the filespec for a file. How many folders (counting the root folder) must you open in My Computer to reach the file?

6. Suppose the filespec for a file is A:\Animal\Birds\Robin.doc. How many folders must you open in My Computer to reach the file?

7. The folder Windows contains a folder named System. How many folders does System contain?

8. The file Vb6.exe is created when Visual Basic is installed on a computer. Determine the filespec for this file.

The folder Windows contains a folder named System. Open System and then press Alt/V/D to select the Details option from the View menu. In Exercises 9-12, give the effect of clicking on the specified button in the bar just below the toolbar.

9. Size

10. Type

11. Modified

12. Name

13. Suppose your computer has just one diskette drive. How could you use the procedures discussed in this section to copy a file in the root folder of a diskette onto another diskette?

14. Open the folder on your hard disk containing Visual Basic. How many sub-folders does the folder contain directly? How many files does the folder contain directly?

In Exercises 15 and 16, carry out the stated tasks.

15. (a) Take a blank diskette and create two folders (directories) named Laurel and Hardy.
    (b) Create a subfolder of Laurel called Stan.
    (c) Use Notepad to create a file containing the sentence "Here's another nice mess you've gotten me into." and save the file with the name Quote.txt in the directory Laurel.
    (d) Copy the file Quote.txt into the folder Hardy.
    (e) Rename the new copy of the file Quote.txt as Line.txt.
    (f) Delete the original copy of the file Quote.txt.

16. (a) Take a blank diskette, create a folder (directory) named Slogans, and create two subfolders of Slogans named Coke and CocaCola.
    (b) Use Notepad to create a file containing the sentence "It's the real thing." and save the file with the name Coke1970.txt in the folder (directory) Coke.

(c) Use Notepad to create a file containing the phrase "The ideal brain tonic." and save the file with the name Coke1892.txt in the folder (directory) Coke.

(d) Copy the two files in Coke into the folder (directory) CocaCola.

(e) Delete the folder (directory) Coke.

(f) Rename the folder (directory) CocaCola as Coke.

✔✔ Solutions to Practice Problems 1.3

1. First way: Use the Delete command from the File menu of My Computer. Second way: Format the diskette.

2. Three, counting the root folder. You can think of clicking on the C: icon as opening the root folder. After that, you must open folder Games and then folder Board. Chess.exe will be in the folder Board.

1.4   AN INTRODUCTION TO VISUAL BASIC

Visual Basic is one of the most exciting developments in programming in many years. Visual Basic is the next generation of BASIC and is designed to make user-friendly programs easier to develop.

Prior to the creation of Visual Basic, developing a friendly user interface usually required teams of programmers using arcane languages like "C" that came in 10-pound boxes with thousands of pages of documentation. Now it can be done by a few people using a language that is a direct descendant of BASIC—the language most accessible to beginning programmers.

Visual Basic 6.0 requires the Microsoft Windows operating system. Although you don't need to be an expert user of Microsoft Windows, you do need to know the basics before you can master Visual Basic—that is, you need to be comfortable with manipulating a mouse, you need to know how to manipulate a window, and you need to know how to use Notepad and My Computer. However, there is no better way to master Microsoft Windows than to write applications for it—and that is what Visual Basic is all about.

Why Windows, and Why Visual Basic?

What people call **graphical user interfaces**, or GUIs (pronounced "gooies"), have revolutionized the microcomputer industry. Instead of the cryptic C:\> prompt that DOS users have long seen (and that some have long feared), users are presented with a desktop filled with little pictures called icons. Icons provide a visual guide to what the program can do.

Accompanying the revolution in how programs look was a revolution in how they feel. Consider a program that requests information for a database. Figure 1.14 shows how such a DOS-based BASIC program gets its information. The program requests the six pieces of data one at a time, with no opportunity to go back and alter previously entered information. After the program requests the six pieces of data, the screen clears and the six inputs are again requested one at a time. Figure 1.15 shows how an equivalent Visual Basic program gets its information. The boxes may be filled in any order. When the user clicks on a box with the mouse, the cursor moves to that box. The user can either type in new information or edit the existing information. When the user is satisfied that all the information is correct, he or she just clicks on the Write to Database button. The boxes will clear and the data for another person can be entered. After all names have been entered, the user clicks on the Exit button. In Figure 1.14, the program is in control; in Figure 1.15, the user is in control!

```
Enter Name (Enter EOD to terminate): Mr. President
Enter Address: 1600 Pennsylvania Avenue
Enter City: Washington
Enter State: DC
Enter Zipcode: 20500
Enter Phone Number: 202-395-3000
```

Figure 1.14 Input screen of a DOS-based BASIC program to fill a database.

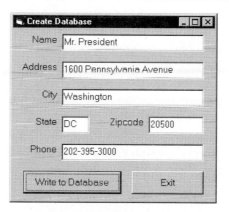

Figure 1.15 Input screen of a Visual Basic program to fill a database.

How You Develop a Visual Basic Application

One of the key elements of planning a Visual Basic application is deciding what the user sees—in other words, designing the screen. What data will he or she be entering? How large a window should the application use? Where will you place the command buttons—the "buttons" the user clicks on to activate the applications? Will the applications have places to enter text (text boxes) and places to display output? What kind of warning boxes (message boxes) should the application use? In Visual Basic, the responsive objects a program designer places on windows are called **controls**.

Two features make Visual Basic different from traditional programming tools.

1. You literally draw the user interface, much like using a paint program. Next, and perhaps more important,

2. When you're done drawing the interface, the command buttons, text boxes, and other objects that you have placed in a blank window will automatically recognize user actions such as mouse movements and button clicks. That is, the sequence of procedures executed in your program is controlled by "events" that the user initiates rather than by a predetermined sequence of procedures in your program.

In any case, only after you design the interface does anything like traditional programming occur. Objects in Visual Basic recognize events like mouse clicks; how the objects respond to them depends on the instructions you write. You always need to write instructions in order to make controls respond to events. This makes Visual Basic programming fundamentally different from conventional programming.

Programs in conventional programming languages run from the top down. For conventional programming languages, execution starts from the first line and moves with the flow of the program to different parts as needed. A Visual Basic program works completely differently. The core of a Visual Basic program is a set of independent groups of instructions that are activated by the events they have been told to recognize. This is a fundamental shift. Instead of doing what the programmer thinks should happen, the program gives the user control.

Most of the programming instructions in Visual Basic that tell your program how to respond to events like mouse clicks occur in what Visual Basic calls *event procedures*. Essentially, anything executable in a Visual Basic program is either in an event procedure or is used by an event procedure to help the procedure carry out its job. In fact, to stress that Visual Basic is fundamentally different from traditional programming languages, Microsoft uses the term *project*, rather than *program*, to refer to the combination of programming instructions and user interface that makes a Visual Basic application possible.

Here is a summary of the steps you take to design a Visual Basic application:

1. Decide how the windows that the user sees will look.

2. Determine which events the objects on the window should recognize.

3. Write the event procedures for those events.

Now here is what happens when the program is running:

1. Visual Basic monitors the window and the objects in the window to detect any event that an object can recognize (mouse movements, clicks, keystrokes, and so on).

2. When Visual Basic detects an event, it examines the program to see if you've written an event procedure for that event.

3. If you have written an event procedure, Visual Basic executes the instructions that make up that event procedure and goes back to Step 1.

4. If you have not written an event procedure, Visual Basic waits for the next event and goes back to Step 1.

These steps cycle continuously until the application ends. Usually, an event must happen before Visual Basic will do anything. Event-driven programs are reactive more than active—and that makes them more user friendly.

The Different Versions of Visual Basic

Visual Basic 1.0 first appeared in 1991. It was followed by version 2.0 in 1992, version 3.0 in 1993, version 4.0 in 1995, version 5.0 in 1997, and version 6.0 in 1998. Because Microsoft has publicly announced that Visual Basic is a key product for the company, Microsoft will continue to add further enhancements to the language. For example, Microsoft is using versions of Visual Basic to control all its applications, such as Microsoft Office. Master Visual Basic and you will be well-prepared for almost any office computer environment.

Visual Basic 6.0 comes in four editions—Learning, Professional, Enterprise, and Working Model Edition. All editions require either Windows 95, Windows 98, or Windows NT (4.0 or later). You can use any edition of Visual Basic 6.0 with this textbook.

1.5 PROGRAMMING TOOLS

An **algorithm** is a logical sequence of steps that solve a problem. This section discusses some specific algorithms and develops three tools used to convert algorithms into computer programs: flowcharts, pseudocode, and hierarchy charts.

You use algorithms every day to make decisions and perform tasks. For instance, whenever you mail a letter, you must decide how much postage to put on the envelope. One rule of thumb is to use one stamp for every five sheets of paper or fraction thereof. Suppose a friend asks you to determine the number of stamps to place on an envelope. The following algorithm will accomplish the task.

1. Request the number of sheets of paper; call it Sheets.   *(input)*

2. Divide Sheets by 5.   *(processing)*

3. Round the quotient up to the next highest whole number; call it Stamps.   *(processing)*

4. Reply with the number Stamps.   *(output)*

The preceding algorithm takes the number of sheets (Sheets) as input, processes the data, and produces the number of stamps needed (Stamps) as output. We can test the algorithm for a letter with 16 sheets of paper.

1. Request the number of sheets of paper; Sheets = 16.

2. Dividing 5 into 16 gives 3.2.

3. Rounding 3.2 up to 4 gives Stamps = 4.

4. Reply with the answer, 4 stamps.

This problem-solving example can be pictured by

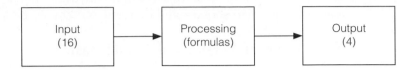

Of the program design tools available, the three most popular are the following:

Flowcharts: Graphically depict the logical steps to carry out a task and show how the steps relate to each other.

Pseudocode: Uses English-like phrases with some Visual Basic terms to outline the task.

Hierarchy charts: Show how the different parts of a program relate to each other.

Flowcharts

A flowchart consists of special geometric symbols connected by arrows. Within each symbol is a phrase presenting the activity at that step. The shape of the symbol indicates the type of operation that is to occur. For instance, the parallelogram denotes input or output. The arrows connecting the symbols, called **flowlines**, show the progression in which the steps take place. Flowcharts should "flow" from the top of the page to the bottom. Although the symbols used in flowcharts are standardized, no standards exist for the amount of detail required within each symbol.

A table of the flowchart symbols adopted by the American National Standards Institute (ANSI) follows. Figure 1.16 shows the flowchart for the postage stamp problem.

Symbol	Name	Meaning
⟶	*Flowline*	Used to connect symbols and indicate the flow of logic.
⬭	*Terminal*	Used to represent the beginning (Start) or the end (End) of a task.
▱	*Input/Output*	Used for input and output operations, such as reading and printing. The data to be read or printed are described inside.
▭	*Processing*	Used for arithmetic and data-manipulation operations. The instructions are listed inside the symbol.
◇	*Decision*	Used for any logic or comparison operations. Unlike the input/output and processing symbols, which have one entry and one exit flowline, the decision symbol has one entry and two exit paths. The path chosen depends on whether the answer to a question is "yes" or "no."

◯	*Connector*	Used to join different flowlines.
	Offpage Connector	Used to indicate that the flowchart continues to a second page.
	Predefined Process	Used to represent a group of statements that perform one processing task.
	Annotation	Used to provide additional information about another flowchart symbol.

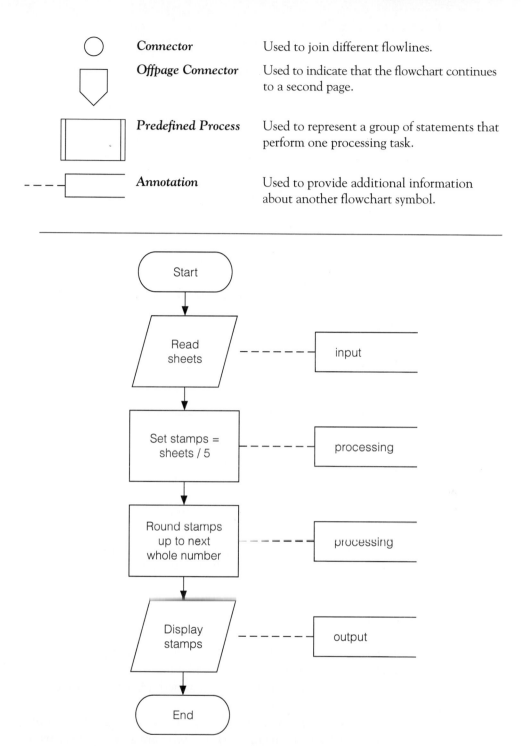

Figure 1.16 Flowchart for the postage stamp problem.

The main advantage of using a flowchart to plan a task is that it provides a pictorial representation of the task, which makes the logic easier to follow. We can clearly see every step and how each step is connected to the next. The major disadvantage with flowcharts is that when a program is very large, the flowcharts may continue for many pages, making them difficult to follow and modify.

Pseudocode

Pseudocode is an abbreviated version of actual computer code (hence, *pseudocode*). The geometric symbols used in flowcharts are replaced by English-like statements that outline the process. As a result, pseudocode looks more like computer code than does a flowchart. Pseudocode allows the programmer to focus on the steps required to solve a problem rather than on how to use the computer language. The programmer can describe the algorithm in Visual Basic-like form without being restricted by the rules of Visual Basic. When the pseudocode is completed, it can be easily translated into the Visual Basic language.

The following is pseudocode for the postage stamp problem:

> **Program:** Determine the proper number of stamps for a letter
> Read Sheets   (*input*)
> Set the number of stamps to Sheets / 5   (*processing*)
> Round the number of stamps up to the next whole number   (*processing*)
> Display the number of stamps   (*output*)

Pseudocode has several advantages. It is compact and probably will not extend for many pages as flowcharts commonly do. Also, the plan looks like the code to be written and so is preferred by many programmers.

Hierarchy Charts

The last programming tool we'll discuss is the **hierarchy chart,** which shows the overall program structure. Hierarchy charts are also called structure charts, HIPO (Hierarchy plus Input-Process-Output) charts, top-down charts, or VTOC (Visual Table of Contents) charts. All these names refer to planning diagrams that are similar to a company's organization chart.

Hierarchy charts depict the organization of a program but omit the specific processing logic. They describe what each part, or **module**, of the program does and they show how the modules relate to each other. The details on how the modules work, however, are omitted. The chart is read from top to bottom and from left to right. Each module may be subdivided into a succession of submodules that branch out under it. Typically, after the activities in the succession of submodules are carried out, the module to the right of the original module is considered. A quick glance at the hierarchy chart reveals each task performed in the program and where it is performed. Figure 1.17 shows a hierarchy chart for the postage stamp problem.

The main benefit of hierarchy charts is in the initial planning of a program. We break down the major parts of a program so we can see what must be done in general. From this point, we can then refine each module into more detailed plans using flowcharts or pseudocode. This process is called the **divide-and-conquer** method.

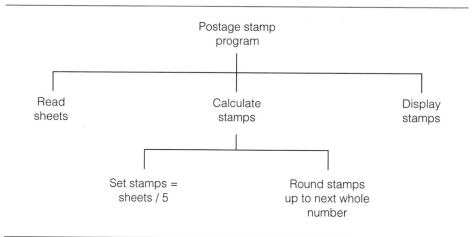

Figure 1.17 Hierarchy chart for the postage stamp problem.

The postage stamp problem was solved by a series of instructions to read data, perform calculations, and display results. Each step was in a sequence; that is, we moved from one line to the next without skipping over any lines. This kind of structure is called a **sequence structure**. Many problems, however, require a decision to determine whether a series of instructions should be executed. If the answer to a question is "Yes," then one group of instructions is executed. If the answer is "No," then another is executed. This structure is called a **decision structure**. Figure 1.18 contains the pseudocode and flowchart for a decision structure.

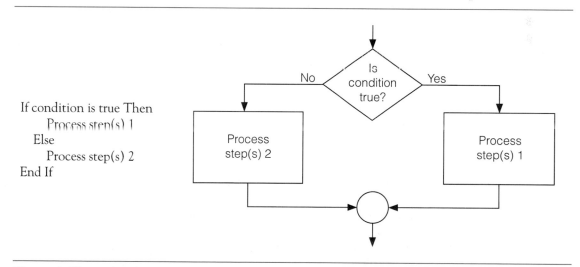

```
If condition is true Then
      Process step(s) 1
Else
      Process step(s) 2
End If
```

Figure 1.18 Pseudocode and flowchart for a decision structure.

The sequence and decision structures are both used to solve the following problem:

Direction of Numbered NYC Streets Algorithm

Problem: Given a street number of a one-way street in New York, decide the direction of the street, either eastbound or westbound.

Discussion: There is a simple rule to tell the direction of a one-way street in New York: Even numbered streets run eastbound.

Input: Street number

Processing: Decide if the street number is divisible by 2.

Output: "Eastbound" or "Westbound"

Figures 1.19 through 1.21 show the flowchart, pseudocode, and hierarchy chart for the New York numbered streets problem.

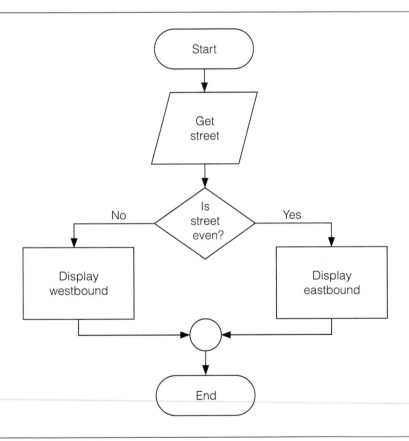

Figure 1.19 Flowchart for the New York numbered streets problem.

Program: Determine the direction of a numbered NYC street.

```
Get Street
If Street is even Then
    Display Eastbound
  Else
    Display Westbound
End If
```

Figure 1.20 Pseudocode for the New York numbered streets problem.

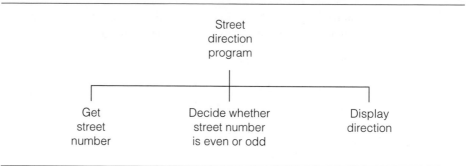

Figure 1.21 Hierarchy chart for the New York numbered streets problem.

The solution to the next problem requires the repetition of a series of instructions. A programming structure that executes instructions many times is called a **loop structure**.

We need a test (or decision) to tell when the loop should end. Without an exit condition, the loop would repeat endlessly (an infinite loop). One way to control the number of times a loop repeats (often referred to as the number of passes or iterations) is to check a condition before each pass through the loop and continue executing the loop as long as the condition is true. See Figure 1.22.

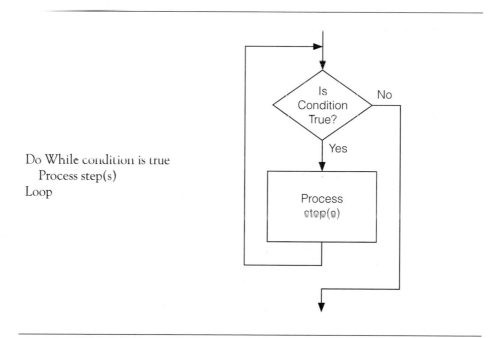

Do While condition is true
   Process step(s)
Loop

Figure 1.22 Pseudocode and flowchart for a loop.

Class-Average Algorithm

Problem: Calculate and report the grade-point average for a class.

Discussion: The average grade equals the sum of all grades divided by the number of students. We need a loop to read and then add (accumulate) the grades for each student in the class. Inside the loop, we also need to total (count) the number of students in the class. See Figures 1.23 to 1.25.

Input: Student grades

Processing: Find the sum of the grades; count the number of students; calculate average grade = sum of grades / number of students.

Output: Average grade

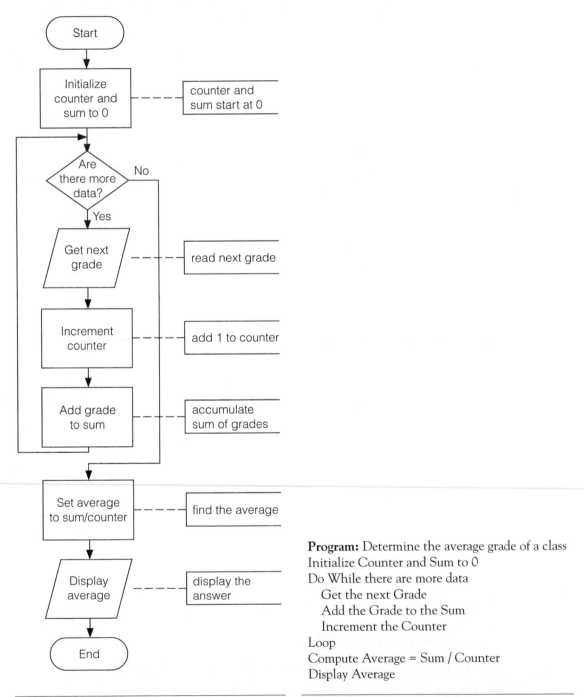

Program: Determine the average grade of a class
Initialize Counter and Sum to 0
Do While there are more data
    Get the next Grade
    Add the Grade to the Sum
    Increment the Counter
Loop
Compute Average = Sum / Counter
Display Average

Figure 1.23 Flowchart for the class-average problem.

Figure 1.24 Pseudocode for the class-average problem.

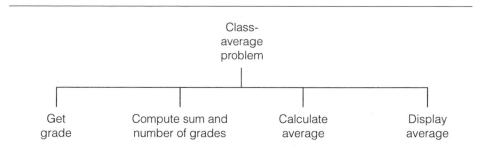

Figure 1.25 Hierarchy chart for the class-average problem.

Comments

1. Tracing a flowchart is like playing a board game. We begin at the Start symbol and proceed from symbol to symbol until we reach the End symbol. At any time, we will be at just one symbol. In a board game, the path taken depends on the result of spinning a spinner or rolling a pair of dice. The path taken through a flowchart depends on the input.

2. The algorithm should be tested at the flowchart or pseudocode stage before being coded into a program. Different data should be used as input, and the output checked. This process is known as **desk checking**. The test data should include nonstandard data as well as typical data.

3. Flowcharts, pseudocode, and hierarchy charts are universal problem-solving tools. They can be used to construct programs in any computer language, not just Visual Basic.

4. Flowcharts are used throughout this text to provide a visualization of the flow of certain programming tasks and Visual Basic control structures. Major examples of pseudocode and hierarchy charts appear in the case studies.

5. There are four primary logical programming constructs: sequence, decision, loop, and unconditional branch. Unconditional branch, which appears in some languages as Goto statements, involves jumping from one place in a program to another. Structured programming uses the first three constructs but forbids the fourth. One advantage of pseudocode over flowcharts is that pseudocode has no provision for unconditional branching and thus forces the programmer to write structured programs.

6. Flowcharts are time-consuming to write and difficult to update. For this reason, professional programmers are more likely to favor pseudocode and hierarchy charts. Because flowcharts so clearly illustrate the logical flow of programming techniques, however, they are a valuable tool in the education of programmers.

7. There are many styles of pseudocode. Some programmers use an outline form, whereas others use a form that looks almost like a programming language. The pseudocode appearing in the case studies of this text focuses on the primary tasks to be performed by the program and leaves many of the routine details to be completed during the coding process. Several Visual Basic keywords, such as, Print, If, Do, and While, are used extensively in the pseudocode appearing in this text.

8. Many people draw rectangles around each item in a hierarchy chart. In this text, rectangles are omitted to encourage the use of hierarchy charts by making them easier to draw.

2 Fundamentals of Programming in Visual Basic

2.1 VISUAL BASIC OBJECTS

Visual Basic programs display a Windows style screen (called a **form**) with boxes into which users type (and edit) information and buttons that they click to initiate actions. The boxes and buttons are referred to as **controls**. Forms and controls are called **objects**. In this section, we examine forms and four of the most useful Visual Basic controls.

Note: If Visual Basic has not been installed on your computer, you can install it by following the steps outlined on the first page of Appendix B.

Invoking Visual Basic 6.0: To invoke Visual Basic, click the Start button, point to Programs, point to Microsoft Visual Basic 6.0, and click on Microsoft Visual Basic 6.0 in the final list.

With all versions of Visual Basic 6.0, the center of the screen will contain the New Project window of Figure 2.1. The main part of the window is a tabbed dialog box with three tabs—New, Existing, and Recent. (If the New tab is not in the foreground, click on it to bring it to the front.) The number of project icons showing are either three (with the Working Model and Learning Editions) or thirteen (with the Professional and Enterprise Editions).

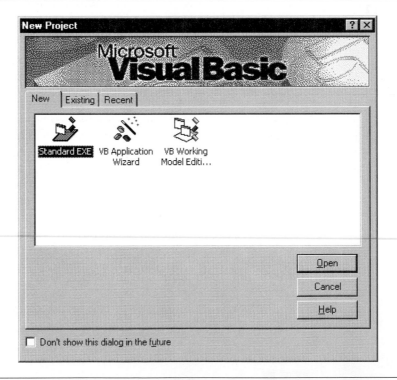

Figure 2.1 New Project window from Working Model Edition of VB 6.0.

Double-click the Standard EXE icon to bring up the initial Visual Basic screen in Figure 2.2. The appearance of this screen varies slightly with the different editions of Visual Basic.

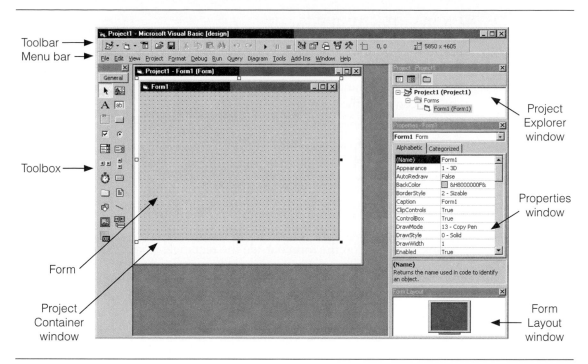

Figure 2.2 The initial Visual Basic screen.

The **Toolbar** is a collection of icons that carry out standard operations when clicked. For example, the fifth icon, which looks like a diskette, can be used to save the current program to a disk. To reveal the function of a Toolbar icon, position the mouse pointer over the icon for a few seconds.

The **Menu bar** of the Visual Basic screen displays the commands you use to work with Visual Basic. Some of the menus, like File, Edit, View, and Window, are common to most Windows applications. Others, such as Project, Format, and Debug, provide commands specific to programming in Visual Basic.

The large stippled **Form window**, or **form** for short, becomes a Windows window when a program is executed. Most information displayed by the program appears on the form. The information usually is displayed in controls that have been placed on the form. The **Form Layout window** allows you to position the location of the form at run time relative to the entire screen using a small graphical representation of the screen.

The **Project Explorer window** is not needed for our purposes. The **Properties window** is used to change how objects look and react.

The icons in the **Toolbox** represent controls that can be placed on the form. The four controls discussed in this chapter are text boxes, labels, command buttons, and picture boxes.

Text boxes: You use a text box primarily to get information, referred to as **input**, from the user.

Labels: You place a label to the left of a text box to tell the user what type of information to enter into the text box. You also use labels to display output.

Command buttons: The user clicks a command button to initiate an action.

Picture boxes: You use a picture box to display text or graphics output.

▣ A Text Box Walkthrough

1. Double-click on the text box icon. (The text box icon consists of the letters ab and a vertical bar cursor inside a rectangle and is the fourth icon in the Toolbox.) A rectangle with eight small squares, called sizing handles, appears at the center of the form. See Figure 2.3.

Figure 2.3 A text box with sizing handles.

2. Click anywhere on the form outside the rectangle to remove the handles.

3. Click on the rectangle to restore the handles. An object showing its handles is (said to be) **selected**. A selected object can have its size altered, location changed, and other properties modified.

4. Move the mouse arrow to the handle in the center of the right side of the text box. The cursor should change to a double arrow (↔). Hold down the left mouse button, and move the mouse to the right. The text box is stretched to the right. Similarly, grabbing the text box by one of the other handles and moving the mouse stretches the text box in another direction. For instance, you use the handle in the upper-left corner to stretch the text box up and to the left. Handles also can be used to make the text box smaller.

5. Move the mouse arrow to any point of the text box other than a handle, hold down the left mouse button, and move the mouse. You can now drag the text box to a new location. Using Steps 4 and 5, you can place a text box of any size anywhere on the form.

   Note: The text box should now be selected; that is, its sizing handles should be showing. If not, click anywhere inside the text box to select it.

6. Press the delete key, Del, to remove the text box from the form. Step 7 gives an alternative way to place a text box of any size at any location on the form.

7. Click on the text box icon in the Toolbox. Then move the mouse pointer to any place on the form. (When over the form, the mouse pointer becomes a pair of crossed thin lines.) Hold down the left mouse button, and move the mouse on a diagonal to generate a rectangle. Release the mouse button to obtain a selected text box. You can now alter the size and location as before.

   Note: The text box should now be selected; that is, its sizing handles should be showing. If not, click anywhere inside the text box to select it.

8. Press F4 to activate the Properties window. (You can also activate the properties window by clicking on it or clicking on the Properties Window icon in the Toolbar.) See Figure 2.4. The first line of the Properties window (called the **Object box**) reads "Text1 TextBox". Text1 is the current name of the text box. The two tabs permit you to view the list of properties either alphabetically or grouped into categories. Text boxes have 43 properties that

can be grouped into 7 categories. Use the up- and down-arrow keys (or the up- and down-scroll arrows) to glance through the list. The left column gives the property and the right column gives the current setting of the property. We discuss four properties in this walkthrough.

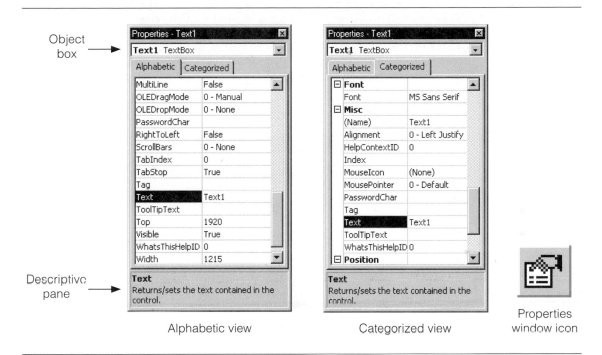

Figure 2.4 Text box Properties window.

9. Move to the Text property with the up- and down-arrow keys. (Alternatively, scroll until the property is visible and click on the property.) The Text property is now highlighted. The Text property determines the words in the text box. Currently, the words are set to "Text1" in the **Settings box** on the right.

10. Type your first name. As you type, your name replaces "Text1" in both the Settings box and the text box. See Figure 2.5. (Alternatively, you could have clicked on the Settings box and edited its contents.)

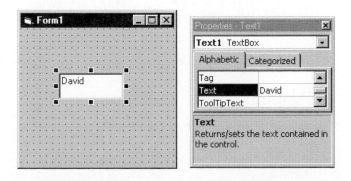

Figure 2.5 Setting the text property to David.

11. Click at the beginning of your name in the Settings box and add your title, such as Mr., Ms., or The Honorable. (If you mistyped your name, you can easily correct it now.)

12. Press Shift+Ctrl+F to move to the first property that begins with the letter F. Now use the down-arrow key or the mouse to highlight the property ForeColor. The foreground color is the color of the text.

13. Click on the down arrow in the right part of the Settings box, and then click on the Palette tab to display a selection of colors. See Figure 2.6. Click on one of the solid colors, such as blue or red. Notice the change in the color of your name.

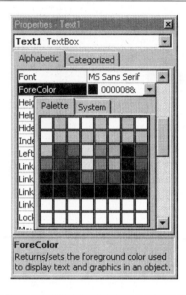

Figure 2.6 Setting the ForeColor property.

14. Highlight the Font property with a single click of the mouse. The current font is named MS Sans Serif.

15. Click on the ellipsis (...) box in the right part of the Settings box to display a dialog box. See Figure 2.7. The three lists give the current name (MS Sans Serif), current style (Regular), and current size (8) of the font. You can change any of these attributes by clicking. Click on Bold in the style list, and click on 12 in the size list. Now click on the OK button to see your name displayed in a larger bold font.

16. Click on the text box and resize it to be about 3 inches wide and 1 inch high.

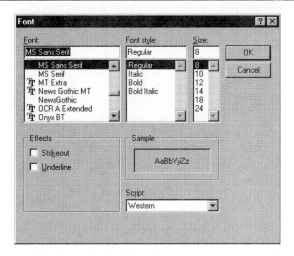

Figure 2.7 The Font dialog box.

Visual Basic programs consist of three parts—interface, values of properties, and code. Our interface consists of a form with a single object, a text box. We have set a few properties for the text box—the text (namely, your name), the foreground color, the font style, and the font size. In Section 2.2, we see how to place code into a program. Visual Basic endows certain capabilities to programs that are independent of any code. We will now run the existing codeless program and experience these capabilities.

17. Press F5 to run the program. (Alternatively, a program can be run from the menu by pressing Alt/R/S or by clicking on the Start icon ▶, the 12th icon on the Toolbar.) Notice that the dots have disappeared from the form.

18. The cursor is at the beginning of your name. Press the End key to move the cursor to the end of your name. Now type in your last name, and then keep typing. Eventually, the words will scroll to the left.

19. Press Home to return to the beginning of the text. You have a full-fledged word processor at your disposal. You can place the cursor anywhere you like to add or delete text. You can drag the cursor across text to create a block, place a copy of the block in the clipboard with Ctrl+C, and then duplicate it anywhere with Ctrl+V.

20. To terminate the program, press Alt+F4. Alternatively, you can end a program by clicking on the End icon ■, the 14th icon on the Toolbar, or clicking on the form's close button ☒.

21. Select the text box, activate the Properties window, select the MultiLine property, click on the down-arrow button, and finally click on True. The MultiLine property has been changed from False to True.

22. Run the program, and type in the text box. Notice that now words wrap around when the end of a line is reached. Also, text will scroll up when it reaches the bottom of the text box.

23. End the program.

24. Press Alt/F/V or click on the Save Project icon 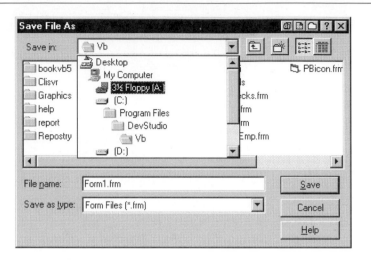 to save the work done so far. A Save File As dialog box appears. See Figure 2.8. Visual Basic creates two disk files to store a program. The first, with the extension .frm, is entered into the Save File As dialog box and the second, with the extension .vbp, into a Save Project As dialog box. Visual Basic refers to programs as **projects**.

Figure 2.8 The Save File As dialog box.

25. Type a file name, such as *testprog,* into the "File name" box. The extension .frm automatically will be appended to the name. Do not press the Enter key yet. (Pressing the Enter key has the same effect as clicking Save.) The selection in the "Save in" box tells where your program will be saved. Alter it as desired. (**Suggestion:** If you are using a computer in a campus computer lab, you probably should use a diskette to save your work. If so, place the diskette in a drive, say, the A drive, and select 3^1/$_2$ Floppy (A:) in the "Save in" box.)

26. Click the Save button when you are ready to go on. (Alternatively, press Tab several times until the Save button is highlighted and then press Enter.) The Save Project As dialog box appears.

27. Type a file name into the File name box. You can use the same name, such as *testprog,* as before. Then proceed as in Steps 25 and 26. (The extension .vbp will be added.)

28. Press Alt/F/N to begin a new program. (As before, select Standard EXE.)

29. Place three text boxes on the form. (Move each text box out of the center of the form before creating the next.) Notice that they have the names Text1, Text2, and Text3.

30. Run the program. Notice that the cursor is in Text1. We say that Text1 has the **focus**. (This means that Text1 is the currently selected object and any keyboard actions will be sent directly to this object.) Any text typed will display in that text box.

31. Press Tab once. Now, Text2 has the focus. When you type, the characters appear in Text2.

32. Press Tab several times, and then press Shift+Tab a few times. With Tab, the focus cycles through the objects on the form in the order the objects were created. With Shift+Tab, the focus cycles in the reverse order.

33. End the program.

34. Press Alt/F/O, or click on the Open Project icon 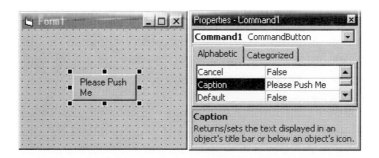 to reload your first program. When a dialog box asks if you want to save your changes, click the No button or press N. An Open Project dialog box appears on the screen. Click on the Recent tab to see a list of the programs most recently opened or saved. Your first program and its location should appear at the top of the list. (**Note:** You can also find any program by clicking on the Existing tab and using the dialog box to search for the program.) Click on the name of your first program and then click on the Open button. Alternatively, double-click on the name. (You also have the option of typing the name into the "File name" box and then clicking the Open button.)

Note: Whenever you open a program that has been saved, you will not see the program's form. To view the form, select Object from the View menu by pressing Alt/V/B. If the word "Object" is grayed, run the program, terminate the program, and then try Alt/V/B again.

▣ A Command Button Walkthrough

1. Press Alt/F/N and double-click on Standard EXE to start a new program. There is no need to save anything.

2. Double-click on the command button icon to place a command button in the center of the form. (The rectangular-shaped command button icon is the sixth icon in the Toolbox.)

3. Activate the Properties window, highlight the Caption property, and type "Please Push Me". See Figure 2.9. Notice that the letters appear on the command button as they are typed. The button is too small.

Figure 2.9 Setting the Caption property.

4. Click on the command button to select it, and then enlarge it to accommodate the phrase "Please Push Me" on one line.

5. Run the program, and click on the command button. The command button appears to move in and then out. In Section 2.2, we write code that is activated when a command button is pushed.

6. End the program, and select the command button.

7. From the Properties window, edit the Caption setting by inserting an ampersand (&) before the first letter, P. Notice that the ampersand does not show on the button. However, the letter following the ampersand is now underlined. See Figure 2.10. Pressing Alt+P while the program is running executes the same code as clicking the command button. Here, P is referred to as the **access key** for the command button. (The access key is always specified as the character following the ampersand.)

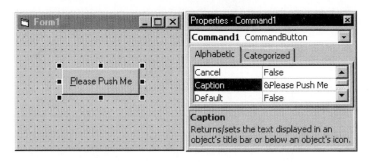

Figure 2.10 Designating P as an access key.

A A Label Walkthrough

1. Press Alt/F/N and double-click on Standard EXE to start a new program. There is no need to save anything.

2. Double-click on the label icon to place a label in the center of the form. (The label icon, a large letter A, is the third icon in the Toolbox.)

3. Activate the Properties window, highlight the Caption property, and type "Enter Your Phone Number". Such a label would be placed next to a text box into which the user will enter a phone number.

4. Click on the label to select it, and then widen it until all words are on the same line.

5. Make the label narrower until the words occupy two lines.

6. Activate the Properties window, and double-click on the Alignment property. Double-click two more times and observe the label's appearance. The combination of sizing and alignment permits you to design a label easily.

7. Run the program. Nothing happens, even if you click on the label. Labels just sit there. The user cannot change what a label displays unless you write code to allow the change.

8. End the program.

A Picture Box Walkthrough

1. Press Alt/F/N, and double-click on Standard EXE to start a new program. There is no need to save anything.

2. Double-click on the picture box icon to place a picture box in the center of the form. (The picture box icon is the second icon in the Toolbox. It contains a picture of the sun shining over a desert.)

3. Enlarge the picture box.

4. Run the program. Nothing happens and nothing will, no matter what you do. Although picture boxes look like text boxes, you can't type in them. However, you can display text in them with statements discussed later in this chapter, you can draw lines and circles in them with statements discussed in Chapter 5, and you can insert pictures into them.

5. End the program and click the picture box to select it.

6. Activate the Properties window, and double-click on the Picture property. A Load Picture dialog box appears. See Figure 2.11.

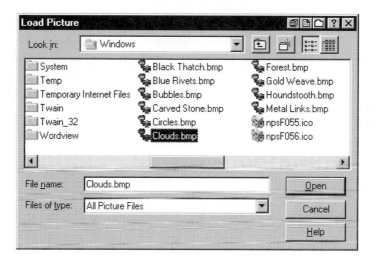

Figure 2.11 The Load Picture dialog box.

7. Select the Windows folder and then double-click on one of the picture files. Good candidates are Clouds.bmp, shown in Figure 2.12, and Setup.bmp. (Also, the CD accompanying this textbook contains several picture files in the folder Pictures.)

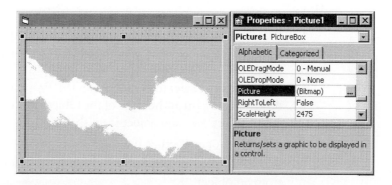

Figure 2.12 A picture box filled with the Clouds.bmp picture.

8. Click on the picture box and press Del to remove the picture box.

Comments

1. When selecting from a list, double-clicking has the same effect as clicking once and pressing Enter.

2. On a form, the Tab key cycles through the objects that can get the focus, and in a dialog box, it cycles through the items.

3. The form itself is also an object and has properties. For instance, you can change the text in the title bar with the Caption property. You can move the form by dragging the title bar of its Project Container window.

4. The name of an object is used in code to refer to the object. By default, objects are given names like Text1 and Text2. You can use the Properties window to change the Name property of an object to a more suggestive name. (The Name property is always the first property in the list of properties. An object's Name must start with a letter and can be a maximum of 40 characters. It can include numbers and underline (_) characters, but can't include punctuation or spaces.) Also, Microsoft recommends that each name begin with a three-letter prefix that identifies the type of the control. See the table below. Beginning with Section 2.2, we will use suggestive names and these prefixes whenever possible.

Object	Prefix	Example
command button	cmd	cmdComputeTotal
form	frm	frmPayroll
label	lbl	lblInstructions
picture box	pic	picClouds
text box	txt	txtAddress

5. The Name and Caption properties of a command button are both initially set to something like Command1. However, changing one of these properties does not affect the setting of the other property. The same is true for the Name and Caption properties of forms and labels, and for the Name and Text properties of text boxes.

6. The color settings appear as strings of digits and letters preceded by &H and trailed with &. Don't concern yourself with this notation.

7. Here are some fine points on the use of the Properties window.

   (a) Press Shift+Ctrl+*letterkey* to highlight the first property that begins with that letter. Successive pressings highlight successive properties that begin with that letter.

   (b) To change the selected object from the Properties window, click on the down-arrow icon at the right of the Object box of the Properties window. Then select the new object from the drop-down list.

8. Some useful properties that have not been discussed are the following:

   (a) BorderStyle: Setting the BorderStyle to "0 – None" removes the border from an object.

   (b) Visible: Setting the Visible property to False hides an object when the program is run. The object can be made to reappear with code.

(c) BackColor: Specifies the background color for a text box, label, picture box, or form. Also specifies the background color for a command button having the Style property set to "1 – Graphical." (Such a command button can display a picture.)

(d) BackStyle: The BackStyle property of a label is opaque by default. The rectangular region associated with the label is filled with the label's background color and caption. Setting the background style of a label to transparent causes whatever is behind the label to remain visible; the background color of the label essentially becomes "see through."

(e) Font: Can be set to any of Windows' fonts, such as Courier or Times New Roman. Two unusual fonts are Symbol and Wingdings. For instance, with the Wingdings font, pressing the keys for %, &, ', and J yield a bell, a book, a candle, and a smiling face, respectively. To view the character sets for the different Windows' fonts, click on the Start button, and successively select Programs, Accessories, and Character Map. Then click on Character Map or press the Enter key. After selecting a font, hold down the left mouse button on any character to enlarge it and obtain the keystroke that produces that character.

9. When you click on a property in the Properties window, a description of the property appears just below the window. With the Learning, Professional, and Enterprise Editions of VB 6.0 you can obtain very detailed (and somewhat advanced) information about a property by clicking on the property and pressing F1 for Help.

10. Most properties can be set or altered with code as the program is running instead of being preset from the Properties window. For instance, a command button can be made to disappear with a line such as Command1.Visible = False. See Section 2.2 for details.

11. The BorderStyle and MultiLine properties of a text box can be set only from the Properties window. You cannot alter them during run time.

12. Of the objects discussed in this section, only command buttons have true access keys.

13. If you inadvertently double-click on an object in a form, a window containing two lines of text will appear. (The first line begins Private Sub.) This is a code window and is discussed in the next section. To remove this window, click on its Close button.

14. To enlarge (or decrease) the Project Container window, position the mouse cursor anywhere on the right or bottom edge and drag the mouse. To enlarge (or decrease) the form, select the form and drag one of its sizing handles. Alternatively, you can enlarge either the Project Container window or the form by clicking on its Maximize button.

15. We will always be selecting the Standard EXE icon from the New Project window.

✔ **PRACTICE PROBLEMS 2.1**

1. What is the difference between the Caption and the Name of a command button?

2. Suppose in an earlier session you created an object that looks like an empty rectangle. It might be a picture box, a text box with Text property set to nothing (blanked out by deleting all characters), or a label with a blank caption and BorderStyle property set to Fixed Single. How might you determine which it is?

➤ **EXERCISES 2.1**

1. Why are command buttons sometimes called "push buttons"?

2. How can you tell if a program is running by looking at the screen?

3. Create a form with two command buttons, run the program, and click on each button. Do you notice anything different about a button after it has been clicked?

4. Place a text box on a form and select the text box. What is the effect of pressing the various arrow keys while holding down the Ctrl key? The Shift key?

5. Place three text boxes vertically on a form with Text3 above Text2, and Text2 above Text1. Then run the program and successively press Tab. Notice that the text boxes receive the focus from bottom to top. Experiment with various configurations of command buttons and text boxes to convince yourself that objects get the focus in the order in which they were created.

6. While a program is running, an object is said to **lose focus** when the focus moves from that object to another object. In what three ways can the user cause an object to lose focus?

In Exercises 7 to 28, carry out the task. Use a new form for each exercise.

7. Place CHECKING ACCOUNT in the title bar of a form.

8. Create a text box containing the words PLAY IT, SAM in blue letters.

9. Create an empty text box with a yellow background.

10. Create a text box containing the word HELLO in large italic letters.

11. Create a text box containing the sentence "After all is said and done, more is said than done." The sentence should occupy three lines and each line should be centered in the text box.

12. Create a borderless text box containing the words VISUAL BASIC in bold white letters on a red background.

13. Create a text box containing the words VISUAL BASIC in Courier font.

14. Create a command button containing the word PUSH.

15. Create a command button containing the word PUSH in large italic letters.

16. Create a command button containing the word PUSH in nonbold letters with the letter P underlined.

17. Create a command button containing the word PUSH with the letter H as access key.

18. Create a command button containing the caption HALF MOON, a white background, and the picture file MOON7.BMP from the Pictures folder of the CD accompanying this book.

19. Create a label containing the word ALIAS.

20. Create a label containing the word ALIAS in white on a blue background.

21. Create a label with a border containing the centered italicized word ALIAS.

22. Create a label containing VISUAL on the first line and BASIC on the second line. Each word should be right justified. (**Note:** An extra space will appear after "VISUAL.")

23. Create a label containing a picture of a diskette. (**Hint:** Use the Wingdings character <.) Make the diskette large.

24. Create a label with a border and containing the bold word ALIAS in the Terminal font.

25. Create a picture box with a yellow background.

26. Create a picture box with no border and a red background.

27. Create a picture box containing two command buttons.

28. Create a picture box with a blue background containing a picture box with a white background.

In Exercises 29 to 36, create the interface shown in the figure. (These exercises give you practice creating objects and assigning properties. The interfaces do not necessarily correspond to actual programs.)

29.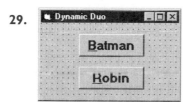

30.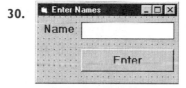

31.

32.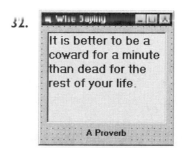

33.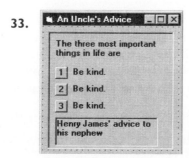

34.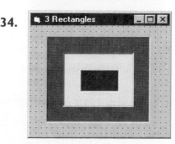

35.

This picture is contained in the file picbox.bmp in the Pictures folder of the CD accompanying this book.

36.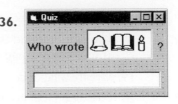

37. Create a replica of your bank check on a form. Words common to all checks, such as PAY TO THE ORDER OF, should be contained in labels. Items specific to your checks, such as your name at the top left, should be contained in text boxes. Make the check on the screen resemble your check as much as possible.

38. Create a replica of your campus ID on a form. Words that are on all student IDs, such as the name of the college, should be contained in labels. Information specific to your ID, such as your name and social security number, should be contained in text boxes. Simulate your picture with a text box containing a smiling face—a size 24 Wingdings J.

39. If you are familiar with Paint (one of the programs in the group Accessories), use Paint to make a drawing and then save it as a .bmp file. In Visual Basic, create a picture box containing the picture.

✔✔ **Solutions to Practice Problems 2.1**

1. The Caption is the text appearing on the command button, whereas the Name is the designation used to refer to the command button. Initially, they have the same value, such as Command1. However, they can each be changed independently of the other.

2. Click on the object to select it, and then press F4 to activate its Properties window. The Object box gives the Name of the object (in bold letters) and its type, such as Label, TextBox, or PictureBox.

We have examined only four of the objects from the Toolbox. To determine the type of one of the other objects, hold the mouse pointer over it for a few seconds.

2.2 VISUAL BASIC EVENTS

When a Visual Basic program is run, a form and its controls appear on the screen. Normally, nothing happens until the user takes an action, such as clicking a control or pressing the Tab key. Such an action is called an **event**.

The three steps to creating a Visual Basic program are as follows:

1. Create the interface; that is, generate, position, and size the objects.

2. Set properties; that is, set relevant properties for the objects.

3. Write the code that executes when the events occur.

This section is devoted to Step 3.

Code consists of statements that carry out tasks. Visual Basic has a repertoire of over 200 statements, and we will use many of them in this text. In this section, we limit ourselves to statements that change properties of objects while a program is running.

Properties of an object are changed in code with statements of the form

```
objectName.property = setting
```

where *objectName* is the name of the form or a control, *property* is one of the properties of the object, and *setting* is a valid setting for that object. Such statements are called **assignment statements**. They assign values to properties. Here are three other assignment statements.

The statement

```
txtBox.Font.Size = 12
```

sets the size of the characters in the text box named txtBox to 12.

The statement

```
txtBox.Font.Bold = True
```

converts the characters in the text box to boldface.

The statement

```
txtBox.Text = ""
```

clears the contents of the text box; that is, it invokes the blank setting.

Most events are associated with objects. The event *clicking cmdButton* is different from the event *clicking picBox*. These two events are specified cmdButton_Click and picBox_Click. The statements to be executed when an event occurs are written in a block of code called an **event procedure**. The structure of an event procedure is

```
Private Sub objectName_event()
    statements
End Sub
```

The word Sub in the first line signals the beginning of the event procedure, and the first line identifies the object and the event occurring to that object. The last line signals the termination of the event procedure. The statements to be executed appear between these two lines. (**Note:** The word Private indicates that the event procedure cannot be invoked by an event from another form. This will always be the case in this text. The word *Sub* is an abbreviation of *Subprogram*.) For instance, the event procedure

```
Private Sub cmdButton_Click()
    txtBox.Text = ""
End Sub
```

clears the contents of the text box when the command button is clicked.

An Event Procedure Walkthrough

The form in Figure 2.13, which contains a text box and a command button, will be used to demonstrate what event procedures are and how they are created. Three event procedures will be used to alter the appearance of a phrase that is typed into the text box. The event procedures are txtPhrase_LostFocus, txtPhrase_GotFocus, and cmdBold_Click.

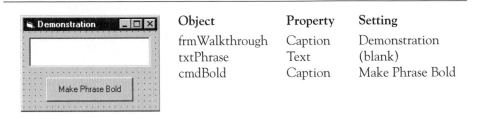

Object	Property	Setting
frmWalkthrough	Caption	Demonstration
txtPhrase	Text	(blank)
cmdBold	Caption	Make Phrase Bold

Figure 2.13 The interface for the event procedure walkthrough.

1. Create the interface in Figure 2.13. The Name properties of the form, text box, and command button should be set as shown in the Object column. The Caption property of the form should be set to Demonstration, the Text property of the text box should be made blank, and the Caption property of the command button should be set to Make Phrase Bold.

2. Double-click on the text box. A window, called a **code window**, appears. See Figure 2.14. Just below the title bar are two drop-down list boxes. The left box is called the **Object box** and the right box is called the **Procedure box**. (When you position the mouse pointer over one of these list boxes, its type appears.)

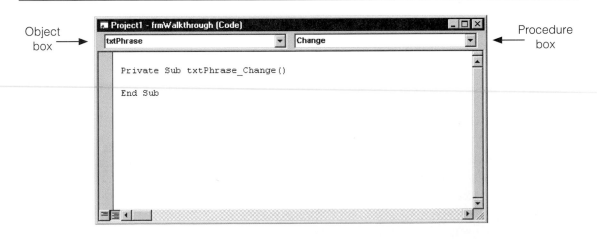

Figure 2.14 A code window.

3. Click on the down-arrow button to the right of the Procedure box. The drop-down menu that appears contains a list of all possible event procedures associated with text boxes. See Figure 2.15.

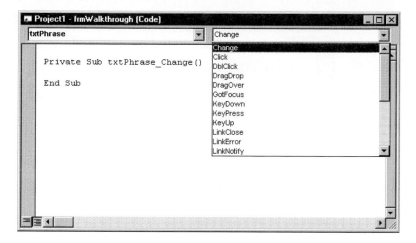

Figure 2.15 Drop-down menu of event procedures.

4. Scroll down the list of event procedures and click on LostFocus. (LostFocus is the 14th event procedure.) The lines

```
Private Sub txtPhrase_LostFocus()

End Sub
```

appear in the code window with a blinking cursor poised at the beginning of the blank line.

5. Type the line

```
txtPhrase.Font.Size = 12
```

between the existing two lines. (We usually indent lines inside procedures.) (After you type each period, the editor displays a list containing possible choices of items to follow the period. See Figure 2.16. This feature is called "List Properties/Methods." In Figure 2.16, instead of typing the word "Size," you can double-click on "Size" in the displayed list or highlight the word "Size" and press Tab.) The screen appears as in Figure 2.17. We have now created an event procedure that is activated whenever the text box loses the focus.

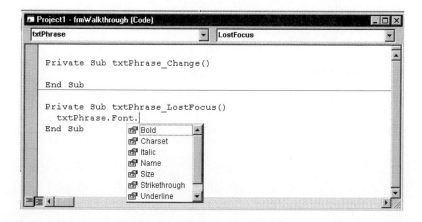

Figure 2.16 A LostFocus event procedure.

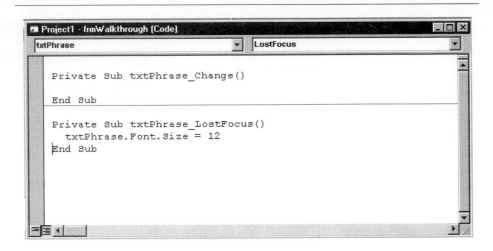

Figure 2.17 A LostFocus event procedure.

6. Let's create another event procedure for the text box. Click on the down-arrow button to the right of the Procedure box, scroll up the list of event procedures, and click on GotFocus. Then type the lines

```
txtPhrase.Font.Size = 8
txtPhrase.Font.Bold = False
```

between the existing two lines. See Figure 2.18.

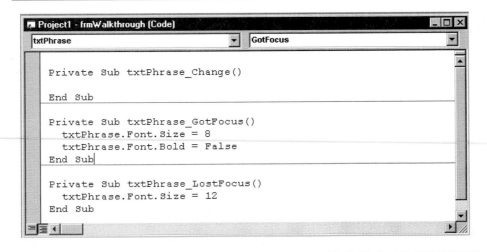

Figure 2.18 A GotFocus event procedure.

7. The txtPhrase_Change event procedure in Figure 2.18 was not used and can be deleted. To delete the procedure, highlight it by dragging the mouse across the two lines of code, and then press the Del key.

8. Let's now create an event procedure for the command button. Click on the down-arrow button to the right of the Object box. The drop-down menu contains a list of the objects, along with a mysterious object called (General). See Figure 2.19. [We'll discuss (General) later in this chapter.]

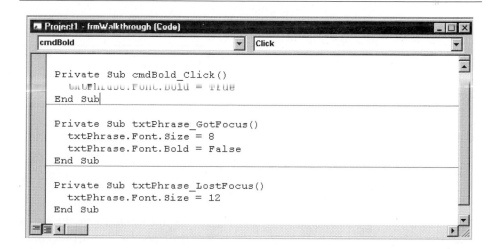

Figure 2.19 List of objects.

9. Click on cmdBold. The event procedure cmdBold_Click is displayed. Type in the line

```
txtPhrase.Font.Bold = True
```

The screen appears as in Figure 2.20, and the program is complete.

```
Private Sub cmdBold_Click()
   txtPhrase.Font.Bold = True
End Sub

Private Sub txtPhrase_GotFocus()
   txtPhrase.Font.Size = 8
   txtPhrase.Font.Bold = False
End Sub

Private Sub txtPhrase_LostFocus()
   txtPhrase.Font.Size = 12
End Sub
```

Figure 2.20 The three event procedures.

10. Now run the program by pressing F5.

11. Type something into the text box. In Figure 2.21, the words "Hello Friend" have been typed. (A text box has the focus whenever it is ready to accept typing; that is, whenever it contains a blinking cursor.)

Figure 2.21 Text box containing input.

12. Press the Tab key. The contents of the text box will be enlarged as in Figure 2.22. When Tab was pressed, the text box lost the focus; that is, the event LostFocus happened to txtPhrase. Thus, the event procedure txtPhrase_LostFocus was called, and the code inside the procedure was executed.

Figure 2.22 Text box after it has lost the focus.

13. Click on the command button. This calls the event procedure cmdBold_Click, which converts the text to boldface. See Figure 2.23.

Figure 2.23 Text box after the command button has been clicked.

14. Click on the text box or press the Tab key to move the cursor (and, therefore, the focus) to the text box. This calls the event procedure txtPhrase_GotFocus, which restores the text to its original state.

15. You can repeat Steps 11 to 14 as many times as you like. When you are finished, end the program by pressing Alt+F4, clicking the End icon on the Toolbar, or clicking the Close button (X) on the form.

Comments

1. To hide the code window, press the right mouse button and click on Hide. You can also hide it by clicking on the icon at the left side of the title bar and clicking on Close. To view a hidden code window, press Alt/View/Code. To hide a form, close its container. To view a hidden form, press Alt/View/Object.

2. The form is the default object in Visual Basic code. That is, code such as

```
Form1.property = setting
```

can be written as

```
property = setting
```

Also, event procedures associated with Form1 appear as

```
Form_event()
```

rather than

```
Form1_event()
```

3. Another useful command is SetFocus. The statement

```
object.SetFocus
```

moves the focus to the object.

4. We have ended our programs by clicking the End icon or pressing Alt+F4. A more elegant technique is to create a command button, call it cmdQuit, with caption Quit and the event procedure:

```
Private Sub cmdQuit_Click()
    End
End Sub
```

5. Certain words, such as Sub, End, and False, have special meanings in Visual Basic and are referred to as **keywords** or **reserved words**. The Visual Basic editor automatically capitalizes the first letter of a keyword and displays the word in blue.

6. Visual Basic can detect certain types of errors. For instance, consider the line

```
txtPhrase.Font.Bold = False
```

from the walkthrough. Suppose you neglected to type the word False to the right of the equal sign before leaving the line. Visual Basic would tell you something was missing by displaying the left message box at the top of page 58. (Also, the line would turn red.) On the other hand, suppose in the cmdBold.Click event procedure you misspell the keyword "Bold" as "bolt." You might notice something is wrong when the letter "b" is not capitalized. If not, you will certainly know about the problem when the program is run because Visual Basic will display the right message box at the top of page 58 when you click on the command button. After you click on Debug, the line containing the offending word will be highlighted.

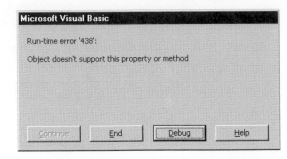

7. At design time, colors are selected from a palette. At run time, the eight most common colors can be assigned with the color constants vbBlack, vbRed, vbGreen, vbYellow, vbBlue, vbMagenta, vbCyan, and vbWhite. For instance, the statement

```
picBox.BackColor = vbYellow
```

gives picBox a yellow background.

8. For statements of the form *object.property* = *setting*, with properties Caption, Text, or Font.Name, the setting must be surrounded by quotes. (For instance, lblTwo.Caption = "Name", txtBox.Text = "Fore", and picBox.Font.Name = "Courier".) When the words True or False appear to the right of the equal sign, they should *not* be surrounded by quotation marks.

9. Code windows have many features of word processors. For instance, the operations cut, copy, paste, find, undo, and redo can be carried out with the sixth through eleventh icons of the Toolbar. These operations, and several others, also can be initiated from the Edit menu.

10. Names of existing event procedures associated with an object are *not* automatically changed when you rename the object. You must change them yourself and also must change any references to the object. Therefore, you should finalize the names of your objects before you put any code into their event procedures.

11. If you find the automatic List Properties/Methods feature distracting, you can turn it off by pressing Alt/Tools/Options, selecting the Editor page, and deselecting Auto List Members. If you do so, you can still display a list manually at the appropriate time by pressing Ctrl+J.

12. Earlier versions of Visual Basic used the property FontSize instead of Font.Size. Although Font.Size is preferred, FontSize is allowed for compatibility. Similarly, properties such as FontBold, FontItalic, and FontName have been included for compatibility with earlier versions of Visual Basic.

13. Assignment statements can be written preceded with the keyword Let. For instance, txtBox.Text = "Hello", also can be written Let txtBox.Text = "Hello". Therefore, assignment statements are also known as Let statements.

✔ PRACTICE PROBLEM 2.2

1. You can always locate an existing event procedure by searching through the code window with the Pg Up and Pg Dn keys. Give another way.

➤ **EXERCISES 2.2**

In Exercises 1 to 6, describe the contents of the text box after the command button is clicked.

1.
```
Private Sub cmdButton_Click()
    txtBox.Text = "Hello"
End Sub
```

2.
```
Private Sub cmdButton_Click()
    txtBox.ForeColor = vbRed
    txtBox.Text = "Hello"
End Sub
```

3.
```
Private Sub cmdButton_Click()
    txtBox.Font.Italic = True
    txtBox.Text = "Hello"
End Sub
```

4.
```
Private Sub cmdButton_Click()
    txtBox.Font.Size = 24
    txtBox.Text = "Hello"
End Sub
```

5.
```
Private Sub cmdButton_Click()
    txtBox.Text = "Hello"
    txtBox.Visible = False
End Sub
```

6.
```
Private Sub cmdButton_Click()
    txtBox.Font.Bold = True
    txtBox.Text = "Hello"
End Sub
```

In Exercises 7 to 10, assume the three objects on the form were created in the order txtOne, txtTwo, and lblOne. Also assume that txtOne has the focus. Determine the output displayed in lblOne when Tab is pressed.

7.
```
Private Sub txtOne_LostFocus()
    lblOne.ForeColor = vbGreen
    lblOne.Caption = "Hello"
End Sub
```

8.
```
Private Sub txtOne_LostFocus()
    lblOne.Caption = "Hello"
End Sub
```

9.
```
Private Sub txtTwo_GotFocus()
    lblOne.Font.Name = "Courier"
    lblOne.Font.Size = 24
    lblOne.Caption = "Hello"
End Sub
```

10.
```
Private Sub txtTwo_GotFocus()
    lblOne.Font.Italic = True
    lblOne.Caption = "Hello"
End Sub
```

In Exercises 11 to 16, determine the errors.

11.
```
Private Sub cmdButton_Click()
    frmHi = "Hello"
End Sub
```

12.
```
Private Sub cmdButton_Click()
    txtOne.ForeColor = "red"
End Sub
```

13.
```
Private Sub cmdButton_Click()
    txtBox.Caption = "Hello"
End Sub
```

14.
```
Private Sub cmdButton_Click()
    lblTwo.Text = "Hello"
End Sub
```

15.
```
Private Sub cmdButton_Click()
    lblTwo.BorderStyle = 2
End Sub
```

16.
```
Private Sub cmdButton_Click()
    txtOne.MultiLine = True
End Sub
```

In Exercises 17 to 32, write a line (or lines) of code to carry out the task.

17. Display "E.T. phone home." in lblTwo.

18. Display "Play it, Sam." in lblTwo.

19. Display "The stuff that dreams are made of." in red letters in txtBox.

20. Display "Life is like a box of chocolates." in Courier font in txtBox.

21. Delete the contents of txtBox.

22. Delete the contents of lblTwo.

23. Make lblTwo disappear.

24. Remove the border from lblTwo.

25. Give picBox a blue background.

26. Place a bold red "Hello" in lblTwo.

27. Place a bold italic "Hello" in txtBox.

28. Make picBox disappear.

29. Give the focus to cmdButton.

30. Remove the border from picBox.

31. Place a border around lblTwo and center its contents.

32. Give the focus to txtBoxTwo.

33. Describe the GotFocus event in your own words.

34. Describe the LostFocus event in your own words.

35. Labels and picture boxes have an event called DblClick that responds to a double-clicking of the left mouse button. Write a simple program to test this event. Determine whether or not you can trigger the DblClick event without also triggering the Click event.

36. Write a simple program to demonstrate that a command button's Click event is triggered when you press the Enter key while the command button has the focus. Does this also happen with text boxes and picture boxes?

In Exercises 37 to 42, the interface and initial properties are specified. Write the code to carry out the stated task.

37. When one of the three command buttons is pressed, the words on the command button are displayed in the label with the stated alignment.

Object	Property	Setting
frmEx37	Caption	Alignment
lblShow	BorderStyle	1-Fixed Single
cmdLeft	Caption	Left Justify
cmdCenter	Caption	Center
cmdRight	Caption	Right Justify

38. When one of the command buttons is pressed, the face changes to a smiling face (Wingdings character "J") or a frowning face (Wingdings character "L").

Object	Property	Setting
frmEx38	Caption	Face
lblFace	Font	Wingdings
	Caption	K
	Font Size	24
cmdSmile	Caption	Smile
cmdFrown	Caption	Frown

39. Pressing the command buttons alters the background and foreground colors in the text box.

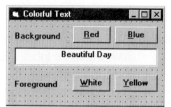

Object	Property	Setting
frmEx39	Caption	Colorful Text
lblBack	Caption	Background
cmdRed	Caption	&Red
cmdBlue	Caption	&Blue
txtShow	Text	Beautiful Day
	Alignment	2 – Center
lblFore	Caption	Foreground
cmdWhite	Caption	&White
cmdYellow	Caption	&Yellow

40. While one of the three text boxes has the focus, its text is bold. When it loses the focus, it ceases to be bold. The command buttons enlarge text (Font.Size = 12) or return text to normal size (Font.Size = 8).

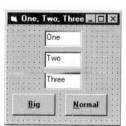

Object	Property	Setting
frmEx40	Caption	One, Two, Three
txtOne	Text	One
txtTwo	Text	Two
txtThree	Text	Three
cmdBig	Caption	&Big
cmdNormal	Caption	&Normal

41. When you click on one of the three small text boxes at the bottom of the form, an appropriate saying is displayed in the large text box. Use the sayings "I like life, it's something to do."; "The future isn't what it used to be."; and "Tell the truth and run."

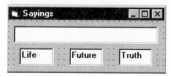

Object	Property	Setting
frmEx41	Caption	Sayings
txtQuote	Text	(blank)
txtLife	Text	Life
txtFuture	Text	Future
txtTruth	Text	Truth

42. After the user types something into the text box, the user can change the font by clicking on one of the command buttons.

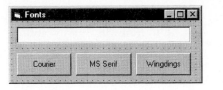

Object	Property	Setting
frmEx42	Caption	Fonts
txtShow	Text	(blank)
cmdCour	Caption	Courier
cmdSerif	Caption	MS Serif
cmdWing	Caption	Wingdings

In Exercises 43 to 48, write a program with a Windows-style interface to carry out the task.

43. Allow the user to click on command buttons to change the size of the text in a text box and alter its appearance between bold and italics.

44. A form contains two text boxes and one large label between them with no preset caption. When the focus is on the first text box, the label reads "Enter your full name." When the focus is on the second text box, the label reads "Enter your phone number, including area code."

45. Use the same form and properties as in Exercise 38, with the captions for the command buttons replaced with Vanish and Reappear. Clicking a button should produce the stated result.

46. Simulate a traffic light with three small square picture boxes placed vertically on a form. Initially, the bottom picture box is solid green and the other picture boxes are white. When the Tab key is pressed, the middle picture box turns yellow and the bottom picture box turns white. The next time Tab is pressed, the top picture box turns red and the middle picture box turns white. Subsequent pressing of the Tab key cycles through the three colors. *Hint:* First, place the bottom picture box on the form, then the middle picture box, and finally the top picture box.

47. The form contains four square buttons arranged in a rectangular array. Each button has the caption "Push Me." When you click on a button, the button disappears and the other three become or remain visible.

48. The form contains two text boxes into which the user types information. When the user clicks on one of the text boxes, it becomes blank and its contents are displayed in the other text box.

✔✔ **Solution to Practice Problem 2.2**

1. With the code window showing, click on the arrow to the right of the Object box and then select the desired object. Then click on the arrow to the right of the Procedure box, and select the desired event procedure.

2.3 NUMBERS

Much of the data processed by computers consists of numbers. In "computerese," numbers are often called **numeric constants**. This section discusses the operations that are performed with numbers and the ways numbers are displayed.

Arithmetic Operations

The five arithmetic operations in Visual Basic are addition, subtraction, multiplication, division, and exponentiation. Addition, subtraction, and division are denoted in Visual Basic by the standard symbols +, −, and /, respectively. However, the notations for multiplication and exponentiation differ from the customary mathematical notations.

Mathematical Notation	Visual Basic Notation
$a \cdot b$ or $a \times b$	$a * b$
a^r	$a \wedge r$

(The asterisk [*] is the upper character of the 8 key. The caret [∧] is the upper character of the 6 key.) **Note:** In this book, the proportional font used for text differs from the fixed-width font used for programs. In the program font, the asterisk appears as a five-pointed star (*).

One way to show a number on the screen is to display it in a picture box. If n is a number, then the instruction

```
picBox.Print n
```

displays the number n in the picture box. If the picBox.Print instruction is followed by a combination of numbers and arithmetic operations, it carries out the operations and displays the result. Print is a reserved word and the Print operation is called a **method**. Another important method is Cls. The statement

```
picBox.Cls
```

erases all text and graphics from the picture box picBox.

EXAMPLE 1 The following program applies each of the five arithmetic operations to the numbers 3 and 2. Notice that 3 / 2 is displayed in decimal form. Visual Basic never displays numbers as common fractions. **Note 1:** The star in the fifth and eighth lines is the computer-font version of the asterisk. **Note 2:** The word "Run" in the phrasing [Run ...] indicates that F5 should be pressed to execute the program. **Note 3:** All programs appearing in examples and case studies are provided on the CD accompanying this book. See the discussion of the CD near the end of the book for details.

Below is the form design and a table showing the names of the objects on the form and the settings, if any, for properties of these objects. This form design is also used in the discussion and examples in the remainder of this section.

Object	Property	Setting
frm2_3_1	Caption	2-3-1
picResults		
cmdCompute	Caption	Compute

```
Private Sub cmdCompute_Click()
  picResults.Cls
  picResults.Print 3 + 2
  picResults.Print 3 - 2
  picResults.Print 3 * 2
  picResults.Print 3 / 2
  picResults.Print 3 ^ 2
  picResults.Print 2 * (3 + 4)
End Sub
```

[Run, and then click the command button.]

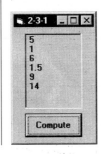

Scientific Notation

Let us review powers of 10 and scientific notation. Our method of decimal notation is based on a systematic use of exponents.

$$10^1 = 10 \qquad\qquad 10^{-1} = 1/10 = .1$$
$$10^2 = 100 \qquad\qquad 10^{-2} = .01$$
$$10^3 = 1000 \qquad\qquad 10^{-3} = .001$$
$$\vdots \qquad\qquad\qquad\qquad \vdots$$
$$10^n = \underbrace{1000...0}_{n\ zeros} \qquad\qquad 10^{-n} = \underbrace{.000...01}_{n\ digits}$$

Scientific notation provides a convenient way of writing numbers by using powers of 10 to stand for zeros. Numbers are written in the form $b \cdot 10^r$, where b is a number from 1 up to (but not including) 10, and r is an integer. For example, it is much more convenient to write the diameter of the sun (1,400,000,000 meters) in scientific notation: $1.4 \cdot 10^9$ meters. Similarly, rather than write .0000003 meters for the diameter of a bacterium, it is simpler to write $3 \cdot 10^{-7}$ meters.

Any acceptable number can be entered into the computer in either standard or scientific notation. The form in which Visual Basic displays a number depends on many factors, with size being an important consideration. In Visual Basic, $b \cdot 10^r$ is usually written as bEr. (The letter E is an abbreviation for *exponent*.) The following forms of the numbers just mentioned are equivalent.

1.4 * 10^9	1.4E+09	1.4E+9	1.4E9	1400000000
3 * 10^–7	3E–07	3E–7	.0000003	

The computer displays r as a two-digit number, preceded by a plus sign if r is positive and a minus sign if r is negative.

EXAMPLE 2 The following program illustrates scientific notation. The computer's choice of whether to display a number in scientific or standard form depends on the magnitude of the number.

```
Private Sub cmdCompute_Click()
  picResults.Cls
  picResults.Print 1.2 * 10 ^ 34
  picResults.Print 1.2 * 10 ^ 8
  picResults.Print 1.2 * 10 ^ 3
  picResults.Print 10 ^ -20
  picResults.Print 10 ^ -2
End Sub
```

[Run, and then click the command button.]

Variables

In applied mathematics problems, quantities are referred to by names. For instance, consider the following high school algebra problem. "If a car travels at 50 miles per hour, how far will it travel in 14 hours? Also, how many hours are required to travel 410 miles?" The solution to this problem uses the well-known formula

$$\text{distance} = \text{speed} \times \text{time elapsed}$$

Here's how this problem would be solved with a computer program.

```
Private Sub cmdCompute_Click()
  picResults.Cls
  speed = 50
  timeElapsed = 14
  distance = speed * timeElapsed
  picResults.Print distance
  distance = 410
  timeElapsed = distance / speed
  picResults.Print timeElapsed
End Sub
```

[Run, and then click the command button. The following is displayed in the picture box.]

```
700
8.2
```

The third line of the event procedure sets the speed to 50, and the fourth line sets the time elapsed to 14. The fifth line multiplies the value for the speed by the value for the time elapsed and sets the distance to this product. The next line displays the answer to the first question. The three lines before the End Sub statement answer the second question in a similar manner.

The names *speed*, *timeElapsed*, and *distance*, which hold numbers, are referred to as **variables**. Consider the variable *timeElapsed*. In the fourth line, its value was set to 14. In the eighth line, its value was changed as the result of a computation. On the other hand, the variable *speed* had the same value, 50, throughout the program.

In general, a variable is a name that is used to refer to an item of data. The value assigned to the variable may change during the execution of the program. In Visual Basic, variable names can be up to 255 characters long, must begin with a letter, and can consist only of letters, digits, and underscores. (The shortest variable names consist of a single letter.) Visual Basic does not distinguish between uppercase and lowercase letters used in variable names. Some examples of variable names are *total*, *numberOfCars*, *taxRate_1998*, and *n*. As a convention, we write variable names in lowercase letters except for the first letters of additional words (as in *numberOfCars*).

If *var* is a variable and *num* is a constant, then the statement

```
var = num
```

assigns the number *num* to the variable *var*. (Such a statement is another example of an assignment statement.) Actually, the computer sets aside a location in memory with the name *var* and places the number *num* in it. The statement

```
picBox.Print var
```

looks into this memory location for the value of the variable and displays the value in the picture box.

A combination of constants, variables, and arithmetic operations that can be evaluated to yield a number is called a **numeric expression**. Expressions are evaluated by replacing each variable by its value and carrying out the arithmetic. Some examples of expressions are 2 * distance + 7, n + 1, and (a + b) / 3.

EXAMPLE 3

The following program displays the value of an expression.

```
Private Sub cmdCompute_Click()
  picResults.Cls
  a = 5
  b = 4
  picResults.Print a * (2 + b)
End Sub
```

[Run, and then click the command button. The following is displayed in the picture box.]

```
30
```

If *var* is a variable, then the statement

```
var = expression
```

first evaluates the expression on the right and *then* assigns its value to the variable. For instance, the event procedure in Example 3 can be written as

```
Private Sub cmdCompute_Click()
  picResults.Cls
  a = 5
  b = 4
  c = a * (2 + b)
  picResults.Print c
End Sub
```

The expression a * (2 + b) is evaluated to 30 and then this value is assigned to the variable *c*.

Because the expression on the right side of an assignment statement is evaluated *before* an assignment is made, a statement such as

```
n = n + 1
```

is meaningful. It first evaluates the expression on the right (that is, it adds 1 to the original value of the variable *n*), and then assigns this sum to the variable *n*. The effect is to increase the value of the variable *n* by 1. In terms of memory locations, the statement retrieves the value of *n* from *n*'s memory location, uses it to compute *n* + 1, and then places the sum back into *n*'s memory location.

Print Method

Consider the following event procedure.

```
Private Sub cmdDisplay_Click()
  picResults.Cls
  picResults.Print 3
  picResults.Print -3
End Sub
```

[Run, and then click the command button.]

Notice that the negative number –3 begins directly at the left margin, whereas the positive number 3 begins one space to the right. The Print method always displays nonnegative numbers with a leading space. The Print method also displays a trailing space after every number. Although the trailing spaces are not apparent here, we will soon see evidence of their presence.

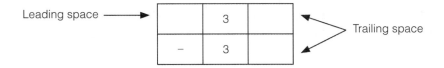

The Print methods used so far display only one number per line. After displaying a number, the cursor moves to the leftmost position and down a line for the next display. Borrowing from typewriter terminology, we say that the computer performs a carriage return and a line feed after each number is displayed. The carriage return and line feed, however, can be suppressed by placing a semicolon at the end of the number.

EXAMPLE 4 The following program illustrates the use of semicolons in Print methods. The output reveals the presence of the space trailing each number. For instance, the space trailing –3 combines with the leading space of 99 to produce two spaces between the numbers.

```
Private Sub cmdDisplay_Click()
  picResults.Cls
  picResults.Print 3;
  picResults.Print -3;
  picResults.Print 99;
  picResults.Print 100
End Sub
```

[Run, and then click the command button.]

Semicolons can be used to display several numbers with one Print method. If *m*, *n*, and *r* are numbers, a line of the form

```
picBox.Print m; n; r
```

displays the three numbers, one after another, separated only by their leading and trailing spaces. For instance, the Print methods in preceding Example 4 can be replaced by the single line

```
picResults.Print 3; -3; 99; 100
```

Relational Operators

Relational operators compare the size of two numbers. Table 2.1 shows the different mathematical relational operators, their representations in Visual Basic, their meanings, and examples. A **condition** is an expression involving relational operators that is either true or false.

Mathematical Notation	Visual Basic Notation	Meaning	Example
=	=	equal to	$2 = 2$
$\neq$	<>	unequal to	$1 <> 2$
<	<	less than	$2 < 3$
>	>	greater than	$1.6 > 1$
$\leq$	<=	less than or equal to	$2 <= 3$
$\geq$	>=	greater than or equal to	$5 >= 5$

Table 2.1 Relational operators.

EXAMPLE 5   Determine whether each of the following conditions is true or false.

(a) $1 <= 1$ (c) $-2 <> 2$
(b) $1 < 1$ (d) $-2 < -3$

SOLUTION   (a) True. The notation <= means "less than *or* equal to." That is, the condition is true provided either of the two circumstances holds. The second one (equal to) holds.
(b) False. The notation < means "strictly less than" and no number can be strictly less than itself.
(c) True. Two numbers are equal only if they are identical. Because −2 is different from 2, they are not equal.
(d) False. The relationship $a < b$ holds only if the number *a* is to the left of the number *b* on the number line.

EXAMPLE 6   Suppose the value of *num1* is 4 and the value of *num2* is 3. Is the condition (*num1* + *num2*) < 2 * *num1* true or false?

SOLUTION   The value of *num1* + *num2* is 7 and the value of 2 * *num1* is 8. Since $7 < 8$, the condition is true.

Numeric Functions: Sqr, Int, Round

Visual Basic has a number of built-in functions that greatly extend its mathematical capability. Functions associate with one or more values, called the *input*, a single value, called the *output*. The function is said to **return** the output value.

The function Sqr calculates the square root of a number. The function Int finds the greatest integer less than or equal to a number. Therefore, Int discards the decimal part of positive numbers. The value of Round(n, r) is the number n rounded to r decimal places. The parameter r can be omitted. If so, n is rounded to a whole number. Some examples follow:

```
Sqr(9) is 3.          Int(2.7) is 2.        Round(2.7) is 3.
Sqr(0) is 0.          Int(3) is 3.          Round(2.317, 2) is 2.32.
Sqr(2) is 1.414214.   Int(-2.7) is -3.      Round(2.317, 1) is 2.3.
```

The terms inside the parentheses can be either numbers (as shown), numeric variables, or numeric expressions. Expressions are first evaluated to produce the input.

EXAMPLE 7 The following program evaluates each of the functions for a specific input given by the value of the variable n.

```
Private Sub cmdEvaluate_Click()
  picResults.Cls
  n = 6.76
  root = Sqr(n)
  picResults.Print root; Int(n), Round(n, 1)
End Sub
```

[Run, and then click the command button. The following is displayed in the picture box.]

```
2.6  6  6.8
```

EXAMPLE 8 The following program evaluates each of the preceding functions at an expression.

```
Private Sub cmdEvaluate_Click()
  picResults.Cls
  a = 2
  b = 3
  picResults.Print Sqr(5 * b + 1); Int(a ^ b); Round(a / b, 3)
End Sub
```

[Run, and then click the command button. The following is displayed in the picture box.]

```
4  8  0.667
```

Comments

1. Numbers must not contain commas, dollar signs, or percent signs. Also, mixed numbers, such as 8 1/2, are not allowed.

2. Parentheses should be used when necessary to clarify the meaning of an expression. When there are no parentheses, the arithmetic operations are performed in the following order: (1) exponentiations; (2) multiplications and divisions; (3) additions and subtractions. In the event of ties, the leftmost operation is carried out first. Table 2.2 summarizes these rules.

( )	Inner to outer, left to right
^	Left to right in expression
* /	Left to right in expression
+ −	Left to right in expression

Table 2.2 Level of precedence for arithmetic operations.

3. Restricted keywords cannot be used as names of variables. For instance, the statements "print = 99" and "end = 99" are not valid. Some other common keywords are Call, If, Select, and Sub. If a keyword is used as a variable name, you will soon be warned that something is wrong. As soon as the cursor is moved from the line, an error message will appear, and the line will turn red. The use of some other keywords (such as Error, Height, Name, Rate, Time, Val, Width, and Year) as variable names does not trigger an immediate warning, but generates an error message when the program is run. Although there is a way to get Visual Basic to accept this last group of keywords as variable names, we will never use keywords as variable names. You can tell immediately when you inadvertently use a reserved word as a variable in an assignment statement because Visual Basic automatically capitalizes the first letter of keywords. For instance, if you type "rate = 50" and press the Enter key, the line will change to "Rate = 50".

4. Grammatical errors, such as misspellings or incorrect punctuations, are called **syntax errors**. Certain types of syntax errors are spotted by the smart editor when they are entered, whereas others are not detected until the program is executed. When Visual Basic spots an error, it displays a dialog box. Some incorrect statements and their errors are given below.

Statement	Reason for Error
picBox.Primt 3	Misspelling of keyword
picBox.Print 2 +	No number follows the plus sign
9W = 5	9W is not a valid variable name

5. Errors detected while a program is running are called **run-time errors**. Although some run-time errors are due to improper syntax, others result from the inability of the computer to carry out the intended task. For instance, if the value of *numVar* is 0, then the statement

```
numVarInv = 1/numVar
```

interrupts the program with the run-time error "Division by zero." If the file Data.txt is not in the root folder of the C drive, then a statement that refers to the file by the filespec "C:\Data.txt" produces the run-time error "File not found."

The dialog box generated by a run-time error states the type of error and has a row of four command buttons captioned Continue, End, Debug, and Help. If you click on the Debug command button, Visual Basic will highlight in yellow the line of code that caused the error. (**Note:** After a run-time error occurs, the program is said to be in break mode. See the first page of Appendix C for a discussion of the three program modes.)

6. A third type of error is the so-called **logical error**. Such an error occurs when a program does not perform the way it was intended. For instance, the line

```
ave = firstNum + secondNum / 2
```

is syntactically correct. However, the missing parentheses in the first line are responsible for an incorrect value being generated. Appendix C discusses debugging tools that can be used to detect and correct logical errors.

7. The omission of the asterisk to denote multiplication is a common error. For instance, the expression a(b + c) is not valid. It should read a * (b + c).

8. When n is a number that is halfway between two successive whole numbers (such as 1.5, 2.5, 3.5, and 4.5), then n is rounded by Round(n) to the nearest even number. That is, half the time n is rounded up and half the time it is rounded down. For instance, Round(2.5) is 2 and Round(3.5) is 4. Similar results hold for any number whose decimal part ends in 5. For instance, Round(3.65, 1) is 3.6 and Round(3.75, 1) is 3.8.

9. When you first open a program that has been saved on disk, the Code window may not appear. If so, run and then terminate the program to see the Code window. To see the Form window, click on Object in the View menu or press Shift+F7. To return to the Code window, click on Code in the View window or press F7.

PRACTICE PROBLEMS 2.3

1. Evaluate 2 + 3 * 4.

2. Complete the table by filling in the value of each variable after each line is executed.

	a	b	c
`Private Sub cmdCompute_Click()`			
`a = 3`	3	–	–
`b = 4`	3	4	–
`c = a + b`			
`a = c * a`			
`picResults.Print   a - b`			
`b = b * b`			
`End Sub`			

➤ **EXERCISES 2.3**

In Exercises 1 to 6, evaluate the numeric expression without the computer, and then use Visual Basic to check your answer.

1. 3 * 4

2. 7 ^ 2

3. 1 / (2 ^ 5)

4. 3 + (4 * 5)

5. (5 − 3) * 4

6. 3 * ((−2) ^ 5)

In Exercises 7 to 10, write the number in scientific notation as it might be displayed by the computer.

7. 3 billion

8. 12,300,000

9. 4 / (10 ^ 8)

10. 32 * (10 ^ 20)

In Exercises 11 to 16, determine whether or not the name is a valid variable name.

11. balance

12. room&Board

13. fOrM_1040

14. 1040B

15. expenses?

16. INCOME 1987

In Exercises 17 to 22, evaluate the numeric expression where a = 2, b = 3, and c = 4.

17. (a * b) + c

18. a * (b + c)

19. (1 + b) * c

20. a ^ c

21. b ^ (c − a)

22. (c − a) ^ b

In Exercises 23 to 28, write an event procedure to calculate and display the value of the expression.

23. $7 \cdot 8 + 5$

24. $(1 + 2 \cdot 9)^3$

25. 5.5% of 20

26. $15 - 3(2 + 3^4)$

27. 17 (3 + 162)

28. 4 1/2 − 3 5/8

In Exercises 29 to 34, determine whether the condition is true or false. Assume a = 2 and b = 3.

29. 3 * a = 2 * b

30. (5 − a) * b < 7

31. b <= 3

32. a ^ b = b ^ a

33. a ^ (5 − 2) > 7

34. 3E−02 < .01 * a

In Exercises 35 to 40, find the value of the given function. Assume a = 5.

35. Sqr(64)

36. Int(10.75)

37. Round(3.1279, 3)

38. Sqr (4 + a)

39. Int(9 − 2)

40. Round(−2.6)

In Exercises 41 and 42, complete the table by filling in the value of each variable after each line is executed.

41.

	x	y
Private Sub cmdCompute_Click()	_	_
x = 2		
y = 3 * x		
x = y + 5		
picResults.Cls		
picResults.Print x + 4		
y = y + 1		
End Sub	_	_

42.

	bal	inter	withDr
Private Sub cmdCompute_Click()	_	_	_
bal = 100			
inter = .05			
withDr = 25			
bal = bal + inter * bal			
bal = bal - withDr			
End Sub	_	_	_

In Exercises 43 to 50, determine the output displayed in the picture box by the lines of code.

43.
```
amount = 10
    picOutput.Print amount - 4
```

44.
```
a = 4
b = 5 * a
picOutput.Print a + b; b - a
```

45.
```
picOutput.Print 1; 2;
picOutput.Print 3; 4
picOutput.Print 5 + 6
```

46.
```
number = 5
number = 2 * number
picOutput.Print number
```

47.
```
picOutput.Print a + 1
a = 4
b = a ^ 2
picOutput.Print a * b
```

48.
```
tax = 200
tax = 25 + tax
picOutput.Print tax
```

49. x = 3
    picOutput.Print x ^ x; x + 3 * x

50. n = 2
    picOutput.Print 3 * n
    n = n + n
    picOutput.Print n + n

In Exercises 51 to 54, identify the errors.

51. a = 2
    b = 3
    a + b = c
    picOutput.Print c

52. a = 2
    b = 3
    c = d = 4
    picOutput.Print 5((a + b) / (c + d)

53. balance = 1,234
    deposit = $100
    picOutput.Print balance + deposit

54. .05 = interest
    balance = 800
    picOutput.Print interest * balance

In Exercises 55 and 56, rewrite the code with fewer lines.

55. picOutput.Print 1;
    picOutput.Print 2;
    picOutput.Print 1 + 2

56. a = 1
    b = a + 2
    picOutput.Print b

In Exercises 57 to 64, write code starting with Private Sub cmdCompute_ Click() and picOutput.Cls statements, ending with an End Sub statement, and having one line for each step. Lines that display data should use the given variable names.

57. The following steps calculate a company's profit.

   (a) Assign the value 98456 to the variable *revenue*.
   (b) Assign the value 45000 to the variable *costs*.
   (c) Assign the difference between the variables *revenue* and *costs* to the variable *profit*.
   (d) Display the value of the variable *profit* in a picture box.

58. The following steps calculate the amount of a stock purchase.

   (a) Assign the value 25.625 to the variable *costPerShare*.
   (b) Assign the value 400 to the variable *numberOfShares*.
   (c) Assign the product of *costPerShare* and *numberOfShares* to the variable *amount*.
   (d) Display the value of the variable *amount* in a picture box.

59. The following steps calculate the price of an item after a 30% reduction.

   (a) Assign the value 19.95 to the variable *price*.
   (b) Assign the value 30 to the variable *discountPercent*.
   (c) Assign the value of (*discountPercent* divided by 100) times *price* to the variable *markDown*.
   (d) Decrease price by *markDown*.
   (e) Display the value of *price* in a picture box.

60. The following steps calculate a company's break-even point, the number of units of goods the company must manufacture and sell in order to break even.

    (a) Assign the value 5000 to the variable *fixedCosts*.
    (b) Assign the value 8 to the variable *pricePerUnit*.
    (c) Assign the value 6 to the variable *costPerUnit*.
    (d) Assign the value *fixedCosts* divided by (the difference of *pricePerUnit* and *costPerUnit*) to the variable *breakEvenPoint*.
    (e) Display the value of the variable *breakEvenPoint* in a picture box.

61. The following steps calculate the balance after 3 years when $100 is deposited in a savings account at 5% interest compounded annually.

    (a) Assign the value 100 to the variable *balance*.
    (b) Increase the variable *balance* by 5% of its value.
    (c) Increase the variable *balance* by 5% of its value.
    (d) Increase the variable *balance* by 5% of its value.
    (e) Display the value of the variable *balance* in a picture box.

62. The following steps calculate the balance at the end of 3 years when $100 is deposited at the beginning of each year in a savings account at 5% interest compounded annually.

    (a) Assign the value 100 to the variable *balance*.
    (b) Increase the variable *balance* by 5% of its value, and add 100.
    (c) Increase the variable *balance* by 5% of its value, and add 100.
    (d) Increase the variable *balance* by 5% of its value.
    (e) Display the value of the variable *balance* in a picture box.

63. The following steps calculate the balance after 10 years when $100 is deposited in a savings account at 5% interest compounded annually.

    (a) Assign the value 100 to the variable *balance*.
    (b) Multiply the variable *balance* by 1.05 raised to the 10th power.
    (c) Display the value of the variable *balance* in a picture box.

64. The following steps calculate the percentage profit from the sale of a stock:

    (a) Assign the value 10 to the variable *purchasePrice*.
    (b) Assign the value 15 to the variable *sellingPrice*.
    (c) Assign to the variable *percentProfit* 100 times the value of the difference between *sellingPrice* and *purchasePrice* divided by *purchasePrice*.
    (d) Display the value of the variable *percentProfit* in a picture box.

In Exercises 65 to 70, write an event procedure to solve the problem and display the answer in a picture box. The program should use variables for each of the quantities.

65. Suppose each acre of farmland produces 18 tons of corn. How many tons of corn can be produced on a 30-acre farm?

66. Suppose a ball is thrown straight up in the air with an initial velocity of 50 feet per second and an initial height of 5 feet. How high will the ball be after 3 seconds? **Note:** The height after t seconds is given by the expression $-16t^2 + v_o t + h_o$, where v_o is the initial velocity and h_o is the initial height.

67. If a car left Washington, D.C., at 2 o'clock and arrived in New York at 7 o'clock, what was its average speed? *Note:* New York is 233 miles from Washington.

68. A motorist wants to determine her gas mileage. At 23,340 miles (on the odometer) the tank is filled. At 23,695 miles the tank is filled again with 14.1 gallons. How many miles per gallon did the car average between the two fillings?

69. A U.S. geological survey showed that Americans use an average of 1600 gallons of water per person per day, including industrial use. How many gallons of water are used each year in the United States? *Note:* The current population of the United States is about 270 million people.

70. According to FHA specifications, each room in a house should have a window area equal to at least 10% of the floor area of the room. What is the minimum window area for a 14- by 16-ft room?

✔✔ **Solutions to Practice Problems 2.3**

1. 14. Multiplications are performed before additions. If the intent is for the addition to be performed first, the expression should be written (2 + 3) * 4.

2.

	a	b	c
`Private Sub cmdCompute_Click()`	—	—	—
`a = 3`	3	—	—
`b = 4`	3	4	—
`c = a + b`	3	4	7
`a = c * a`	21	4	7
`picResults.Print a - b`	21	4	7
`b = b * b`	21	16	7
`End Sub`	—	—	—

Each time an assignment statement is executed, only one variable has its value changed (the variable to the left of the equal sign).

2.4 STRINGS

Two primary types of data can be processed by Visual Basic: numbers and strings. Sentences, phrases, words, letters of the alphabet, names, telephone numbers, addresses, and social security numbers are all examples of strings. Formally, a **string constant** is a sequence of characters that is treated as a single item. Strings can be assigned names with assignment statements, can be displayed with Print methods, and can be combined by an operation called concatenation (denoted by &).

Variables and Strings

A **string variable** is a name used to refer to a string. The allowable names of string variables are identical to those of numeric variables. The value of a string variable is assigned or altered with assignment statements and displayed with Print methods just like the value of a numeric variable.

EXAMPLE I The following code shows how assignment statements and Print are used with strings. The string variable *today* is assigned a value by the fourth line and this value is displayed by the fifth line. The quotation marks surrounding each string constant are not part of the constant and are not displayed by the Print method. (The form design for Examples 1 through 5 consists of a command button and picture box.)

```
Private Sub cmdButton_Click()
  picBox.Cls
  picBox.Print "hello"
  today = "9/17/99"
  picBox.Print today
End Sub
```

[Run, and then click the command button. The following is displayed in the picture box.]

```
hello
9/17/99
```

If *x*, *y*, ..., *z* are characters and *strVar1* is a string variable, then the statement

```
strVar1 = "xy...z"
```

assigns the string constant *xy...z* to the variable, and the statement

```
picBox.Print "xy...z"
```

or

```
picBox.Print strVar1
```

displays the string *xy...z* in a picture box. If *strVar2* is another string variable, then the statement

```
strVar2 = strVar1
```

assigns the value of the variable *strVar1* to the variable *strVar2*. (The value of *strVar1* will remain the same.) String constants used in assignment or picBox.Print statements must be surrounded by quotation marks, but string variables are never surrounded by quotation marks.

As with numbers, semicolons can be used with strings in picBox.Print statements to suppress carriage returns and line feeds. However, picBox.Print statements do not display leading or trailing spaces along with strings.

EXAMPLE 2 | The following program illustrates the use of the assignment statement and Print method with text.

```
Private Sub cmdShow_Click()
  picOutput.Cls
  phrase = "win or lose that counts."
  picOutput.Print "It's not whether you "; phrase
  picOutput.Print "It's whether I "; phrase
End Sub
```

[Run, and then click the command button. The following is displayed in the picture box.]

```
It's not whether you win or lose that counts.
It's whether I win or lose that counts.
```

EXAMPLE 3 | The following program has strings and numbers occurring together in a picBalance.Print instruction.

```
Private Sub cmdCompute_Click()
  picBalance.Cls
  interestRate = 0.0655
  principal = 100
  phrase = "The balance after a year is"
  picBalance.Print phrase; (1 + interestRate) * principal
End Sub
```

[Run, and then click the command button. The following is displayed in the picture box.]

```
The balance after a year is 106.55
```

Concatenation

Two strings can be combined to form a new string consisting of the strings joined together. The joining operation is called **concatenation** and is represented by an ampersand (&). For instance, "good" & "bye" is "goodbye". A combination of strings and ampersands that can be evaluated to form a string is called a **string expression**. The assignment statement and Print method evaluate expressions before assigning them to variables or displaying them.

EXAMPLE 4 | The following program illustrates concatenation.

```
Private Sub cmdDisplay_Click()
  picQuote.Cls
  quote1 = "The ballgame isn't over,"
  quote2 = "until it's over."
  quote = quote1 & quote2
  picQuote.Print quote & "   Yogi Berra"
End Sub
```

[Run, and then click the command button. The following is displayed in the picture box.]

```
The ballgame isn't over, until it's over.   Yogi Berra
```

Declaring Variable Types

So far, we have not distinguished between variables that hold strings and variables that hold numbers. There are several advantages to specifying the type of values, string or numeric, that can be assigned to a variable. A statement of the form

```
Dim variableName As String
```

specifies that only strings can be assigned to the named variable. A statement of the form

```
Dim variableName As Single
```

specifies that only numbers can be assigned to the named variable. The term Single derives from *single-precision real number*. After you type the space after the word "As," the editor displays a list of all the possible next words. In this text we use only a few of the items from this list.

A Dim statement is said to **declare** a variable. From now on we will declare all variables. However, all the programs will run correctly even if the Dim statements are omitted. Declaring variables at the beginning of each event procedure is regarded as good programming practice because it makes programs easier to read and helps prevent certain types of errors.

EXAMPLE 5   The following rewrite of Example 3 declares all variables.

```
Private Sub cmdCompute_Click()
  Dim interestRate As Single
  Dim principal As Single
  Dim phrase As String
  picBalance.Cls
  interestRate = 0.0655
  principal = 100
  phrase = "The balance after a year is"
  picBalance.Print phrase; (1 + interestRate) * principal
End Sub
```

Several Dim statements can be combined into one. For instance, the first three Dim statements of Example 5 can be replaced by

```
Dim interestRate As Single, principal As Single, phrase As String
```

Visual Basic actually has several different types of numeric variables. So far, we have used only single-precision numeric variables. Single-precision numeric variables can hold numbers of magnitude from as small as 1.4×10^{-45} to as large as 3.4×10^{38}. Another type of numeric variable, called **Integer**, can hold only whole numbers from −32768 to 32767. Integer-type variables are declared with a statement of the form

```
Dim intVar As Integer
```

The Integer data type uses less memory than the Single data type and statements using the Integer type execute faster. (This is only useful in programs with many calculations, such as the programs in later chapters that use For . . . Next loops.) Of course, Integer variables are limited because they cannot hold decimals or large numbers. We will use Integer variables extensively with For . . . Next loops in Chapter 3 and occasionally when the data clearly consist of small whole numbers.

Other types of numeric variables are Long, Double, and Currency. We do not use them in this text. Whenever we refer to a numeric variable without mentioning a type, we mean Single or Integer.

Scope of Variables

As soon as a variable is declared inside an event procedure with a Dim statement, it is assigned a **default value**. The default value for numeric variables is 0. The default value for string variables is the **null string** "", the string containing no characters. After the event procedure is exited (that is, when End Sub is reached) the variable ceases to exist. The next time the event procedure is invoked, the variable again initially will assume its default value. Such a variable is said to have **local** scope. If two different event procedures have local variables of the same name, these variables are treated as separate entities; they have absolutely no relationship to each other.

There is another way to declare a variable so that its value persists and so that the variable can be recognized by every event procedure associated with the form. Such a variable is said to have **form-level** scope. To declare a form-level variable, place its Dim statement at the top of the code window in the (Declarations) section of (General). Also, do not include a Dim statement for that variable inside any event procedure.

EXAMPLE 6 In the following program, x is a form-level variable and y is a local variable.

```
Dim x As Single

Private Sub cmdOne_Click()
  Dim y As Single
  x = x + 1
  y = y + 1
  picBox.Print "x ="; x; " y ="; y
End Sub

Private Sub cmdTwo_Click()
  Dim y As Single
  x = x + 1
  y = y + 1
  picBox.Print "x ="; x; " y ="; y
End Sub
```

[Run, click the first command button twice, and click the second command button. The following is displayed in the picture box.]

```
x = 1   y = 1
x = 2   y = 1
x = 3   y = 1
```

Using Text Boxes for Input and Output

The contents of a text box is always a string. Therefore, statements such as

```
strVar = txtBox.Text
```

and

```
txtBox.Text = strVar
```

can be used to assign the contents of the text box to the string variable *strVar* and vice versa.

Numbers are stored in text boxes as strings. Therefore, they should be converted to numbers before being assigned to numeric variables. If *str* is a string representation of a number, then

```
Val(str)
```

is that number. Conversely, if *num* is a number, then

```
Str(num)
```

is a string representation of the number. Therefore, statements such as

```
numVar = Val(txtBox.Text)
```

and

```
txtBox.Text = Str(numVar)
```

can be used to assign the contents of the text box to the numeric variable *numVar* and vice versa. **Note:** When a non-negative number is converted to a string with Str, its first character (but not its last character) is a blank space.

EXAMPLE 7 The following program converts miles to furlongs and vice versa. **Note:** A furlong is one-eighth of a mile.

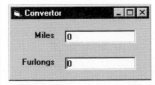

Object	Property	Setting
frm2_4_7	Caption	Convertor
lblMile	Caption	Miles
txtMile	Text	0
lblFurlong	Caption	Furlongs
txtFurlong	Text	0

The two text boxes have been named txtMile and txtFurlong. With the Event procedures shown, typing a number into a text box and pressing Tab results in the converted number being displayed in the other text box.

```
Private Sub txtMile_LostFocus()
  txtFurlong.Text = Str(8 * Val(txtMile.Text))
End Sub

Private Sub txtFurlong_LostFocus()
  txtMile.Text = Str(Val(txtFurlong.Text) / 8)
End Sub
```

ANSI Character Set

Each of the 47 different keys in the center typewriter portion of the keyboard can produce two characters, for a total of 94 characters. Adding 1 for the space character produced by the space bar makes 95 characters. These characters have numbers ranging from 32 to 126 associated with them. These values, called the ANSI (or ASCII) values of the characters, are given in Appendix A. Table 2.3 shows a few of the values.

32 (space)	48 0	66 B	122 z
33 !	49 1	90 Z	123 {
34 "	57 9	97 a	125 }
35 #	65 A	98 b	126 ~

Table 2.3 A few ANSI values.

Most of the best-known fonts, such as Ariel, Courier, Helvetica, and Times New Roman, are essentially governed by the ANSI standard, which assigns characters to the numbers from 32 to 255. Table 2.4 shows a few of the higher ANSI values.

162 ¢	177 ±	181 µ	190 $\frac{3}{4}$
169 ©	178 ^{2}	188 $\frac{1}{4}$	247 ÷
176 °	179 ^{3}	189 $\frac{1}{2}$	248 ø

Table 2.4 A few higher ANSI values.

If n is a number between 32 and 255, then

```
Chr(n)
```

is the string consisting of the character with ANSI value n. If *str* is any string, then

```
Asc(str)
```

is the ANSI value of the first character of *str*. For instance, the statement

```
txtBox.Text = Chr(65)
```

displays the letter A in the text box and the statement

```
picBox.Print Asc("Apple")
```

displays the number 65 in the picture box.

Concatenation can be used with Chr to obtain strings using the higher ANSI characters. For instance, with one of the fonts that conforms to the ANSI standard, the statement

```
txtBox.Text = "32" & Chr(176) & " Fahrenheit"
```

displays 32° Fahrenheit in the text box.

String Relationships

The string *a* is said to be less than the string *b* if *a* precedes *b* alphabetically when using the ANSI (or ASCII) table to alphabetize their values. For instance, "cat" < "dog", "cart"< "cat", and "cat" < "catalog". Digits precede uppercase letters, which precede lowercase letters. Two strings are compared left to right, character by character, to determine which one should precede the other. Therefore, "9W" < "bat", "Dog" < "cat", and "Sales-98" < "Sales-retail".

Table 2.5 shows the different relational operators, their representations in Visual Basic, their meanings, and examples.

Mathematical Notation	Visual Basic Notation	Meaning	Example
=	=	identical to	"a" = "a"
≠	<>	different from	"a" <> "A"
<	<	precedes alphabetically	"a" < "b"
>	>	follows alphabetically	"b" > "a"
≤	<=	precedes alphabetically or is identical to	"A" <= "B"
≥	>=	follows alphabetically or is identical to	"b" >= "a"

Table 2.5 Relational Operators

EXAMPLE 8   A relationship (or condition) between two strings is either true or false. Determine whether each of the following conditions is true or false.

(a) "G" <= "a"   (c) "bar" < "bat"
(b) "A" <= "G"   (d) "Bat" < "bat"

SOLUTION   (a) True. The uppercase letters come before the lowercase letters in the ANSI table.
(b) True. The symbol <= means less than *or* equal. Of course, the condition "A" < "G" is also true.
(c) True. The characters of the strings are compared one at a time working from left to right. Because the first two match, the third character decides the order.
(d) True. The first character of "Bat" precedes the first character of "bat" in the ANSI table.

String Functions: Left, Mid, Right, UCase, Trim

The functions Left, Mid, and Right are used to extract characters from the left end, middle, and right end of a string. Suppose *str* is a string and *m* and *n* are positive integers. Then Left(*str*, *n*) is the string consisting of the first *n* characters of *str* and Right(*str*, *n*) is the string consisting of the last *n* characters of *str*. Mid(*str*, *m*, *n*) is the string consisting of *n* characters of *str*, beginning with the *m*th character. UCase(*str*) is the string *str* with all of its lowercase letters capitalized. Trim(*str*) is the string *str* with all leading and trailing spaces removed. Some examples are as follows:

```
Left("fanatic", 3) is "fan".        Right("fanatic", 3) is "tic".
Left("12/15/99", 2) is "12".        Right("12/15/99", 2) is "99".
Mid("fanatic", 5, 1) is "t".        Mid("12/15/99", 4, 2) is "15".
UCase("Disk") is "DISK".            UCase("12three") is "12THREE".
Trim(" 1  2 ") is "1  2".           Trim("-12 ") is "-12".
```

The strings produced by Left, Mid, and Right are referred to as **substrings** of the strings from which they were formed. For instance, "fan" and "t" are substrings of "fanatic". The substring "fan" is said to begin at position 1 of "fanatic" and the substring "t" is said to begin at position 5.

Like the numeric functions discussed in Section 2.3, Left, Mid, Right, UCase, and Trim also can be evaluated for variables and expressions.

EXAMPLE 9

The following program evaluates the functions above for variables and expressions. Note that spaces are counted as characters.

```
Private Sub cmdEvaluate_Click()
  Dim str1 As String, str2 As String
  picResults.Cls
  str1 = "Quick as "
  str2 = "a wink"
  picResults.Print Left(str1, 7)
  picResults.Print Mid(str1 & str2, 7, 6)
  picResults.Print UCase(str1 & str2)
  picResults.Print "The average "; Right(str2, 4); " lasts .1 second."
  picResults.Print Trim(str1); str2
End Sub
```

[Run, and then click the command button. The following is displayed in the picture box.]

```
Quick a
as a w
QUICK AS A WINK
The average wink lasts .1 second.
Quick asa wink
```

String-Related Numeric Functions: Len, InStr

The functions Len and InStr operate on strings but produce numbers. The function Len gives the number of characters in a string. The function InStr searches for the first occurrence of one string in another and gives the position at which the string is found. Suppose *str1* and *str2* are strings. The value of Len(*str1*) is the number of characters in *str1*. The value of InStr(*str1*, *str2*) is 0 if *str2* is not a substring of *str1*. Otherwise, its value is the first position of *str2* in *str1*. Some examples of Len and InStr follow:

```
Len("Shenandoah") is 10.          InStr("Shenandoah", "nand") is 4.
Len("Just a moment") is 13.       InStr("Just a moment", " ") is 5.
Len(" ") is 1.                    InStr("Croissant", "ist") is 0.
```

EXAMPLE 10 The following program evaluates functions at variables and expressions. The eighth line locates the position of the space separating the two names. The first name will end one position to the left of this position and the last name will consist of all but the first *n* characters of the full name.

```
Private Sub cmdAnalyze_Click()
  Dim nom As String
  Dim n As Integer
  Dim first As String
  Dim last As String
  picResults.Cls
  nom = txtFullName.Text
  n = InStr(nom, " ")
  first = Left(nom, n - 1)
  last = Right(nom, Len(nom) - n)
  picResults.Print "Your first name is "; first
  picResults.Print "Your last name has"; Len(last); "letters."
End Sub
```

[Run, type John Doe into the text box, and then click the command button.]

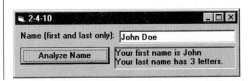

Format Functions

The Format functions are used to display numbers and dates in familiar forms and to right-justify numbers. Here are some examples of how numbers are converted to strings with Format functions.

Function	String Value
FormatNumber(12345.628, 1)	12,345.6
FormatCurrency(12345.628, 2)	$12,345.63
FormatPercent(0.185, 2)	18.50%

The value of FormatNumber(n, r) is the string containing the number n rounded to r decimal places and displayed with commas every three digits to the left of the decimal point. The value of FormatCurrency(n, r) is the string consisting of a dollar sign followed by the value of FormatNumber(n, r). FormatCurrency uses the accountant's convention of using surrounding parentheses to denote negative amounts. The value of FormatPercent(n, r) is the string consisting of the number n displayed as a percent and rounded to r decimal places.

With all three functions, r can be omitted. If so, the number is rounded to 2 decimal places. Strings corresponding to numbers less than 1 in magnitude have a zero to the left of the decimal point. Also, n can be a number, a numeric expression, or even a string corresponding to a number.

Function	String Value
`FormatNumber(1 + Sqr(2), 3)`	2.414
`FormatCurrency(-1000)`	($1,000.00)
`FormatPercent(".005")`	0.50%

If *dateString* represents a date in a form such as 7-4-1999, 7-4-99, or 7/4/99, then the value of FormatDateTime(*dateString*, vbLongDate) is a string giving the date in a form such as Sunday, July 04, 1999.

Function	String Value
`FormatDateTime("9-15-99", vbLongDate)`	Wednesday, September 15, 1999
`FormatDateTime("10-23-00", vbLongDate)`	Monday, October 23, 2000

The value of Format(*expr*, "@@ . . . @"), where "@@ . . . @" is a string of n "at" symbols, is the string consisting of the value of *expr* right-justified in a field of n spaces. This function is used with fixed-width fonts, such as Courier, to display columns of numbers so that the decimal points and commas are lined up or to display right-justified lists of words. The following examples use a string of 10 "at" symbols.

Function	String Value
`Format(1234567090, "@@@@@@@@@@")`	1234567090
`Format(FormatNumber(1234.5), "@@@@@@@@@@")`	1,234.50
`Format(FormatNumber(12345.67), "@@@@@@@@@@")`	12,345.67
`Format(FormatCurrency(13580.17), "@@@@@@@@@@")`	$13,580.17

Comments

1. The string "", which contains no characters, is different from " ", the string consisting of a single space.

2. The statement picBox.Print, with no string or number, simply skips a line in the picture box.

3. Good programming practice dictates that only string values be assigned to string variables and only numeric values be assigned to numeric variables. Although Visual Basic allows this convention to be violated, so doing sometimes results in the error message "Type mismatch."

4. The quotation-mark character (") can be placed into a string constant by using Chr(34). For example, after the statement

```
txtBox.Text = "George " & Chr(34) & "Babe" & Chr(34) & " Ruth"
```

is executed, the text box contains

```
George "Babe" Ruth
```

5. Most major programming languages require that all variables be declared before they can be used. Although declaring variables with Dim statements is optional in Visual Basic, you can tell Visual Basic to make declaration mandatory by typing:

```
Option Explicit
```

as the first line in the code window.

Then, if you use a variable without first declaring it in a Dim statement, the message "Variable not defined" will appear as soon as you attempt to run the program. One big advantage of using Option Explicit is that mistypings of variable names will be detected. Otherwise, malfunctions due to typing errors are often difficult to detect.

You can have Visual Basic automatically place Option Explicit at the top of every program you write. The steps are as follows:

(a) Press Alt/T/O and click on the Editor tab to invoke the editor options.
(b) If the square to the left of "Require Variable Declaration" does not contain a check mark, click on the square and press the OK button.

6. If Val is omitted from the statement

```
numVar = Val(txtBox.Text)
```

or Str is omitted from the statement

```
txtBox.Text = Str(numVar)
```

Visual Basic does not complain, but simply makes the conversion for you. However, errors can arise from omitting Val and Str. For instance, if the contents of txtBox1.Text is 34 and the contents of txtBox2.Text is 56, then the statement

```
numVar = txtBox1.Text + txtBox2.Text
```

assigns the number 3456 rather than 90 to *numVar*. (This is because Visual Basic does not perform the conversion until just before the assignment.) If txtBox1 is empty, then the statement

```
numVar = 3 * txtBox1.Text
```

will stop the program and produce the error message "Type mismatch." We follow the standards of good programming practice by always using Val and Str to convert values between text boxes and numeric variables. Similar considerations apply to conversions involving label captions.

7. Variable names should describe the role of the variable. Also, some programmers use a prefix, such as sng or str, to identify the type of a variable. For example, they would use names like sngInterestRate and strFirstName.

8. Trim is useful when reading data from a text box. Sometimes users type spaces at the end of input. Unless the spaces are removed, they can cause havoc elsewhere in the program. Also, Trim is useful in trimming the leading spaces from numbers that have been converted to strings with Str.

9. Several exercises involve a percentage change, which is calculated as 100 * (newValue – oldValue) / oldValue. This amount is often coded as

```
perChange = (newValue - oldValue) / oldValue
picOutput.Print "The change is "; FormatPercent(perChange)
```

The variable perChange holds the decimal form of the percentage change. The FormatPercent function multiplies the decimal form by 100 and appends a percent symbol.

10. FormatCurrency(n, r) indicates negative numbers with parentheses instead of minus signs. If you prefer minus signs, use FormatCurrency(n, r, vbFalse). For instance, the value of FormatCurrency(–1234, 2, vbFalse) is "–$1,234.00".

11. As we saw in Comment 9 of the previous section, numbers ending in 5 are sometimes rounded down. Such is never the case with FormatNumber, FormatCurrency, and FormatPercent. For instance, FormatNumber(2.5) is "3.00" and FormatCurrency(8.945) is "$8.95".

12. The value of `FormatDateTime(Now, vbLongDate)` is today's date. For any positive number n, `FormatDateTime(Now + n, vbLongDate)` is the date n days from today and `FormatDateTime(Now - n, vbLongDate)` is the date n days ago.

13. The functions FormatNumber, FormatCurrency, FormatPercent, and FormatDateTime were added to Visual Basic in VB6.0. The same results can be obtained with the Format function alone. However, these new functions execute faster than Format and are easier to use. In addition, they can be placed in VBScript programs that are used to make Web pages interactive.

✔ PRACTICE PROBLEMS 2.4

1. Compare the following two statements, where *phrase* is a string variable and *balance* is a numeric variable.

```
picBox.Print "It's whether I "; phrase
picBox.Print "The balance is"; balance
```

Why is the space preceding the second quotation mark necessary for the first picBox.Print statement but not for the second picBox.Print statement?

2. A label's caption is a string and can be assigned a value with a statement of the form

```
lblOne.Caption = strVar
```

What is one advantage to using a label for output as opposed to a text box?

3. Write code to add the numbers in txtBox1 and txtBox2, and place the sum in lblThree.

➤   **EXERCISES 2.4**

In Exercises 1 to 12, determine the output displayed in the picture box by the lines of code.

1.
```
picOutput.Print "Hello"
picOutput.Print "12" & "34"
```

2.
```
picOutput.Print "Welcome; my friend."
picOutput.Print "Welcome"; "my friend."
```

3.
```
picOutput.Print "12"; 12; "TWELVE"
```

4.
```
picOutput.Print Chr(104) & Chr(105)
```

5.
```
Dim r As String, b As String
r = "A ROSE"
b = " IS "
picOutput.Print r; b; r; b; r
```

6.
```
Dim n As Single, x As String
n = 5
x = "5"
picOutput.Print n
picOutput.Print x
```

7.
```
Dim houseNumber As Single
Dim street As String
houseNumber = 1234
street = "Main Street"
picOutput.Print houseNumber; street
```

8.
```
Dim p As String, word As String
p = "f"
word = "lute"
picOutput.Print p & word
```

9.
```
Dim quote As String, person As String, qMark As String
quote = "We're all in this alone."
person = "Lily Tomlin"
qMark = Chr(34)
picOutput.Print qMark & quote & qMark & "   " & person
```

10.
```
Dim letter As String
letter = "D"
picOutput.Print letter; " is the"; Asc(letter) - Asc("A") + 1;
picOutput.Print "th letter of the alphabet."
```

11.
```
Dim a As Single
a = 1
picOutput.Font.Name = "Courier"
picOutput.Print "12345678"
picOutput.Print Str(a + 2); Val(Str(a)); Str(4 - a)
```

12.
```
Dim num1 As Single, num2 As String
num1 = 3567
num2 = Str(num1)
picOutput.Print "The number of characters in"; num2; " is"; Len(num2)
```

In Exercises 13 to 15, identify any errors.

13.
```
Dim phone As Single
phone = "234-5678"
picOutput.Print "My phone number is "; phone
```

14.
```
Dim quote As String
quote = I came to Casablanca for the waters.
picOutput.Print quote; "   "; "Bogart"
```

15.
```
Dim end As String
end = "happily ever after."
PicOutput.Print "They lived "; end
```

In Exercises 16 to 19, determine whether the condition is true or false.

16. "9W" <> "9w"

17. "Inspector" < "gadget"

18. "Car" < "Train"

19. "99" < "ninety-nine"

In Exercises 20 to 29, determine the output of the given function.

20. `UCase("McD's")`

21. `Left("harp", 2)`

22. `Mid("ABCDE", 2, 3)`

23. `Instr("shoe", "h")`

24. `Left("ABCD", 2)`

25. `UCase("$2 bill")`

26. `Instr("shoe", "f")`

27. `Mid("shoe", 4, 1)`

28. `Right("snow", 3)`

29. `Right("123", 1)`

In Exercises 30 to 47, determine what will be displayed in the picture box by the given lines of code.

30. `picBox.Print FormatNumber(-12.3456, 3)`

31. `picBox.Print FormatNumber(12345)`

32.
```
numVar = Round(12345.9)
picBox.Print FormatNumber(numVar, 3)
```

33. `picBox.Print FormatCurrency(12345.67, 0)`

34. `picBox.Print FormatPercent(3 / 4, 1)`

35. `picBox.Print FormatDateTime(Now + 1, vbLongDate)`

36. `picBox.Print FormatDateTime("7-4-1776", vbLongDate)`

(**Note:** The Declaration of Independence was signed on a Thursday.)

37. `picBox.Print FormatDateTime("12-31-99", vbLongDate)`

(**Note:** The year 2000 begins on a Saturday.)

38.
```
strVar = FormatDateTime(Now, vbLongDate)
picBox.Print Left(strVar, Instr(strVar, ",") - 1)
```

39.
```
strVar = FormatDateTime(Now, vbLongDate)
picBox.Print Right(strVar, 4)
```

40. `picBox.Print "Pay to France "; FormatCurrency(27267622)`

41. `picBox.Print "The interest rate is "; FormatPercent(0.045)`

42. `picBox.Print "On 1/1/98, the US pop. was "; FormatNumber(268924000, 0)`

43. `picBox.Print "The minimum wage is "; FormatCurrency(5.15)`

44. `picBox.Print FormatPercent(.893); " of new computers use Windows."`

45.
```
picBox.Font.Name = "Courier"
picBox.Print "12345678"
strVar = FormatNumber(1999.958, 0)
picBox.Print Format(strVar, "@@@@@@@@")
```

46.
```
picBox.Font.Name = "Courier"
picBox.Print "1234567890"
strVar = FormatCurrency(1234.567)
picBox.Print Format(strVar, "@@@@@@@@@@")
```

47.
```
picBox.Font.Name = "Courier"
picBox.Print "1234567890"
picBox.Print Format("abcd", "@@@@@@@@")
```

48. In the following program, determine the output displayed in the picture box when the command buttons are pressed in the following order: First, Second, First.

```
Dim word As String

Private Sub cmdFirst_Click()
  word = word & "Yada "
  picOutput.Print word
End Sub


Private Sub cmdSecond_Click()
  picOutput.Print word
End Sub
```

49. Repeat Exercise 48 with the statement Dim word As String inserted as the first line of code in the second event procedure.

50. Repeat Exercise 48, where the Dim statement is removed from the top of the program and inserted as the first line of code in each event procedure.

In Exercises 51 to 54, write code starting with Private Sub cmdDisplay_ Click() and picOutput.Cls statements, ending with an End Sub statement, and having one line for each step. Lines that display data should use the given variable names.

51. The following steps give the name and birth year of a famous inventor.

(a) Declare all variables used in the steps below.
(b) Assign "Thomas" to the variable *firstName*.
(c) Assign "Alva" to the variable *middleName*.
(d) Assign "Edison" to the variable *lastName*.
(e) Assign 1847 to the variable *yearOfBirth*.
(f) Display the inventor's full name followed by a comma and his year of birth.

52. The following steps compute the price of ketchup.

(a) Declare all variables used in the steps below.
(b) Assign "ketchup" to the variable *item*.
(c) Assign 1.80 to the variable *regularPrice*.
(d) Assign .27 to the variable *discount*.
(e) Display the phrase "1.53 is the sale price of ketchup."

53. The following steps display a copyright statement.

(a) Declare all variables used in the steps below.
(b) Assign "Prentice Hall, Inc." to the variable *publisher*.
(c) Display the phrase "© Prentice Hall, Inc."

54. The following steps give advice.

(a) Declare all variables used in the steps below.
(b) Assign "Fore" to the variable *prefix*.
(c) Display the phrase "Forewarned is Forearmed."

In Exercises 55 to 60, the interface and initial properties are specified. Write the code to carry out the stated task.

55. After values are placed in the x and y text boxes, pressing Compute Sum places x + y in the sum picture box.

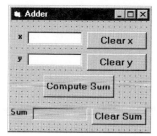

Object	Property	Setting
frmEx55	Caption	Adder
lblX	Caption	x
txtNum1	Text	(blank)
cmdClearX	Caption	Clear x
lblY	Caption	y
txtNum2	Text	(blank)
cmdClearY	Caption	Clear y
cmdCompute	Caption	Compute Sum
lblSum	Caption	Sum
picSum		
cmdClearSum	Caption	Clear Sum

56. When cmdCelsius is pressed, the temperature is converted from Fahrenheit to Celsius, the title bar changes to Celsius, cmdCelsius is hidden, and cmdFahr becomes visible. If cmdFahr is now pressed, the temperature is converted from Celsius to Fahrenheit, the title bar reverts to Fahrenheit, cmdFahr is hidden, and cmdCelsius becomes visible. Of course, the user can change the temperature in the text box at any time. (**Note:** The conversion formulas are $C = (5/9) * (F - 32)$ and $F = (9/5) * C + 32$.)

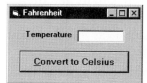

Object	Property	Setting
frmEx46	Caption	Fahrenheit
lblTemp	Caption	Temperature
txtTemp	Text	(blank)
cmdCelsius	Caption	Convert to Celsius
cmdFahr	Caption	Convert to Fahrenheit
	Visible	False

57. If *n* is the number of seconds between lightning and thunder, the storm is *n*/5 miles away. Write a program that requests the number of seconds between lightning and thunder and reports the distance of the storm.

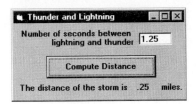

Object	Property	Setting
frmStorm	Caption	Thunder and Lightning
lblNumSec	Caption	Number of seconds between lightning and thunder
txtNumSec	Text	(blank)
cmdCompute	Caption	Compute Distance
lblDistance	Caption	The distance of the storm is
lblNumMiles	Caption	(blank)
lblMiles	Caption	miles.

58. Write a program to request as input the name of a baseball team, the number of games won, and the number of games lost, and then display the percentage of games won.

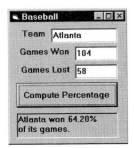

Object	Property	Setting
frmBaseball	Caption	Baseball
lblTeam	Caption	Team
txtTeam	Text	(blank)
lblWon	Caption	Games Won
txtWon	Text	(blank)
lblLost	Caption	Games Lost
txtLost	Text	(blank)
cmdCompute	Caption	Compute Percentage
picPercent		

59. The numbers of calories burned per hour by bicycling, jogging, and swimming are 200, 475, and 275, respectively. A person loses 1 pound of weight for each 3500 calories burned. Write a program that allows the user to input the number of hours spent at each activity and then calculates the number of pounds worked off.

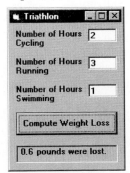

Object	Property	Setting
frmTriathlon	Caption	Triathlon
lblCycle	Caption	Number of Hours Cycling
txtCycle	Text	(blank)
lblRun	Caption	Number of Hours Running
txtRun	Text	(blank)
lblSwim	Caption	Number of Hours Swimming
txtSwim	Text	(blank)
cmdCompute	Caption	Compute Weight Loss
picWtLoss		

60. The American College of Sports Medicine recommends that you maintain your *training heart rate* during an aerobic workout. Your training heart rate is computed as .7 * (220 – a) + .3 * r, where a is your age, and r is your resting heart rate (your pulse when you first awaken). Write a program to request a person's age and resting heart rate and then calculate the training heart rate. (Determine *your* training heart rate.)

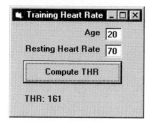

Object	Property	Setting
frmWorkout	Caption	Training Heart Rate
lblAge	Caption	Age
txtAge	Text	(blank)
lblRestHR	Caption	Resting Heart Rate
txtRestHR	Text	(blank)
cmdCompute	Caption	Compute THR
lblTHR	Caption	THR:
lblTrainHR	Caption	(blank)

In Exercises 61 to 66, write a program with a Windows-style interface to carry out the task. The program should use variables for each of the quantities and display the outcome with a complete explanation, as in Example 5.

61. If a company's annual revenue is $550,000 and its expenses are $410,000, what is its net income (revenue minus expenses)?

62. When P dollars are deposited in a savings account at interest rate r compounded annually, the balance after n years is $P(1 + r)^n$. Write a program to request the principal P and the interest rate r as input, and compute the balance after 10 years, as shown in the sample output on the left below.

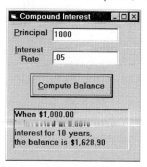 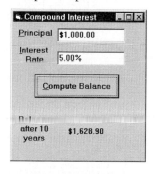

63. Redo Exercise 62 to achieve the output shown on the right above. The principal and interest should be entered as 1000 and .05, but should be converted to nice forms when the button is pressed. (The balance is displayed in a label.) Also, the two text boxes should become empty when they receive the focus to allow for additional computations.

64. Write a program that requests a letter, converts it to uppercase, and gives its first position in the sentence "THE QUICK BROWN FOX JUMPS OVER A LAZY DOG." For example, if the user responds by typing *b* into the text box, then the message B *first occurs in position 11* is displayed.

65. Calculate the amount of a waiter's tip, given the amount of the bill and the percentage tip. (Test the program with $20 and 15 percent.)

66. Write a program that requests a sentence, a word in the sentence, and another word, and then displays the sentence with the first word replaced by the second. For example, if the user responds by typing "What you don't know won't hurt you" into the first text box and *know* and *owe* into the second and third text boxes, then the message "What you don't owe won't hurt you" is displayed.

✔✔ **Solutions to Practice Problems 2.4**

1. In the second picBox.Print statement, the item following the second quotation mark is a positive number, which is displayed with a leading space. Because the corresponding item in the first picBox.Print statement is a string, which is *not* displayed with a leading space, a space had to be inserted before the quotation mark.

2. The user cannot enter data into a label from the keyboard. Therefore, if a control is to be used for output only, a label is preferred. *Note:* When using a label for output, you might want to set its BorderStyle property to "1-Fixed Single," so it will be discernable.

3. `lblThree.Caption = Str(Val(txtBox1.Text) + Val(txtBox2.Text))`

2.5 INPUT AND OUTPUT

So far we have relied on assignment statements to assign values to variables. Data also can be stored in files and accessed through Input # statements, or data can be supplied by the user in a text box or input box. The Print method, with a little help from commas and the Tab function, can spread out and align the display of data in a picture box or on a printer. Message boxes grab the user's attention and display temporary messages. Comment statements allow the programmer to document all aspects of a program, including a description of the input used and the output to be produced.

Reading Data from Files

In Chapter 1, we saw how to create data files with Windows' Notepad. (As a rule of thumb, and simply as a matter of style, we enclose each string in quotation marks.) A file can have either one item per line or many items (separated by commas) can be listed on the same line. Usually, related items are grouped together on a line. For instance, if a file consisted of payroll information, each line would contain the name of a person, that person's hourly wage, and the number of hours that person worked during the week, as shown in Figure 2.24.

```
"Mike Jones", 7.35, 35
"John Smith", 6.75, 33
```

Figure 2.24 Contents of Staff.txt.

The items of data will be assigned to variables one at a time in the order they appear in the file. That is, "Mike Jones" will be the first value assigned to a variable. After all the items from the first line have been assigned to variables, subsequent requests for values will be read from the next line.

Data stored in a file can be read in order (that is, sequentially) and assigned to variables with the following steps.

1. Choose a number from 1 to 255 to be the **reference number** for the file.

2. Execute the statement

```
Open "filespec" For Input As #n
```

where *n* is the reference number. This procedure is referred to as **Opening a file for input**. It establishes a communications link between the computer and the disk drive for reading data *from* the disk. Data then can be input from the specified file and assigned to variables in the program.

3. Read items of data in order, one at a time, from the file with Input # statements. The statement

```
Input #n, var
```

causes the program to look in the file for the next available item of data and assign it to the variable *var*. In the file, individual items are separated by commas or line breaks. The variable in the Input # statement should be the same type (that is, string or numeric) as the data to be assigned to it from the file.

4. After the desired items have been read from the file, close the file with the statement

```
Close #n
```

EXAMPLE 1   Write a program that uses a file for input and produces the same output as the following code. (The form design for all examples in this section consists of a command button and a picture box.)

```
Private Sub cmdDisplay_Click()
  Dim houseNumber As Single, street As String
  picAddress.Cls
  houseNumber = 1600
  street = "Pennsylvania Ave."
  picAddress.Print "The White House is located at"; houseNumber; street
End Sub
```

[Run, and then click the command button. The following is displayed in the picture box.]

```
The White House is located at 1600 Pennsylvania Ave.
```

SOLUTION   Use Windows' Notepad to create the file Data.txt containing the following two lines:

1600
"Pennsylvania Ave."

In the following code, the fifth line looks for the first item of data, 1600, and assigns it to the numeric variable *houseNumber*. (Visual Basic records that this piece of data has been used.) The sixth line looks for the next available item of data, "Pennsylvania Ave.", and assigns it to the string variable *street*. **Note:** You will have to alter the Open statement in the fourth line to tell it where the file Data.txt is located. For instance, if the file is in the root directory (that is, folder) of a diskette in drive A, then the line should read Open "A:\Data.txt" For Input As #1. If the file is located in the subdirectory (that is, folder) Vb6 of the C drive, then the statement should be changed to Open "C:\Vb6\Data.txt" For Input As #1. See Comment 1 for another option.

```
Private Sub cmdDisplay_Click()
  Dim houseNumber As Single, street As String
  picAddress.Cls
  Open "Data.txt" For Input As #1
  Input #1, houseNumber
  Input #1, street
  picAddress.Print "The White House is located at"; houseNumber; street
  Close #1
End Sub
```

A single Input # statement can assign values to several different variables. For instance, the two Input # statements in the solution of Example 1 can be replaced by the single statement

```
    Input #1, houseNumber, street
```

In general, a statement of the form

```
    Input #n, var1, var2, ..., varj
```

has the same effect as the sequence of statements

```
    Input #n, var1
    Input #n, var2
        .
        .
    Input #n, varj
```

EXAMPLE 2   The following program uses the file Staff.txt in Figure 2.24 to compute weekly pay. Notice that the variables in the Input # statement are the same types (String, Single, Single) as the constants in each line of the file.

```
Private Sub cmdCompute_Click()
  Dim nom As String, wage As Single, hrs As Single
  picPay.Cls
  Open "Staff.txt" For Input As #1
  Input #1, nom, wage, hrs
  picPay.Print nom; hrs * wage
  Input #1, nom, wage, hrs
  picPay.Print nom; hrs * wage
  Close #1
End Sub
```

[Run, and then click the command button. The following will be displayed in the picture box.]

```
Mike Jones 257.25
John Smith 222.75
```

In certain situations, we must read the data in a file more than once. This is accomplished by closing the file and reopening it. After a file is closed and then reopened, subsequent Input # statements begin reading from the first entry of the file.

EXAMPLE 3

The following program takes the average annual amounts of money spent by single-person households for several categories and converts these amounts to percentages. The data are read once to compute the total amount of money spent and then read again to calculate the percentage for each category. *Note:* These figures were compiled for the year 1995 by the Bureau of Labor Statistics.

Costs.txt consists of the following four lines:

"Transportation", 3887
"Housing", 7643
"Food", 3017
"Other", 7804

```
Private Sub cmdCompute_Click()
  Dim total As Single, category As String, amount As Single
  Open "Costs.txt" For Input As #1
  picPercent.Cls
  total = 0
  Input #1, category, amount
  total = total + amount
  Input #1, category, amount
  total = total + amount
  Input #1, category, amount
  total = total + amount
  Input #1, category, amount
  total = total + amount
  Close #1
  Open "Costs.txt" For Input As #1
  Input #1, category, amount
  picPercent.Print category, FormatPercent(amount / total)
  Input #1, category, amount
  picPercent.Print category, FormatPercent(amount / total)
  Input #1, category, amount
  picPercent.Print category, FormatPercent(amount / total)
  Input #1, category, amount
  picPercent.Print category, FormatPercent(amount / total)
  Close #1
End Sub
```

[Run, and then click the command button. The following is displayed in the picture box.]

```
Transportation   17.39%
Housing          34.20%
Food             13.50%
Other            34.92%
```

Input from an Input Box

Normally, a text box is used to obtain input described by a label. Sometimes, we want just one piece of input and would rather not have a text box and label stay on the screen forever. The problem can be solved with an **input box**. When a statement of the form

```
stringVar = InputBox(prompt, title)
```

is executed, an input box similar to the one shown in Figure 2.25 pops up on the screen. After the user types a response into the text box at the bottom of the screen and presses Enter (or clicks OK), the response is assigned to the string variable. The *title* argument is optional and gives the caption to appear in the Title bar. The *prompt* argument is a string that tells the user what information to type into the text box.

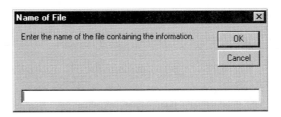

Figure 2.25 Sample input box.

When you type the parenthesis following the word InputBox, the editor displays a line containing the general form of the InputBox statement. See Figure 2.26. This feature, which was added in Visual Basic 5.0, is called **Quick Info**. Optional parameters are surrounded by brackets. All the parameters in the general form of the InputBox statement are optional except for *prompt*.

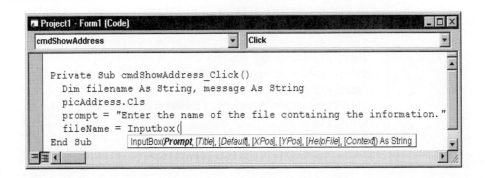

Figure 2.26 Quick Info feature.

EXAMPLE 4

In the following solution to Example 1, the file name is provided by the user in an input box.

```
Private Sub cmdDisplay_Click()
  Dim fileName As String, prompt As String, title As String
  Dim houseNumber As Single, street As String
  picAddress.Cls
  prompt = "Enter the name of the file containing the information."
  title = "Name of File"
  fileName = InputBox(prompt, title)
  Open fileName For Input As #1
  Input #1, houseNumber
  Input #1, street
  picAddress.Print "The White House is located at"; houseNumber; street
  Close #1
End Sub
```

[Run, and then click the command button. The input box of Figure 2.25 appears on the screen. Type Data.txt (possibly preceded with a path) into the input box and click on OK. The input box disappears and the following appears in the picture box.]

```
The White House is located at 1600 Pennsylvania Ave.
```

The response typed into an input box is treated as a single string value, no matter what is typed. (Quotation marks are not needed and, if included, are considered as part of the string.) Numeric data typed into an input box should be converted to a number with Val before it is assigned to a numeric variable or used in a calculation.

Formatting Output with Print Zones

Each line in a picture box can be thought of as being subdivided into zones, as shown in Figure 2.27. Each zone contains 14 positions, where the width of a position is the average width of the characters in the font.

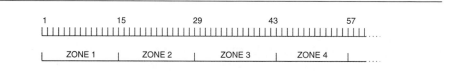

Figure 2.27 Print zones.

We have seen that when the Print method is followed by several items separated by semicolons, the items are displayed one after another. When commas are used instead of semicolons, the items are displayed in consecutive zones. For instance, if the Font property of picBox is set to Courier, when the motto of the state of Alaska is displayed with the statements

```
picBox.Print "North", "to", "the", "future."
picBox.Print "12345678901234567890123456789012345678901234567890"
```

the resulting picture box is

```
North           to          the          future.
12345678901234567890123456789012345678901234567890
```

where each word is in a separate print zone. This same output can be achieved with the code

```
Dim a As String, b As String, c As String, d As String
a = "North"
b = "to"
c = "the"
d = "future."
picBox.Print a, b, c, d
picBox.Print "12345678901234567890123456789012345678901234567890"
```

EXAMPLE 5

The following program uses Print zones to organize expenses for public and private schools into columns of a table. The data represent the average expenses for 1995–96. (The Font setting for picTable is the default font MS Sans Serif.)

```
Private Sub cmdDisplay_Click()
  picTable.Cls
  picTable.Print " ", "Pb 2-yr", "Pr 2-yr", "Pb 4-yr", "Pr 4-yr"
  picTable.Print
  picTable.Print "Tuit & Fees", 1387, 6350, 2860, 12432
  picTable.Print "Bks & Suppl", 577, 567, 591, 601
  picTable.Print "Board", 1752, 1796, 1721, 1845
  picTable.Print "Trans", 894, 902, 929, 863
  picTable.Print "Other Exp", 1142, 1220, 1348, 1169
  picTable.Print " ", "----------", "----------", "----------", "----------"
  picTable.Print "Total", 5752, 10835, 7449, 16910
End Sub
```

[Run, and then click the command button. The following is displayed in the picture box.]

	Pb 2-yr	Pr 2-yr	Pb 4-yr	Pr 4-yr
Tuit & Fees	1387	6350	2860	12432
Bks & Suppl	577	567	591	601
Board	1752	1796	1721	1845
Trans	894	902	929	863
Other Exp	1142	1220	1348	1169
Total	5752	10835	7449	16910

Tab Function

If an item appearing in a Print statement is preceded by

```
Tab(n);
```

where n is a positive integer, that item will be displayed (if possible) beginning at the nth position of the line. (Exceptions are discussed in Comment 10.)

EXAMPLE 6 The following program uses the Tab function to organize data into columns of a table. The data represent the number of bachelor's degrees conferred (in units of 1000). (*Source:* National Center of Educational Statistics.)

```
Private Sub cmdDisplay_Click()
  picTable.Cls
  picTable.Print Tab(10); "1970-71"; Tab(20); "1980-81"; Tab(30); "1990-91"
  picTable.Print
  picTable.Print "Male"; Tab(10); 476; Tab(20); 470; Tab(30); 490
  picTable.Print "Female"; Tab(10); 364; Tab(20); 465; Tab(30); 560
  picTable.Print "Total"; Tab(10); 840; Tab(20); 935; Tab(30); 1050
End Sub
```

[Run, and then click the command button. The resulting picture box is shown.]

	1970-71	1980-81	1990-91
Male	476	470	490
Female	364	465	560
Total	840	935	1050

Using a Message Box for Output

Sometimes you want to grab the user's attention with a brief message such as "Correct" or "Nice try, but no cigar." You want this message only to appear on the screen until the user has read it. This mission is easily accomplished with a **message box** such as the one shown in Figure 2.28. When a statement of the form

```
MsgBox prompt, , title
```

is executed, where *prompt* and *title* are strings, a message box with *prompt* displayed and the title bar caption *title* appears, and stays on the screen until the user presses Enter or clicks OK. For instance, the statement MsgBox "Nice try, but no cigar", , "Consolation" produces Figure 2.28. If you use double quotation marks ("") for *title*, the title bar will be blank.

Figure 2.28 Sample message box.

Line Continuation Character

Up to 1023 characters can be typed in a line of code. If you use a line with more characters than can fit in the window, Visual Basic scrolls the window toward the right as needed. However, most programmers prefer having lines that are no longer than the width of the code window. This can be achieved with the underscore character (_) preceded by a space. Make sure the underscore doesn't appear inside quotation marks though. For instance, the line

```
msg = "640K ought to be enough for anybody. (Bill Gates, 1981)"
```

can be written as

```
msg = "640K ought to be enough for " & _
        "anybody. (Bill Gates, 1981)"
```

Output to the Printer

You print text on a sheet of paper in the printer in much the same way you display text in a picture box. Visual Basic treats the printer as an object named Printer. If *expr* is a string or numeric expression, then the statement

```
Printer.Print expr
```

sends *expr* to the printer in exactly the same way picBox.Print sends output to a picture box. You can use semicolons, commas for print zones, and Tab.

Font properties can be set with statements like

```
Printer.Font.Name = "Script"
Printer.Font.Bold = True
Printer.Font.Size = 12
```

Another useful printer command is

```
Printer.NewPage
```

which starts a new page.

Windows' print manager usually waits until an entire page has been completed before starting to print. To avoid losing information, execute the statement

```
Printer.EndDoc
```

when you are finished printing.

The statement

```
PrintForm
```

prints the content of the form.

Internal Documentation

Now that we have the capability to write more complicated programs, we must concern ourselves with program documentation. **Program documentation** is the inclusion of comments that specify the intent of the program, the purpose of the variables, the nature of the data in the files, and the tasks performed by individual portions of the program. To create a comment line, just begin the line with an apostrophe. Such a line is completely ignored when the program is executed. (The keyword Rem can be used instead of the apostrophe. Rem is an abbreviation for Remark.) Program documentation appears whenever the program is displayed or printed. Also, a line of code can be documented by adding an apostrophe followed by the desired information to the end of the line. Comments (also known as Rem statements) appear green on the screen.

EXAMPLE 7   Document the program in Example 2.

SOLUTION   In the following program, the first comment describes the entire program, the next three comments give the meanings of the variables, and the final comment describes the items in each line of the file.

```
Private Sub cmdCompute_Click()
  'Compute weekly pay
  Dim nom As String     'Employee name
  Dim wage As Single    'Hourly pay
  Dim hrs As Single     'Number of hours worked during week
  picPay.Cls
  Open "Staff.txt" For Input As #1
  'person's name, person's wage, person's hours worked
  Input #1, nom, wage, hrs
  picPay.Print nom; hrs * wage
  Input #1, nom, wage, hrs
  picPay.Print nom; hrs * wage
  Close #1
End Sub
```

Some of the benefits of documentation are as follows:

1. Other people can easily comprehend the program.

2. The program can be understood when read later.

3. Long programs are easier to read because the purposes of individual pieces can be determined at a glance.

Comments

1. Visual Basic provides a convenient device for accessing a file that resides in the same folder as the (saved) program. After a program has been saved in a folder, the value of App.Path is the string consisting of the name of the folder. Therefore, if a program contains a line such as

```
Open App.Path & "\Data.txt" For Input As #1
```

Visual Basic will look for the file Data.txt in the folder containing the program.

The programs from this book, as well as the data files they use, all are contained in the folder Programs on the CD accompanying this book. On the CD, App.Path is used in every Open statement. Therefore, even after you copy the contents of the Programs folder onto your hard drive or a diskette, the programs will continue to execute properly without your having to alter any paths.

2. The text box and input box provide a whole new dimension to the capabilities of a program. The user, rather than the programmer, can provide the data to be processed.

3. A string used in a file does not have to be enclosed by quotation marks. The only exceptions are strings containing commas or leading and trailing spaces.

4. If an Input # statement looks for a string and finds a number, it will treat the number as a string. Suppose the first two entries in the file Data.txt are the numbers 2 and 3.

```
Private Sub cmdButton_Click()
  Dim a As String, b As String
  picBox.Cls
  Open "Data.txt" For Input As #1
  Input #1, a, b
  picBox.Print a + b
  Close #1
End Sub
```

[Run and then click the command button. The following is displayed in the picture box.]

23

5. If an Input # statement looks for a number and finds a string, the Input # statement will assign the value 0 to the numeric variable. For instance, suppose the first two entries in the file Data.txt are "ten" and 10. Then after the statement

```
Input #1, num1, num2
```

is executed, where *num1* and *num2* are numeric variables, the values of these variables will be 0 and 10.

6. If all the data in a file have been read by Input # statements and another item is requested by an Input # statement, a box will appear displaying the message "Input past end of file."

7. Numeric data in a text box, input box, or file must be a constant. It *cannot* be a variable or an expression. For instance, num, 1 / 2, and 2 + 3 are not acceptable.

8. To skip a Print zone, just include two consecutive commas.

9. Print zones are usually employed to align information into columns. Since most fonts have proportionally-spaced characters, wide characters occupy more than one fixed-width column and narrow characters occupy less. The best and most predictable results are obtained when a fixed-pitch font (such as Courier) is used with print zones.

10. The Tab function cannot be used to move the cursor to the left. If the position specified in a Tab function is to the left of the current cursor position, the cursor will move to that position on the next line. For instance, the line

```
picBox.Print "hello"; Tab(3); "good-bye"
```

results in the output

```
hello
  good-bye
```

11. The statement Close, without any reference number, closes all open files.

PRACTICE PROBLEMS 2.5

1. What is the difference in the outcomes of the following sets of lines of code?

```
Input #1, num1, num2
picOutput.Print num1 + num2
```

```
Input #1, num1
Input #1, num2
picOutput.Print num1 + num2
```

2. What is the difference in the outcomes of the following sets of lines of code?

```
strVar = InputBox("How old are you?", "Age")
numVar = Val(strVar)
picOutput.Print numVar
```

```
numVar = Val(InputBox("How old are you?", "Age"))
picOutput.Print numVar
```

EXERCISES 2.5

In Exercises 1 to 14, assume that the file **Data.txt** (shown to the right of the code) has been opened for input with reference number 1. Determine the output displayed in the picture box by the lines of code.

1.
```
Dim num As Single
Input #1, num
picOutput.Print num * num
```
Data.txt
4

2.
```
Dim word As String
Input #1, word
picOutput.Print "un" & word
```
Data.txt
"speakable"

3.
```
Dim str1 As String, str2 As String
Input #1, str1, str2
picOutput.Print str1; str2
```
Data.txt
"base"
"ball"

4.
```
Dim num1 As Single, num2 As Single
Dim num3 As Single
Input #1, num1, num2, num3
picOutput.Print (num1 + num2) * num3
```
Data.txt
3
4
5

5.
```
Dim yrOfBirth As Single, curYr As Single
Input #1, yrOfBirth
Input #1, curYr        'Current year
picOutput.Print "Age:"; curYr - yrOfBirth
```
Data.txt
1979
1999

6.
```
Dim str1 As String, str2 As String
Input #1, str1
Input #1, str2
picOutput.Print str1 & str2
```
Data.txt
"A, my name is "
"Alice"

7.
```
Dim word1 As String, word2 As String
Input #1, word1
Input #1, word2
picOutput.Print word1 & word2
```
Data.txt
"set", "up"

8.
```
Dim num As Single, sum As Single
sum = 0
Input #1, num
sum = sum + num
Input #1, num
sum = sum + num
picOutput.Print "Sum:"; sum
```
Data.txt
123, 321

9.
```
Dim building As String
Dim numRooms As Single
Input #1, building, numRooms
picOutput.Print "The "; building;
picOutput.Print " has"; numRooms; "rooms."
```
Data.txt
"White House", 132

10.
```
Dim nom As String       'Name of student
Dim grade1 As Single    'Grade on 1st exam
Dim grade2 As Single    'Grade on 2nd exam
Dim average As Single   'Ave of grades
Input #1, nom, grade1, grade2
average = (grade1 + grade2) / 2
picOutput.Print nom; " ======> "; average
Input #1, nom, grade1, grade2
average = (grade1 + grade2) / 2
picOutput.Print nom; " ======> "; average
```
Data.txt
"Al Adams", 72, 88
"Betty Brown", 76, 82

11.
```
Dim num1 As Single, num2 As Single
Dim str1 As String, str2 As String
Input #1, num1, str1
Input #1, str2, num2
picOutput.Print num1; str1; str2; num2
Close #1
Open "Data.txt" For Input As #1
picOutput.Print num2
Input #1, num2
picOutput.Print num2
```
Data.txt
1, "One", "Two", 2

12.
```
Dim num As Integer, str As String
Input #1, num, str
picOutput.Print num; str
Close #1
Open "Data.txt" For Input As #1
Input #1, num, str
picOutput.Print num, str
```

Data.txt
4, "calling birds"
3, "French hens"

13.
```
Dim college As String
Dim yrFounded As Single
Dim yrStr As String, yr As Single
Input #1, college, yrFounded
yrStr = InputBox("What is the current year?")
yr = Val(yrStr)
picOutput.Print college; " is";
picOutput.Print yr - yrFounded; "years old."
```

Data.txt
"Harvard University", 1636

(Assume that the response is *1999*.)

14.
```
Dim hourlyWage As Single, nom As String
Dim hoursWorked As Single, message As String
Input #1, hourlyWage, nom
message = "Hours worked by " & nom & ":"
hoursWorked = Val(InputBox(message))
picOutput.Print "Pay for "; nom; " is";
picOutput.Print hoursWorked * hourlyWage
```

Data.txt
7.50, "Joe Smith"

(Assume that the response is *10*.)

In Exercises 15 to 28, determine the output displayed in the picture box by the following lines of code.

15.
```
Dim bet As Single      'Amount bet at roulette
bet = Val(InputBox("How much do you want to bet?", "Wager"))
picOutput.Print "You might win"; 36 * bet; "dollars."
```

(Assume that the response is *5*.)

16.
```
Dim word As String
word = InputBox("Word to negate:")
picOutput.Print "un"; word
```

(Assume that the response is *tied.*)

17.
```
Dim lastName As String, message As String, firstName As String
lastName = "Jones"
message = "What is your first name Mr. " & lastName
firstName = InputBox(message)
picOutput.Print "Hello "; firstName; " "; lastName
```

(Assume that the response is *John.*)

18.
```
Dim intRate As Single  'Current interest rate
intRate = Val(InputBox("Current interest rate?"))
picOutput.Print "At the current interest rate, ";
picOutput.Print "your money will double in";
picOutput.Print 72 / intRate; "years."
```

(Assume that the response is *6*.)

19. `picOutput.Print 1; "one", "won"`

20. `picOutput.Print 1, 2; 3`

21. `picOutput.Print "one",`
`    picOutput.Print "two"`

22. `picOutput.Print "one", , "two"`

23. `picOutput.Font.Name = "Courier"    'Fixed-width font`
`    picOutput.Print "1234567890"`
`    picOutput.Print Tab(4); 5`

24. `picOutput.Font.Name = "Courier"    'Fixed-width font`
`    picOutput.Print "1234567890"`
`    picOutput.Print "Hello"; Tab(3); "Good-bye"`

25. `picOutput.Font.Name = "Courier"`
`    picOutput.Print "1234567890"`
`    picOutput.Print Tab(3); "one"; Tab(8); "two"`

26. `picOutput.Font.Name = "Courier"`
`    picOutput.Print "1234567890"`
`    picOutput.Print Tab(3); "one"`
`    picOutput.Print "   "; "two"`

27. `picOutput.Font.Name = "Courier"`
`    picOutput.Print "12345678901234"`
`    picOutput.Print "one", Tab(12); "two"`

28. `picOutput.Font.Name = "Courier"`
`    picOutput.Print "1234567890"`
`    picOutput.Print Tab(2); "1"; Tab(5); "2"`
`    picOutput.Print 1; 2`

In Exercises 29 to 40, assume that the file Data.txt (shown to the right of the code) has been opened for input with reference number 1. Identify any errors.

29. `Dim str1 As String, str2 As String`
`    Input #1, str1, str2`
`    picOutput.Print "Hello "; str1`

Data.txt
"John Smith"

30. `Dim num As Single`
`    Input #1, num`
`    picOutput.Print 3 * num`

Data.txt
1 + 2

31. `'Each line of Data.txt contains`
`    'building, height, # of stories`
`    Dim building As String`
`    Dim ht As Single`
`    Input #1, building, ht`
`    picOutput.Print building, ht`
`    Input #1, building, ht`
`    picOutput.Print building, ht`

Data.txt
"World Trade Center", 1350, 110
"Sears Tower", 1454, 110

32.
```
Dim num As Single
num = InputBox(Pick a number from 1 to 10.)
picOutput.Print "Your number is"; num
```

33.
```
Dim statePop As Single
statePop = Val(InputBox("State Population?"))
picOutput.Print "The population should grow to";
picOutput.Print 1.01 * statePop; "by next year."
```

(Assume that the response is 8,900,000)

34. `info = InputBox()`

35. `Printer.Name = Courier`

36. `txtBox.Text = "one", "two"`

37. `lblTwo.Caption = 1, 2`

38. `Printer.Print "Hello"; Tab(200); "Good-bye"`

39. `Form.Caption = "one"; Tab(10); "two"`

40.
```
Dim rem As Single   'Number to remember        Data.txt
Input #1, rem                                  4
picOutput.Print "Don't forget to ";
picOutput.Print "remember the number"; rem
```

41. Fill in the table with the value of each variable after each line is executed. Assume the file Data.txt consists of the two lines

"phone", 35.25
"postage", 14.75

Event Procedure	category	amount	total
`Private Sub cmdDetermineTotal_Click()`			
`Dim category As String`			
`Dim amount As Single`			
`Dim total As Single`			
`Open "Data.txt" For Input As #1`			
`Input #1, category, amount`			
`total = total + amount`			
`Input #1, category, amount`			
`total = total + amount`			
`picOutput.Print total`			
`Close #1`			
`End Sub`			

42. Fill in the table with the value of each variable after each line is executed. Assume the file Data.txt consists of the single line

2, 3, 5

Event Procedure	num1	num2	num3
`Private Sub cmdButton_Click()`			
`   Dim num1 As Single, num2 As Single`			
`   Dim num3 As Single`			
`   Open "Data.txt" For Input As #1`			
`   Input #1, num1, num2, num3`			
`   num1 = num2 + num3`			
`   Close #1`			
`   Open "Data.txt" For Input As #2`			
`   Input #2, num1, num3`			
`   num3 = num3 + 1`			
`   Close #2`			
`End Sub`			

In Exercises 43 to 46, write code starting with Private Sub cmdDisplay_ Click() and picOutput.Cls statements, ending with an End Sub statement, and having one or two lines for each step. Lines that display data should use the given variable names.

43. The following steps display the changes in political activities for first-year college students from 1996 to 1997. Assume the file Politics.txt consists of the two lines

"frequently discuss politics", 16.2, 13.7
"worked on a political campaign", 6.6, 8.2

(a) Declare all variables used in the steps below.
(b) Use an Input # statement to assign values to the variables *activity*, *percent96*, and *percent97*.
(c) Display a sentence giving the change in the percentage of students engaged in the activity.
(d) Repeat steps (b) and (c).

44. The following steps display information about Americans' eating habits. Assume the file Data.txt consists of the single line

"soft drinks", "million gallons", 23

(a) Declare all variables used in the steps below.
(b) Open the file Data.txt for input.

(c) Use an Input # statement to assign values to the variables *food*, *units*, and *quantityPerDay*.

(d) Display a sentence giving the quantity of a food item consumed by Americans in 1 day.

45. The following steps calculate the percent increase in a typical grocery basket of goods:

(a) Declare all variables used in the steps below.

(b) Assign 200 to the variable *begOfYearPrice*.

(c) Request the price at the end of the year with an input box and assign it to the variable *endOfYearPrice*.

(d) Assign 100 ∗ (*endOfYearPrice* – *begOfYearPrice*) / *begOfYearPrice* to the variable *percentIncrease*.

(e) Display a sentence giving the percent increase for the year.

(Test the program with a $215 end-of-year price.)

46. The following steps calculate the amount of money earned in a walk-a-thon.

(a) Declare all variables used in the steps below.

(b) Request the amount pledged per mile from an input box and assign it to the variable *pledge*.

(c) Request the number of miles walked from an input box and assign it to the variable *miles*.

(d) Display a sentence giving the amount to be paid.

(Test the program with a pledge of $2.00 and a 15-mile walk.)

In Exercises 47 and 48, write a line of code to carry out the task.

47. Pop up a message box stating "The future isn't what it used to be."

48. Pop up a message box with "Taking Risks Proverb" in the title bar and the message "You can't steal second base and keep one foot on first."

49. Table 2.6 summarizes the month's activity of three checking accounts. Write a program that displays the account number and the end-of-month balance for each account and then displays the total amount of money in the three accounts. Assume the data are stored in a data file.

Account Number	Beginning-of-Month Balance	Deposits	Withdrawals
AB4057	1234.56	345.67	100.00
XY4321	789.00	120.00	350.00
GH2222	321.45	143.65	0.00

Table 2.6 Checking-account activity.

50. Table 2.7 contains a list of colleges with their student enrollments and faculty sizes. Write a program to display the names of the colleges and their student/faculty ratios, and the ratio for the total collection of students and faculty. Assume the data for the colleges are stored in a data file.

	Enrollment	Faculty
Ohio State	48352	3518
Univ. of MD, College Park	31471	1849
Princeton	6340	890

Table 2.7 Colleges.

Source: The World Almanac, 1998.

51. Write a program to compute semester averages. Each line in a data file should contain a student's Social Security number and the grades for three hourly exams and the final exam. (The final exam counts as two hourly exams.) The program should display each student's Social Security number and semester average, and then the class average. Use the data in Table 2.8.

Soc. Sec. No.	Exam 1	Exam 2	Exam 3	Final Exam
123-45-6789	67	85	90	88
111-11-1111	93	76	82	80
123-32-1234	85	82	89	84

Table 2.8 Student grades.

52. Table 2.9 gives the projected year 2000 populations of three New England states. Write a program that calculates the average population and then displays the name of each state and the difference between its population and the average population. The states and their populations should be stored in a data file.

Maine	1259
Massachusetts	6199
Connecticut	3284

Table 2.9 2000 Population (in thousands) of three New England states.

53. Write a program to produce Table 2.10. (The amounts are given in millions of dollars.) The name, sport, salary or winnings, and endorsements for the four people should be contained in a data file. The totals should be computed by the program.

Athlete	Sport	Salary or Winnings	Endorsements	Total
M. Jordan	basketball	29.3	193.2	222.5
E. Holyfield	boxing	110.3	7.5	117.8
A. Agassi	tennis	11.3	63.5	74.8
W. Gretsky	hockey	36.8	31.5	68.3

Table 2.10 1990–96 earnings (in millions) of athletes.

54. Write a program to calculate the amount of a waiter's tip given the amount of the bill and the percentage tip. The output should be a complete sentence that reiterates the inputs and gives the resulting tip. For example, if $20 and 15% are the inputs, then the output might read "A 15 percent tip on 20 dollars is 3 dollars."

55. Design a form with two text boxes labeled "Name" and "Phone number". Then write an event procedure that shows a message box stating "Be sure to include the area code!" when the second text box receives the focus.

In Exercises 56 and 57, write lines of code corresponding to the given flow-chart. Assume that the data needed are contained in a file.

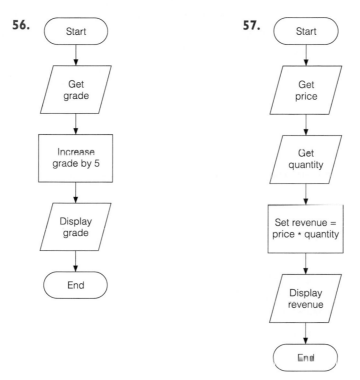

56.
- Start
- Get grade
- Increase grade by 5
- Display grade
- End

57.
- Start
- Get price
- Get quantity
- Set revenue = price * quantity
- Display revenue
- End

✔✔ **Solutions to Practice Problems 2.5**

1. The outputs are identical. In this text, we tend to use a single Input # statement for each line of the file.

2. The outcomes are identical. In this text, we use the second style.

2.6 GENERAL PROCEDURES

An event procedure contains a block of code (enclosed by Private Sub and End Sub statements) that is executed when the associated event occurs. A **general procedure** is similar to an event procedure. The primary difference is that an event procedure is executed as the result of an event occurring (usually determined by the user), whereas a general procedure is executed whenever the programmer decides to execute it. There are two types of general procedures—**Sub procedures** and **Function procedures**.

Sub Procedures

The simplest type of Sub procedure has the form

```
Private Sub ProcedureName()
  block of code
End Sub
```

A Sub procedure is invoked with a statement of the form

```
Call ProcedureName
```

General procedures allow a problem to be broken into small problems to be solved one at a time. Also, they eliminate repetitive code, can be reused in other programs, and allow a team of programmers to work on a single program.

The rules for naming general procedures are identical to the rules for naming variables. The name chosen for a Sub procedure should describe the task it performs. Sub procedures can be either typed (in entirety) directly into the code window, or into a template created with the following steps:

1. Press Alt/T/P to select Add Procedure from the Tools menu.

2. Type in the name of the procedure. (Omit parentheses.)

3. Select Sub from the Type box and Private from the Scope box.

4. Press the Enter key or click on OK.

Consider the following program that calculates the sum of two numbers. This program will be revised to incorporate Sub procedures.

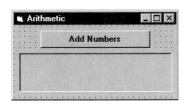

Object	Property	Setting
frmArithmetic	Caption	Arithmetic
cmdAdd	Caption	Add Numbers
picResult		

```
Private Sub cmdAdd_Click()
  Dim num1 As Single, num2 As Single
  'Display the sum of two numbers
  picResult.Cls
  picResult.Print "This program displays a sentence "
  picResult.Print "identifying two numbers and their sum."
  picResult.Print
  num1 = 2
  num2 = 3
  picResult.Print "The sum of"; num1; "and"; num2; "is"; num1 + num2
End Sub
```

[Run, and then click the command button. The following is displayed in the picture box.]

```
This program displays a sentence
identifying two numbers and their sum.

The sum of 2 and 3 is 5
```

The tasks performed by this program can be summarized as follows:

Explain purpose of program.

Display numbers and their sum.

Sub procedures allow us to write and read the program in such a way that we first focus on the tasks and later on how to accomplish each task.

EXAMPLE I

The following program uses a Sub procedure to accomplish the first task of the preceding program. When the statement Call ExplainPurpose is reached, execution jumps to the Private Sub ExplainPurpose statement. The lines between Private Sub ExplainPurpose and End Sub are executed, and then execution continues with the line following the Call statement.

```
Private Sub cmdAdd_Click()
  Dim num1 As Single, num2 As Single
  'Display the sum of two numbers
  picResult.Cls
  Call ExplainPurpose
  picResult.Print
  num1 = 2
  num2 = 3
  picResult.Print "The sum of"; num1; "and"; num2; "is"; num1 + num2
End Sub

Private Sub ExplainPurpose()
  'Explain the task performed by the program
  picResult.Print "This program displays a sentence"
  picResult.Print "identifying two numbers and their sum."
End Sub
```

In Example 1, the cmdAdd_Click event procedure is referred to as the **calling procedure** and the ExplainPurpose Sub procedure is referred to as the called procedure. The second task performed by the program in Example 1 also can be handled by a Sub procedure. The values of the two numbers, however, must be transmitted to the Sub procedure. This transmission is called **passing**.

EXAMPLE 2

The following revision of the program in Example 1 uses a Sub procedure to accomplish the second task. The statement Call Add(2, 3) causes execution to jump to the Private Sub Add(num1 As Single, num2 As Single) statement, which assigns the number 2 to *num1* and the number 3 to *num2*.

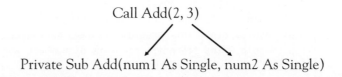

After the lines between Private Sub Add (num1 As Single, num2 As Single) and End Sub are executed, execution continues with the line following Call Add(2, 3), namely, the End Sub statement in the event procedure. **Note:** If you use Add Procedure to create a template for the Sub procedure, you must type in "num1 As Single, num2 As Single" after leaving the Add Procedure dialog box.

```
Private Sub cmdAdd_Click()
  'Display the sum of two numbers
  picResult.Cls
  Call ExplainPurpose
  picResult.Print
  Call Add(2, 3)
End Sub

Private Sub Add(num1 As Single, num2 As Single)
  'Display numbers and their sum
  picResult.Print "The sum of"; num1; "and"; num2; "is"; num1 + num2
End Sub

Private Sub ExplainPurpose()
  'Explain the task performed by the program
  picResult.Print "This program displays a sentence"
  picResult.Print "identifying two numbers and their sum."
End Sub
```

Sub procedures make a program easy to read, modify, and debug. The event procedure gives an unencumbered description of what the program does and the Sub procedures fill in the details. Another benefit of Sub procedures is that they can be called several times during the execution of the program. This feature is especially useful when there are many statements in the Sub procedure.

EXAMPLE 3

The following extension of the program in Example 2 displays several sums.

```
Private Sub cmdAdd_Click()
  'Display the sums of several pairs of numbers
  picResult.Cls
  Call ExplainPurpose
  picResult.Print
  Call Add(2, 3)
  Call Add(4, 6)
  Call Add(7, 8)
End Sub

Private Sub Add(num1 As Single, num2 As Single)
  'Display numbers and their sum
  picResult.Print "The sum of"; num1; "and"; num2; "is"; num1 + num2
End Sub

Private Sub ExplainPurpose()
  'Explain the task performed by the program
  picResult.Print "This program displays sentences"
  picResult.Print "identifying pairs of numbers and their sums."
End Sub
```

[Run, and then click the command button. The following is displayed in the picture box.]

```
This program displays sentences
identifying pairs of numbers and their sums.

The sum of 2 and 3 is 5
The sum of 4 and 6 is 10
The sum of 7 and 8 is 15
```

The variables *num1* and *num2* appearing in the Sub procedure Add are called **parameters**. They are merely temporary place holders for the numbers passed to the Sub procedure; their names are not important. The only essentials are their type, quantity, and order. In this Add Sub procedure, the parameters must be numeric variables and there must be two of them. For instance, the Sub procedure could have been written

```
Private Sub Add(this As Single, that As Single)
   'Display numbers and their sum
   picResult.Print "The sum of"; this; "and"; that; "is"; this + that
End Sub
```

A string also can be passed to a Sub procedure. In this case, the receiving parameter in the Sub procedure must be followed by the declaration As String.

EXAMPLE 4 The following program passes a string and two numbers to a Sub procedure. When the Sub procedure is first called, the string parameter *state* is assigned the string constant "Hawaii", and the numeric parameters *pop* and *area* are assigned the numeric constants 1134750 and 6471, respectively. The Sub procedure then uses these parameters to carry out the task of calculating the population density of Hawaii. The second Call statement assigns different values to the parameters.

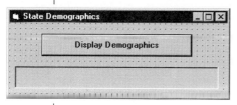

Object	Property	Setting
frmStates	Caption	State Demographics
cmdDisplay	Caption	Display Demographics
picDensity		

```
Private Sub cmdDisplay_Click()
   'Calculate the population densities of states
   picDensity.Cls
   Call CalculateDensity("Hawaii", 1134750, 6471)
   Call CalculateDensity("Alaska", 570345, 591000)
End Sub

Private Sub CalculateDensity(state As String, pop As Single, area As Single)
   Dim rawDensity As Single, density As Single
   'The density (number of people per square mile)
   'will be displayed rounded to a whole number
   rawDensity = pop / area
   density = Round(rawDensity)   'round to whole number
   picDensity.Print "The density of "; state; " is"; density;
   picDensity.Print "people per square mile."
End Sub
```

[Run, and then click the command button. The following is displayed in the picture box.]

```
The density of Hawaii is 175 people per square mile.
The density of Alaska is 1 people per square mile.
```

The parameters in the density program can have any names, as with the parameters in the addition program of Example 3. The only restriction is that the first parameter be a string variable and that the last two parameters be numeric variables of type Single. For instance, the Sub procedure could have been written

```
Private Sub CalculateDensity(x As String, y As Single, z As Single)
  Dim rawDensity As Single, density As Single
  'The density (number of people per square mile)
  'will be rounded to a whole number
  rawDensity = y / z
  density = Round(rawDensity)
  picDensity.Print "The density of "; x; " is"; density;
  picDensity.Print "people per square mile."
End Sub
```

When nondescriptive names are used for parameters, the Sub procedure should contain comment statements giving the meanings of the variables. Possible comment statements for the preceding program are

```
'x    name of the state
'y    population of the state
'z    area of the state
```

Variables and Expressions as Arguments

The items appearing in the parentheses of a Call statement are called **arguments**. These should not be confused with parameters, which appear in the heading of a Sub procedure. In Example 3, the arguments of the Call Add statements were constants. These arguments also could have been variables or expressions. For instance, the event procedure could have been written as follows. See Figure 2.29.

```
Private Sub cmdAdd_Click()
  Dim x As Single, y As Single, z As Single
  'Display the sum of two numbers
  picResult.Cls
  Call ExplainPurpose
  picResult.Print
  x = 2
  y = 3
  Call Add(x, y)
  Call Add(x + 2, 2 * y)
  z = 7
  Call Add(z, z + 1)
End Sub
```

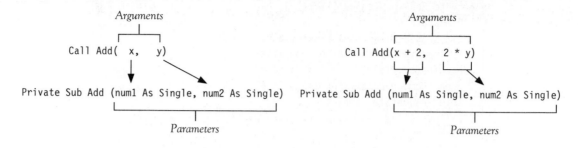

Figure 2.29 Passing arguments to parameters.

This feature allows values obtained as input from the user to be passed to a Sub procedure.

EXAMPLE 5

The following variation of the addition program requests the two numbers as input from the user. Notice that the names of the arguments, *x* and *y*, are different than the names of the parameters. The names of the arguments and parameters may be the same or different; what matters is that the order, number, and types of the arguments and parameters match.

```
Private Sub cmdCompute_Click()
 Dim x As Single, y As Single
 'This program requests two numbers and
 'displays the two numbers and their sum.
 x = Val(InputBox("FirstNumber:", "Add Two Numbers"))
 y = Val(InputBox("Second Number:", "Add Two Numbers"))
 Call Add(x, y)
End Sub

Private Sub Add(num1 As Single, num2 As Single)
 'Display numbers and their sum
 picResult.Cls
 picResult.Print "The sum of"; num1; "and"; num2; "is"; num1 + num2
End Sub
```

[Run, click the command button, and respond to the requests for numbers with 23 and 67. The following is displayed in the picture box.]

```
The sum of 23 and 67 is 90
```

EXAMPLE 6

The following variation of Example 4 obtains its input from the file Demograp.txt. The second Call statement uses different variable names for the arguments to show that using the same argument names is not necessary. See Figure 2.30.

Demograp.txt contains the following two lines:

"Hawaii", 1134750, 6471
"Alaska", 570345, 591000

```
Private Sub cmdDisplay_Click()
  Dim state As String, pop As Single, area As Single
  Dim s As String, p As Single, a As Single
  'Calculate the population densities of states
  picDensity.Cls
  Open "Demograp.txt" For Input As #1
  Input #1, state, pop, area
  Call CalculateDensity(state, pop, area)
  Input #1, s, p, a
  Call CalculateDensity(s, p, a)
  Close #1
End Sub

Private Sub CalculateDensity(state As String, pop As Single, area As Single)
  Dim rawDensity As Single, density As Single
  'The density (number of people per square mile)
  'will be rounded to a whole number
  rawDensity = pop / area
  density = Round(rawDensity)
  picDensity.Print "The density of "; state; " is "; density;
  picDensity.Print "people per square mile."
End Sub
```

[Run, and then click the command button. The following is displayed in the picture box.]

```
The density of Hawaii is 175 people per square mile.
The density of Alaska is 1 people per square mile.
```

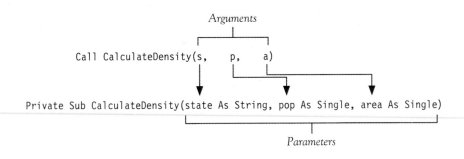

Figure 2.30 Passing arguments to parameters in Example 6.

Passing Values Back from Sub Procedures

Suppose a variable, call it *arg*, appears as an argument in a Call statement, and its corresponding parameter in the Sub statement is *par*. After the Sub procedure is executed, *arg* will have whatever value *par* had in the Sub procedure. Hence, not only is the value of *arg* passed to *par*, but the value of *par* is passed back to *arg*.

EXAMPLE 7   The following program illustrates the transfer of the value of a parameter to its calling argument.

```
Private Sub cmdDisplay_Click()
  Dim amt As Single
  'Illustrate effect of value of parameter on value of argument
  picResults.Cls
  amt = 2
  picResults.Print amt;
  Call Triple(amt)
  picResults.Print amt
End Sub

Private Sub Triple(num As Single)
  'Triple a number
  picResults.Print num;
  num = 3 * num
  picResults.Print num;
End Sub
```

[Run, and then click the command button. The following is displayed in the picture box.]

```
2   2   6   6
```

Although this feature may be surprising at first glance, it provides a vehicle for passing values from a Sub procedure back to the place from which the Sub procedure was called. Different names may be used for an argument and its corresponding parameter, but only one memory location is involved. Initially, the cmdDisplay_Click( ) event procedure allocates a memory location to hold the value of *amt* (Figure 2.31(a)). When the Sub procedure is called, the parameter *num* becomes the Sub procedure's name for this memory location (Figure 2.31(b)). When the value of *num* is tripled, the value in the memory location becomes 6 (Figure 2.31(c)). After the completion of the procedure, the parameter name *num* is forgotten; however, its value lives on in *amt* (Figure 2.31(d)). The variable *amt* is said to be **passed by reference**.

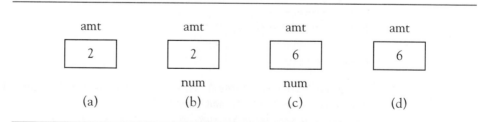

Figure 2.31 Passing a variable by reference to a Sub procedure.

Passing by reference has a wide variety of uses. In the next example, it is used as a vehicle to transport a value from a Sub procedure back to an event procedure.

EXAMPLE 8 The following variation of Example 5 uses a Sub procedure to acquire the input. The variables *x* and *y* are not assigned values prior to the execution of the first Call statement. Therefore, before the Call statement is executed, they have the value 0. After the Call statement is executed, however, they have the values 2 and 3. These values then are passed by the second Call statement to the Sub procedure Add.

```
Private Sub cmdCompute_Click()
  Dim x As Single, y As Single
  'Display the sum of the two numbers
  Call GetNumbers(x, y)
  Call Add(x, y)
End Sub

Private Sub Add(num1 As Single, num2 As Single)
  Dim sum As Single
  'Display numbers and their sum
  picResult.Cls
  sum = num1 + num2
  picResult.Print "The sum of"; num1; "and"; num2; "is"; sum
End Sub

Private Sub GetNumbers(num1 As Single, num2 As Single)
  'Get the two numbers
  num1 = Val(InputBox("First number:", "Add Two Numbers"))
  num2 = Val(InputBox("Second number:", "Add Two Numbers"))
End Sub
```

In most situations, a variable with no preassigned value is used as an argument of a Call statement for the sole purpose of carrying back a value from the Sub procedure.

EXAMPLE 9 The following variation of Example 8 allows the cmdCompute_Click event procedure to be written in the input-process-output style:

```
Private Sub cmdCompute_Click()
  Dim x As Single, y As Single, s As Single
  'Display the sum of two numbers
  Call GetNumbers(x, y)
  Call CalculateSum(x, y, s)
  Call DisplayResult(x, y, s)
End Sub

Private Sub CalculateSum(num1 As Single, num2 As Single, sum As Single)
  'Add the values of num1 and num2
  'and assign the value to sum
  sum = num1 + num2
End Sub

Private Sub DisplayResult(num1 As Single, num2 As Single, sum As Single)
  'Display a sentence giving the two numbers and their sum
  picResult.Cls
  picResult.Print "The sum of"; num1; "and"; num2; "is"; sum
End Sub
```

```
Private Sub GetNumbers(num1 As Single, num2 As Single)
  'Get the two numbers
  num1 = Val(InputBox("First number:", "Add Two Numbers"))
  num2 = Val(InputBox("Second number:", "Add Two Numbers"))
End Sub
```

Function Procedures

A **Function procedure** (also known as a **user-defined function**) is a function created by the programmer in the same manner as a Sub procedure. A Function procedure is used in the same way as a built-in function. Like a built-in function, a user-defined function has a single output that is usually either a string or a number. A Function procedure is defined in a function block of the form

```
Private Function FunctionName(var1 As Type1, var2 As Type2, ...) As dataType
  statement(s)
  FunctionName = expression
End Function
```

Function names should be suggestive of the role performed and must conform to the rules for naming variables. The type *dataType*, which specifies the type of the output, will be one of String, Integer, Single, and so on. In the preceding general code, the next-to-last line assigns the output, which must be of type *dataType*, to the function name. Two examples of functions are as follows:

```
Private Function FtoC(t As Single) As Single
  'Convert Fahrenheit temperature to Celsius
  FtoC = (5 / 9) * (t - 32)
End Function

Private Function FirstName(nom As String) As String
  Dim firstSpace As Integer
  'Extract the first name from the full name nom
  firstSpace = InStr(nom, " ")
  FirstName = Left(nom, firstSpace - 1)
End Function
```

In each of the preceding functions, the value of the function is assigned by a statement of the form *FunctionName = expression*. The variables *t* and *nom* appearing in the preceding functions are parameters. They can be replaced with any variable of the same type without affecting the function definition. For instance, the function FtoC could have been defined as

```
Private Function FtoC(temp As Single) As Single
  'Convert Fahrenheit temperature to Celsius
  FtoC = (5 / 9) * (temp - 32)
End Function
```

Like Sub procedures, functions can be created from a code window with Alt/T/P. The only difference is that the circle next to the word Function should be selected.

EXAMPLE 10   The following program uses the function FtoC.

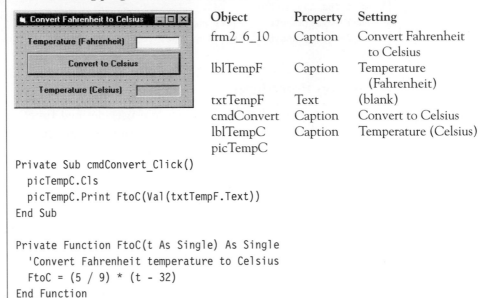

Object	Property	Setting
frm2_6_10	Caption	Convert Fahrenheit to Celsius
lblTempF	Caption	Temperature (Fahrenheit)
txtTempF	Text	(blank)
cmdConvert	Caption	Convert to Celsius
lblTempC	Caption	Temperature (Celsius)
picTempC		

```
Private Sub cmdConvert_Click()
  picTempC.Cls
  picTempC.Print FtoC(Val(txtTempF.Text))
End Sub

Private Function FtoC(t As Single) As Single
  'Convert Fahrenheit temperature to Celsius
  FtoC = (5 / 9) * (t - 32)
End Function
```

[Run, type 212 into the text box, and then click the command button.]

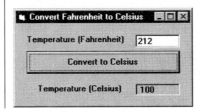

EXAMPLE 11   The following program uses the function FirstName.

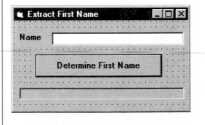

Object	Property	Setting
frm2_6_11	Caption	Extract First Name
lblName	Caption	Name
txtFullName	Text	(blank)
cmdDetermine	Caption	Determine First Name
picFirstName		

```
Private Sub cmdDetermine_Click()
  Dim nom As String
  'Determine a person's first name
  nom = txtFullName.Text
  picFirstName.Cls
  picFirstName.Print "The first name is "; FirstName(nom)
End Sub

Private Function FirstName(nom As String) As String
  Dim firstSpace As Integer
  'Extract the first name from a full name
  firstSpace = InStr(nom, " ")
  FirstName = Left(nom, firstSpace - 1)
End Function
```

[Run, type Thomas Woodrow Wilson into the text box, and then click the command button.]

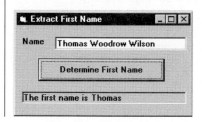

The input to a user-defined function can consist of one or more values. The function in the next example has four parameters. One-letter parameter and variable names have been used so the mathematical formulas will look familiar and be readable. Because the names are not descriptive, the meanings of these variables are carefully stated in comment statements.

EXAMPLE 12   The following program computes the future value of a bank savings account. With the responses shown, the program computes the balance in a savings account when $100 is deposited for 5 years at 4 percent interest compounded quarterly. Interest is earned 4 times per year at the rate of 1 percent per interest period. There will be 4 * 5 or 20 interest periods.

Object	Property	Setting
frm2_6_12	Caption	Bank Deposit
lblAmount	Caption	Amount of bank deposit
txtAmount	Text	(blank)
lblRate	Caption	Annual rate of interest
txtRate	Text	(blank)
lblNumComp	Caption	Number of times interest is compounded per year
txtNumComp	Text	(blank)
lblNumYrs	Caption	Number of years
txtNumYrs	Text	(blank)
cmdCompute	Caption	Compute Balance
lblBalance	Caption	Balance
picBalance		

```
Private Sub cmdCompute_Click()
  Dim p As Single, r As Single, c As Single, n As Single
  'Find the future value of a bank deposit
  Call InputData(p, r, c, n)
  Call DisplayBalance(p, r, c, n)
End Sub

Private Sub DisplayBalance(p As Single,r As Single,c As Single,n As Single)
  Dim balance As Single
  'Display the balance in the picture box
  picBalance.Cls
  balance = FV(p, r, c, n)
  picBalance.Print FormatCurrency(balance)
End Sub
```

```
Private Function FV(p As Single,r As Single,c As Single,n As Single) As Single
  Dim i As Single, m As Single
  'Find the future value of a bank savings account
  'p  principal, the amount deposited
  'r  annual rate of interest
  'c  number of times interest is compounded per year
  'n  number of years
  'i  interest rate per period
  'm  total number of times interest is compounded
  i = r / c
  m = c * n
  FV = p * ((1 + i) ^ m)
End Function

Private Sub InputData(p As Single, r As Single, c As Single, n As Single)
  'Get the four values from the text boxes
  p = Val(txtAmount.Text)
  r = Val(txtRate.Text)
  c = Val(txtNumComp.Text)
  n = Val(txtNumYrs.Text)
End Sub
```

[Run, type 100, .04, 4, and 5 into the text boxes, then click the command button.]

Comments

1. Variables dimensioned inside general procedures have local scope, just as they do with event procedures. Variables declared in the (Declarations) section of (General) are recognized by every procedure—event and general.

2. After a general procedure has been defined, Visual Basic automatically reminds you of the procedure's parameters when you type in a statement that calls the procedure. As soon as you type in the left parenthesis following the procedure name, a banner appears giving the names and types of the parameters. The help feature is called **Parameter Info**. See Figure 2.32.

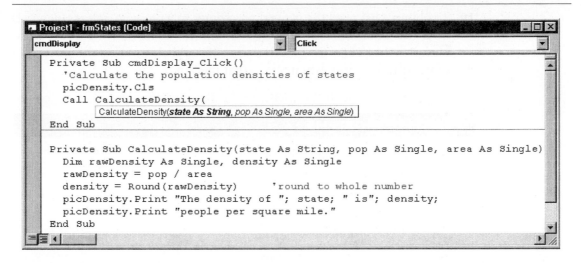

Figure 2.32 The Parameter Info help feature.

3. A Sub procedure can call another Sub procedure. If so, after the End Sub of the called Sub procedure is reached, execution continues with the line in the calling Sub procedure that follows the Call statement.

4. When you create a general procedure without parameters, Visual Basic automatically adds a pair of empty parentheses at the end of the procedure name. Call statements should not use the empty parentheses. (See Example 3.) The use of parentheses is optional for function calls.

5. When a variable argument is passed by reference to a general procedure, any changes to the corresponding parameter inside the procedure will change the value of the original argument when the procedure finishes. This change can be prevented by surrounding the argument by an extra pair of parentheses or by preceding the parameter in the top line of the procedure definition with ByVal. In this case, the argument is said to be **passed by value**.

6. Sub procedures are easily distinguished from event procedures. The names of event procedures always begin with the name of control, followed by an underscore character and the name of an event.

7. In Appendix C, the section "Stepping Through a Program Containing a General Procedure: Chapter 2" uses the Visual Basic debugger to trace the flow through a program and observe the interplay between arguments and parameters.

8. Functions can perform the same tasks as Sub procedures. For instance, they can request input and display text; however, they are primarily used to calculate a single value. Normally, Sub procedures are used to carry out other tasks.

9. Functions differ from Sub procedures in the way they are accessed. Sub procedures are invoked with Call statements, whereas functions are invoked by placing them where you would otherwise expect to find a constant, variable, or expression.

10. To obtain a list of all the general procedures in a program, select (General) from the Code window's Object box, and then click on the down-arrow button to the right of the Procedure box. If you click on one of the procedures in the list, the cursor will move to that procedure.

 PRACTICE PROBLEMS 2.6

1. What is wrong with the following code?

```
Private Sub cmdDisplay_Click()
  Dim phone As String
  phone = txtPhoneNum.Text
  Call AreaCode(phone)
End Sub

Private Sub AreaCode()
  picOutput.Print "Your area code is "; Left(phone, 3)
End Sub
```

2. What is displayed in the picture box when cmdCompute is clicked?

```
Private Sub cmdCompute_Click()
  Dim gallonsPerBushel As Single, apples As Single
  'How many gallons of apple cider can we make?
  Call GetData(gallonsPerBushel, apples)
  Call DisplayNumOfGallons(gallonsPerBushel, apples)
End Sub


Private Function Cider(g As Single, x As Single) As Single
  Cider = g * x
End Function


Private Sub DisplayNumOfGallons(galPerBu As Single, apples As Single)
  picOutput.Cls
  picOutput.Print "You can make"; Cider(galPerBu, apples);
  picOutput.Print "gallons of cider."
End Sub


Private Sub GetData(gallonsPerBushel As Single, apples As Single)
  'gallonsPerBushel    Number of gallons of cider one bushel
  '                    of apples makes
  'apples              Number of bushels of apples available
  gallonsPerBushel = 3
  apples = 9
End Sub
```

> **EXERCISES 2.6**

In Exercises 1 to 26, determine the output displayed in the picture box when the command button is clicked.

1.
```
Private Sub cmdDisplay_Click()
    Call Question
    Call Answer
End Sub

Private Sub Answer()
    picOutput.Print "Because they were invented in the northern"
    picOutput.Print "hemisphere where sundials move clockwise."
End Sub

Private Sub Question()
    picOutput.Print "Why do clocks run clockwise?"
End Sub
```

2.
```
Private Sub cmdDisplay_Click()
    'The fates of Henry the Eighth's six wives
    Call CommonFates
    picOutput.Print "died;"
    Call CommonFates
    picOutput.Print "survived."
End Sub

Private Sub CommonFates()
    'The most common fates
    picOutput.Print "Divorced, beheaded, ";
End Sub
```

3.
```
Private Sub cmdDisplay_Click()
    'Good advice to follow
    Call Advice
End Sub

Private Sub Advice()
    picOutput.Print "Keep cool, but don't freeze."
    Call Source
End Sub

Private Sub Source()
    picOutput.Print "Source: A jar of mayonnaise."
End Sub
```

4.
```
Private Sub cmdDisplay_Click()
    'Opening lines of Tale of Two Cities
    Call Times("best")
    Call Times("worst")
End Sub

Private Sub Times(word As String)
    'Display line
    picOutput.Print "It was the "; word; " of times."
End Sub
```

5.
```
Private Sub cmdDisplay_Click()
    'Sentence using number, thing, and place
    Call Sentence(168, "hour", "a week")
    Call Sentence(76, "trombone", "the big parade")
End Sub

Private Sub Sentence(num As Single, thing As String, where As String)
    picOutput.Print num; thing; "s in "; where
End Sub
```

6.
```
Private Sub cmdDisplay_Click()
    Dim word As String
    word = "worldly"
    Call Negative("un" & word, word)
End Sub

Private Sub Negative(neg As String, word As String)
    picOutput.Print "The negative of "; word; " is "; neg
End Sub
```

7.
```
Private Sub cmdDisplay_Click()
    Call HowMany(24)
    picOutput.Print "a pie."
End Sub

Private Sub HowMany(num As Integer)
    Call What(num)
    picOutput.Print " baked in ";
End Sub

Private Sub What(num As Integer)
    picOutput.Print num; "blackbirds";
End Sub
```

8.
```
Private Sub cmdDisplay_Click()
    picOutput.Print "All's";
    Call PrintWell
    Call PrintWords(" that ends")
    picOutput.Print "."
End Sub

Private Sub PrintWell()
    picOutput.Print " well";
End Sub

Private Sub PrintWords(words As String)
    picOutput.Print words;
    Call PrintWell
End Sub
```

9.
```
Private Sub cmdDisplay_Click()
    Dim num As Single
    num = 7
    Call AddTwo(num)
    picOutput.Print num
End Sub

Private Sub AddTwo(num As Single)
    num = num + 2
End Sub
```

10.
```
Private Sub cmdDisplay_Click()
    Dim term As String
    term = "Fall"
    Call Plural(term)
    picOutput.Print term
End Sub

Private Sub Plural(term As String)
    term = term & "s"
End Sub
```

11.
```
Private Sub cmdDisplay_Click()
    Dim a As Single
    a = 5
    Call Square(a)
    picOutput.Print a
End Sub

Private Sub Square(num As Single)
    num = num * num
End Sub
```

12.
```
Private Sub cmdDisplay_Click()
    Dim state As String
    state = "NEBRASKA"
    Call Abbreviate(state)
    picOutput.Print state
End Sub

Private Sub Abbreviate(a As String)
    a = Left(a, 2)
End Sub
```

13.
```
Private Sub cmdDisplay_Click()
    Dim word As String
    Call GetWord(word)
    picOutput.Print "Less is "; word
End Sub

Private Sub GetWord(w As String)
    w = "more"
End Sub
```

14.
```
Private Sub cmdDisplay_Click()
    Dim word1 As String, word2 As String
    word1 = "fail"
    word2 = "plan"
    picOutput.Print "If you ";
    Call Sentence(word1, word2)
    Call Exchange(word1, word2)
    picOutput.Print " then you ";
    Call Sentence(word1, word2)
End Sub

Private Sub Exchange(word1 As String, word2 As String)
    Dim temp As String
    temp = word1
    word1 = word2
    word2 = temp
End Sub

Private Sub Sentence(word1 As String, word2 As String)
    picOutput.Print word1; " to "; word2;
End Sub
```

15.
```
Private Sub cmdDisplay_Click()
  Dim state As String
  state = "Ohio "
  Call Team
End Sub

Private Sub Team()
  Dim state As String
  picOutput.Print state;
  picOutput.Print "Buckeyes"
End Sub
```

16.
```
Private Sub cmdDisplay_Click()
  Dim a As Single
  a = 5
  Call Multiply(7)
  picOutput.Print a * 7
End Sub

Private Sub Multiply(num As Single)
  Dim a As Single
  a = 11
  picOutput.Print a * num
End Sub
```

17.
```
Private Sub cmdDisplay_Click()
  Dim num As Single
  num = 1
  Call Amount(num)
  Call Amount(num)
End Sub

Private Sub Amount(num As Single)
  Dim total As Single
  total = total + num
  picOutput.Print total;
End Sub
```

18.
```
Private Sub cmdDisplay_Click()
  Dim river As String
  river = "Wabash"
  Call Another
  picOutput.Print river
  Call Another
End Sub

Private Sub Another()
  Dim river As String
  picOutput.Print river;
  river = "Yukon"
End Sub
```

19.
```
Private Sub cmdConvert_Click()
  Dim temp As Single
  'Convert Celsius to Fahrenheit
  temp = 95
  picOutput.Print CtoF(temp)
End Sub

Private Function CtoF(t As Single) As Single
  CtoF = (9 / 5) * t + 32
End Function
```

20.
```
Private Sub cmdDisplay_Click()
  Dim acres As Single
  'acres      Number of acres in a parking lot
  acres = 5
  picOutput.Print "You can park about"; Cars(acres); "cars."
End Sub

Private Function Cars(x As Single) As Single
  'Parking cars
  Cars = 100 * x
End Function
```

21.
```
Private Sub cmdDisplay_Click()
  Dim p As Single
  'Rule of 72
  p = Val(txtPopGr.Text)        'Population growth as a percent
  picOutput.Print "The population will double in";
  picOutput.Print DoublingTime(p); "years."
End Sub
```

```
Private Function DoublingTime(x As Single) As Single
  'Estimate time required for a population to double
  'at a growth rate of x percent
  DoublingTime = 72 / x
End Function
```

(Assume that the text box contains the number 3.)

22.
```
Private Sub cmdDisplay_Click()
  Dim days As String, num As Integer
  'Determine the day of the week from its number
  days = "SunMonTueWedThuFriSat"
  num = Val(InputBox("Enter the number of the day"))
  picOutput.Print "The day is "; DayOfWeek(days, num)
End Sub

Private Function DayOfWeek(x As String, n As Integer) As String
  Dim position As Integer
  'x    string containing 3-letter abbreviations of days of the week
  'n    the number of the day
  position = 3 * n - 2
  DayOfWeek = Mid(x, position, 3)
End Function
```

(Assume that the response is 4.)

23.
```
Private Sub cmdDisplay_Click()
  Dim a As String
  'Demonstrate local variables
  a = "Choo "
  picOutput.Print TypeOfTrain()
End Sub

Private Function TypeOfTrain() As String
  Dim a As String
  a = a & a
  TypeOfTrain = a & "train"
End Function
```

24.
```
Private Sub cmdDisplay_Click()
  Dim num As Single
  'Triple a number
  num = 5
  picOutput.Print Triple(num);
  picOutput.Print num
End Sub

Private Function Triple(x As Single) As Single
  Dim num As Single
  num = 3
  Triple = num * x
End Function
```

25.
```
Private Sub cmdDisplay_Click()
  Dim word As String
  word = "moral"
  Call Negative(word)
  word = "political"
  Call Negative(word)
End Sub

Private Function AddA(word As String) As String
  AddA = "a" & word
End Function

Private Sub Negative(word As String)
  picOutput.Print word; " has the negative "; AddA(word)
End Sub
```

26.
```
Private Sub cmdDisplay_Click()
  Dim city As String, pop As Single, shrinks As Single
  Open "Docs.txt" For Input as #1
  Input #1, city, pop, shrinks
  Call DisplayData(city, pop, shrinks)
  Input #1, city, pop, shrinks
  Call DisplayData(city, pop, shrinks)
  Close #1
End Sub

Private Sub DisplayData(city As String, pop As Single, shrinks As Single)
  picOutput.Print city; " has"; ShrinkDensity(pop, shrinks);
  picOutput.Print "psychiatrists per 100,000 people."
End Sub

Private Function ShrinkDensity(pop As Single,shrinks As Single) As Integer
  ShrinkDensity = Int(100000 * (shrinks / pop))
End Function
```

(Assume that the file Docs.txt contains the following two lines.)

"Boston", 2824000, 8602
"Denver", 1633000, 3217

In Exercises 27 to 32, find the errors.

27.
```
Private Sub cmdDisplay_Click()
  Dim n As Integer
  n = 5
  call Alphabet
End Sub

Private Sub Alphabet(n As Integer)
  picOutput.Print Left("abcdefghijklmnopqrstuvwxyz", n)
End Sub
```

28.
```
Private Sub cmdDisplay_Click()
  Dim word As String, number As String
  word = "seven"
  number = 7
  Call Display(word, number)
End Sub
```

29.
```
Private Sub cmdDisplay_Click()
  Dim num As Integer
  num = 2
  Call Tea(num)
End Sub

Private Sub Tea()
  picOutput.Print "Tea for"; num
End Sub
```

30.
```
Private Sub cmdDisplay_Click()
  Dim ano As String
  Call GetYear(ano)
  picOutput.Print ano
End Sub

Private Sub GetYear(yr As Single)
  yr = 1998
End Sub
```

31.
```
Private Sub cmdDisplay_Click()
  Dim answer As Single
  'Select a greeting
  answer = Val(InputBox("Enter 1 or 2."))
  picOutput.Print Greeting(answer)
End Sub

Private Function Greeting(x As Single) As Single
  Greeting = Mid("hellohi ya", 5 * x - 4, 5)
End Function
```

32.
```
Private Sub cmdDisplay_Click()
  Dim word As String
  word = InputBox("What is your favorite word?")
  picOutput.Print "When the word is written twice,";
  picOutput.Print Twice (word); "letters are used."
End Sub

Private Function Twice(w As String) As Single
  'Compute twice the length of a string
  Twice(w) = 2 * Len(w)
End Function
```

In Exercises 33 and 34, rewrite the program so input, processing, and output are each performed by Calls to Sub procedures.

33.
```
Private Sub cmdDisplay_Click()
    Dim price As Single, tax As Single, cost As Single
    'Calculate sales tax
    picOutput.Cls
    price = Val(InputBox("Enter the price of the item:"))
    tax = .05 * price
    cost = price + tax
    picOutput.Print "Price: "; price
    picOutput.Print "Tax: "; tax
    picOutput.Print "--------------"
    picOutput.Print "Cost: "; cost
End Sub
```

34.
```
Private Sub cmdDisplay_Click()
    Dim length As Single, wdth As Single, area As Single
    'Determine the area of a rectangle
    picOutput.Cls
    length = Val(txtLength.Text)
    wdth = Val(txtWidth.Text)
    area = length * wdth
    picOutput.Print "The area of the rectangle is"; area
End Sub
```

35. Write a program to display four verses of *Old McDonald Had a Farm*. The primary verse, with variables substituted for the animals and sounds, should be contained in a Sub procedure. The program should use the file Farm.txt.

Farm.txt contains the following four lines:

"lamb", "baa"
"firefly", "blink"
"chainsaw", "brraap"
"computer", "beep"

The first verse of the output should be

```
Old McDonald had a farm. Eyi eyi oh.
And on his farm he had a lamb. Eyi eyi oh.
With a baa baa here, and a baa baa there.
Here a baa, there a baa, everywhere a baa baa.
Old McDonald had a farm. Eyi eyi oh.
```

36. Write a program to display the data from Table 2.11. The occupations and numbers of people for 1994 and 2005 should be contained in the file Growth.txt. A Sub procedure, to be called four times, should read the three pieces of data for an occupation, calculate the percent change from 1994 to 2005, and display the four items. **Note:** The percent increase is calculated as 100 * (2005 value − 1994 value) / (1994 value).

Occupation	1994	2005	Increase
Personal home care aides	179	391	118%
Home health aides	420	848	102%
System analysts	483	928	92%
Computer engineers	195	372	91%

Table 2.11 Occupations projected to experience fastest job growth, 1994–2005 (numbers in thousands).

Source: U.S. Bureau of the Census, Statistical Abstract of the U.S.

37. The Hat Rack is considering locating its new branch store in one of three malls. The following file gives the monthly rent per square foot and the total square feet available at each of the three locations. Write a program to display a table exhibiting this information along with the total monthly rent for each mall.

    Malls.txt contains the following three lines:

    "Green Mall", 6.50, 583
    "Red Mall", 7.25, 426
    "Blue Mall", 5.00, 823

38. Write a program to produce a sales receipt. Each time the user clicks on a command button, an item and its price should be read from a pair of text boxes and displayed in a picture box. Use a form-level variable to track the sum of the prices. When the user clicks on a second command button (after all the entries have been made), the program should display the sum of the prices, the sales tax (5 percent of total), and the total amount to be paid. Figure 2.33 shows a sample output of the program.

Light bulbs	2.65
Soda	3.45
Soap	1.15

Sum	7.25
Tax	0.36
Total	7.61

Figure 2.33 Sales receipt for Exercise 38.

In Exercises 39 through 42, construct user-defined functions to carry out the primary task(s) of the program.

39. In 1998, the federal government developed the body mass index (BMI) to determine ideal weights. Body mass index is calculated as 703 times the weight in pounds, divided by the square of the height in inches, and then rounded to the nearest whole number. Write a program that accepts a person's weight and height as input and gives the person's body mass index. (*Note:* A BMI of 19 to 25 corresponds to a healthy weight.)

40. In order for exercise to be beneficial to the cardiovascular system, the heart rate (number of heart beats per minute) must exceed a value called the training heart rate, THR. A person's THR can be calculated from his age and resting heart rate (pulse when first awakening) as follows:

(a) Calculate the maximum heart rate as 220 – age.
(b) Subtract the resting heart rate from the maximum heart rate.
(c) Multiply the result in step (b) by 60 percent and then add the resting heart rate.

Write a program to request a person's age and resting heart rate as input and display their THR. (Test the program with an age of 20 and a resting heart rate of 70, and then determine *your* training heart rate.)

41. Write a program to request the name of a United States senator as input and display the address and greeting for a letter to the senator. Assume the name has two parts and use a function to determine the senator's last name. A sample outcome when Robert Smith is typed into the text box holding the senator's name follows:

```
The Honorable Robert Smith
United States Senate
Washington, DC 20001

Dear Senator Smith,
```

42. Rewrite the population density program from Example 4 of Section 2.6 using a function to calculate the population density.

✔✔ Solutions to Practice Problems 2.6

1. The statement Private Sub AreaCode( ) must be replaced by Private Sub AreaCode(phone As String). Whenever a value is passed to a Sub procedure, the Sub statement must provide a parameter to receive the value.

2. You can make 27 gallons of cider. In this program, the function was used by a Sub procedure rather than by an event procedure.

CHAPTER 2   SUMMARY

1. The Visual Basic screen consists of a collection of objects for which various properties can be set. Some examples of *objects* are text boxes, labels, command buttons, picture boxes, and the form itself. Objects placed on the form are called *controls*. Some useful properties are Text (set the text displayed by a text box), Caption (set the title of a form, the contents of a label, or the words on a command button), Font.Size (set the size of the characters displayed), Alignment (set the placement of the contents of a label), MultiLine (text box to display text on several lines), Picture (display drawing in picture box), ForeColor (set foreground color), BackColor (set background color), Visible (show or hide object), BorderStyle (alter and possibly remove border), Font.Bold (display boldface text), and Font.Italic (display italic text).

2. An event procedure is called when a specific event occurs to a specified object. Some event procedures are *object*_Click (*object* is clicked), *object*_LostFocus (*object* loses the focus), and *object*_GotFocus (*object* receives the focus).

3. Visual Basic methods such as Print and Cls are applied to objects and are coded as *object*.Print and *object*.Cls.

4. Two types of *constants* that can be stored and processed by Visual Basic are *numbers* and *strings*.

5. The arithmetic *operations* are +, −, *, /, and ^. The only string operation is &, concatenation. An *expression* is a combination of constants, variables, functions, and operations that can be evaluated.

6. A *variable* is a name used to refer to data. Variable names can be up to 255 characters long, must begin with a letter, and may contain letters, digits, and underscores. Dim statements explicitly declare variables and specify the types of the variables. In this book, variables primarily have types Single, Integer, and String.

7. Values are assigned to variables by assignment and Input # statements. The values appearing in assignment statements can be constants, variables, or expressions. Input # statements look to data files for constants. String constants used in assignment statements must be surrounded by quotation marks, whereas quotation marks are optional for string constants input with Input #. InputBox can be used to request that the user type in data.

8. The Print method displays information in a picture box or on the printer. *Semicolons, commas,* and *Tab* control the placement of the items on a particular line. A temporary message can be displayed on the screen using the MsgBox statement.

9. You control the printer with the Printer object and write to it with statements of the form Printer.Print *expression*. You set properties with statements of the form Printer.*property* = *setting*. Printer.NewPage starts a new page and PrintForm does a screen dump. A series of commands to the Printer object must end with EndDoc, which actually produces the final printed page.

10. Comments (explanatory text beginning with an apostrophe) are used to explain formulas, state the purposes of variables, and articulate the purposes of various parts of a program.

11. The Format functions provides control of how numbers are displayed.

12. *Functions* can be thought of as accepting numbers or strings as input and returning numbers or strings as output.

Function	Input	Output
Asc	string	number
Chr	number	string
Format	number, string	string
InStr	string, string	number
Int	number	number
Left	string, number	string
Len	string	number
Mid	string, number, number	string
Right	string, number	string
Round	number, number	number
Sqr	number	number
Str	number	string
Trim	string	string
UCase	string	string
Val	string	number

13. A *general procedure* is a portion of a program that is accessed by event procedures or other general procedures. The two types of general procedures are *Sub procedures* and *Function procedures*.

14. Sub procedures are defined in blocks beginning with Private Sub statements and ending with End Sub statements. They are accessed by Call statements.

15. Function procedures are defined in blocks beginning with Private Function statements and ending with End Function statements. A function is activated by a reference in an expression and returns a value.

16. In any procedure, the arguments appearing in the calling statement must match the parameters of the Sub or Function statement in number, type, and order. They need not match in name.

CHAPTER 2   PROGRAMMING PROJECTS

1. Write a program that allows the user to specify two numbers and then adds, subtracts, or multiplies them when the user clicks on the appropriate command button. The output should give the type of arithmetic performed and the result.

2. Suppose automobile repair customers are billed at the rate of $35 per hour for labor. Also, costs for parts and supplies are subject to a 5% sales tax. Write a program to print out a simplified bill. The customer's name, the number of hours of labor, and the cost of parts and supplies should be entered into the program via text boxes. When a command button is clicked, the customer's name (indented) and the three costs should be displayed in a picture box, as shown in the sample run in Figure 2.34.

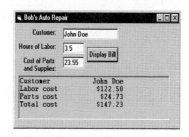

Figure 2.34 Sample run for Programming Project 2.

3. Write a program to generate the following personalized form letter. The person's name and address should be read from text boxes.

```
Mr. John Jones
123 Main Street
Juneau, Alaska  99803

Dear Mr. Jones,

    The Jones family has been selected as the
first family on Main Street to have the opportunity
to purchase an Apex solar-powered flashlight. Due to limited
supply, only 1000 of these amazing inventions will be available
in the entire state of Alaska. Don't delay. Order today.

                        Sincerely,
                        Cuthbert J. Twillie
```

4. At the end of each month, a credit card company constructs the table in Figure 2.35 to summarize the status of the accounts. Write a program to produce this table. The first four pieces of information for each account should be read from a data file. The program should compute the finance charges (1.5% of the unpaid past due amount) and the current amount due. Format the last column to be aligned right.

Account Number	Past Due Amount	Payments	Purchases	Finance Charges	Current Amt Due
123-AB	123.45	10.00	934.00	1.70	$1,049.15
456-CD	134.56	134.56	300.00	0.00	$300.00

Figure 2.35 Status of credit card accounts.

5. Table 2.12 gives the distribution of the U.S. population (in thousands) by age group and sex. Write a program to produce the table shown in Figure 2.36. For each age group, the column labeled %Males gives the percentage of the people in that age group that are male and similarly for the column labeled %Females. The last column gives the percentage of the total population in each age group. (**Note:** Store the information in Table 2.12 in a data file. For instance, the first line in the file should be "Under 20", 39168, 37202. Read and add up the data once to obtain the total population, and then read the data again to produce the table.)

Age Group	Males	Females
Under 20	39,168	37,202
20–64	76,761	78,291
Over 64	13,881	19,980

Table 2.12 U.S. resident population (1996) in thousands.

```
                   U.S. Population (in thousands)

Age group   Males   Females  %Males   %Females  %Total

Under 20   39,168   37,202   51.29%   48.71%    28.79%
20-64      76,761   78,291   49.51%   50.49%    58.45%
Over 64    13,881   19,980   40.99%   59.01%    12.76%
```

Figure 2.36 Output of Programming Project 5.

6. About seven million notebook computers were sold in 1997. Table 2.13 gives the market share for the four largest vendors. Write a program that displays the number of computers sold by each of the Big Four. The input and output should be handled by Sub procedures and the number of computers calculated by a Function procedure.

Company	Market Share
Toshiba	20%
IBM	11%
Compaq	9%
Dell	6%

Table 2.13 1997 Market Shares of the Top Notebook Vendors
Source: PC Magazine, January 20, 1998

7. Table 2.14 gives the advertising expenditures (in millions of dollars) for the four most advertised soft drink brands during the first nine months of 1995 and 1996. Write a program that displays the percentage change in advertising for each brand. Sub procedures should be used for input and output and the percentage change should be computed with a Function procedure. **Note:** The percentage change is 100*([1996 expenditure] – [1995 expenditure]) / [1995 expenditure].

Brand	1995 Expenditure	1996 Expenditure
Coca-Cola Classic	60.7	121.6
Pepsi-Cola	94.8	83.0
Diet Coke	43.7	70.0
Dr. Pepper	46.3	51.8

Table 2.14 Most Advertised Soft Drinks.
Source: Beverage World, March 1997.

3 Controlling Program Flow

3.1 DECISION STRUCTURES

An **If block** allows a program to decide on a course of action based on whether a certain condition is true or false. A block of the form

```
If condition Then
    action1
  Else
    action2
End If
```

causes the program to take *action1* if *condition* is true and *action2* if *condition* is false. Each action consists of one or more Visual Basic statements. After an action is taken, execution continues with the line after the If block. Figure 3.1 contains the pseudocode and flowchart for an If block.

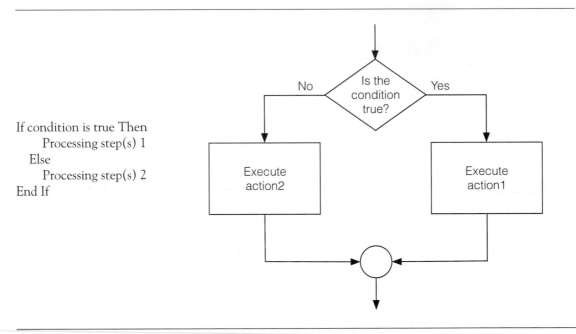

```
If condition is true Then
    Processing step(s) 1
Else
    Processing step(s) 2
End If
```

Figure 3.1 Pseudocode and flowchart for an If block.

EXAMPLE 1 Write a program to find the larger of two numbers input by the user.

SOLUTION In the following program, the condition is Val(txtFirstNum.Text) > Val(txt-SecondNum.Text), and each action consists of a single assignment statement. With the input 3 and 7, the condition is false, and so the second action is taken.

Object	Property	Setting
frmMaximum	Caption	Maximum
lblFirstNum	Caption	First Number
txtFirstNum	Text	(blank)
lblSecondNum	Caption	Second Number
txtSecondNum	Text	(blank)
cmdFindLarger	Caption	Find Larger Number
picResult		

```
Private Sub cmdFindLarger_Click()
  Dim largerNum As Single
  picResult.Cls
  If Val(txtFirstNum.Text) > Val(txtSecondNum.Text) Then
      largerNum = Val(txtFirstNum.Text)
    Else
      largerNum = Val(txtSecondNum.Text)
  End If
  picResult.Print "The larger number is"; largerNum
End Sub
```

[Run, type 3 and 7 into the text boxes, and press the command button.]

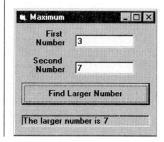

EXAMPLE 2 Write a program that requests the costs and revenue for a company and displays the message "Break even" if the costs and revenue are equal or otherwise displays the profit or loss.

SOLUTION In the following program, the action following Else is another If block. We say that the program uses **nested If blocks**.

Object	Property	Setting
frm3_1_2	Caption	Profit/Loss
lblCosts	Caption	Costs
txtCosts	Text	(blank)
lblRev	Caption	Revenue
txtRev	Text	(blank)
cmdShow	Caption	Show Financial Status
picResult		

```
Private Sub cmdShow_Click()
  Dim costs As Single, revenue As Single, profit As Single, loss As Single
  costs = Val(txtCosts.Text)
  revenue = Val(txtRev.Text)
  picResult.Cls
  If costs = revenue Then
      picResult.Print "Break even"
    Else
      If costs < revenue Then
          profit = revenue - costs
          picResult.Print "Profit is "; FormatCurrency(profit)
        Else
          loss = costs - revenue
          picResult.Print "Loss is "; FormatCurrency(loss)
      End If
  End If
End Sub
```

[Run, type 9500 and 8000 into the text boxes, and press the command button.]

The Else part of an If block can be omitted. This important type of If block appears in the next example.

EXAMPLE 3 The following program offers assistance to the user before presenting a quotation.

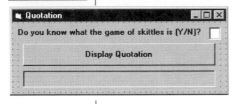

Object	Property	Setting
frm3_1_3	Caption	Quotation
lblQuestion	Caption	Do you know what the game of skittles is (Y/N)?
txtAnswer	Text	(blank)
cmdDisplay	Caption	Display Quotation
picQuotation		

```
Private Sub cmdDisplay_Click()
  Dim message As String
  message = "Skittles is an old form of bowling in which a wooden" & _
            " disk is used to knock down nine pins arranged in a square."
  If UCase(txtAnswer.Text) = "N" Then
      MsgBox message, , ""
  End If
  picQuote.Cls
  picQuote.Print "Life ain't all beer and skittles. - Du Maurier (1894)"
End Sub
```

[Run, type N into the text box, and press the command button.]

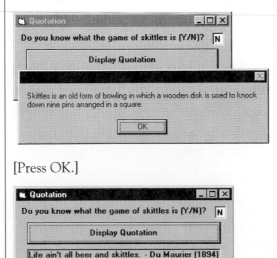

[Press OK.]

Note: Rerun the program, type Y into the text box, press the command button, and observe that the description of the game is bypassed

Select Case Blocks

A Select Case block is an efficient decision-making structure that simplifies choosing among several actions. It avoids complex nested If constructs. If blocks make decisions based on the truth value of a condition; Select Case choices are determined by the value of an expression called a **selector**. Each of the possible actions is preceded by a clause of the form

```
Case valueList
```

where *valueList* itemizes the values of the selector for which the action should be taken.

EXAMPLE 4 The following program converts the finishing position in a horse race into a descriptive phrase. After the variable *position* is assigned a value from txtPosition, the computer searches for the first Case clause whose value list contains that value and executes the succeeding statement. If the value of *position* is greater than 5, then the statement following Case Else is executed.

Object	Property	Setting
frmRace	Caption	Horse Race
lblPosition	Caption	Finishing position (1, 2, 3, . . .)
txtPosition	Text	(blank)
cmdDescribe	Caption	Describe Position
picOutcome		

```
Private Sub cmdDescribe_Click()
  Dim position As Integer     'Selector
  position = Val(txtPosition.Text)
  picOutcome.Cls
  Select Case position
    Case 1
      picOutcome.Print "Win"
    Case 2
      picOutcome.Print "Place"
    Case 3
      picOutcome.Print "Show"
    Case 4, 5
      picOutcome.Print "You almost placed"
      picOutcome.Print "in the money."
    Case Else
      picOutcome.Print "Out of the money."
  End Select
End Sub
```

[Run, type 2 into the text box, and press the command button.]

EXAMPLE 5

In the following variation of Example 4, the value lists specify ranges of values. The first value list provides another way to specify the numbers 1 to 3. The second value list covers all numbers from 4 on.

```
Private Sub cmdDescribe_Click()
  Dim position As Integer
  'Describe finishing positions in a horse race
  picOutcome.Cls
  position = Val(txtPosition.Text)
  Select Case position
    Case 1 To 3
      picOutcome.Print "In the money."
      picOutcome.Print "Congratulations"
    Case Is > 3
      picOutcome.Print "Not in the money."
  End Select
End Sub
```

[Run, type 2 into the text box, and press the command button.]

The general form of the Select Case block is

```
Select Case selector
  Case valueList1
    action1
  Case valueList2
    action2
      .
      .
  Case Else
    action of last resort
End Select
```

where Case Else (and its action) is optional, and each value list contains one or more of the following types of items separated by commas:

1. A constant

2. A variable

3. An expression

4. An inequality sign preceded by Is and followed by a constant, variable, or expression

5. A range expressed in the form *a* To *b*, where *a* and *b* are constants, variables, or expressions

Different items appearing in the same list must be separated by commas. Each action consists of one or more statements. After the selector is evaluated, the computer looks for the first value-list item containing the value of the selector and carries out its associated action.

EXAMPLE 6 | The following program uses several different types of value lists. With the response shown, the first action was selected because the value of y − x is 1.

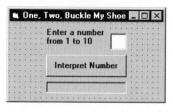

Object	Property	Setting
frm3_1_6	Caption	One, Two, Buckle My Shoe
lblEnterNum	Caption	Enter a number from 1 to 10
txtNumber	Text	(blank)
cmdInterpret	Caption	Interpret Number
picPhrase		

```
Private Sub cmdInterpret_Click()
  Dim x As Integer, y As Integer, num As Integer
  'One, Two, Buckle My Shoe
  picPhrase.Cls
  x = 2
  y = 3
  num = Val(txtNumber.Text)
  Select Case num
    Case y - x, x
      picPhrase.Print "Buckle my shoe."
    Case Is <= 4
      picPhrase.Print "Shut the door."
    Case x + y To x * y
      picPhrase.Print "Pick up sticks."
    Case 7, 8
      picPhrase.Print "Lay them straight."
    Case Else
      picPhrase.Print "Start all over again."
  End Select
End Sub
```

[Run, type 4 into the text box, and press the command button.]

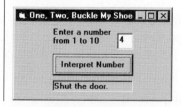

In each of the three preceding examples the selector was a numeric variable; however, the selector also can be a string variable or an expression.

EXAMPLE 7   The following program has the string variable *firstName* as a selector.

Object	Property	Setting
frmQuiz	Caption	Quiz
lblQuestion	Caption	"What was President Wilson's first name ?"
txtName	Text	(blank)
cmdInterpret	Caption	Interpret Answer
picAnswer		

```
Private Sub cmdInterpret_Click()
  Dim firstName As String
  'Quiz
  picAnswer.Cls
  firstName = txtName.Text
  Select Case firstName
    Case "Thomas"
      picAnswer.Print "Correct."
    Case "Woodrow"
      picAnswer.Print "Sorry, his full name was"
      picAnswer.Print "Thomas Woodrow Wilson."
    Case "President"
      picAnswer.Print "Are you for real?"
    Case Else
      picAnswer.Print "Nice try, but no cigar."
  End Select
End Sub
```

[Run, type Woodrow into the text box, and press the command button.]

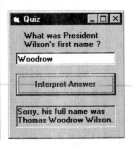

Logical Operators

Programming situations often require more complex conditions than those considered so far. For instance, suppose we would like to state that the value of a numeric variable, *n*, is strictly between 2 and 5. The proper Visual Basic condition is

$$(2 < n) \text{ And } (n < 5)$$

The condition $(2 < n)$ And $(n < 5)$ is a combination of the two conditions $2 < n$ and $n < 5$ with the logical operator And.

The three main logical operators are And, Or, and Not. If *cond1* and *cond2* are conditions, then the condition

    cond1 And *cond2*

is true if both *cond1* and *cond2* are true. Otherwise, it is false. The condition

    cond1 Or *cond2*

is true if either *cond1* or *cond2* (or both) is true. Otherwise, it is false. The condition

    Not *cond1*

is true if *cond1* is false, and is false if *cond1* is true.

EXAMPLE 8   The If block in the following program has a logical operator in its condition.

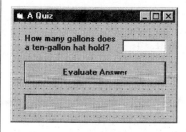

Object	Property	Setting
frmQuiz	Caption	A Quiz
lblQuestion	Caption	How many gallons does a ten-gallon hat hold?
txtAnswer	Text	(blank)
cmdEvaluate	Caption	Evaluate Answer
picSolution		

```
Private Sub cmdEvaluate_Click()
  Dim answer As Single
  'Evaluate answer
  picSolution.Cls
  answer = Val(txtAnswer.Text)
  If (answer >= .5) And (answer <= 1) Then
      picSolution.Print "Good, ";
    Else
      picSolution.Print "No, ";
  End If
  picSolution.Print "it holds about 3/4 of a gallon."
End Sub
```

[Run, type 10 into the text box, and press the command button.]

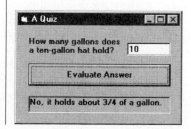

Comments

1. Conditions evalutate to either True or False. These two values are called the **truth values** of the condition.

2. The actions of an If block and the word Else do not have to be indented. For instance, the If block of Example 1 can be written

```
If Val(txtFirstNum.Text) > Val(txtSecondNum.Text) Then
largerNum = Val(txtFirstNum.Text)
Else
largerNum = Val(txtSecondNum.Text)
End If
```

However, because indenting improves the readability of the block, it is regarded as good programming style. As soon as you see the word If, your eyes can easily scan down the program to find the matching End If and the enclosed Else clause. You then immediately have a good idea of the size and complexity of the block.

3. Care should be taken to make If blocks easy to understand. For instance, in Figure 3.2, the block on the left is difficult to follow and should be replaced by the clearer block on the right.

```
If cond1 Then                     If cond1 And cond2 Then
    If cond2 Then                     action
        action                    End If
    End If
End If
```

Figure 3.2 A confusing If block and an improvement.

4. In Appendix C, the section "Stepping Through Programs Containing Decision Structures: Chapter 3" uses the Visual Basic debugging tools to trace the flow through an If block and a Select Case block.

5. Visual Basic also has a single-line If statement of the form

```
If condition Then action1 Else action2
```

which is a holdover from earlier, unstructured versions of BASIC; it is seldom used in this text.

6. Some programming languages do not allow a value to appear in two different value lists; Visual Basic does. If a value appears in two different value lists, the action associated with the first value list will be carried out.

7. In Visual Basic, if the value of the selector does not appear in any of the value lists and there is no Case Else clause, execution of the program will continue with the statement following the Select Case block.

8. If the word Is, which should precede an inequality sign in a value list, is accidentally omitted, the smart editor will automatically insert it when checking the line.

9. A Case clause of the form Case b To c selects values from b to c inclusive. However, the extreme values can be excluded by placing the action inside an If block beginning with If (*selector* <> b) And (*selector* <> c) Then.

10. The value of b must be less than or equal to the value of c in a Case clause of the form Case b To c.

11. A condition such as $2 < n < 5$ should never be used, because Visual Basic will not evaluate it as intended. The correct condition is $(2 < n)$ And $(n < 5)$.

12. A common error is to replace the condition Not $(n < 3)$ by condition $(3 > n)$. The correct replacement is $(3 >= n)$.

✔ **PRACTICE PROBLEMS 3.1**

1. Suppose the user is asked to input a number into txtNumber for which the square root is to be taken. Fill in the If block so that the lines of code below either will display the message "Number can't be negative" or will display the square root of the number.

```
Private Sub cmdTakeSquareRoot_Click()
  Dim num As Single
  'Check reasonableness of data
  num = Val(txtNumber.Text)
  If

  End If
End Sub
```

2. Suppose the selector of a Select Case block is the numeric variable *num*. Determine whether each of the following Case clauses is valid

(a) `Case 1, 4, Is < 10`

(b) `Case Is < 5, Is >= 5`

(c) `Case num = 2`

3. Complete Table 3.1.

cond1	cond2	cond1 And cond2	cond1 Or cond2	Not cond2
True	True	True		
True	False		True	
False	True			False
False	False			

Table 3.1 Truth values of logical operators.

➤ **EXERCISES 3.1**

In Exercises 1 to 10, determine the output displayed in the picture box when the command button is clicked.

1.
```
Private Sub cmdDisplay_Click()
    Dim num As Single
    num = 4
    If num <= 9 Then
        picOutput.Print "Less than ten"
      Else
        If num = 4 Then
            picOutput.Print "Equal to four"
        End If
    End If
End Sub
```

2.
```
Private Sub cmdDisplay_Click()
    Dim change As Single
    change = 356            'Amount of change in cents
    If change >= 100 Then
        picOutput.Print "Your change contains";
        picOutput.Print Int(change / 100); "dollars."
      Else
        picOutput.Print "Your change contains no dollars."
    End If
End Sub
```

3.
```
Private Sub cmdDisplay_Click()
    Dim a As Single, b As Single, c As Single
    a = 2
    b = 3
    c = 5
    If a * b < c Then
        b = 7
      Else
        b = c * a
    End If
    picOutput.Print b
End Sub
```

4.
```
Private Sub cmdDisplay_Click()
    Dim num As Single
    num = 5
    If num < 0 Then
        picOutput.Print "neg"
      Else
        If num = 0 Then
            picOutput.Print "zero"
          Else
            picOutput.Print "positive"
        End If
    End If
End Sub
```

5.
```
Private Sub cmdDisplay_Click()
   Dim length As Single
    'Cost of phone call from NY to LA
   Call InputLength(length)
   Call DisplayCost(length)
End Sub

Private Function Cost(length As Single) As Single
  If length < 1 Then
      Cost = .46
    Else
      Cost = .46 + (length - 1) * .36
  End If
End Function

Private Sub DisplayCost(length As Single)
   'Display the cost of a call
   picOutput.Print "Cost of call: "; FormatCurrency(Cost(length))
End Sub

Private Sub InputLength(length As Single)
   'Request the length of a phone call
   length = Val(InputBox("Duration of the call in minutes?"))
End Sub
```
(Assume that the response is *31*.)

6.
```
Private Sub cmdDisplay_Click()
   Dim age As Single, price As Single
   age = Val(InputBox("What is your age?"))
   Select Case age
     Case Is < 6
       price = 0
     Case 6 To 17
       price = 3.75
     Case Is >= 17
       price = 5
   End Select
   picOutput.Print "The price is "; FormatCurrency(price)
End Sub
```
(Determine the output for each of the following responses: 8, 5, 17)

7.
```
Private Sub cmdDisplay_Click()
   Dim nom As String
   nom = InputBox("Who developed the stored program concept?")
   Select Case UCase(nom)
     Case "JOHN VON NEUMANN", "VON NEUMANN"
       picOutput.Print "Correct"
     Case "JOHN MAUCHLY", "MAUCHLY", "J. PRESPER ECKERT", "ECKERT"
       picOutput.Print "He worked with the developer, von Neumann, on the ENIAC."
     Case Else
       picOutput.Print "Nope"
   End Select
End Sub
```
(Determine the output for each of the following responses: Grace Hopper, Eckert, John von Neumann)

8.
```
Private Sub cmdDisplay_Click()
    Dim n As Single
    n = Val(InputBox("Enter a number from 5 to 12"))
    Select Case n
      Case 5
        picOutput.Print "case 1"
      Case 5 To 7
        picOutput.Print "case 2"
      Case 7 To 12
        picOutput.Print "case 3"
    End Select
End Sub
```
(Determine the output for each of the following responses: 7, 5, 11.2)

9.
```
Private Sub cmdDisplay_Click()
    Dim num1 As Single, word As String, num2 As Single
    'State a quotation
    num1 = 3
    word = "hello"
    num2 = Val(InputBox("Enter a number"))
    Select Case 2 * num2 - 1
      Case num1 * num1
        picOutput.Print "Less is more."
      Case Is > Len(word)
        picOutput.Print "Time keeps everything from happening at once."
      Case Else
        picOutput.Print "The less things change, the more they remain the same."
    End Select
End Sub
```
(Determine the output for each of the following responses: 2, 5, 6)

10.
```
Private Sub cmdDisplay_Click()
    Dim whatever As Single
    whatever = Val(InputBox("Enter a number"))
    Select Case whatever
      Case Else
        picOutput.Print "Hi"
    End Select
End Sub
```
(Determine the output for each of the following responses: 7, –1)

In Exercises 11 to 20, identify the errors.

11.
```
Private Sub cmdDisplay_Click()
    Dim num As Single
    num = .5
    If 1 < num < 3 Then
        picOutput.Print "Number is between 1 and 3."
    End If
End Sub
```

```
12. Private Sub cmdDisplay_Click()
        Dim major As String
        If major = "Business" Or "Computer Science" Then
            picOutput.Print "Yes"
        End If
    End Sub

13. Private Sub cmdDisplay_Click()
        If 2 <> 3
            picOutput.Print "Numbers are not equal"
        End If
    End Sub

14. Private Sub cmdDisplay_Click()
        Dim switch As String
        'Change switch from "on" to "off", or from "off" to "on"
        switch = InputBox("Enter on or off.")
        If switch = "off" Then
            switch = "on"
        End If
        If switch = "on" Then
            switch = "off"
        End If
    End Sub

15. Private Sub cmdDisplay_Click()
        Dim j As Single, k As Single
        'Display "OK" if either j or k equals 4
        j = 2
        k = 3
        If j Or k = 4 Then
            picOutput.Print "OK"
        End If
    End Sub

16. Private Sub cmdDisplay_Click()
        Dim query As String, answer1 As String, answer2 As String
        'Is your program correct?
        query = "Are you certain everything in your program is correct?"
        answer1 = InputBox(query)
        answer1 = UCase(Left(answer1, 1))
        If answer1 = "N" Then
            picOutput.Print "Don't patch bad code, rewrite it."
          Else
            query = "Does your program run correctly"
            answer2 = InputBox(query)
            answer2 = UCase(Left(answer2, 1))
            If answer2 = "Y" Then
                picOutput.Print "Congratulations"
              Else
                picOutput.Print "One of the things you are certain"
                picOutput.Print "about is wrong."
            End If
    End Sub
```

```
17. Private Sub cmdDisplay_Click()          18. Private Sub cmdDisplay_Click()
        Dim num As Single                           Dim num1 As Single, num2 As Single
        num = 2                                     num1 = 5
        Select Case num                             num2 = 7
          picOutput.Print "Two"                     Select Case num1
        End Select                                    Case 3 <= num1 <= 10
    End Sub                                              picOutput.Print "Between 3 and 10"
                                                        Case num2 To 5; 4
                                                          picOutput.Print "Near 5"
                                                    End Select
                                                End Sub
```

```
19. Private Sub cmdDisplay_Click()
        Dim word As String
        word = InputBox("Enter a word from the United States motto")
        Select Case UCase(word)
          Case "E"
            picOutput.Print "This is the first word of the motto."
          Case Left(word, 1) = "P"
            picOutput.Print "The second word is PLURIBUS."
          Case Else
            picOutput.Print "The third word is UNUM."
        End Select
    End Sub
```

```
20. Private Sub cmdDisplay_Click()
        Dim num As Single
        num = 5
        Select Case num
          Case 5, Is <> 5
            picOutput.Print "Five"
          Case Is > 5
            picOutput.Print "Greater than 5"
    End Sub
```

In Exercises 21 to 24, simplify the code.

```
21. If a = 2 Then
        a = 3 + a
    Else
        a = 5
    End If
```

```
22. If Not (answer <> "y") Then
        picOutput.Print "YES"
    Else
        If (answer = "y") Or (answer = "Y") Then
            picOutput.Print "YES"
        End If
    End If
```

```
23. If j = 7 Then
        b = 1
      Else
        If j <> 7 Then
            b = 2
        End If
    End If

24. If a < b Then
        If b < c Then
            picOutput.Print b; "is between"; a; "and"; c
        End If
    End If
```

In Exercises 25 to 28, rewrite the code using a Select Case block.

```
25. If a = 1 Then          26. If a = 1 Then
        picOutput.Print "one"        picOutput.Print "lambs"
      Else                        End If
        If a > 5 Then             If a <= 3 And a < 4 Then
            picOutput.Print "two"     picOutput.Print "eat"
        End If                    End If
    End If                        If a = 5 Or a > 7 Then
                                      picOutput.Print "ivy"
                                  End If
```

```
27. If a < 5 Then          28. If a = 3 Then
        If a = 2 Then                 a = 1
            picOutput.Print "yes"  End If
          Else                     If a = 2 Then
            picOutput.Print "no"       a = 3
        End If                     End If
      Else                         If a = 1 Then
        If a = 2 Then                  a = 2
            picOutput.Print "maybe"  End If
        End If
    End If
```

29. Write a program to determine how much to tip the waiter in a fine restaurant. The tip should be 15 percent of the check, with a minimum of $1.

30. A computer store sells diskettes at 50 cents each for small orders or at 30 cents each for orders of 25 diskettes or more. Write a program that requests the number of diskettes ordered and displays the total cost. (Test the program for purchases of 5, 25, and 35 diskettes.)

31. Write a program to handle a savings account withdrawal. The program should request the current balance and the amount of the withdrawal as input and then display the new balance. If the withdrawal is greater than the original balance, the program should display: "Withdrawal denied." If the new balance is less than $150, the message: "Balance below $150" should be displayed.

32. Write a program that requests three scores as input and displays the average of the two highest scores. The input and output should be handled by Sub procedures and the average should be determined by a user-defined function.

33. Write a program that requests a word (with lowercase letters) as input and translates the word into pig latin. The rules for translating a word into pig latin are as follows:

(a) If the word begins with a consonant, move the first letter to the end of the word and add *ay*. For instance, *chip* becomes *hipcay*.

(b) If the word begins with a vowel, add *way* to the end of the word. For instance, *else* becomes *elseway*.

34. Federal law requires hourly employees be paid "time-and-a-half" for work in excess of 40 hours in a week. For example, if a person's hourly wage is $8 and he works 60 hours in a week, his gross pay should be

$$(40 \times 8) + (1.5 \times 8 \times (60 - 40)) = \$560.$$

Write a program that requests as input the number of hours a person works in a given week and his hourly wage, and then displays his gross pay.

35. Table 3.2 gives the terms used by the National Weather Service to describe the degree of cloudiness. Write a program that requests the percentage of cloud cover as input and then displays the appropriate descriptor.

Percentage of Cloud Cover	Descriptor
0–30	clear
31–70	partly cloudy
71–99	cloudy
100	overcast

Table 3.2 Cloudiness descriptors.

36. Table 3.3 shows the location of books in the library stacks according to their call numbers. Write a program that requests the call number of a book as input and displays the location of the book.

Call Numbers	Location
100 to 199	basement
200 to 500 and over 900	main floor
501 to 900 except 700 to 750	upper floor
700 to 750	archives

Table 3.3 Location of library books.

37. Write a program that requests a month of the year and then gives the number of days in the month. If the month is February, the user should be asked whether or not the current year is a leap year.

38. IRS informants are paid cash awards based on the value of the money recovered. If the information was specific enough to lead to a recovery, the informant receives 10 percent of the first $75,000, 5 percent of the next $25,000, and 1 percent of the remainder, up to a maximum award of $50,000. Write a program that requests the amount of the recovery as input and displays the award. (Test the program on the amounts $10,000, $125,000, and $10,000,000.) (**Note:** The source of this formula is *The Book of Inside Information*, Boardroom Books, 1993.)

39. Write a program that, given the last name of one of the four most recent presidents, displays his state and a colorful fact about him.

Note: Carter: Georgia; The only soft drink served in the Carter White House was Coca-Cola. Reagan: California; His secret service code name was Rawhide. Bush: Texas; He was the third left-handed president. Clinton: Arkansas; In college he did a good imitation of Elvis Presley.

40. Table 3.4 contains information on several states. Write a program that requests a state and category (flower, motto, and nickname) as input and displays the requested information. If the state or category requested is not in the table, the program should so inform the user.

State	Flower	Nickname	Motto
California	Golden poppy	Golden State	Eureka
Indiana	Peony	Hoosier State	Crossroads of America
Mississippi	Magnolia	Magnolia State	By valor and arms
New York	Rose	Empire State	Ever upward

Table 3.4 State flowers, nicknames, and mottos.

41. The current calendar, called the Gregorian calendar, was introduced in 1582. Every year divisible by 4 was declared to be a leap year with the exception of the years ending in 00 (that is, those divisible by 100) and not divisible by 400. For instance, the years 1600 and 2000 are leap years, but 1700, 1800, and 1900 are not. Write a program that requests a year as input and states whether or not it is a leap year. (Test the program on the years 1994, 1995, 1900, and 2000.)

✔✔ **Solutions to Practice Problems 3.1**

```
1. If num < 0 Then
      MsgBox "Number can't be negative.", , "Input Error"
      txtNumber.Text = ""
      txtNumber.SetFocus
   Else
      picSquareRoot.Print Sqr(num)
   End If
```

2. (a) Valid. These items are redundant because 1 and 4 are just special cases of Is < 10. However, this makes no difference in Visual Basic.

(b) Valid. These items are contradictory. However, Visual Basic looks at them one at a time until it finds an item containing the value of the selector. The action following this Case clause will always be carried out.

(c) Not valid. It should be Case 2.

3. cond1	cond2	cond1 And cond2	cond1 Or cond2	Not cond2
True	True	True	True	False
True	False	False	True	True
False	True	False	True	False
False	False	False	False	True

3.2 DO LOOPS

A **loop**, one of the most important structures in Visual Basic, is used to repeat a sequence of statements a number of times. At each repetition, or **pass**, the statements act upon variables whose values are changing.

The **Do loop** repeats a sequence of statements either as long as or until a certain condition is true. A Do statement precedes the sequence of statements, and a Loop statement follows the sequence of statements. The condition, along with either the word While or Until, follows the word Do or the word Loop. When Visual Basic executes a Do loop of the form

```
Do While condition
   statement(s)
Loop
```

it first checks the truth value of *condition*. If *condition* is false, then the statements inside the loop are not executed, and the program continues with the line after the Loop statement. If *condition* is true, then the statements inside the loop are executed. When the statement Loop is encountered, the entire process is repeated, beginning with the testing of *condition* in the Do While statement. In other words, the statements inside the loop are repeatedly executed only as long as (that is, while) the condition is true. Figure 3.3 contains the pseudocode and flowchart for this loop.

Do While condition is true
   Processing step(s)
Loop

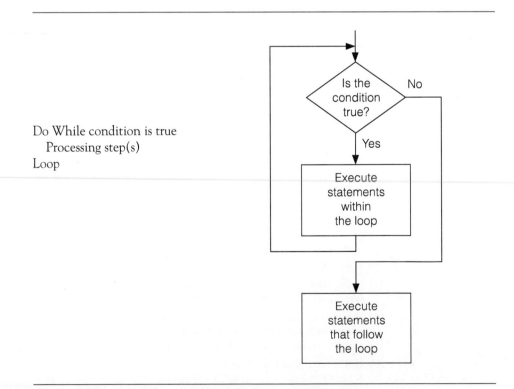

Figure 3.3 Pseudocode and flowchart for a Do While loop.

EXAMPLE I   Write a program that displays the numbers from 1 to 10.

SOLUTION   The condition in the Do loop is "num <= 10".

```
Private Sub cmdDisplay_Click()
  Dim num As Integer
  'Display the numbers from 1 to 10
  num = 1
  Do While num <= 10
    picNumbers.Print num;
    num = num + 1
  Loop
End Sub
```

[Run, and click the command button. The following is displayed in the picture box.]

1 2 3 4 5 6 7 8 9 10

Do loops are commonly used to ensure that a proper response is received from the InputBox function.

EXAMPLE 2   The following program requires the user to give a password before a secret file can be accessed.

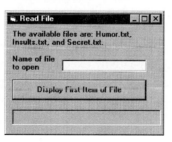

Object	Property	Setting
frm3_2_2	Caption	Read File
lblFiles	Caption	The available files are: Humor.txt, Insults.txt, and Secret.txt.
lblName	Caption	Name of file to open
txtName	Text	(blank)
cmdDisplay	Caption	Display First Item of File
picItem		

```
Private Sub cmdDisplay_Click()
  Dim passWord As String, info As String
  If UCase(txtName.Text) = "SECRET.TXT" Then
      passWord = ""
      Do While passWord <> "SHAZAM"
        passWord = InputBox("What is the password?")
        passWord = UCase(passWord)
      Loop
  End If
  Open txtName.Text For Input As #1
  Input #1, info
  picItem.Cls
  picItem.Print info
  Close #1
End Sub
```

[Run, type Secret.txt into the text box, and click the command button.]

Note: If a file other than Secret.txt is requested, the statements inside the loop are not executed.

In Examples 1 and 2 the condition was checked at the top of the loop, that is, before the statements were executed. Alternatively, the condition can be checked at the bottom of the loop when the statement Loop is reached. When Visual Basic encounters a Do loop of the form

```
Do
    statement(s)
Loop Until condition
```

it executes the statements inside the loop and then checks the truth value of *condition*. If *condition* is true, then the program continues with the line after the Loop statement. If *condition* is false, then the entire process is repeated beginning with the Do statement. In other words, the statements inside the loop are executed at least once and then are repeatedly executed *until* the condition is true. Figure 3.4 shows the pseudocode and flowchart for this type of Do loop.

Do
    statement(s)
Loop Until condition is true

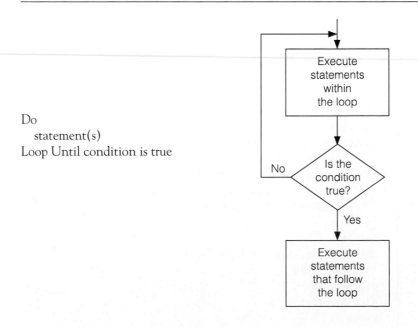

Figure 3.4 Pseudocode and flowchart for a Do loop with condition tested at the bottom.

EXAMPLE 3   The following program is equivalent to Example 2, except that the condition is tested at the bottom of the loop.

```
Private Sub cmdDisplay_Click()
  Dim passWord As String, info As String
  If UCase(txtName.Text) = "SECRET.TXT" Then
      Do
        passWord = InputBox("What is the password?")
        passWord = UCase(passWord)
      Loop Until passWord = "SHAZAM"
  End If
  Open txtName.Text For Input As #1
  Input #1, info
  picItem.Cls
  picItem.Print info
  Close #1
End Sub
```

Do loops allow us to calculate useful quantities for which we might not know a simple formula.

EXAMPLE 4   Suppose you deposit $100 into a savings account and let it accumulate at 7 percent interest compounded annually. The following program determines when you will be a millionaire.

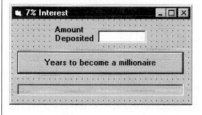

Object	Property	Setting
frmInterest	Caption	7% Interest
lblAmount	Caption	Amount Deposited
txtAmount	Text	(blank)
cmdYears	Caption	Years to become a millionaire
picWhen		

```
Private Sub cmdYears_Click()
  Dim balance As Single, numYears As Integer
  'Compute years required to become a millionaire
  picWhen.Cls
  balance = Val(txtAmount.Text)
  numYears = 0
  Do While balance < 1000000
    balance = balance + .07 * balance
    numYears = numYears + 1
  Loop
  picWhen.Print "In"; numYears; "years you will have a million dollars."
End Sub
```

[Run, type 100 into the text box, and press the command button.]

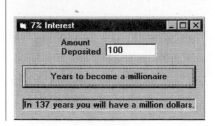

One of the main applications of programming is the processing of lists of data stored in files. Do loops are used to display selected items from the file, search the file for specific items, and perform calculations on the numerical entries of the file. Several devices facilitate working with files. A **counter** is a variable that calculates the number of elements in a file, an **accumulator** is a variable that sums numerical values from a file, a **flag** is a variable that keeps track of whether a certain type of item appears in a file, and the **EOF function** tells us when the end of a file has been reached. The counter and accumulator are initialized with the value 0. Each time a group of data is read from the file, the counter is increased by 1, and the accumulator is increased by the value of one of the numbers in the group. The data type most suited to flags is the **Boolean data type**. Variables of type Boolean can assume just two values—True and False. Suppose a file has been opened with reference number n. At any time, the condition

    EOF(n)

will be true if the end of the file has been reached, and false otherwise.

EXAMPLE 5 The following program uses the counter *numPeople*, the accumulator *total*, and the flag *perfectFlag*. The first Do loop reads the entire contents of the file. The second Do loop stops reading the file when the person whose name is specified in the text box is located. The first three lines of the file Grades.txt are

"Michael", 85
"Brittany", 82
"Christopher", 100

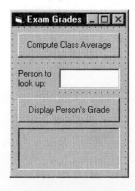

Object	Property	Setting
frm3_2_5	Caption	Exam Grades
cmdAverage	Caption	Compute Class Average
lblPerson	Caption	Person to look up:
txtPerson	Text	(blank)
cmdGrade	Caption	Display Person's Grade
picOutput		

```
Private Sub cmdAverage_Click()
  Dim numPeople As Integer, total As Integer, perfectFlag As Boolean
  Dim nom As String, grade As Integer
  Open "Grades.txt" For Input As #1
```

```
    numPeople = 0
    total = 0
    perfectFlag = False
    Do While Not EOF(1)
      Input #1, nom, grade
      numPeople = numPeople + 1
      total = total + grade
      If grade = 100 Then
          perfectFlag = True
      End If
    Loop
    Close #1
    picOutput.Cls
    picOutput.Print "Class average is"; total / numPeople
    If perfectFlag = True Then
        picOutput.Print "Someone had 100."
    End If
End Sub

Private Sub cmdGrade_Click()
  Dim nom As String, grade As Integer
  Open "Grades.txt" For Input As #1
  Do While (nom <> txtPerson.Text) And (Not EOF(1))
    Input #1, nom, grade
  Loop
  Close #1
  If nom = txtPerson.Text Then
      picOutput.Print nom; grade
    Else
      picOutput.Print "Person not found."
  End If
End Sub
```

[Run, press the first command button, type Brittany into the text box, and press the second command button.]

The first Do loop in Example 5 illustrates the proper way to process a list of data contained in a file. The Do loop should be tested at the top with an end-of-file condition. (If the file is empty, no attempt is made to input data from the file.) The first set of data should be input *after* the Do statement, and then the data should be processed. Figure 3.5 contains the pseudocode and flowchart for this technique.

Do While there are still data in the file
  Get an item of data
  Process the item
Loop

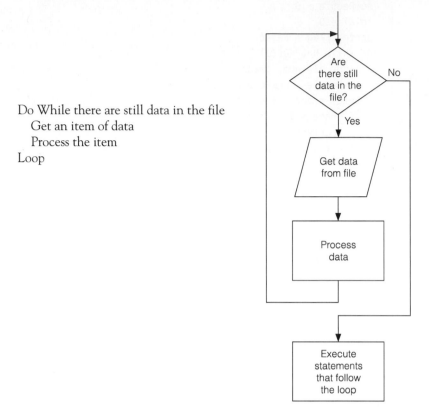

Figure 3.5 Pseudocode and flowchart for processing data from a file.

Comments

1. Be careful to avoid infinite loops—that is, loops that are never exited. The following loop is infinite because the condition "num < > 0" will always be true. **Note:** The loop can be terminated by pressing Ctrl+Break.

```
Private Sub cmdButton_Click()
  Dim num As Single
  'An infinite loop
  num = 7
  Do While num <> 0
    num = num - 2
  Loop
End Sub
```

Notice that this slip-up can be avoided by changing the condition to "num >= 0".

2. Visual Basic allows the use of the words While and Until either at the top or bottom of a Do loop. In this text, the usage of these words is restricted for the following reasons.

(a) Restricting the use simplifies reading the program. The word While proclaims testing at the top, and the word Until proclaims testing at the bottom.

(b) Standard pseudocode uses the word While to denote testing a loop at the top and the word Until to denote testing at the bottom.

3. Good programming practice requires that all variables appearing in a Do loop be assigned values before the loop is entered rather than relying on default values. For instance, the code at the left in what follows should be replaced with the code at the right.

```
'Add 1 through 10          'Add 1 through 10
Do While num < 10            num = 0
  num = num + 1              sum = 0
  sum = sum + num            Do While num < 10
Loop                           num = num + 1
                               sum = sum + num
                             Loop
```

4. When flagVar is a variable of Boolean type, the statements

```
If flagVar = True Then  and  If flagVar = False Then
```

can be replaced by

```
If flagVar Then  and  If Not flagVar Then
```

Similarly, the statements

```
Do While flagVar = True  and  Do While flagVar = False
```

can be replaced by

```
Do While flagVar  and  Do While Not flagVar
```

✔ PRACTICE PROBLEMS 3.2

1. How do you decide whether a condition should be checked at the top of a loop or at the bottom?

2. Change the following loop so it will be executed at least once.

```
Do While continue = "Yes"
  answer = InputBox("Do you want to continue? (Y or N)")
  If UCase(answer) = "Y" Then
      continue = "Yes"
    Else
      continue = "No"
  End If
Loop
```

➤ EXERCISES 3.2

In Exercises 1 to 6, determine the output displayed in the picture box when the command button is clicked.

```
1. Private Sub cmdDisplay_Click()
    Dim q As Single
    q = 3
    Do While q < 15
      q = 2 * q - 1
    Loop
    picOutput.Print q
  End Sub
```

2.
```
Private Sub cmdDisplay_Click()
    Dim info As String, counter As Integer, letter As String
    'Simulate InStr; search for the letter t
    info = "Potato"
    counter = 0
    letter = ""
    Do While (letter <> "t") And (counter < Len(info))
      counter = counter + 1
      letter = Mid(info, counter, 1)
      If letter = "t" Then
          picOutput.Print counter
      End If
    Loop
    If letter <> "t" Then
        picOutput.Print 0
    End If
End Sub
```

3.
```
Private Sub cmdDisplay_Click()
    Dim total As Single, num As Single
    total = 0
    Open "Data.txt" For Input As #1
    Do While Not EOF(1)
      Input #1, num
      total = total + num
    Loop
    Close #1
    picOutput.Print total
End Sub
```

(Assume that the file Data.txt contains the following entries.)

5, 2, 6

4.
```
Private Sub cmdDisplay_Click()
    Dim firstLetter As String, fruit As String
    firstLetter = ""
    Open "Fruits.txt" For Input As #1
    Do While Not EOF(1)
      Input #1, fruit
      If Left(fruit, 1) <> firstLetter Then
          If firstLetter <> "" Then
              picOutput.Print
          End If
          firstLetter = Left(fruit, 1)
          picOutput.Print Tab(3); firstLetter
      End If
      picOutput.Print fruit
    Loop
    Close #1
End Sub
```

(Assume that the file Fruits.txt contains the following entries.)

"Apple", "Apricot", "Avocado", "Banana", "Blueberry", "Grape", "Lemon", "Lime"

5.
```
Private Sub cmdDisplay_Click()
   Dim dessert As String
   'Display list of desserts
   Open "Desserts.txt" For Input As #1
   Do While Not EOF(1)
     Input #1, dessert
     picOutput.Print dessert
   Loop
   Close #1
End Sub
```

(Assume that the file Desserts.txt contains the following entries.)

"pie", "cake", "melon"

6.
```
Private Sub cmdDisplay_Click()
   Dim num As Single
   'Display list of numbers
   Open "Data.txt" For Input As #1
   Input #1, num
   Do While Not EOF(1)
     picOutput.Print num;
     Input #1, num
   Loop
   Close #1
End Sub
```

(Assume that the file Data.txt contains the following entries.)

2, 3, 8, 5

In Exercises 7 to 10, identify the errors.

7.
```
Private Sub cmdDisplay_Click()
   Dim q As Single
   q = 1
   Do While q > 0
     q = 3 * q - 1
     picOutput.Print q;
   Loop
End Sub
```

8.
```
Private Sub cmdDisplay_Click()
   Dim answer As String
   'Repeat until a yes response is given
   Loop
     answer = InputBox("Did you chop down the cherry tree (Y/N)?")
   Do Until UCase(answer) = "Y"
End Sub
```

9.
```
Private Sub cmdDisplay_Click()
   Dim num As Single
   Open "Data.txt" For Input As #1
   Do While (Not EOF(1)) And (num > 0)
     Input #1, num
     picOutput.Print num
   Close #1
End Sub
```

(Assume that the file Data.txt contains the following entries.)

7, 6, 0, –1, 2

10.
```
Private Sub cmdDisplay_Click()
   Dim president As String
   'Display names of some U.S. Presidents
   Open "Pres.txt" For Input As #1
   Input #1, president
   Do
     picOutput.Print president
     Input #1, president
   Loop Until EOF(1)
   Close #1
End Sub
```

(Assume that the file Pres.txt contains the following entries.)

"Lincoln", "Washington", "Kennedy", "Jefferson"

In Exercises 11 to 16, replace each phrase containing Until with an equivalent phrase containing While and vice versa. For instance, the phrase Until sum = 100 would be replaced by While sum < > 100.

11. `Until num < 7`

12. `Until nom = "Bob"`

13. `While response = "Y"`

14. `While total = 10`

15. `While nom <> ""`

16. `Until balance >= 100`

In Exercises 17 and 18, write simpler and clearer code that performs the same task as the given code.

17.
```
Private Sub cmdDisplay_Click()
   Dim nom As String
   nom = InputBox("Enter a name:")
   picOutput.Print nom
   nom = InputBox("Enter a name:")
   picOutput.Print nom
   nom = InputBox("Enter a name:")
   picOutput.Print nom
End Sub
```

18.
```
Private Sub cmdDisplay_Click()
    Dim loopNum As Integer, answer As String
    loopNum = 0
    Do
        If loopNum >= 1 Then
            answer = InputBox("Do you want to continue (Y/N)?")
            answer = UCase(answer)
        Else
            answer = "Y"
        End If
        If (answer = "Y") Or (loopNum = 0) Then
            loopNum = loopNum + 1
            picOutput.Print loopNum
        End If
    Loop Until answer <> "Y"
End Sub
```

19. Write a program that displays a Celsius-to-Fahrenheit conversion table. Entries in the table should range from −40 to 40 degrees Celsius in increments of 5 degrees. **Note:** The formula $f = (9 / 5) * c + 32$ converts Celsius to Fahrenheit.

20. The world population reached 6 billion people in 1999 and was growing at the rate of 1.4 percent each year. Write a program to determine when the population will exceed 10 billion.

21. Table 3.5 gives the prices of various liquids. Write a program that requests an amount of money as input and displays the names of all liquids for which a gallon could be purchased with that amount of money. The information from the table should be read from a file. As an example, if the user has $2.35, then the following should be displayed in the picture box:

You can purchase one gallon of any of the following liquids.

Bleach
Gasoline
Milk

Liquid	Price	Liquid	Price
Apple Cider	2.60	Milk	2.30
Beer	6.00	Gatorade	4.20
Bleach	1.40	Perrier	6.85
Coca-Cola	2.55	Pancake Syrup	15.50
Gasoline	1.30	Spring Water	4.10

Table 3.5 Some comparative prices per gallon of various liquids.

22. Illustrate the growth of money in a savings account. When the user presses the command button, values for Amount and Interest Rate are obtained from text boxes and used to calculate the number of years until the money doubles and the number of years until the money reaches a million dollars. Use the following form design. **Note:** The balance at the end of each year is $(1 + r)$ times the previous balance, where r is the annual rate of interest in decimal form. Use Do loops to determine the number of years.

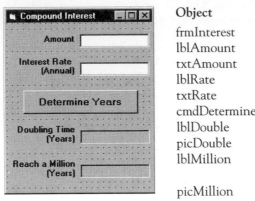

Object	Property	Setting
frmInterest	Caption	Compound Interest
lblAmount	Caption	Amount
txtAmount	Text	(blank)
lblRate	Caption	Interest Rate (Annual)
txtRate	Text	(blank)
cmdDetermine	Caption	Determine Years
lblDouble	Caption	Doubling Time (Years)
picDouble		
lblMillion	Caption	Reach a Million (Years)
picMillion		

Form for Exercise 22   Objects and Major Properties for Exercise 22

23. Write a program to find and display the largest of a collection of positive numbers contained in a data file. (Test the program with the collection of numbers 89, 77, 95, and 86.)

24. Write a program to find and display those names that are repeated in a data file. Assume the file has already been sorted into alphabetical order. When a name is found to be repeated, display it only once.

25. Suppose the file Final.txt contains student grades on a final exam. Write a program that displays the average grade on the exam and the percentage of grades that are above average.

26. Suppose the file Bids.txt contains a list of bids on a construction project. Write a program to analyze the list and report the two highest bids.

27. Suppose the file Uspres.txt contains the names of the United States presidents in order from Washington to Clinton. Write a program that asks the user to type a number from 1 to 42 into a text box, and then, when a command button is clicked, displays the name of the president corresponding to that number.

28. Table 3.6 shows the different grades of eggs and the minimum weight required for each classification. Write a program that processes a data file that lists the weights of a sample of eggs. The program should report the number of eggs in each grade and the weight of the lightest and heaviest egg in the sample. (*Note:* Eggs weighing less than 1.5 ounces cannot be sold in supermarkets.) Figure 3.6 shows a sample output of the program.

Grade	Weight (in ounces)
Jumbo	2.5
Extra Large	2.25
Large	2
Medium	1.75
Small	1.5

```
57 Jumbo eggs
95 Extra Large eggs
76 Large eggs
96 Medium eggs
77 Small eggs
Lightest egg: 1 ounces
Heaviest egg: 2.69 ounces
```

Table 3.6 Grades of Eggs.   **Figure 3.6** Output for Exercise 28.

 **Solutions to Practice Problems 3.2**

1. As a rule of thumb, the condition is checked at the bottom if the loop should be executed at least once.

2. Either precede the loop with the statement `continue = "Yes"` or change the first line to `Do` and replace the `Loop` statement with `Loop Until continue <> "Yes"`.

3.3 FOR...NEXT LOOPS

When we know exactly how many times a loop should be executed, we can use a special type of loop, called a For...Next loop. For...Next loops are easy to read and write, and have features that make them ideal for certain common tasks. The following code uses a For...Next loop to display a table.

```
Private Sub cmdDisplayTable_Click()
  Dim i As Integer
  'Display a table of the first 5 numbers and their squares
  picTable.Cls
  For i = 1 To 5
    picTable.Print i; i ^ 2
  Next i
End Sub
```

[Run and click on cmdDisplayTable. The following is displayed in the picture box.]

```
1   1
2   4
3   9
4   16
5   25
```

The equivalent program written with a Do loop is as follows.

```
Private Sub cmdDisplayTable_Click()
  Dim i As Integer
  'Display a table of the first 5 numbers and their squares
  picTable.Cls
  i = 1
  Do While i <= 5
    picTable.Print i; i ^ 2
    i = i + 1
  Loop
End Sub
```

In general, a portion of a program of the form

initial value ———————— For $i = m$ To n ◄———————— terminating value
control variable ————————   statement(s) ◄———————— body
                              Next i

constitutes a For...Next loop. The pair of statements For and Next cause the statements between them to be repeated a specified number of times. The For statement designates a numeric variable, called the **control variable**, that is initialized and then automatically changes after each execution of the loop. Also, the For statement gives the range of values this variable will assume. The Next statement increments the control variable. If $m \leq n$, then i is assigned the values m, $m + 1, \ldots, n$ in order, and the body is executed once for each of these values. If $m > n$, then the statements in the body are not executed, and execution continues with the statement after the For...Next loop.

When program execution reaches a For...Next loop, such as the one shown previously, the For statement assigns to the control variable i the initial value m and checks to see whether i is greater than the terminating value n. If so, then execution jumps to the line following the Next statement. If $i <= n$, the statements inside the loop are executed. Then, the Next statement increases the value of i by 1 and checks this new value to see if it exceeds n. If not, the entire process is repeated until the value of i exceeds n. When this happens, the program moves to the line following the loop. Figure 3.7 contains the pseudocode and flowchart of a For...Next loop.

For i = m to n
    Processing step(s)
Next i

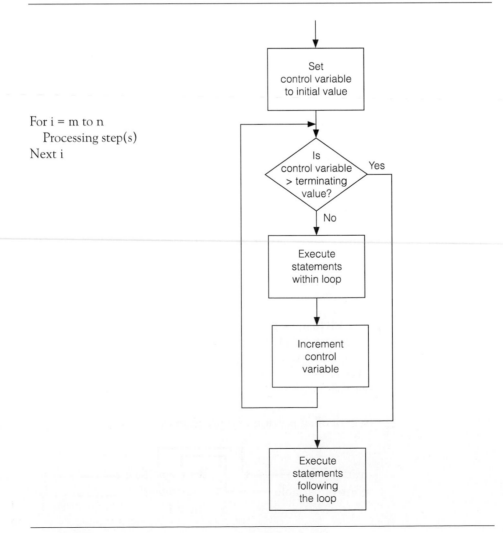

Figure 3.7 Pseudocode and flowchart of a For...Next loop.

The control variable can be *any* numeric variable. The most common single letter names are *i*, *j*, and *k*; however, if appropriate, the name should suggest the purpose of the control variable.

EXAMPLE 1

Suppose the population of a city is 300,000 in the year 1998 and is growing at the rate of 3 percent per year. The following program displays a table showing the population each year until 2002.

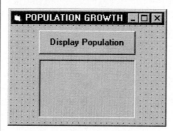

Object	Property	Setting
frm3_3_1	Caption	POPULATION GROWTH
cmdDisplay	Caption	Display Population
picTable		

```
Private Sub cmdDisplay_Click()
  Dim pop As Single, yr As Integer
  'Display population from 1998 to 2002
  picTable.Cls
  pop = 300000
  For yr = 1998 To 2002
    picTable.Print yr, FormatNumber(pop, 0)
    pop = pop + .03 * pop
  Next yr
End Sub
```

[Run, and click the command button.]

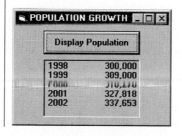

The initial and terminating values can be constants, variables, or expressions. For instance, the For statement in the preceding program can be replaced by

```
firstYr = 1998
lastYr = 2002
For yr = firstYr To lastYr
```

In Example 1, the control variable was increased by 1 after each pass through the loop. A variation of the For statement allows any number to be used as the increment. The statement

```
For i = m To n Step s
```

instructs the Next statement to add *s* to the control variable instead of 1. The numbers *m*, *n*, and *s* do not have to be whole numbers. The number *s* is called the **step value** of the loop.

EXAMPLE 2 The following program displays the values of the index of a For...Next loop for terminating and step values input by the user.

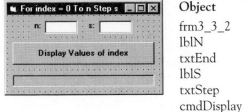

Object	Property	Setting
frm3_3_2	Caption	For index = 0 To n Step s
lblN	Caption	n:
txtEnd	Text	(blank)
lblS	Caption	s:
txtStep	Text	(blank)
cmdDisplay	Caption	Display Values of index
picValues		

```
Private Sub cmdDisplay_Click()
  Dim n As Single, s As Single, index As Single
  'Display values of index ranging from 0 to n Step s
  picValues.Cls
  n = Val(txtEnd.Text)
  s = Val(txtStep.Text)
  For index = 0 To n Step s
    picValues.Print index;
  Next index
End Sub
```

[Run, type 3.2 and .5 into the text boxes, and click the command button.]

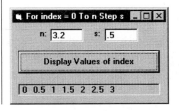

In the examples considered so far, the control variable was successively increased until it reached the terminating value. However, if a negative step value is used and the initial value is greater than the terminating value, then the control value is decreased until reaching the terminating value. In other words, the loop counts backward or downward.

EXAMPLE 3 The following program accepts a word as input and displays it backwards:

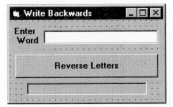

Object	Property	Setting
frm3_3_3	Caption	Write Backwards
lblWord	Caption	Enter Word
txtWord	Text	(blank)
cmdReverse	Caption	Reverse Letters
picTranspose		

```
Private Sub cmdReverse_Click()
  Dim m As Integer, j As Integer
  Dim word As String, reverse As String
```

```
    'Write a word backwards
    picTranspose.Cls
    word = txtWord.Text
    m = Len(word)
    reverse = ""
    For j = m To 1 Step -1
      reverse = reverse + Mid(word, j, 1)
    Next j
    picTranspose.Print reverse
End Sub
```

[Run, type SUEZ into the text box, and click the command button.]

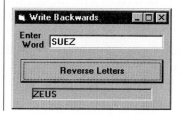

Note: The initial and terminating values of a For...Next loop can be expressions. For instance, the seventh and ninth lines of the event procedure in Example 3 can be consolidated to

```
For j = Len(word) To 1 Step -1
```

The body of a For...Next loop can contain *any* sequence of Visual Basic statements. In particular, it can contain another For...Next loop. However, the second loop must be completely contained inside the first loop and must have a different control variable. Such a configuration is called **nested loops**. Figure 3.8 shows several examples of valid nested loops.

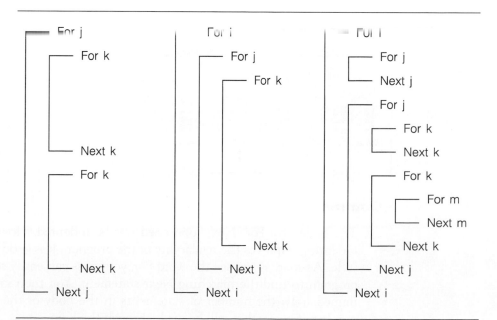

Figure 3.8 Nested loops.

EXAMPLE 4   Write a program to display the products of the integers from 1 to 4.

SOLUTION   In the following program, *j* denotes the left factors of the products, and *k* denotes the right factors. Each factor takes on a value from 1 to 4. The values are assigned to *j* in the outer loop and to *k* in the inner loop. Initially, *j* is assigned the value 1 and then the inner loop is traversed four times to produce the first row of products. At the end of these four passes, the value of *j* will still be 1, and the value of *k* will have been incremented to 5. The picTable.Print statement just before Next j guarantees that no more products will be displayed in that row. The first execution of the outer loop is then complete. Following this, the statement Next j increments the value of *j* to 2. The statement beginning For k is then executed. It resets the value of *k* to 1. The second row of products is displayed during the next four executions of the inner loop and so on.

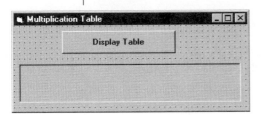

Object	Property	Setting
frmMultiply	Caption	Multiplication Table
cmdDisplay	Caption	Display Table
picTable		

```
Private Sub cmdDisplay_Click()
  Dim j As Integer, k As Integer
  picTable.Cls
  For j = 1 To 4
    For k = 1 To 4
      picTable.Print j; "x"; k; "="; j * k,
    Next k
    picTable.Print
  Next j
End Sub
```

[Run and press the command button.]

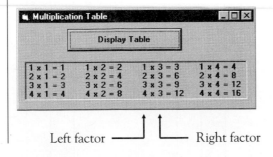

Left factor ——⌐   ⌐—— Right factor

Comments

1. The body of a For...Next loop need not be indented. However, because indenting improves the readability of the program, it is good programming style. As soon as you see the word For, your eyes can easily scan down the program to find the matching Next statement. You then know two facts immediately: the number of statements in the body of the loop and the number of passes that will be made through the loop.

2. For and Next statements must be paired. If one is missing, the program will generate the error message "For without Next" or "Next without For."

3. Consider a loop beginning with For $i = m$ To n Step s. The loop will be executed exactly once if m equals n no matter what value s has. The loop will not be executed at all if m is greater than n and s is positive, or if m is less than n and s is negative.

4. The value of the control variable should not be altered within the body of the loop; doing so might cause the loop to repeat indefinitely or have an unpredictable number of repetitions.

5. Noninteger step values can lead to roundoff errors with the result that the loop is not executed the intended number of times. For instance, a loop beginning with For i = 1 To 2 Step .1 will be executed only 10 times instead of the intended 11 times. It should be replaced with For i = 1 To 2.01 Step .1.

PRACTICE PROBLEMS 3.3

1. Why won't the following lines of code work as intended?

```
For i = 15 To 1
  picBox.Print i;
Next i
```

2. When is a For...Next loop more appropriate than a Do loop?

EXERCISES 3.3

In Exercises 1 to 10, determine the output displayed in the picture box when the command button is clicked.

1.
```
Private Sub cmdDisplay_Click()
    Dim i As Integer
    For i = 1 To 4
      picOutput.Print "Pass #"; i
    Next i
End Sub
```

2.
```
Private Sub cmdDisplay_Click()
    Dim i As Integer
    For i = 3 To 6
      picOutput.Print 2 * i;
    Next i
End Sub
```

3.
```
Private Sub cmdDisplay_Click()
    Dim j As Integer
    For j = 2 To 8 Step 2
      picOutput.Print j;
    Next j
    picOutput.Print "Who do we appreciate?"
End Sub
```

4.
```
Private Sub cmdDisplay_Click()
    Dim countdown As Integer
    For countdown = 10 To 1 Step -1
      picOutput.Print countdown;
    Next countdown
    picOutput.Print "blastoff"
End Sub
```

5.
```
Private Sub cmdDisplay_Click()
    Dim num As Integer, i As Integer
    num = 5
    For i = num To 2 * num + 3
      picOutput.Print i;
    Next i
End Sub
```

6.
```
Private Sub cmdDisplay_Click()
    Dim i As Single
    For i = 3 To 5 Step .25
      picOutput.Print i;
    Next i
    picOutput.Print i
End Sub
```

7.
```
Private Sub cmdDisplay_Click()
    Dim recCount As Integer, miler As Integer
    Dim nom As String, mileTime As String
    'First entry in data file is number of records in file
    Open "Miler.txt" For Input As #1
    Input #1, recCount
    For miler = 1 To recCount
      Input #1, nom, mileTime
      picOutput.Print nom, mileTime
    Next miler
    Close #1
End Sub
```
(Assume that the file Miler.txt contains the following four lines.)

3

"Steve Cram", "3:46.31"

"Steve Scott", "3:51.6"

"Mary Slaney", "4:20.5"

8.
```
Private Sub cmdDisplay_Click()
    Dim recCount As Integer, total As Integer
    Dim i As Integer, score As Integer
    'First entry in data file is number of records in file
    Open "Scores.txt" For Input As #1
    Input #1, recCount
    total = 0
    For i = 1 To recCount
      Input #1, score
      total = total + score
    Next i
    Close #1
    picOutput.Print "Average ="; total / recCount
End Sub
```
(Assume that the file Scores.txt contains the following entries.)

4, 89, 85, 88, 98

9.
```
Private Sub cmdDisplay_Click()
    Dim i As Integer, j As Integer
    For i = 0 To 2
      For j = 0 To 3
        picOutput.Print i + 3 * j + 1; "  ";
      Next j
      picOutput.Print
    Next i
End Sub
```

```
10. Private Sub cmdDisplay_Click()
      Dim i As Integer, j As Integer
      For i = 1 To 5
        For j = 1 To i
          picOutput.Print "*";
        Next j
        picOutput.Print
      Next i
    End Sub
```

In Exercises 11 to 14, identify the errors.

```
11. Private Sub cmdDisplay_Click()
      Dim j As Single
      For j = 1 To 25.5 Step -1
        picOutput.Print j
      Next j
    End Sub
```

```
12. Private Sub cmdDisplay_Click()
      Dim i As Integer
      For i = 1 To 3
        picOutput.Print i; 2 ^ i
    End Sub
```

```
13. Private Sub cmdDisplay_Click()
      Dim i As Integer
      For i = 1 To 99
        If Int (i / 2) = i / 2 Then
          Next i
        Else
          picOutput.Print i
        End If
      Next i
    End Sub
```

```
14. Private Sub cmdDisplay_Click()
      Dim i As Integer, j As Integer
      For i = 1 To 6
        For j = 1 To 3
          picOutput.Print i / j;
      Next i
    Next j
    End Sub
```

In Exercises 15 and 16, rewrite the program using a For...Next loop.

```
15. Private Sub cmdDisplay_Click()
      Dim num As Integer
      num = 1
      Do While num <= 10
        picOutput.Print num
        num = num + 2
      Loop
    End Sub
```

```
16. Private Sub cmdDisplay_Click()
      picOutput.Print "hello"
      picOutput.Print "hello"
      picOutput.Print "hello"
      picOutput.Print "hello"
    End Sub
```

In Exercises 17 to 36, write a program to complete the stated task.

17. Display a row of 10 stars (asterisks).

18. Request a number from 1 to 20 and display a row of that many stars (asterisks).

19. Display a 10-by-10 array of stars.

20. Request a number, and call a Sub procedure to display an array having that number of stars on each side.

21. Find the sum $1 + 1/2 + 1/3 + 1/4 + \ldots + 1/100$.

22. Find the sum of the odd numbers from 1 to 99.

23. You are offered two salary options for 10 days of work. Option 1: $100 per day. Option 2: $1 the first day, $2 the second day, $4 the third day, and so on, with the amount doubling each day. Write a program to determine which option pays better.

24. When $1000 is deposited at 5 percent simple interest, the amount grows by $50 each year. When money is invested at 5 percent compound interest, the amount at the end of each year is 1.05 times the amount at the beginning of that year. Write a program to display the amounts for 10 years for a $1000 deposit at 5 percent simple and compound interest. The first few lines displayed in the picture box should appear as in Figure 3.9.

Year	Amount Simple Interest	Amount Compound Interest
1	$1,050.00	$1,050.00
2	$1,100.00	$1,102.50
3	$1,150.00	$1,157.63

Figure 3.9 Growth of $1000 at simple and compound interest.

25. According to researchers at Stanford Medical School (as cited in *Medical Self Care*), the ideal weight for a woman is found by multiplying her height in inches by 3.5 and subtracting 108. The ideal weight for a man is found by multiplying his height in inches by 4 and subtracting 128. Request a lower and upper bound for heights and then produce a table giving the ideal weights for women and men in that height range. For example, when a lower bound of 62 and an upper bound of 65 are specified, Figure 3.10 shows the output displayed in the picture box:

Height	Wt - Women	Wt - Men
62	109	120
63	112.5	124
64	116	128
65	119.5	132

Figure 3.10 Output for Exercise 25.

26. Table 3.7 gives data (in millions) on personal computer shipments and revenues. Read this data from the file Pc.txt and generate an extended table with two additional columns, Pct Foreign (percent of personal computers sold outside the United States) and Ave Rev (average revenue per computer).

Year	U.S. Shipments	Worldwide Shipments	Worldwide Revenue
1995	22.6	60.2	$123,643
1996	25.7	70.9	150,712
1997	29.9	84.3	177,337
1998	34.6	98.4	217,357

Table 3.7 Personal Computer Shipments and Revenues.

Source: Wall Street Journal Almanac, 1998.

27. Request a sentence, and display the number of sibilants (that is, letters S or Z) in the sentence.

28. Request a number, *n*, from 1 to 30 and one of the letters S or P. Then calculate the sum or product of the numbers from 1 to *n* depending on whether S or P was selected. The calculations should be carried out in Function procedures.

29. Suppose $800 is deposited into a savings account earning 4 percent interest compounded annually, and $100 is added to the account at the end of each year. Calculate the amount of money in the account at the end of 10 years. (Determine a formula for computing the balance at the end of 1 year based on the balance at the beginning of the year. Then write a program that starts with a balance of $800 and makes 10 passes through a loop containing the formula to produce the final answer.)

30. A TV set is purchased with a loan of $563 to be paid off with five monthly payments of $116. The interest rate is 1 percent per month. Display a table giving the balance on the loan at the end of each month.

31. *Radioactive decay.* Cobalt 60, a radioactive form of cobalt used in cancer therapy, decays or dissipates over a period of time. Each year, 12 percent of the amount present at the beginning of the year will have decayed. If a container of cobalt 60 initially contains 10 grams, determine the amount remaining after 5 years.

32. *Supply and demand.* This year's level of production and price for most agricultural products greatly affects the level of production and price next year. Suppose the current crop of soybeans in a certain country is 80 million bushels and experience has shown that for each year,

[price this year] = 20 – .1 * [quantity this year]

[quantity next year] = 5 * [price this year] –10

where quantity is measured in units of millions of bushels. Generate a table to show the quantity and price for each of the next 12 years.

33. Request a number greater than 3, and display a hollow rectangle of stars (asterisks) with each outer row and column having that many stars. Use a fixed-width font such as Courier so that the spaces and asterisks will have the same width. (See Figure 3.11(a).)

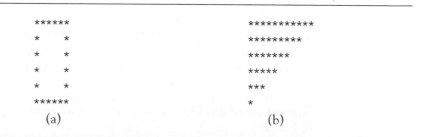

Figure 3.11 Outputs for Exercises 33 and 34.

34. Request an odd number, and display a triangle similar to the one in Figure 3.10(b) with the input number of stars in the top row.

35. Create the histogram in Figure 3.12. A file should hold the years and values. The first two entries in the file could be used to hold the title for the histogram.

```
1994  ******************  20
1995  ***********************  25
1996  *****************  19
1997  ****************  16
1998  ***************  15

Percentage Growth (by number of units) in Worldwide
Retail Sales of Personal Computers
```

Figure 3.12 Histogram for Exercise 35.

36. Write a program to estimate how much a young worker will make before retiring at age 65. Request the worker's name, age, and starting salary as input. Assume the worker receives a 5 percent raise each year. For example, if the user enters Helen, 25, and 20000, then the picture box should display the following:

Helen will earn about $2,415,995

✔✔ **Solutions to Practice Problems 3.3**

1. The loop will never be entered, since 15 is greater than 1. The intended first line might have been

   `For i = 15 To 1 Step -1`

   or

   `For i = 1 To 15`

2. If the exact number of times the loop will be executed is known before entering the loop, then a For...Next loop should be used. Otherwise, a Do loop is more appropriate.

3.4 A CASE STUDY: WEEKLY PAYROLL

This case study processes a weekly payroll using the 1998 Employer's Tax Guide. Table 3.8 shows typical data used by a company's payroll office. These data are processed to produce the information in Table 3.9 that is supplied to each employee along with his or her paycheck. The program should read the employee data for each individual from the text file Payroll.txt (see Table 3.8) and produce output similar to that in Table 3.9. The items in Table 3.9 should be calculated as follows:

Current earnings: Hourly wage times hours worked (with time and a half after 40 hours).

Year-to-date earnings: Previous year-to-date earnings plus current earnings.

FICA tax: Sum of 6.2% of first $68,400 of earnings (Social Security benefits tax) and 1.45% of total wages (Medicare tax)

Federal income tax withheld: Subtract $51.92 from the current earnings for each withholding exemption and use Table 3.10 or Table 3.11, depending on marital status.

Check amount: [Current earnings] – [FICA taxes] – [Income tax withheld]

Name	Hourly Wage	Hours Worked	Withholding Exemptions	Marital Status	Previous Year-to-Date Earnings
Al Clark	$45.50	38	4	Married	$68,925.50
Ann Miller	$44.00	35	3	Married	$68,200.00
John Smith	$17.95	50	1	Single	$30,604.75
Sue Taylor	$25.50	43	2	Single	$36,295.50

Table 3.8 Employee data.

Name	Current Earnings	Yr. to date Earnings	FICA Taxes	Income Tax Withheld	Check Amount
Al Clark	$1,729.00	$70,654.50	$25.07	$290.50	$1,413.43
Ann Miller	$1,540.00	$69,740.00	$34.73	$252.12	$1,253.15
John Smith	$987.25	$31,592.00	$75.52	$186.73	$725.00
Sue Taylor	$1,134.75	$37,430.25	$86.81	$213.49	$834.45

Table 3.9 Payroll information.

Adjusted Weekly Income	Income Tax Withheld
$0 to $51	$0
Over $51 to $517	15% of amount over $51
Over $517 to $1,105	$69.90 + 28% of excess over $517
Over $1,105 to $2,493	$234.54 + 31% of excess over $1,105
Over $2,493 to $5,385	$664.82 + 36% of excess over $2,493
Over $5,385	$1,705.94 + 39.6% of excess over $5,385

Table 3.10 1998 Federal income tax withheld for a single person paid weekly.

Adjusted Weekly Income	Income Tax Withheld
$0 to $124	$0
Over $124 to $899	15% of excess over $124
Over $899 to $1,855	$116.25 + 28% of excess over $899
Over $1,855 to $3,084	$383.93 + 31% of excess over $1,855
Over $3,084 to $5,439	$764.92 + 36% of excess over $3,084
Over $5,439	$1,612.72 + 39.6% of excess over $5,439

Table 3.11 1998 Federal income tax withheld for a married person paid weekly.

Designing the Weekly Payroll Program

After displaying a single heading for the output, the program must repeatedly read the data for an employee, compute the five items appearing in Table 3.9, and then display the payroll information. Five computations form the basic tasks of the program.

A. Compute current earnings.

B. Compute year-to-date earnings.

C. Compute FICA tax.

D. Compute Federal Income Tax withheld.

E. Compute paycheck amount (that is, take-home pay).

Tasks A, B, C, and E are fairly simple. Each involves applying a formula to given data. (For instance, if hours worked is at most 40, then Current Earnings = Hourly Wage times Hours Worked.) Thus, we won't break down these tasks any further. Task D is more complicated, so we continue to divide it into smaller subtasks.

D. *Compute Federal Income Tax Withheld.* First the employee's pay is adjusted for exemptions, and then the amount of income tax to be withheld is computed. The computation of the income tax withheld differs for married and single individuals. Task D is, therefore, divided into the following subtasks:

D.1 Compute pay adjusted by exemptions.
D.2 Compute income tax withheld for single employee.
D.3 Compute income tax withheld for married employee.

The top-down chart in Figure 3.13 shows the stepwise refinement of the problem.

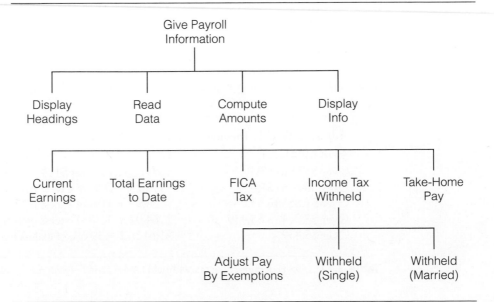

Figure 3.13 Top-down chart for the weekly payroll program.

Pseudocode for the Weekly Payroll Program

Display headings and determine output format
Do While there is still data in the file Payroll.txt
   Get an employee's payroll data
   Compute current gross pay
   Compute total earnings to date
   Compute FICA tax
   Compute income tax withheld
     Adjust pay for exemptions
     If employee is single Then
        Compute income tax withheld from adjusted pay using tax brackets
        for single taxpayers
      Else
        Compute income tax withheld from adjusted pay using tax brackets
        for married taxpayers
     End If
   Compute check
   Display payroll information
Loop

Writing the Weekly Payroll Program

The program calls a sequence of eight tasks, seven of which are executed repeatedly within a large loop. Table 3.12 shows these tasks as well as their subtasks.

---

1. Display headings.
2. Read employee payroll data as long as data still are in the employee data file.
3. Compute current earnings.
4. Compute year-to-date earnings.
5. Compute FICA tax.
6. Compute Federal Income Tax withheld.
   6.1 Compute adjusted pay.
   6.2 Compute amount withheld for single employee.
   6.3 Compute amount withheld for married employee.
7. Compute paycheck amounts.
8. Display payroll information.

Table 3.12 Tasks and their subtasks.

```
Private Sub cmdComputePayroll_Click()
   Dim exemptions As Integer 'Number of exemptions for employee
   Dim fedTax As Single       'Federal income tax withheld this week
   Dim ficaTax As Single      'Social Security plus Medicare tax for this week
   Dim hrsWorked As Single    'Hours worked this week
   Dim hrWage As Single       'Hourly wage
   Dim mStatus As String      'Marital status (SINGLE or MARRIED)
   Dim nom As String          'Name of employee
   Dim grossPay As Single     'This week's pay before taxes
   Dim check As Single        'Paycheck this week (take-home pay)
   Dim prevPay As Single      'Total pay for year excluding this week
   Dim totalPay As Single     'Total pay for year including this week
```

```
     'Compute and display payroll information table
     Call ShowHeading                                               'Task 1
     Open "Payroll.txt" For Input As #1
     Do While Not EOF(1)
       Input #1, nom, hrWage, hrsWorked, exemptions, mStatus, prevPay   'Task 2
       grossPay = Gross_Pay(hrWage, hrsWorked)                     'Task 3
       totalPay = prevPay + grossPay                               'Task 4
       ficaTax = FICA_Tax(grossPay, prevPay, totalPay)            'Task 5
       fedTax = Fed_Tax(grossPay, exemptions, mStatus)            'Task 6
       check = grossPay - ficaTax - fedTax                         'Task 7
       Call ShowPayroll(nom, grossPay, totalPay, ficaTax, fedTax, check) 'Task 8
     Loop
     Close #1
   End Sub


   Private Function Fed_Tax(grossPay As Single, exemptions As Integer, _
                   mStatus As String) As Single
     Dim adjPay As Single
     'Task 6.1: Compute the adjusted pay, adjPay
     adjPay = grossPay - (51.92 * exemptions)
     If adjPay < 0 Then
         adjPay = 0
     End If
     If UCase(mStatus) = "SINGLE" Then
         Fed_Tax = TaxSingle(adjPay)    'Task 6.2
       Else
         Fed_Tax = TaxMarried(adjPay)   'Task 6.3
     End If
     Fed_Tax = Round(Fed_Tax, 2)        'Round to nearest cent
   End Function


   Private Function FICA_Tax(grossPay As Single, _
           prevPay As Single, totalPay As Single) As Single
     'Task 5: Compute social security plus medicare tax
     If totalPay <= 68400 Then
         FICA_Tax = 0.062 * grossPay
       Else
         If prevPay < 68400 Then        'Compute social security component
            FICA_Tax = 0.062 * (68400 - prevPay)
          Else
            FICA_Tax = 0
         End If
     End If
     FICA_Tax = FICA_Tax + 0.0145 * grossPay    'Add medicare component
     FICA_Tax = Round(FICA_Tax, 2)              'Round to nearest cent
   End Function


   Private Function Gross_Pay(hrWage As Single, hrsWorked As Single) As Single
     'Task 3: Compute current earnings
     If hrsWorked <= 40 Then
         Gross_Pay = hrsWorked * hrWage
       Else
         Gross_Pay = 40 * hrWage + (hrsWorked - 40) * 1.5 * hrWage
     End If
   End Function
```

```vb
Private Sub ShowHeading()
  'Task 1: Display headings for paychecks
  picOutput.Cls
  picOutput.Print , "Current", "Yr. to date", "FICA", "Income Tax", "Check"
  picOutput.Print "Name", "Earnings", "Earnings", "Taxes", "Withheld", "Amount"
End Sub


Private Sub ShowPayroll(nom As String, grossPay As Single, _
  totalPay As Single, ficaTax As Single, fedTax As Single, check As Single)
  'Task 8: Display payroll information
  picOutput.Print nom, FormatCurrency(grossPay),
  picOutput.Print FormatCurrency(totalPay), FormatCurrency(ficaTax),
  picOutput.Print FormatCurrency(fedTax), FormatCurrency(check)
End Sub


Private Function TaxMarried(adjPay As Single) As Single
  'Task 6.3: Compute federal tax for married person based on adjusted pay
  Select Case adjPay
    Case 0 To 124
      TaxMarried = 0
    Case 124 To 899
      TaxMarried = 0.15 * (adjPay - 124)
    Case 899 To 1855
      TaxMarried = 116.25 + 0.28 * (adjPay - 899)
    Case 1855 To 3084
      TaxMarried = 383.93 + 0.31 * (adjPay - 1855)
    Case 3084 To 5439
      TaxMarried = 764.92 + 0.36 * (adjPay - 3084)
    Case Is > 5439
      TaxMarried = 1612.72 + 0.396 * (adjPay - 5439)
  End Select
End Function


Private Function TaxSingle(adjPay As Single) As Single
  'Task 6.2: Compute federal tax for single person based on adjusted pay
  Select Case adjPay
    Case 0 To 51
      TaxSingle = 0
    Case 51 To 517
      TaxSingle = 0.15 * (adjPay - 51)
    Case 517 To 1105
      TaxSingle = 69.6 + 0.28 * (adjPay - 517)
    Case 1105 To 2493
      TaxSingle = 234.54 + 0.31 * (adjPay - 1105)
    Case 2493 To 5385
      TaxSingle = 664.82 + 0.36 * (adjPay - 2493)
    Case Is > 5385
      TaxSingle = 1705.94 + 0.396 * (adjPay - 5385)
  End Select
End Function
```

Comments

1. In task 5, care has been taken to avoid computing Social Security tax on income in excess of $68,400 per year. The logic of the program makes sure an employee whose income crosses the $68,400 threshold during a given week is taxed on only the difference between $68,400 and his previous year-to-date income.

2. Tasks 6.2 and 6.3 use Select Case to incorporate the tax brackets given in Tables 3.10 and 3.11 for the amount of Federal Income Tax withheld. The upper limit of each Case clause is the same as the lower limit of the next Case clause. This ensured fractional values for adjPay, such as 51.50 in task 6.2, would be properly treated as part of the higher salary range.

CHAPTER 3 SUMMARY

1. An If block decides what action to take depending on the truth values of one or more conditions. To allow several courses of action, the If and Else parts of an If statement can contain other If statements.

2. A Select Case block selects one of several actions depending on the value of an expression, called the *selector*. The entries in the *value* lists should have the same type (string or numeric) as the selector.

3. The principal *logical operators* are And, Or, and Not.

4. A Do loop repeatedly executes a block of statements either as long as or until a certain condition is true. The condition can be checked either at the top of the loop or at the bottom.

5. The EOF function tells us if we have read to the end of a file.

6. As various items of data are processed by a loop, a *counter* can be used to keep track of the number of items, and an *accumulator* can be used to sum numerical values.

7. A *flag* is a Boolean variable used to indicate whether or not a certain event has occurred.

8. A For...Next loop repeats a block of statements a fixed number of times. The *control variable* assumes an initial value and increments by one after each pass through the loop until it reaches the terminating value. Alternative increment values can be specified with the Step keyword.

CHAPTER 3 PROGRAMMING PROJECTS

1. Table 3.13 gives the price schedule for Eddie's Equipment Rental. Full-day rentals cost one-and-a-half times half-day rentals. Write a program that displays Table 3.13 in a picture box when an appropriate command button is clicked and displays a bill in another picture box based on the item number and time period chosen by a customer. The bill should include a $30.00 deposit.

Piece of Equipment	Half-Day	Full Day
1. Rug cleaner	$16.00	$24.00
2. Lawn mower	$12.00	$18.00
3. Paint sprayer	$20.00	$30.00

Table 3.13 Price schedule for Eddie's Equipment Rental.

A possible form layout and sample run is shown in Figure 3.14.

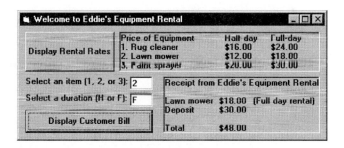

Figure 3.14 Form layout and sample run for Programming Project 1.

2. The American Heart Association suggests that at most 30 percent of the calories in our diet come from fat. Although food labels give the number of calories and amount of fat per serving, they might not give the percentage of calories from fat. This percentage can be calculated by multiplying the number of grams of fat in one serving by 9, dividing that number by the total number of calories per serving, and multiplying the result by 100. Write a program that requests the name, number of calories per serving, and the grams of fat per serving as input, and tells us whether the food meets the American Heart Association recommendation. A sample run is as follows:

3. Table 3.14 contains seven proverbs and their truth values. Write a program that presents these proverbs one at a time and asks the user to evaluate them as true or false. The program should then tell the user how many questions were answered correctly and display one of the following evaluations: Perfect (all correct), Excellent (5 or 6 correct), You might consider taking Psychology 101 (less than 5 correct).

Proverb	Truth Value
The squeaky wheel gets the grease.	True
Cry and you cry alone.	True
Opposites attract.	False
Spare the rod and spoil the child.	False
Actions speak louder than words.	True
Familiarity breeds contempt.	False
Marry in haste, repent at leisure.	True

Table 3.14 Seven proverbs.

Source: "You Know What They Say . . .," by Alfie Kohn, *Psychology Today*, April 1988.

4. Table 3.15 shows the number of bachelor degrees conferred in 1980 and 1994 in certain fields of study. Tables 3.16 and 3.17 show the percentage change and a histogram of 1994 levels, respectively. Write a program that allows the user to display any one of these tables as an option and quit as a fourth option.

Field of Study	1980	1994
Business and management	185,361	246,654
Computer and info. science	11,154	24,200
Education	118,169	167,600
Engineering	68,893	62,220
Social sciences	103,519	133,680

Table 3.15 Bachelor's degrees conferred in certain fields.

Source: U.S. National Center of Educational Statistics.

Field of Study	% Change (1980–1994)
Business and management	33.1
Computer and info. science	117.0
Education	41.8
Engineering	–9.7
Social sciences	29.1

Table 3.16 Percentage change in bachelor's degrees conferred.

Business and management	************************	246,654
Computer and info. science	**	24,200
Education	*****************	167,600
Engineering	******	62,220
Social sciences	*************	133,680

Table 3.17 Bachelor's degrees conferred in 1994 in certain fields.

5. *The Twelve Days of Christmas.* Each year, Provident National Bank of Philadelphia publishes a Christmas price list. See Table 3.18. Write a program that requests an integer from 1 to 12 and then lists the gifts for that day along with that day's cost. On the *n*th day, the *n* gifts are 1 partridge in a pear tree, 2 turtle doves, . . . *n* of the *n*th item. The program also should give the total cost of all twelve days. As an example, Figure 3.15 shows the output in the picture box when the user enters 3.

Item	Cost	Item	Cost
partridge in a pear tree	27.50	swan-a-swimming	1000.00
turtle dove	25.00	maid-a-milking	4.25
French hen	5.00	lady dancing	289.50
calling bird	70.00	lord-a-leaping	292.50
gold ring	60.00	piper piping	95.75
geese-a-laying	25.00	drummer drumming	95.00

Table 3.18 Christmas price index.

```
The gifts for day 3 are
 1 partridge in a pear tree
 2 turtle doves
 3 French hens
Cost:    $92.50

Total cost for the twelve days: $71,613.50
```

Figure 3.15 Sample output for Programming Project 5.

4 Arrays

4.1   CREATING AND ACCESSING ARRAYS

A **variable** (or simple variable) is a name to which Visual Basic can assign a single value. An **array variable** is a collection of simple variables of the same type to which Visual Basic can efficiently assign a list of values.

Consider the following situation. Suppose you want to evaluate the exam grades for 30 students. Not only do you want to compute the average score, but you also want to display the names of the students whose scores are above average. You might place the 30 pairs of student names and scores in a data file and run the program outlined.

```
Private Sub cmdButton_Click()
   Dim student1 As String, score1 As Single
   Dim student2 As String, score2 As Single
   Dim student3 As String, score3 As Single
        .
        .
        .
   Dim student30 As String, score30 As Single
   'Analyze exam grades
   Open "Scores.txt" For Input As #1
   Input #1, student1, score1
   Input #1, student2, score2
   Input #1, student3, score3
        .
        .
        .
   Input #1, student30, score30
   'Compute the average grade
        .
        .
        .
   'Display names of above average students
        .
        .
        .
End Sub
```

This program is going to be uncomfortably long. What's most frustrating is that the 30 Dim statements and 30 Input # statements are very similar and look as if they should be condensed into a short loop. A shorthand notation for the many related variables would be welcome. It would be nice if we could just write

```
For i = 1 To 30
   Input #1, studenti, scorei
Next i
```

Of course, this will not work. Visual Basic will treat *studenti* and *scorei* as two variables and keep reassigning new values to them. At the end of the loop, they will have the values of the 30th student.

Visual Basic provides a data structure called an **array** that lets us do what we tried to accomplish in the loop. The variable names will be similar to those in the Input # statement. They will be

```
student(1), student(2), student(3), ..., student(30)
```

and

```
score(1), score(2), score(3), ..., score(30).
```

We refer to these collections of variables as the array variables *student( )* and *score( )*. The numbers inside the parentheses of the individual variables are called **subscripts**, and each individual variable is called a **subscripted variable** or **element**. For instance, *student*(3) is the third subscripted variable of the array *student( )*, and *score*(20) is the 20th subscripted variable of the array *score( )*. The elements of an array are assigned successive memory locations. Figure 4.1 shows the memory locations for the array *score( )*.

	score(1)	score(2)	score(3)	. . .	score(30)
score( )				. . .	

Figure 4.1 The array *score( )*.

Array variables have the same kinds of names as simple variables. If *array-Name* is the name of an array variable and *n* is a positive whole number, then the statement

```
Dim arrayName(1 To n) As varType
```

reserves space in memory to hold the values of the subscripted variables *array-Name*(1), *arrayName*(2), *arrayName*(3), . . . , *arrayName*(*n*). The spread of the subscripts specified by the Dim statement is called the **range** of the array, and the Dim statement is said to **dimension** the array. The subscripted variables will all have the same data type; namely, the type specified by varType. For instance, they could be all String variables or all Integer variables. In particular, the statements

```
Dim student(1 To 30) As String
Dim score(1 To 30) As Integer
```

dimension the arrays needed for the preceding program.

Frequently arrays are dimensioned at the top of the code window; that is, in the (Declarations) section of (General). As discussed in Section 2.4, such arrays have **form-level scope**. That is, they are recognized by all procedures and retain their value when the procedures are exited.

Values can be assigned to subscripted variables with assignment statements and displayed with Print methods. The statement

```
Dim score(1 To 30) As Integer
```

sets aside a portion of memory for the numeric array *score( )* and places the default value 0 in each element.

	score(1)	score(2)	score(3)	. . .	score(30)
score( )	0	0	0	. . .	0

The statements

```
score(1) = 87
score(3) = 92
```

assign values to the first and third elements.

	score(1)	score(2)	score(3)	. . .	score(30)
score( )	87	0	92	. . .	0

The statements

```
For i = 1 To 4
  picBox.Print score(i);
Next i
```

then produce the output 87 0 92 0   in picBox.

EXAMPLE 1

The following program creates a string array consisting of the names of the first five World Series winners. Figure 4.2 shows the array created by the program.

```
'Create array for five strings
Dim teamName(1 To 5) As String    'in (Declarations) section of (General)

Private Sub cmdWhoWon_Click()
  Dim n As Integer
  'Fill array with World Series Winners
  teamName(1) = "Red Sox"
  teamName(2) = "Giants"
  teamName(3) = "White Sox"
  teamName(4) = "Cubs"
  teamName(5) = "Cubs"
  'Access array of five strings
  n = Val(txtNumber.Text)
  picWinner.Cls
  picWinner.Print "The "; teamName(n); " won World Series number"; n
End Sub
```

[Run, type 2 into the text box, and click the command button.]

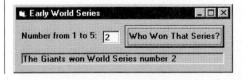

	teamName(1)	teamName(2)	teamName(3)	teamName(4)	teamName(5)
teamName( )	Red Sox	Giants	White Sox	Cubs	Cubs

Figure 4.2 The array *teamName( )* of Example 1.

In Example 1, the array *teamName* was assigned values within the cmdWhoWon_Click event procedure. Every time the command button is clicked, the values are reassigned to the array. This manner of assigning values to an array can be very inefficient, especially in programs with large arrays where the task of the program (in Example 1, looking up a fact) may be repeated numerous times for different user input. When, as in Example 1, the data to be placed in an array are known at the time the program first begins to run, a more efficient location for the statements that fill the array is in Visual Basic's **Form_Load** event procedure. The Form_Load event procedure is executed by Visual Basic once as soon as the program is run, and this execution is guaranteed to occur before the execution of any other event or general procedure in the program. Example 2 uses the Form_Load procedure to improve on Example 1.

EXAMPLE 2   Modify Example 1 to request the name of a baseball team as input and search the array to determine whether or not the team name appears in the array. Load the array values only once.

```
'Create array for five strings
Dim teamName(1 To 5) As String  'in (Declarations) section of (General)

Private Sub cmdDidTheyWin_Click()
  Dim team As String, foundFlag As Boolean, n As Integer
  'Search for an entry in a list of strings
  team = txtName.Text
  foundFlag = False
  n = 0
  Do
    n = n + 1
    If UCase(teamName(n)) = UCase(team) Then
        foundFlag = True
    End If
  Loop Until (foundFlag = True) Or (n = 5)
  'Above line can be replaced with Loop Until (foundFlag) or (n = 5)
  picWinner.Cls
  If foundFlag = False Then    'Can be replaced by If Not foundFlag
      picWinner.Print "The "; team; " did not win any";
      picWinner.Print " of the first five World Series."
    Else
      picWinner.Print "The "; teamName(n); " won World Series number"; n
  End If
End Sub

Private Sub Form_Load()
  'Fill array with World Series winners
  teamName(1) = "Red Sox"
  teamName(2) = "Giants"
  teamName(3) = "White Sox"
  teamName(4) = "Cubs"
  teamName(5) = "Cubs"
End Sub
```

[Run, type White Sox into the text box, and click the command button.]

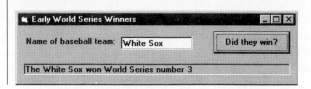

We could have written the program in Example 2 with a For...Next loop beginning For n = 1 To 5. However, such a loop would unnecessarily search the entire list when the sought-after item were found early. The wasted time could be significant for a large array.

In some applications, arrays are needed only temporarily to help a procedure complete a task. Visual Basic also allows us to create array variables that are local to a specific procedure and that exist temporarily while the procedure is executing. If the statement

```
Dim arrayName(1 To n) As varType
```

is placed inside an event procedure, then space for n subscripted variables is set aside in memory each time the procedure is invoked and released when the procedure is exited.

In Example 1, values were assigned to the elements of the array with assignment statements. However, data for large arrays are more often stored in a data file and read with Input # statements. Example 3 uses this technique. Also, because the task of the program is likely to be performed only once during a run of the program, a local array is used.

EXAMPLE 3 Table 4.1 gives names and test scores from a mathematics contest given in 1953. Write a program to display the names of the students scoring above the average for these eight students.

Richard Dolen	135		Paul H. Monsky	150
Geraldine Ferraro	114		Max A. Plager	114
James B. Fraser	92		Robert A. Schade	91
John H. Maltby	91		Barbara M. White	124

Table 4.1 The top scores on the Fourth Annual Mathematics Contest Sponsored by the Metropolitan NY section of the MAA.

Source: The Mathematics Teacher, February 1953.

SOLUTION The following program creates a string array to hold the names of the contestants and a numeric array to hold the scores. The first element of each array holds data for the first contestant, the second element of each array holds data for the second contestant, and so on. See Figure 4.3. Note that the two arrays can be dimensioned in a single Dim statement by placing a comma between the array declarations.

```
Private Sub cmdShow_Click()
  Dim total As Integer, student As Integer, average As Single
  'Create arrays for names and scores
  Dim nom(1 To 8) As String, score(1 To 8) As Integer
  'Assume the data has been placed in the file "Scores.txt"
  '(The first line of the file is "Richard Dolen", 135)
  Open "Scores.txt" For Input As #1
  For student = 1 To 8
    Input #1, nom(student), score(student)
  Next student
  Close #1
  'Analyze exam scores
  total = 0
  For student = 1 To 8
    total = total + score(student)
  Next student
  average = total / 8
  'Display all names with above-average grades
  picTopStudents.Cls
  For student = 1 To 8
    If score(student) > average Then
        picTopStudents.Print nom(student)
    End If
  Next student
End Sub
```

[Run, and click the command button.]

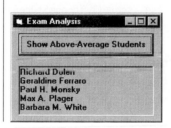

	nom(1)	nom(2)	. . .	nom(8)
nom( )	Richard Dolen	Geraldine Ferraro	. . .	Barbara M. White

	score(1)	score(2)	. . .	score(8)
score( )	135	114	. . .	124

Figure 4.3 Arrays created by Example 3.

In Example 3, the number of students to be processed had to be known at the time the program was written. In actual practice, the amount of data that a program will be processing is not known in advance. Programs should be flexible and incorporate a method for handling varying amounts of data. Visual Basic makes this possible with the statement

```
ReDim arrayName (1 to n) As varType
```

which can use variables or expressions when indicating the subscript range. However, ReDim statements can only be used inside procedures.

EXAMPLE 4 | The following program reworks Example 3 for the case when the amount of data is not known in advance.

```
Private Sub cmdShow_Click()
  Dim numStudents As Integer, nTemp As String, sTemp As Integer
  Dim student As Integer, total As Integer, average As Single
  'Determine amount of data to be processed
  numStudents = 0
  Open "Scores.txt" For Input As #1
  Do While Not EOF(1)
    Input #1, nTemp, sTemp
    numStudents = numStudents + 1
  Loop
  Close #1
  'Create arrays for names and scores
  ReDim nom(1 To numStudents) As String, score(1 To numStudents) As Integer
  Open "Scores.txt" For Input As #1
  For student = 1 To numStudents
    Input #1, nom(student), score(student)
  Next student
  Close #1
  'Analyze exam scores
  total = 0
  For student = 1 To numStudents
    total = total + score(student)
  Next student
  average = total / numStudents
  'Display all names with above-average grades
  picTopStudents.Cls
  For student = 1 To numStudents
    If score(student) > average Then
        picTopStudents.Print nom(student)
    End If
  Next student
End Sub
```

An alternative approach to program flexibility that does not require reading the data file twice is to require that the data file begin with a line that holds the number of records to be processed. If Scores.txt is modified by adding a new first line that gives the number of students, then the 4th through 18th lines of Example 4 can be replaced with

```
'Create arrays for names and scores
Open "Scores.txt" For Input As #1
Input #1, numStudents
ReDim nom(1 To numStudents) As String, score(1 To numStudents) As Integer
For student = 1 To numStudents
  Input #1, nom(student), score(student)
Next student
Close #1
```

The range of an array need not just begin with 1. A statement of the form

```
Dim arrayName(m To n) As varType
```

where m is less than or equal to n, creates an array with elements *arrayName*(m), *arrayName*($m + 1$), *arrayName*($m + 2$), . . . , *arrayName*(n). The same holds for ReDim.

In Example 4, the ReDim statement allowed us to create arrays whose size was not known before the program was run. On the other hand, the arrays that were created were local to the event procedure cmdShow_Click. Many applications require form-level arrays whose size is not known in advance. Unfortunately, Dim statements cannot use variables or expressions to specify the subscript range. The solution offered by Visual Basic is to allow the (Declarations) section of (General) to contain Dim statements of the form

```
Dim arrayName() As varType
```

where no range for the subscripts of the array is specified. An array created in this manner will be form-level but cannot be used until a ReDim statement is executed in a procedure to establish the range of subscripts. The "As *varType*" clause can be omitted from the ReDim statement.

EXAMPLE 5   The first World Series was held in 1903 and has been held in most subsequent years. Suppose the file Winners.txt contains the outcome for each year The first four lines of the file are "Red Sox"; "(no series)"; "Giants"; "White Sox". Write a program to display the years, if any, of the World Series that were won by the team specified by the user.

```
'Create form-level array
Dim teamName() As String
Dim lastYear As Integer      'Last year recorded in Winners.txt

Private Sub cmdDidTheyWin_Click()
  Dim teamToFind As String, numWon As Integer, series As Integer
  'Search for World Series won by user's team
  teamToFind = UCase(txtName.Text)
  picSeriesWon.Cls
```

```
   For series = 1903 To lastYear
     If UCase(teamName(series)) = teamToFind Then
         numWon = numWon + 1
         If numWon = 1 Then
             picSeriesWon.Print "The "; teamName(series);
             picSeriesWon.Print " won the following World Series: ";
           Else
             'Separate from previous
             picSeriesWon.Print ",";
             If (numWon = 5) Or (numWon = 16) Then
                 'Start a new line at 5th and 16th win
                 picSeriesWon.Print
             End If
         End If
         picSeriesWon.Print Str(series);
     End If
   Next series
   If numWon = 0 Then
       picSeriesWon.Print "The "; teamToFind; " did not win any World Series."
   End If
End Sub

Private Sub Form_Load()
  Dim series As Integer, team As String
  'Determine the last year recorded in the file Winners.txt
  lastYear = 1902
  Open "Winners.txt" For Input As #1
  Do While Not EOF(1)
    Input #1, team
    lastYear = lastYear + 1
  Loop
  Close #1
  'Fill array with World Series winners
  Open "Winners.txt" For Input As #1
  ReDim teamName(1903 To lastYear)
  For series = 1903 To lastYear
    Input #1, teamName(series)       .
  Next series
  Close #1
End Sub
```

[Run, type Yankees into the text box, and click the command button.]

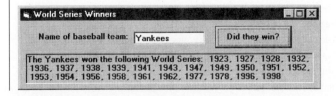

Comments

1. Arrays must be dimensioned in a Dim or ReDim statement before they are used. If a statement such as $a(6) = 3$ appears without a previous Dim or ReDim of the array $a(\ )$, then the error message "Sub or Function not defined" will be displayed when an attempt is made to run the program.

2. Subscripts in ReDim statements can be numeric expressions. Subscripts whose values are not whole numbers are rounded to the nearest whole number. Subscripts outside the range of the array produce an error message as shown below when the last line inside the event procedure is reached.

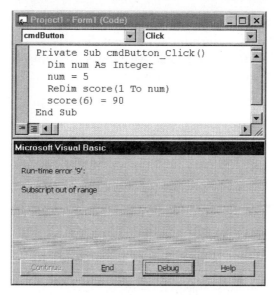

3. The two arrays in Example 3 are referred to as **parallel arrays** because subscripted variables having the same subscript are related.

4. The integers m and n in the statement Dim *arrayName*(m To n) As *varType* can be positive, negative, or zero. The only restriction is that m cannot be greater than n. The same holds true for ReDim statements.

5. Until a value is assigned to an element of an array, the element has its default value. Numeric variables have a default value of 0, and string variables have the default value "", the empty string.

6. The statement Dim *arrayName*(0 To n) As *varType* can be replaced by the statement Dim *arrayName*(n) As *varType*. The same holds for the ReDim statement.

7. An array that is not dimensioned in the (Declarations) section of (General) but rather is declared in a procedure is local to that procedure and unknown in all other procedures. However, an entire local array can be passed to another procedure. The name of the array, followed by an empty set of parentheses, must appear as an argument in the calling statement, and an array variable name of the same type must appear as a corresponding parameter in the procedure definition of the procedure that is to receive the array.

✔ **PRACTICE PROBLEMS 4.1**

1. When should arrays be used to hold data?

2. (a) Give an appropriate Dim statement to declare a string array to hold the names of the *Time* magazine "Man of the Year" awards for the years 1980 through 1989.
   (b) Write a statement to assign to the array element for 1982 the name of that year's winner, "The Computer".

➤ **EXERCISES 4.1**

In Exercises 1 to 6, determine the output displayed in the picture box when the command button is clicked. All Dim statements for arrays are in the (Declarations) section of (General).

1.
```
Dim a(1 To 20) As Integer

Private Sub cmdDisplay_Click()
  a(5) = 1
  a(10) = 2
  a(15) = 7
  picOutput.Print a(5) + a(10);
  picOutput.Print a(5 + 10);
  picOutput.Print a(20)
End Sub
```

2.
```
Dim sq(1 To 5) As Integer

Private Sub cmdDisplay_Click()
  Dim i As Integer, t As Integer
  For i = 1 To 5
    sq(i) = i * i
  Next i
  picOutput.Print sq(3)
  t = 3
  picOutput.Print sq(5 - t)
End Sub
```

3.
```
Dim fh(1 To 4) As String

Private Sub cmdDisplay_Click()
  Dim i As Integer, n As Integer
  Open "Horsemen.txt" For Input As #1
  For i = 1 To 4
    Input #1, fh(i)
  Next i
  Close #1
  picOutput.Print fh(4)
  n = 1
  picOutput.Print fh(2 * n + 1)
End Sub
```

(Assume that the file Horsemen.txt contains the following entries.)

"Miller", "Layden", "Crowley", "Stuhldreher"

4.
```
Dim s(1 To 4) As Integer

Private Sub cmdDisplay_Click()
  Dim t As Integer, k As Integer
  Open "Data.txt" For Input As #1
  t = 0
  For k = 1 To 4
    Input #1, s(k)
    t = t + s(k)
  Next k
```

```
    picOutput.Print t
    Close #1
End Sub
```

(Assume that the file Data.txt contains the following entries: 3, 5, 2, 1)

5. `Dim p(1 To 6) As Integer`

```
Private Sub cmdDisplay_Click()
  Dim k As Integer
  Open "Data.txt" For Input As #1
  For k = 1 To 6
    Input #1, p(k)
  Next k
  Close #1
  For k = 6 To 1 Step -1
    picOutput.Print p(k);
  Next k
End Sub
```

(Assume that the file Data.txt contains the following entries: 4, 3, 11, 9, 2, 6)

6. `Dim a(1 To 4) As Integer`
`Dim b(1 To 4) As Integer`
`Dim c(1 To 4) As Integer`

```
Private Sub cmdDisplay_Click()
  Dim i As Integer
  Open "Data.txt" For Input As #1
  For i = 1 To 4
    Input #1, a(i), b(i)
  Next i
  Close #1
  For i = 1 To 4
    c(i) = a(i) * b(i)
    picOutput.Print c(i);
  Next i
End Sub
```

(Assume that the file Data.txt contains the following entries: 2, 5, 3, 4, 1, 3, 7, 2)

In Exercises 7 to 12, identify the errors.

7. `Dim companies(1 To 100) As String`

```
Private Sub Form_Load()
  Dim recCount As Integer, i As Integer
  Open "Complist.txt" For Input As #1
  Input #1, recCount
  ReDim companies(1 To recCount) As String
  For i = 1 To recCount
    Input #1, companies(i)
  Next i
  Close #1
End Sub
```

8.
```
Dim p(1 To 100) As Single

Private Sub cmdDisplay_Click()
  Dim i As Integer
  For i = 1 To 200
    p(i) = i / 2
  Next i
End Sub
```

9.
```
Dim a(1 To 10) As Integer

Private Sub cmdDisplay_Click()
  Dim i As Integer, k As Integer
  Open "Data.txt" For Input As #1
  For i = 1 To 9
    Input #1, a(i)
  Next i
  Close #1
  For k = 1 To 9
    a(k) = a(5 - k)
  Next k
End Sub
```
(Assume that the file Data.txt contains the following entries.)

1, 2, 3, 4, 5, 6, 7, 8, 9

10.
```
maxRecords = 100
Dim patients(1 To maxRecords) As String

Private Sub cmdDisplay_Click()
  Dim recCount As Integer, i As Integer
  Open "Patients.txt" For Input As #1
  recCount = 0
  Do While (Not EOF(1)) And (recCount < maxRecords)
    recCount = recCount + 1
    Input #1, patients(recCount)
  Loop
  Close #1
  picOutput.Cls
  picOutput.Print recCount; "records were read"
End Sub
```

11.
```
Dim b(2 To 8 Step 2) As Integer

Private Sub cmdDisplay_Click()
  Dim t As Integer
  Open "Data.txt" For Input As #1
  For t = 2 To 8 Step 2
    Input #1, b(t)
  Next t
  Close #1
End Sub
```
(Assume that the file Data.txt contains the following entries.)

1, 4, 8, 19

12. Dim names()

```
Private Sub Form_Load
  Dim i As Integer, recCount As Integer
  Open "Data.txt" For Input As #1
  Input #1, recCount
  ReDim names(1 to recCount) As String
  For i = 1 to recCount
    Input #1, names(i)
  Next i
  Close #1
End Sub
```

(Assume that the file Data.txt contains the following entries.)

3, "Tom", "Dick", "Harry"

13. Assuming the array *river*( ) is as shown below, fill in the empty rectangles to show the progressing status of *river*( ) after the execution of each program segment.

	river(1)	river(2)	river(3)	river(4)	river(5)
river( )	Nile	Ohio	Amazon	Volga	Thames

```
temp = river(1)
river(1) = river(5)
river(5) = temp
```

	river(1)	river(2)	river(3)	river(4)	river(5)
river( )					

```
temp = river(1)
For i = 1 To 4
  river(i) = river(i + 1)
Next i
river(5) = temp
```

	river(1)	river(2)	river(3)	river(4)	river(5)
river( )					

14. Assuming the array *cat*( ) is as shown below, fill in the empty rectangles to show the final status of *cat*( ) after executing the nested loops.

	cat(1)	cat(2)	cat(3)	cat(4)
cat( )	Morris	Garfield	Socks	Felix

```
For i = 1 To 3
  For j = 1 To 4 - i
    If cat(j) > cat(j + 1) Then
        temp = cat(j)
        cat(j) = cat(j + 1)
        cat(j + 1) = temp
    End If
  Next j
Next i
```

	cat(1)	cat(2)	cat(3)	cat(4)
cat( )				

15. The subscripted variables of the array $a(\ )$ have the following values: $a(1) = 6$, $a(2) = 3$, $a(3) = 1$, $a(4) = 2$, $a(5) = 5$, $a(6) = 8$, $a(7) = 7$. Suppose $i = 2$, $j = 4$, and $k = 5$. What values will n have when the following assignment statements are executed?

(a) `n = a(k) - a(i)`

(b) `n = a(k - i) + a(k - j)`

(c) `n = a(k) * a(i + 2)`

(d) `n = a(j - i) * a(i)`

16. The array *monthName( )* holds the following three-character strings.

`monthName(1)="Jan", monthName(2)="Feb", ..., monthName(12)="Dec"`

(a) What is displayed by the following statement?

`picMonth.Print monthName(4), monthName(9)`

(b) What value is assigned to *winter* by the following statement?

`winter = monthName(12) & "," & monthName(1) & "," & monthName(2)`

17. Modify the program in Example 3 to display each student's name and the number of points by which his or her score differs from the average.

18. Modify the program in Example 3 to display only the name(s) of the student(s) with the highest score.

In Exercises 19 to 30, write a line of code or program segment to complete the stated task.

19. Inside a procedure, dimension the string array *bestPicture( )* to have subscripts ranging from 1975 to 1995.

20. In the (Declarations) section of (General), dimension the string array *info( )* to have subscripts ranging from 10 to 100.

21. Dimension the string array *marx( )* with subscripts ranging from 1 to 4 so that the array is visible to all parts of the program. Assign the four values Chico, Harpo, Groucho, and Zeppo to the array as soon as the program is run.

22. Dimension the string array *stooges( )* with subscripts ranging from 1 to 3 so that the array is visible only to the event procedure cmdStooges_Click. Assign the three values Moe, Larry, Curly to the array as soon as the command button is clicked.

23. The arrays $a(\ )$ and $b(\ )$ have been dimensioned to have range 1 to 4, and values have been assigned to $a(1)$ to $a(4)$. Reverse the order of these values, and store them in $b(\ )$.

24. Given two arrays, $p(\ )$ and $q(\ )$, each with range 1 to 20, compute the sum of the products of the corresponding array elements, that is,

```
p(1)*q(1) + p(2)*q(2) + ... + p(20)*q(20)
```

25. Display the values of the array $a(\ )$ of range 1 to 30 in five columns as shown below.

```
a(1)    a(2)    a(3)    a(4)    a(5)
a(6)    a(7)    a(8)    a(9)    a(10)
  .       .       .       .       .
  .       .       .       .       .
a(26)   a(27)   a(28)   a(29)   a(30)
```

26. A list of 20 integers, all between 1 and 10, is contained in a data file. Determine how many times each integer appears and have the program display the frequency of each integer.

27. Compare two arrays $a(\ )$ and $b(\ )$ of range 1 to 10 to see if they hold identical values, that is, if $a(i) = b(i)$ for all i.

28. Calculate the sum of the entries with odd subscripts in an array $a(\ )$ of range 1 to 9.

29. Twelve exam grades are stored in the array $grades(\ )$. Curve the grades by adding 7 points to each grade.

30. Read 10 numbers contained in a data file into an array and then display three columns as follows: Column 1 should contain the original 10 numbers, column 2 should contain these numbers in reverse order, and column 3 should contain the averages of the corresponding numbers in columns 1 and 2.

31. Thirty scores, each lying between 0 and 49, are given in a data file. Write a program that uses these scores to create an array $frequency(\ )$ as follows:

```
frequency(1) = # of scores < 10
frequency(2) = # of scores such that 10 <= score < 20
frequency(3) = # of scores such that 20 <= score < 30
frequency(4) = # of scores such that 30 <= score < 40
frequency(5) = # of scores such that 40 <= score < 50.
```

The program should then display the results in tabular form as follows:

Interval	Frequency
0 to 9	frequency(1)
10 to 19	frequency(2)
20 to 29	frequency(3)
30 to 39	frequency(4)
40 to 49	frequency(5)

32. Given the following flight schedule,

Flight #	Origin	Destination	Departure Time
117	Tucson	Dallas	8:45 a.m.
239	LA	Boston	10:15 a.m.
298	Albany	Reno	1:35 p.m.
326	Houston	New York	2:40 p.m.
445	New York	Tampa	4:20 p.m.

write a program to load this information into four arrays of range 1 to 5, *flightNum( )*, *orig( )*, *dest( )*, and *deptTime( )*, and ask the user to specify a flight number. Have the computer find the flight number, and display the information corresponding to that flight. Account for the case where the user requests a nonexistent flight.

33. Table 4.2 contains the names and number of units of the top 10 pizza chains in 1997. Write a program to place these data into a pair of parallel arrays, compute the total number of units for these 10 chains, and display a table giving the name and percentage of total units for each of the companies.

Name	Units	Name	Units
1. Pizza Hut	14,400	6. Godfather's	554
2. Domino's	5,950	7. Chuck E. Cheese	312
3. Little Caesar's	4,300	8. Picadilly Circus	680
4. Papa John's	1,517	9. Pizza Inn	514
5. Round Table	539	10. California Pizza Kitchen	80

Table 4.2 Top 10 pizza chains for 1997 (and numbers of units).
Source: Restaurants & Institutions, July 1998

34. A retail store has five bins, numbered 1 to 5, each containing a different commodity. At the beginning of a particular day, each bin contains 45 items. Table 4.3 shows the cost per item for each of the bins and the quantity sold during that day.

Bin	Cost per Item	Quantity Sold
1	3.00	10
2	12.25	30
3	37.45	9
4	7.49	42
5	24.95	17

Table 4.3 Costs of items and quantities sold for Exercise 34.

Write a program to

(a) Place the cost per item and the quantity sold from each bin into parallel arrays.
(b) Display a table giving the inventory at the end of the day and the amount of revenue obtained from each bin.
(c) Compute the total revenue for the day.
(d) List the number of each bin that contains fewer than 20 items at the end of the day.

35. Write a program that asks the user for a month by number and then displays the name of that month. For instance, if the user inputs 2, the program should display February. *Hint:* Create an array of 12 strings, one for each month of the year.

✔✔ **Solutions to Practice Problems 4.1**

1. Arrays should be used when

(a) Several pieces of data of the same type will be entered by the user.

(b) Computations must be made on the items in a data file *after* all of the items have been read.

(c) Lists of corresponding data are being analyzed.

2. (a) `Dim manOfTheYear(1980 To 1989) As String`

    (b) `manOfTheYear(1982) = "The Computer"`

4.2 SORTING AND SEARCHING

Ordered Arrays

An array is said to be **ordered** if its values are in either ascending or descending order. The following arrays illustrate the different types of ordered and unordered arrays. In an ascending ordered array, the value of each element is less than or equal to the value of the next element. That is,

$$[\text{each element}] \le [\text{next element}]$$

For string arrays, the ANSI table is used to evaluate the "less than or equal to" condition.

Ordered Ascending Numeric Array

dates( )	1492	1776	1812	1929	1969

Ordered Descending Numeric Array

discov( )	1610	1541	1513	1513	1492

Ordered Ascending String Array

king( )	Edward	Henry	James	John	Kong

Ordered Descending String Array

lake( )	Superior	Ontario	Michigan	Huron	Erie

Unordered Numeric Array

rates( )	8.25	5.00	7.85	8.00	6.50

Unordered String Array

char( )	G	R	E	A	T

A **sort** is an algorithm for ordering an array. Of the many different techniques for sorting an array we discuss the **bubble sort**. It requires the swapping of values stored in a pair of variables. If *var1*, *var2*, and *temp* are all variables of the same type (that is, all numeric or all string), then the statements

```
temp = var1
var1 = var2
var2 = temp
```

assign *var1*'s value to *var2*, and *var2*'s value to *var1*.

EXAMPLE 1   Write a program to alphabetize two words supplied in text boxes.

SOLUTION

```
Private Sub cmdAlphabetize_Click()
  Dim firstWord As String, secondWord As String, temp As String
  'Alphabetize two words
  firstWord = txtFirstWord.Text
  secondWord = txtSecondWord.Text
  If firstWord > secondWord Then
      temp = firstWord
      firstWord = secondWord
      secondWord = temp
  End If
  picResult.Cls
  picResult.Print firstWord; " before "; secondWord
End Sub
```

[Run, type the following text shown into the text boxes, and click the command button.]

Bubble Sort

The bubble sort is an algorithm that compares adjacent items and swaps those that are out of order. If this process is repeated enough times, the list will be ordered. Let's carry out this process on the list Pebbles, Barney, Wilma, Fred, Dino. The steps for each pass through the list are as follows:

1. Compare the first and second items. If they are out of order, swap them.

2. Compare the second and third items. If they are out of order, swap them.

3. Repeat this pattern for all remaining pairs. The final comparison and possible swap are between the next to last and last elements.

The first time through the list, this process is repeated to the end of the list. This is called the first pass. After the first pass, the last item (Wilma) will be in its proper position. Therefore, the second pass does not have to consider it and so requires one less comparison. At the end of the second pass, the last two items will be in their proper position. (The items that must have reached their proper position have been underlined.) Each successive pass requires one less comparison. After four passes, the last four items will be in their proper positions, and, hence, the first will be also.

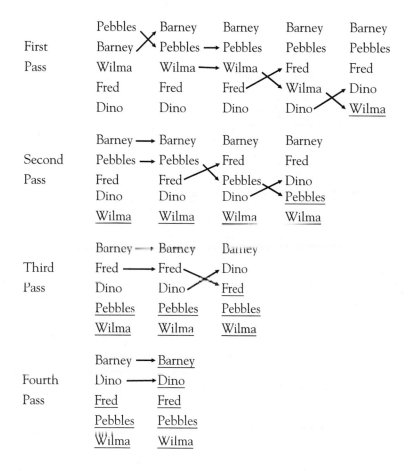

EXAMPLE 2

SOLUTION

Write a program to alphabetize the names Pebbles, Barney, Wilma, Fred, Dino.

Sorting the list requires a pair of nested loops. The inner loop performs a single pass, and the outer loop controls the number of passes.

```
Dim nom(1 To 5) As String

Private Sub cmdSort_Click()
  Dim passNum As Integer, i As Integer, temp As String
  'Bubble sort names
  For passNum = 1 To 4     'Number of passes is 1 less than number of items
    For i = 1 To 5 - passNum            'Each pass needs 1 less comparison
      If nom(i) > nom(i + 1) Then
          temp = nom(i)
          nom(i) = nom(i + 1)
          nom(i + 1) = temp
      End If
```

```
      Next i
    Next passNum
    'Display alphabetized list
    picNames.Cls
    For i = 1 To 5
      picNames.Print nom(i),
    Next i
End Sub

Private Sub Form_Load()
  'Fill array with names
  nom(1) = "Pebbles"
  nom(2) = "Barney"
  nom(3) = "Wilma"
  nom(4) = "Fred"
  nom(5) = "Dino"
End Sub
```

[Run, and click the command button.]

EXAMPLE 3   Table 4.4 contains facts about the 10 most populous metropolitan areas with listings in ascending order by city name. Sort the table in descending order by population.

Metro Area	Population in Millions	Median Income per Household	% Native to State	% Advanced Degree
Boston	4.2	$40,666	73	12
Chicago	8.1	$35,918	73	8
Dallas	3.9	$32,825	64	8
Detroit	4.7	$34,729	76	7
Houston	3.7	$31,488	67	8
Los Angeles	14.5	$36,711	59	8
New York	18.1	$38,445	73	11
Philadelphia	5.9	$35,797	70	8
San Francisco	6.3	$41,459	60	11
Washington	3.9	$47,254	32	17

Note: Column 4 gives the percentage of residents who were born in their current state of residence. Column 5 gives the percentage of residents age 25 or older with a graduate or professional degree.

Table 4.4 The 10 most populous metropolitan areas.
Source: The 1990 Census.

SOLUTION   Data are read from a file into parallel arrays by the Form_Load event procedure. When cmdDisplayStats is clicked, the collection of parallel arrays is sorted based on the array *pop*( ). Each time two items are interchanged in the array *pop*( ), the corresponding items are interchanged in each of the other arrays. This way, for each city, the items of information remain linked by a common subscript.

```
Dim city(1 To 10) As String, pop(1 To 10) As Single, income(1 To 10) As Single
Dim natives(1 To 10) As Single, advDeg(1 To 10) As Single

Private Sub cmdDisplayStats_Click()
  Call SortData
  Call ShowData
End Sub

Private Sub Form_Load()
  Dim j As Integer
  'Assume that the data for city name, population, medium income, % native,
  'and % advanced degree have been placed in the file "Citystat.txt"
  '(First line of file is "Boston",4.2,40666,73,12)
  Open "Citystat.txt" For Input As #1
  For j = 1 To 10
    Input #1, city(j), pop(j), income(j), natives(j), advDeg(j)
  Next j
  Close #1
End Sub

Private Sub ShowData()
  Dim j As Integer
  'Display ordered table
  picTable.Cls
  picTable.Print , "Pop. in", "Med. income", "% Native", "% Advanced"
  picTable.Print "Metro Area", "millions", "per hsd", "to State", "Degree"
  picTable.Print
  For j = 1 To 10
    picTable.Print city(j); Tab(16); pop(j), income(j), natives(j), advDeg(j)
  Next j
End Sub

Private Sub SortData()
  Dim passNum As Integer, index As Integer
  'Bubble sort table in descending order by population
  For passNum = 1 To 9
    For index = 1 To 10 - passNum
      If pop(index) < pop(index + 1) Then
          Call SwapData(index)
      End If
    Next index
  Next passNum
End Sub

Private Sub SwapData(index As Integer)
  'Swap entries
  Call SwapStr(city(index), city(index + 1))
  Call SwapNum(pop(index), pop(index + 1))
  Call SwapNum(income(index), income(index + 1))
  Call SwapNum(natives(index), natives(index + 1))
  Call SwapNum(advDeg(index), advDeg(index + 1))
End Sub
```

```
Private Sub SwapNum(a As Single, b As Single)
  Dim temp As Single
  'Interchange values of a and b
  temp = a
  a = b
  b = temp
End Sub

Private Sub SwapStr(a As String, b As String)
  Dim temp As String
  'Interchange values of a and b
  temp = a
  a = b
  b = temp
End Sub
```

[Run, and click the command button.]

Metropolitan Statistics				
Display Statistics on 10 Most Populous Metropolitan Areas				
Metro Area	Pop. in millions	Med. income per hsd	% Native to State	% Advanced Degree
New York	18.1	38445	73	11
Los Angeles	14.5	36711	59	8
Chicago	8.1	35918	73	8
San Francisco	6.3	41459	60	11
Philadelphia	5.9	35797	70	8
Detroit	4.7	34729	76	7
Boston	4.2	40666	73	12
Dallas	3.9	32825	64	8
Washington	3.9	47254	32	17
Houston	3.7	31488	67	8

Searching

Suppose we had an array of 1000 names in alphabetical order and wanted to locate a specific person in the list. One approach would be to start with the first name and consider each name until a match was found. This process is called a **sequential search**. We would find a person whose name begins with "A" rather quickly, but 1000 comparisons might be necessary to find a person whose name begins with "Z". For much longer lists, searching could be a time-consuming matter. However, there is a method, called a **binary search**, that shortens the task considerably.

Let us refer to the sought item as *quarry*. The binary search looks for *quarry* by determining in which half of the list it lies. The other half is then discarded, and the retained half is temporarily regarded as the entire list. The process is repeated until the item is found. A flag can indicate if *quarry* has been found.

The algorithm for a binary search of an ascending list is as follows (Figure 4.5 shows the flowchart for a binary search):

1. At each stage, denote the subscript of the first item in the retained list by *first* and the subscript of the last item by *last*. Initially, the value of *first* is 1, the value of *last* is the number of items in the list, and the value of *flag* is False.

2. Look at the middle item of the current list, the item having the subscript $middle = \mathrm{Int}((first + last) / 2)$.

3. If the middle item is *quarry*, then *flag* is set to True and the search is over.

4. If the middle item is greater than *quarry*, then *quarry* should be in the first half of the list. So the subscript of *quarry* must lie between *first* and *middle* − 1. That is, the new value of *last* is *middle* − 1.

5. If the middle item is less than *quarry*, then *quarry* should be in the second half of the list of possible items. So the subscript of *quarry* must lie between *middle* + 1 and *last*. That is, the new value of *first* is *middle* + 1.

6. Repeat Steps 2 to 5 until *quarry* is found or until the halving process uses up the entire list. (When the entire list has been used up, *first* > *last*.) In the second case, *quarry* was not in the original list.

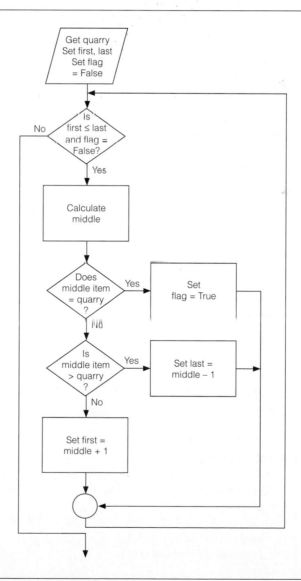

Figure 4.5 Flowchart for a binary search.

EXAMPLE 4 | In the following program, the array *firm( )* contains the alphabetized names of up to 100 corporations. The program requests the name of a corporation as input and uses a binary search to determine whether or not the corporation is in the array.

```
Dim firm(1 To 100) As String
Dim numFirms As Integer

Private Sub BinarySearch(corp As String, result As String)
  Dim foundFlag As Boolean
  Dim first As Integer, middle As Integer, last As Integer
  'Array firm() assumed already ordered alphabetically
  'Binary search of firm() for corp
  foundFlag = False
  first = 1
  last = numFirms
  Do While (first <= last) And (Not foundFlag)
    middle = Int((first + last) / 2)
    Select Case UCase(firm(middle))
      Case corp
        foundFlag = True
      Case Is > corp
        last = middle - 1
      Case Is < corp
        first = middle + 1
    End Select
  Loop
  If foundFlag Then
      result = "found"
    Else
      result = "not found"
  End If
End Sub

Private Sub cmdSearch_Click()
  Dim corp As String, result As String
  corp = UCase(Trim(txtCorporation.Text))
  Call BinarySearch(corp, result)
  'Display results of search
  picResult.Cls
  picResult.Print corp; " "; result
End Sub

Private Sub Form_Load()
  'Fill array with data from FIRMS.TXT
  Open "Firms.txt" For Input As #1
  numFirms = 0
  Do While (Not EOF(1)) And (numFirms < 100)
    numFirms = numFirms + 1
    Input #1, firm(numFirms)
  Loop
End Sub
```

[Run, type IBM into the text box, and click the command button.]

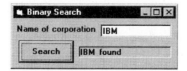

Suppose the array contains 100 corporations and the corporation input in Example 4 is in the second half of the array. On the first pass, *middle* would be assigned Int((1 + 100)/2) = Int(50.5) = 50, and then *first* would be altered to 50 + 1 = 51. On the second pass, *middle* would be assigned Int((51 + 100)/2) = Int(75.5) = 75. If the corporation is not the array element with subscript 75, then either *last* would be assigned 74 or *first* would be assigned 76, depending on whether the corporation appears before or after the 75th element. Each pass through the loop halves the range of subscripts containing the corporation until the corporation is located.

In Example 4, the binary search merely reported whether or not an array contained a certain item. After finding the item, its array subscript was not needed. However, if related data are stored in parallel arrays (as in Table 4.4), the subscript of the found item can be used to retrieve the related information in the other arrays. This process is called a **table lookup**.

Comments

1. In Example 3, parallel arrays already ordered by one field were sorted by another field. Usually, parallel arrays are sorted by the field to be searched when accessing the file. This field is called the **key field**.

2. Suppose an array of 2000 items is searched sequentially—that is, one item after another—in order to locate a specific item. The number of comparisons would vary from 1 to 2000, with an average of 1000. With a binary search, the number of comparisons would be at most 11 because $2^{11} > 2000$.

3. The built-in function UCase converts all the characters in a string to uppercase. UCase is useful in sorting and searching arrays of strings when the alphabetic case (upper or lower) is unimportant. For instance, Example 4 includes UCase in the Select Case comparisons, and so the binary search will locate "Mobil" in the array even if the user entered "MOBIL".

✔ PRACTICE PROBLEMS 4.2

1. The pseudocode for a bubble sort of an array of *n* items follows. Why is the terminating value of the outer loop $n - 1$ and the terminating value of the inner loop $n - j$?

```
For j = 1 To n - 1
  For k = 1 To n - j
    If [kth and (k+1)st items are out of order] Then [interchange them]
  Next k
Next j
```

2. Complete the table below by filling in the values of each variable after successive passes of a binary search of a list of 20 items, where the sought item is in the 13th position.

First	Last	Middle
1	20	10
11	20	

EXERCISES 4.2

In Exercises 1 and 2, decide if the array is ordered.

1. month()

January	February	March	April	May

2. pres()

Adams	Adams	Bush	Johnson	Johnson

In Exercises 3 to 6, determine the output displayed in the picture box when the command button is clicked.

3.
```
Private Sub cmdDisplay_Click()
    Dim p As Integer, q As Integer, temp As Integer
    p = 100
    q = 200
    temp = p
    p = q
    q = temp
    picOutput.Print p; q
End Sub
```

4.
```
Dim gag(1 To 2) As String

Private Sub cmdDisplay_Click()
  If gag(2) < gag(1) Then
     Dim temp As String
     temp = gag(2)
     gag(2) = gag(1)
     gag(1) = temp
  End If
  picOutput.Print gag(1), gag(2)
End Sub

Private Sub Form_Load()
  Open "Data.txt" For Input As #1
  Input #1, gag(1), gag(2)
  Close #1
End Sub
```
(Assume that the file Data.txt contains the following entries.)

"Stan", "Oliver"

5.
```
Private Sub cmdDisplay_Click()
    Dim x As Single, y As Single, temp As Single
    Dim swappedFlag As Boolean
    Open "Data.txt" For Input As #1
    Input #1, x, y
    Close #1
    swappedFlag = False
    If y > x Then
        temp = x
        x = y
        y = temp
        swappedFlag = True
    End If
    picOutput.Print x; y;
    If swappedFlag = True Then
        picOutput.Print "Numbers interchanged."
    End If
End Sub
```

(Assume that the file Data.txt contains the following entries.)

7, 11

6.
```
Dim a(1 To 3) As Integer

Private Sub Form_Load()
    Dim j As Integer
    Open "Data.txt" For Input As #1
    For j = 1 To 3
        Input #1, a(j)
    Next j
    Close #1
End Sub

Private Sub cmdDisplay_Click()
    Dim j As Integer, k As Integer, temp As Integer
    For j = 1 To 2
        For k = 1 To 3 - j
            If a(k) > a(k + 1) Then
                temp = a(k)
                a(k) = a(k + 1)
                a(k + 1) = temp
            End If
        Next k
    Next j
    For j = 1 To 3
        picOutput.Print a(j);
    Next j
End Sub
```

(Assume that the file Data.txt contains the following entries.)

7, 4, 3

In Exercises 7 and 8, identify the errors.

7. `Dim c(1 To 4) As Integer, d(1 To 4) As Integer`

```
Private Sub Form_Load()
  Dim i As Integer
  Open "Data.txt" For Input As #1
  For i = 1 To 4
    Input #1, c(i), d(i)
  Next i
  Close #1
End Sub

Private Sub cmdDisplay_Click()
  'swap two items
  c(4) = d(4)
  d(4) = c(4)
  picOutput.Print c(4), d(4)
End Sub
```

(Assume that the file Data.txt contains the following entries.)

1, 2, 3, 4, 5, 6, 7, 8

8. `Dim a(1 To 3) As Integer, b(1 To 3) As Integer`

```
Private Sub cmdDisplay_Click()
  Dim temp(1 To 3) As Integer
  temp() = a()
  a() = b()
  b() = temp()
End Sub

Private Sub Form_Load()
  Dim i As Integer
  Open "Data.txt" For Input As #1
  For i = 1 To 3
    Input #1, a(i), b(i)
  Next i
  Close #1
End Sub
```

(Assume that the file Data.txt contains the following entries.)

1, 3, 5, 7, 9, 11

9. Which type of search would be best for the following array?

1	2	3	4	5
Paul	Ringo	John	George	Pete

10. Which type of search would be best for the following array?

1	2	3	4	5
Beloit	Green Bay	Madison	Milwaukee	Oshkosh

11. Consider the items Tin Man, Dorothy, Scarecrow, and Lion in that order. After how many swaps in a bubble sort will the list be in alphabetical order?

12. How many comparisons will be made in a bubble sort of six items?

13. How many comparisons will be made in a bubble sort of n items?

14. Modify the program in Example 2 so that it will keep track of the number of swaps and comparisons and display these numbers before ending.

15. Suppose a list of 5000 numbers is to be sorted, but the numbers consist of only 1, 2, 3, and 4. Describe a method of sorting the list that would be much faster than the bubble sort.

In Exercises 16 to 21, write a short program (or procedure) to complete the stated task.

16. Display the names of the seven dwarfs in alphabetical order. For the contents of a data file use

Doc, Grumpy, Sleepy, Happy, Bashful, Sneezy, Dopey

17. Exchange the values of the variables x, y, and z so that x has y's value, y has z's value, and z has x's value.

18. The nation's capital has long been a popular staging area for political, religious, and other large public rallies, protest marches, and demonstrations. The following events have drawn the largest crowds, according to estimates from D.C., U.S. Park, or Capitol police. Read the data into a pair of parallel arrays and display a similar table with the event names in alphabetical order.

Event	Crowd Estimate (in thousands)
LBJ inauguration (1/23/65)	1200
Bicentennial fireworks (7/4/76)	1000
Desert Storm rally (6/8/91)	800
Bill Clinton inauguration (1/20/93)	800
Beach Boys concert (7/4/85)	625
Washington Redskins victory parade (2/3/88)	600
Vietnam moratorium rally (11/15/69)	600
Ronald Reagan inauguration (1/20/81)	500
U.S. Iran hostage motorcade (1/28/81)	500

Table 4.5 Largest Public Displays of Emotion in Washington, D.C.

19. Table 4.6 presents statistics on the five leading athletic footwear brands. Read the data into three parallel arrays and display a similar table with sales in descending order.

Brand	Pairs of Shoes Sold (in millions)	Percentage Share of U.S. market
Adidas USA	21.0	6.0
Fila	23.1	6.6
New Balance	9.5	2.7
Nike	146.7	41.9
Reebok	52.9	15.1

Table 4.6 1997 U.S. market share in athletic footwear.

Source: Morgan Stanley Dean Whitter Research.

20. An airline has a list of 200 flight numbers (between 1 and 1000) in ascending order in the file Flights.txt. Accept a number as input and do a binary search of the list to determine if the flight number is valid.

21. Allow a number n to be input by the user. Then accept as input a list of n numbers. Place the numbers into an array and apply a bubble sort.

22. Write a program that accepts an American word as input and performs a binary search to translate it into its British equivalent. Use the following list of words for data, and account for the case when the word requested is not in the list.

American	British	American	British
attic	loft	ice cream	ice
business suit	lounge suit	megaphone	loud hailer
elevator	lift	radio	wireless
flashlight	torch	sneakers	plimsolls
french fries	chips	truck	lorry
gasoline	petrol	zero	nought

23. Write a program that accepts a student's name and seven test scores as input and calculates the average score after dropping the two lowest grades.

24. Suppose letter grades are assigned as follows:

97 and above	A+	74–76	C
94–96	A	70–73	C–
90–93	A–	67–69	D+
87–89	B+	64–66	D
84–86	B	60–63	D–
80–83	B–	0–59	F
77–79	C+		

Write a program that accepts a grade as input and displays the corresponding letter. *Hint:* This problem shows that when you search an array, you don't always look for equality. Set up an array *range( )* containing the values 97, 94, 90, 87, 84, . . . , 59 and the parallel array *letter( )* containing A+, A, A–, B+, . . . , F. Next, perform a sequential search to find the first i such that *range(i)* is less than or equal to the input grade.

25. The *median* of a set of n measurements is a number such that half the n measurements fall below the median, and half fall above. If the number of measurements n is odd, the median is the middle number when the measurements are arranged in ascending or descending order. If the number of measurements n is even, the median is the average of the two middle measurements when the measurements are arranged in ascending or descending order. Write a program that requests a number n and a set of n measurements as input and then displays the median.

✔✔ **Solutions to Practice Problems 4.2**

1. The outer loop controls the number of passes, one less than the number of items in the list. The inner loop performs a single pass, and the jth pass consists of $n - j$ comparisons.

2.

First	Last	Middle
1	20	10
11	20	15
11	14	12
13	14	13

4.3 ARRAYS AND SEQUENTIAL FILES

Throughout this text we have processed data from files created with Windows' Notepad and saved on a disk. Such files are stored on disk as a sequence of characters. (Two special characters, called the "carriage return" and "line feed" characters, are inserted at the end of each line to indicate where new lines should be started.) Such files are called **sequential files** or **text files**. Sequential files also can be created directly from Visual Basic.

Arrays and sequential files interact in several ways. For instance, the initial values of the elements of arrays are usually loaded from sequential files, and the final values are saved back into sequential files for later use. Also, arrays are used to sort the elements of sequential files. In this section, we first learn how to manage sequential files and then consider some ways that arrays and sequential files interact.

Creating a Sequential File from Visual Basic

The following steps create a new sequential file and write data to it.

1. Choose a file name. A file name can contain up to 255 characters consisting of letters, digits, and a few other assorted characters (including spaces and periods). In this book we use 8.3 format names where each name has a base name of at most 8 characters, and optionally a period followed by a three letter extension. (Such names are recognized by all utility programs.)

2. Choose a number from 1 to 511 to be the **reference number** of the file. While the file is in use, it will be identified by this number.

3. Execute the statement

```
Open "filespec" For Output As #n
```

where n is the reference number. This process is referred to as **opening a file for output**. It establishes a communications link between the computer and the disk drive for storing data *onto* the disk. It allows data to be output from the computer and recorded in the specified file.

4. Place data into the file with the Write # statement. If *a* is a string, then the statement

```
Write #n, a
```

writes the string *a* surrounded by quotation marks into the file. If *c* is a number, then the statement

```
Write #n, c
```

writes the number *c*, without any leading or trailing spaces, into file number *n*. The statement

```
Write #n, a, c
```

writes *a* and *c* as before, but with a comma separating them. Similarly, if the statement Write #n is followed by a list of several strings and/or numbers separated by commas, then all the strings and numbers appear as before, separated by commas. After each Write # statement is executed, the "carriage return" and "line feed" characters are placed into the file.

5. After all the data have been recorded in the file, execute

```
Close #n
```

where *n* is the reference number. This statement breaks the communications link with the file and dissociates the number *n* from the file.

EXAMPLE 1

The following program uses Write # to store the contents of arrays containing names and dates of birth into a sequential file.

```
Dim nom(1 To 3) As String
Dim yr(1 To 3) As Integer

Private Sub cmdCreateFile_Click()
  Dim index As Integer
  Open "Yob.txt" For Output As #1
  For index = 1 To 3
    Write #1, nom(index), yr(index)
  Next index
  Close #1
End Sub

Private Sub Form_Load()
  nom(1) = "Elaine"
  yr(1) = 1961
  nom(2) = "George"
  yr(2) = 1959
  nom(3) = "Kramer"
  yr(3) = 1949
End Sub
```

[Run, click the command button, and then load the file Yob.txt into Windows' Notepad. The following will appear on the screen.]

```
"Elaine",1961
"George",1959
"Kramer",1949
```

Caution: If an existing sequential file is opened for output, the computer will erase the existing data and create a new empty file.

Write # statements allow us to create files just like the Notepad files that appear throughout this text. We already know how to read such files with Input # statements. The remaining major task is adding data to the end of sequential files.

Adding Items to a Sequential File

Data can be added to the end of an existing sequential file with the following steps.

1. Choose a number from 1 to 511 to be the reference number for the file. It need not be the number that was used when the file was created.

2. Execute the statement

```
Open "filespec" For Append As #n
```

where *n* is the reference number. This procedure is called **opening a file for append**. It allows data to be output and recorded at the end of the specified file.

3. Place data into the file with Write # statements.

4. After all the data have been recorded into the file, close the file with the statement Close #*n*.

The Append option for opening a file is intended to add data to an existing file. However, it also can be used to create a new file. If the file does not exist, then the Append option acts just like the Output option and creates the file.

The three options, Output, Input, and Append, are referred to as **modes**. A file should not be open in two modes at the same time. For instance, after a file has been opened for output and data have been written to the file, the file should be closed before being opened for input.

An attempt to open a nonexistent file for input terminates the program with the "File not found" error message. There is a function that tells us whether a certain file has already been created. If the value of

```
Dir("filespec")
```

is the empty string "", then the specified file does not exist. (If the file exists, the value will be the file name.) Therefore, prudence often dictates that files be opened for input with code such as

```
If Dir("filespec") <> "" Then
    Open "filespec" For Input As #1
  Else
    message = "Either no file has yet been created or "
    message = message & "the file is not where expected."
    MsgBox message, , "File Not Found"
End If
```

There is one file-management operation that we have yet to discuss—deleting an item of information from a file. An individual item of a file cannot be changed or deleted directly. A new file must be created by reading each item from the original file and recording it, with the single item changed or deleted, into the new file. The old file is then erased and the new file renamed with the name of the original file. Regarding these last two tasks, the Visual Basic statement

```
Kill "filespec"
```

removes the specified file from the disk and the statement

```
Name "oldfilespec" As "newfilespec"
```

changes the filespec of a file. (**Note:** The Kill and Name statements cannot be used with open files. So doing generates a "File already open" message.)

EXAMPLE 2   The following program modifies the file created in Example 1.

Object	Property	Setting
frm4_3_2	Caption	Modify Yob.txt
lblName	Caption	Name
txtName	Text	(blank)
lblYOB	Caption	Year of Birth
txtYOB	Text	(blank)
cmdAdd	Caption	Add Above Person to File
cmdDelete	Caption	Remove Above Person from File

```
Private Sub cmdAdd_Click()
  Dim message As String
  'Add a person's name and year of birth to file
  If (txtName.Text <> "") And (txtYOB.Text <> "") Then
      Open "Yob.txt" For Append As #1
      Write #1, txtName.Text, Val(txtYOB.Text)
      Close #1
      txtName.Text = ""
      txtYOB.Text = ""
      txtName.SetFocus
    Else
      message = "You must enter a name and year of birth."
      MsgBox message, , "Information Incomplete"
  End If
End Sub

Private Sub cmdDelete_Click()
  'Remove a person from the file if possible
  Dim message As String
  If txtName.Text <> "" Then
      If Dir("Yob.txt") <> "" Then
          Call DeletePerson
        Else
```

```
            message = "Either no file has yet been created or "
            message = message & "the file is not where expected."
            MsgBox message, , "File Not Found."
        End If
      Else
        MsgBox "You must enter a name.", , "Information Incomplete"
    End If
    txtName.SetFocus
End Sub


Private Sub DeletePerson()
  Dim foundFlag As Boolean, nom As String, yr As Integer
  foundFlag = False
  Open "Yob.txt" For Input As #1
  Open "Temp" For Output As #2
  Do While Not EOF(1)
    Input #1, nom, yr
    If nom <> txtName.Text Then
        Write #2, nom, yr
      Else
        foundFlag = True
    End If
    Loop
    Close #1
    Close #2
    Kill "Yob.txt"
    Name "Temp" As "Yob.txt"
    If Not foundFlag Then
        MsgBox "The name was not found.", , ""
      Else
        txtName.Text = ""
        txtYOB.Text = ""
    End If
End Sub
```

The sequential file Yob.txt created in Example 1 is said to consist of three records of two fields each. A **record** holds all the data about a single individual. Each item of data is called a **field**. The two fields are "name" and "year of birth". Sequential files are commonly sorted on a specific field.

EXAMPLE 3   The following program sorts the sequential file Yob.txt by year of birth.

```
Private Sub cmdSort_Click()
  Dim numPeople As Integer
  'Sort data from Yob.txt file by year of birth
  numPeople = NumberOfRecords("Yob.txt")
  'Number of people in file
  ReDim nom(1 To numPeople) As String
  ReDim yearBorn(1 To numPeople) As Integer
  Call ReadData(nom(), yearBorn(), numPeople)
  Call SortData(nom(), yearBorn(), numPeople)
  Call WriteData(nom(), yearBorn(), numPeople)
End Sub
```

```
Private Function NumberOfRecords(filespec As String) As Integer
  Dim nom As String, yearBorn As Integer
  Dim n As Integer   'Used to count records
  Open filespec For Input As #1
  Do While Not EOF(1)
    Input #1, nom, yearBorn
    n = n + 1
  Loop
  Close #1
  NumberOfRecords = n
End Function

Private Sub ReadData(nom() As String, yearBorn() As Integer, _
                     numPeople As Integer)
  Dim index As Integer
  'Read data from file into arrays
  Open "Yob.txt" For Input As #1
  For index = 1 To numPeople
    Input #1, nom(index), yearBorn(index)
  Next index
  Close #1
End Sub

Private Sub SortData(nom() As String, yearBorn() As Integer, _
                     numPeople As Integer)
  Dim passNum As Integer, index As Integer
  'Bubble sort arrays by year of birth
  For passNum = 1 To numPeople - 1
    For index = 1 To numPeople - passNum
      If yearBorn(index) > yearBorn(index + 1) Then
          Call SwapData(nom(), yearBorn(), index)
      End If
    Next index
  Next passNum
End Sub

Private Sub SwapData(nom() As String, yearBorn() As Integer, _
                     index As Integer)
  Dim stemp As String, ntemp As Integer
  'Swap names and years
  stemp = nom(index)
  nom(index) = nom(index + 1)
  nom(index + 1) = stemp
  ntemp = yearBorn(index)
  yearBorn(index) = yearBorn(index + 1)
  yearBorn(index + 1) = ntemp
End Sub
```

```
Private Sub WriteData(nom() As String, yearBorn() As Integer, _
                      numPeople As Integer)
  Dim index As Integer
  'Write data back into file
  Open "Yob.txt" For Output As #1
  For index = 1 To numPeople
    Write #1, nom(index), yearBorn(index)
  Next index
  Close #1
End Sub
```

[Run, click the command button, and then load the file Yob.txt into Windows' Notepad. The following will appear on the screen.]

```
"Kramer",1949
"George",1959
"Elaine",1961
```

Comment

1. In the examples of this section, the files to be processed have been opened and closed within a single procedure. However, the solution to some programming problems requires that a file be opened just once the instant the program is run and stay open until the program is terminated. This is easily accomplished by placing the Open statement in the Form_Load event procedure and the Close and End statements in the click event procedure for a command button labeled "Quit."

PRACTICE PROBLEM 4.3

1. Modify the event procedure cmdAdd_Click() of Example 2 to add a name and year of birth to the end of the file Yob.txt only if the name to be added is not already present in the file. (Assume that the existance of Yob.txt is checked prior to the execution of this event procedure.)

EXERCISES 4.3

In Exercises 1 to 4, determine the output displayed in the picture box when the command button is clicked.

```
1. Private Sub cmdDisplay_Click()
     Dim salutation As String
     Open "Greeting.txt" For Output As #1
     Write #1, "Hello"
     Write #1, "Aloha"
     Close #1
     Open "Greeting.txt" For Input As #1
     Input #1, salutation
     picOutput.Print salutation
     Close #1
   End Sub
```

2.
```
Private Sub cmdDisplay_Click()
    Dim salutation As String, welcome As String
    Open "Greeting.txt" For Output As #2
    Write #2, "Hello", "Aloha"
    Close #2
    Open "Greeting.txt" For Input As #1
    Input #1, salutation, welcome
    picOutput.Print welcome
    Close #1
End Sub
```

3.
```
Private Sub cmdDisplay_Click()
    Dim salutation As String
    Open "Greeting.txt" For Output As #2
    Write #2, "Hello"
    Write #2, "Aloha"
    Write #2, "Bon Jour"
    Close #2
    Open "Greeting.txt" For Input As #1
    Do While Not EOF(1)
      Input #1, salutation
      picOutput.Print salutation
    Loop
    Close #1
End Sub
```

4. Assume the contents of the file Greeting.txt are as shown in Figure 4.6.

```
Private Sub cmdDisplay_Click()
    Dim file As String, salutation As Integer, g As String
    file = "Greeting.txt"
    Open file For Append As #3
    Write #3, "Buenos Dias"
    Close #3
    Open file For Input As #3
    For salutation = 1 To 4
      Input #3, g
      picOutput.Print g
    Next salutation
    Close #3
End Sub
```

"Hello"
"Aloha"
"Bon Jour"

Figure 4.6 Contents of the file Greeting.txt.

In Exercises 5 and 6, identify any errors. Assume Yob.txt is the file created in Example 1.

5.
```
Private Sub cmdDisplay_Click()
    Open Yob.txt For Append As #1
    Write #1, "Jerry", 1958
    Close #1
End Sub
```

6. ```
Private Sub cmdDisplay_Click()
    Dim nom As String, yr As Integer
    Open "Yob.txt" For Output As #2
    Input #2, nom, yr
    picOutput.Print yr
    Close #2
End Sub
```

**Exercises 7 to 14 are related and use the data in Table 4.7. The file created in Exercise 7 should be used in Exercises 8 through 14.**

**7.** Write a program to create the sequential file Cowboy.txt containing the information in Table 4.7.

| | |
|---|---|
| Colt Peacemaker | 12.20 |
| Holster | 2.00 |
| Levi Strauss Jeans | 1.35 |
| Saddle | 40.00 |
| Stetson | 10.00 |

**Table 4.7** Prices paid by cowboys for certain items in mid-1800s.

**8.** Write a program to display all items in the file Cowboy.txt that cost more than $10.

**9.** Write a program to add the data *Winchester rifle, 20.50* to the end of the file Cowboy.txt.

**10.** Suppose an order is placed for 3 Colt Peacemakers, 2 Holsters, 10 pairs of Levi Strauss Jeans, 1 saddle, and 4 Stetsons. Write a program to

(a) Create the sequential file Order.txt to hold the numbers 3, 2, 10, 1, 4.

(b) Use the files Cowboy.txt and Order.txt to display a sales receipt with three columns giving the name of each item, the quantity ordered, and the cost for that quantity.

(c) Compute the total cost of the items and display it at the end of the sales receipt.

**11.** Write a program to request an additional item and price from the user. Then create a sequential file called Cowboy2.txt containing all the information in the file Cowboy.txt with the additional item (and price) inserted in its proper alphabetical sequence. Run the program for both of the following data items: *Boots, 20*; and *Horse, 35*.

**12.** Suppose the price of saddles is reduced by 20 percent. Use the file Cowboy.txt to create a sequential file, Cowboy3.txt, containing the new price list.

**13.** Write a program to create a sequential file called Cowboy4.txt containing all the information in the file Cowboy.txt except for the data *Holster, 2*.

**14.** Write a program to allow additional items and prices to be input by the user and added to the end of the file Cowboy.txt. Include a method to terminate the process.
```

15. Suppose the file Yob.txt contains many names and years, and that the names are in alphabetical order. Write a program that requests a name as input and either gives the person's age or reports that the person is not in the file. **Note:** Because the names are in alphabetical order, usually there is no need to search to the end of the file.

16. Suppose the file Yob.txt contains many names and years. Write a program that creates two files, called Seniors.txt and Juniors.txt, and copies all the data on people born before 1940 into the file Seniors.txt and the data on the others into the file Juniors.txt.

Exercises 17 to 20 are related. They create and maintain the sequential file Average.txt to hold batting averages of baseball players.

17. Suppose the season is about to begin. Compose a program to create the sequential file containing the name of each player, his times at bat, and his number of hits. The program should allow the user to type a name into a text box and then click a command button to add a record to the file. The times at bat and number of hits initially should be set to 0. (**Hint:** Open the file for Output in the Form_Load event procedure and Close the file when a "Quit" command button is clicked.)

18. Each day, the statistics from the previous day's games should be used to update the file. Write a program to read the records one at a time and allow the user to enter the number of times at bat and the number of hits in yesterday's game for each player in appropriate text boxes on a form. When a command button is clicked, the program should update the file by adding these numbers to the previous figures. (**Hint:** Open files in the Form_Load event procedure. Close the files and end the program when all data have been processed.)

19. Several players are added to the league. Compose a program to update the file.

20. Compose a program to sort the file Average.txt with respect to batting averages and display the players with the top 10 batting averages. **Hint:** The file must be read once to determine the number of players and again to load the players into an array.

✔✔ **Solution to Practice Problem 4.3**

1. The file Yob.txt is first opened for Input and scanned for the new name. If the name is not found, Yob.txt is reopened for Append and the name and year of birth are added to the end of the file.

```
Private Sub cmdAdd_Click()
  'Add a new person's name and year of birth to file
  Dim foundFlag As Boolean, nom As String, yr As Integer, message As String
  If (txtName.Text <> "") And (txtYOB.Text <> "") Then
      Open "Yob.txt" for Input as #1
      foundFlag = False
      Do While (Not(EOF(1)) And (Not foundFlag)
        Input #1, nom, yr
        If nom = txtName.Text Then
            foundFlag = True
        End If
      Loop
      Close #1
```

```
        If Not foundFlag Then
            Open "Yob.txt" For Append As #1
            Write #1, txtName.Text, Val(txtYOB.Text)
            Close #1
            txtName.Text = ""
            txtYOB.Text = ""
            txtName.SetFocus
        End If
    Else
        message = "You must enter a name and year of birth."
        MsgBox message, , "Information Incomplete"
    End If
End Sub
```

4.4 A CASE STUDY: CREATING A RECEIPT

Most supermarkets have automated check-out counters. Scanners read coded information on each item and send the information to a computer that produces an itemized receipt after all the items have been scanned. This case study develops a program to produce an itemized check-out receipt after all the coded information has been entered.

The standard code is the Universal Product Code (UPC), which consists of a sequence of 10 digits appearing below a rectangle of bars. (See Figure 4.7.) The bars have these digits encoded in a form that can be read by an optical scanner. The first five digits encode the manufacturer and the second five digits specify the product and the size of the package. The digits 37000 00430 appear on a jar of peanut butter. The string 37000 is the code for Procter & Gamble and 00430 is Procter & Gamble's code for a 22-ounce jar of creamy Jif peanut butter. Of course, the string 00430 will have an entirely different meaning for another manufacturer.

Figure 4.7 Universal Product Code.

Suppose a supermarket carries 10,000 items and a sequential file called Master.txt holds a record for each item consisting of the following information: the UPC, the name of the item, the price. Let us also assume the file has been sorted by the UPC for each record and that the file ends with a fictitious record (called a sentinel) whose sole purpose is to signal the end of the file. The fictitious UPC for the sentinel record should be greater than any actual UPC. (*Note:* The use of a sentinel is a common practice when an entire file will be read sequentially. The advantage of using a sentinel, as opposed to relying solely on EOF, will become apparent when the program is written.) For instance, the master file might contain the following data for three food items.

```
"3700000430","22-oz Jif Peanut Butter",1.76
"4119601012","19-oz Prog Minn Soup",1.70
"7073405307","2.5 oz CS Cinn Rose Tea",1.65
"9999999999","Sentinel",0
```

We wish to write a program that will accept as input UPC codes entered from the keyboard and produce as output a printed itemized receipt. One way to proceed would be to take each UPC as it is input into the computer and then search for it in the master file to find the item description and price. We then would have to search sequentially through a long file many times. A better way to proceed is to first store the input UPCs in an array and then sort the array in increasing order, the same order as the master file. Then all the information can be located in just one sequential pass through the master file.

The program must be able to handle the special case in which a UPC code entered is not in the master file. Suppose the first array item, after the array of UPCs has been sorted, is not in the master file. Then its UPC will never equal one of the UPCs in the master file. At some point during the sequential pass through the master file, the array UPC will be less than the most recently read UPC from the master file. This indicates that the UPC is not in the master file, and that the user must be informed of this fact. After the array of UPCs has been sorted, the search algorithm is as follows.

1. Begin with the first (lowest) array item. (It is most likely higher than the first UPC in the master file.)

2. Read records from the master file until the record is found whose UPC matches or exceeds the array UPC.

3. If the master file UPC matches the array UPC, then print the corresponding description and price of the item from the master file and add the price to the running total. Otherwise, print a message stating that the item is not in the master file.

4. Repeat Steps 2 and 3 for each element of the array.

Designing the Supermarket Check-Out Program

The major tasks of the program are as follows:

1. *Input UPCs from the keyboard* (and count the number of items). Task 1 requests the UPCs of the items purchased. A counter should keep track of the number of items purchased.

2. *Create an itemized receipt.* Task 2 can be divided into smaller subtasks. First sort the array of UPCs of the purchased items into ascending order with a bubble sort. Then, after the master file is opened, the file is searched sequentially for the triplet holding the first array UPC. If this record is found, the item name and price are printed and the price is added to the total. Then, the second item is looked for in the same manner. This process continues until all possible items and prices have been printed. Of course, any unlocatable items must be reported. Finally, the total price is printed and the master file is closed. That is, Task 2 is divided into the following subtasks:

2.1 Sort the array of items purchased.
2.2 Open the master file.
2.3 Search for array UPCs in the master file.
2.4 Print an itemized receipt.
2.5 Close the master file.

Figure 4.8 shows the top-down chart for the program.

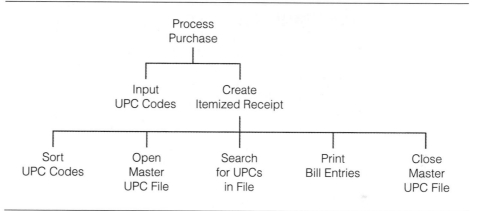

Figure 4.8 Top-down chart for the supermarket check-out program.

Pseudocode for the Supermarket Check-Out Program

INPUT UPC CODES
Initialize numItems counter to 0
Prompt user for input
Do While there are more items to be entered
    Place the UPC into the current array element
    Increment numItems
    Prompt user for more input
Loop

CREATE ITEMIZED RECEIPT
Sort UPCs with the following nested loops
For passNum = 1 To numItems – 1
    For i = 1 To numItems – passNum
        If the ith array UPC is greater than the (i+1)th Then
            Swap the ith and (i+1)th array elements
        End If
    Next i
Next passNum
Open the master file
Initialize total to 0
Read first triplet from the master file
For i = 1 To numItems
    Do While item i's UPC > the current file UPC
        Read the next record from the master file
    Loop
    If item i's UPC = the file UPC then
        Print the corresponding item description and price
        Increase total by price

```
        Else
            Print that the UPC is not in the master file
        End If
Next i
Print total
Close the master file
```

The Supermarket Check-Out Program

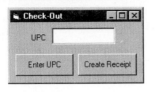

Object	Property	Setting
frm4_4	Caption	Check-Out
lblUPC	Caption	UPC
txtUPC	Text	(blank)
cmdEnterUPC	Caption	Enter UPC
cmdCreateReceipt	Caption	Create Receipt

```
Dim numItems As Integer          'Counts the number of items purchased
Dim itemUPC(1 To 100) As String 'Array of UPCs for the items purchased

Private Sub cmdCreateReceipt_Click()
  Call SortCodes        'Sort array of UPCs
  Call PrintReceipt
End Sub

Private Sub cmdEnterUPC_Click()
  If Len(txtUPC.Text) = 10 Then
      numItems = numItems + 1
      itemUPC(numItems) = txtUPC.Text
      txtUPC.Text = ""
    Else
      MsgBox "UPC must contain 10 digits.", , "Error"
  End If
  txtUPC.SetFocus                 'Move the cursor to the text box txtUPC
End Sub

Private Sub PrintReceipt()
  Dim total As Single        'Total cost of items purchased
  Dim code As String         'First field of record from master file
  Dim descr As String        'Second field of record from master file
  Dim price As Single        'Third field of record from master file
  Dim i As Integer           'Index for For...Next loop
  'Print the receipt
  Open "Master.txt" For Input As #1
  total = 0
  Input #1, code, descr, price
  For i = 1 To numItems
    Do While itemUPC(i) > code
      Input #1, code, descr, price
    Loop
    If itemUPC(i) = code Then
        Printer.Print descr; Tab(37); FormatCurrency(price)
        total = total + price
```

```
            Else
                Printer.Print "** UPC "; itemUPC(i); " not listed **"
            End If
        Next i
        Printer.Print "Total =====================>"; Tab(37); FormatCurrency(total)
        Close #1
        Printer.EndDoc
    End Sub

    Private Sub SortCodes()
        Dim tempUPC As String       'Used for swapping in bubble sort
        Dim passNum As Integer      'Index used in bubble sort
        Dim i As Integer            'Index for For...Next loop
        For passNum = 1 To numItems - 1
          For i = 1 To numItems - passNum
            If itemUPC(i) > itemUPC(i + 1) Then
                'Swap itemUPC(i) and itemUPC(i+1)
                tempUPC = itemUPC(i)
                itemUPC(i) = itemUPC(i + 1)
                itemUPC(i + 1) = tempUPC
            End If
          Next i
        Next passNum
    End Sub
```

CHAPTER 4   SUMMARY

1. For programming purposes, tabular data are most efficiently processed if stored in an *array*. The *ranges* of variable arrays are specified by Dim or ReDim statements.

2. The *bubble sort* is the best-known method for ordering (or *sorting*) arrays.

3. Any array can be searched *sequentially* to find the subscript associated with a sought-after value. Ordered arrays can be searched most efficiently by a *binary search*.

4. When sequential files are *opened*, we must specify whether they will be created and written to, added to, or read from by use of the terms Output, Append, or Input. The file must be *closed* before the operation is changed. Data are written to the file with Write # statements and retrieved with Input # statements. The EOF function tells if we have read to the end of the file.

5. A sequential file can be ordered by placing its data in arrays, sorting the arrays, and then writing the ordered data into a file. This process should precede adding, deleting, or altering items in a master file.

1. Table 4.8 contains some lengths in terms of feet. Write a program that displays the nine different units of measure, requests the unit to convert from, the unit to convert to, and the quantity to be converted, and then displays the converted quantity. A typical outcome is shown in Figure 4.9.

1 inch = .0833 foot	1 rod = 16.5 feet
1 yard = 3 feet	1 furlong = 660 feet
1 meter = 3.2815 feet	1 kilometer = 3281.5 feet
1 fathom = 6 feet	1 mile = 5280 feet

Table 4.8 Equivalent lengths.

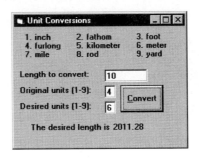

Figure 4.9 Possible outcome of Project 1.

2. Statisticians use the concepts of **mean** and **standard deviation** to describe a collection of data. The mean is the average value of the items, and the standard deviation measures the spread or dispersal of the numbers about the mean. Formally, if $x_1, x_2, x_3, \ldots, x_n$ is a collection of data, then

$$\text{mean} = m = \frac{x_1 + x_2 + x_3 + \ldots + x_n}{n}$$

$$\text{standard deviation} = s = \sqrt{\frac{(x_1 - m)^2 + (x_2 - m)^2 + (x_3 - m)^2 + \ldots + (x_n - m)^2}{n - 1}}$$

Write a computer program to

(a) Place the exam scores 59, 60, 65, 75, 56, 90, 66, 62, 98, 72, 95, 71, 63, 77, 65, 77, 65, 50, 85, and 62 into an array.

(b) Calculate the mean and standard deviation of the exam scores.

(c) Assign letter grades to each exam score, ES, as follows:

$ES \geq m + 1.5s$	A
$m + .5s \leq ES < m + 1.5s$	B
$m - .5s \leq ES < m + .5s$	C
$m - 1.5s \leq ES < m - .5s$	D
$ES < m - 1.5s$	F

For instance, if *m* were 70 and *s* were 12, then grades of 88 or above would receive As, grades between 76 and 87 would receive Bs, and so on. A process of this type is referred to as *curving grades*.

(d) Display a list of the exam scores along with their corresponding grades as shown in Figure 4.10.

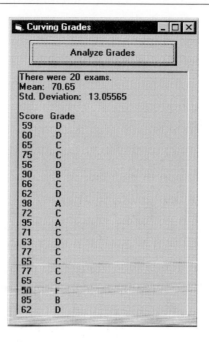

Figure 4.10 Output of Project 2.

3. *Rudimentary translator.* Table 4.9 gives English words and their French and German equivalents. Store these words in a data file and read them into three parallel arrays, one for each language. Write a program that sorts all three arrays according to the array of English words. The program should then request an English sentence as input from the keyboard and translate it into French and German. For example, if the English sentence given is MY PENCIL IS ON THE TABLE, then the French translation will be MON CRAYON EST SUR LA TABLE, and the German translation will be MEIN BLEISTIFT IST AUF DEM TISCH.

YES	OUI	JA	LARGE	GROS	GROSS
TABLE	TABLE	TISCH	NO	NON	NEIN
THE	LA	DEM	HAT	CHAPEAU	HUT
IS	EST	IST	PENCIL	CRAYON	BLEISTIFT
YELLOW	JAUNE	GELB	RED	ROUGE	ROT
FRIEND	AMI	FREUND	ON	SUR	AUF
SICK	MALADE	KRANK	AUTO	AUTO	AUTO
MY	MON	MEIN	OFTEN	SOUVENT	OFT

Table 4.9 English words and their French and German equivalents.

4. Write a program that allows a list of no more than 50 soft drinks and their percent changes in market share during the last 5 years to be input and displays the information in two lists titled *gainers* and *losers*. Each list should be sorted by the *amount* of the percent change. Try your program on the data for the top 8 soft drinks in Table 4.10. **Note:** You will need to store the data initially in an array to determine the number of gainers and losers.

Brand	% Change in Market Share	Brand	% Change in Market Share
Coke Classic	−.2	Sprite	.4
Pepsi-Cola	−.4	Dr. Pepper	.1
Diet Coke	−.2	Diet Pepsi	−.2
Mt. Dew	.5	7-Up	0

Table 4.10 Changes in market share from 1996 to 1997 of leading soft-drink brands.
Source: Beverage Digest, 1998

5. *Create and maintain telephone directories.* Write a program to create and maintain telephone directories. Each directory will be a separate sequential file. The following command buttons should be available:

(a) Select a directory to access. A list of directories that have been created should be stored in a separate sequential file. When a request is made to open a directory, the list of available directories should be displayed as part of an InputBox prompt requesting the name of the directory to be accessed. If the user responds with a directory name not listed, the desire to create a new directory should be confirmed, and then the new directory created and added to the list of existing directories.

(b) Add name and phone number (as given in the text boxes) to the end of the current directory.

(c) Delete name (as given in the text box) from the current directory.

(d) Sort the current directory into name order.

(e) Display the names and phone numbers contained in the current directory.

(f) Terminate the program.

5 Additional Features of Visual Basic

5.1 GRAPHICS

Visual Basic has impressive graphics capabilities. Figure 5.1 shows two types of charts that can be displayed in a picture box.

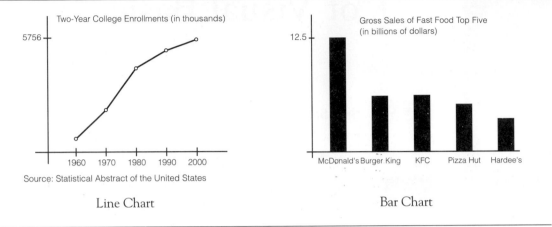

Line Chart

Bar Chart

Figure 5.1 Two Types of Charts

The construction of these charts involves three basic steps: (1) specify a viewing window, (2) use graphics methods to draw the appropriate lines, rectangles, and circles, and (3) place text at appropriate places on the chart. The basic tools for accomplishing each of these steps follows.

Specifying a Viewing Window

Graphics displayed in a picture box have many similarities with graphics displayed on a graphing calculator. Figure 5.2 shows the WINDOW (sometimes called RANGE) settings for a graphing calculator and the resulting coordinate system. After the settings Xmin = a, Xmax = b, Ymin = c, and Ymax = d have been specified, each point on the screen can be identified by an ordered pair of numbers (x, y) where x is between a and b, and y is between c and d. The point at the upper-left corner of the screen will have coordinates (a, d) and the point at the lower-right corner of the screen will have coordinates (b, c). For instance, in Figure 5.2 the coordinates of the upper-left and lower-right points are $(-4, 8)$ and $(4, -5)$. The Visual Basic equivalent of a viewing window setting for a picture box is the statement

```
picBox.Scale (a, d)-(b, c)
```

After the Scale statement has been executed, points can be plotted, and lines and circles can be drawn with statements of the form

```
picBox.PSet (x, y)              'Draw point with coordinates (x, y)
picBox.Line (x1, y1)-(x2, y2)   'Draw line segment from (x1, y1) to (x2, y2)
picBox.Circle (x, y), r         'Draw circle with center (x, y) and radius r
```

For instance, the statement

```
picBox.Scale (-4, 8)-(4, -5)
```

is equivalent to the WINDOW settings of Figure 5.2.

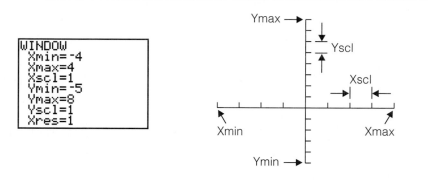

Figure 5.2 Graphing calculator setting for viewing rectangle.

EXAMPLE 1   The following event procedure plots the point (7, 6) in a picture box and draws a circle of radius 3 about the point. The rightmost point to be drawn will have x coordinate 10; therefore the numbers on the x axis must range beyond 10. In the following event procedure, we allow the numbers to range from −2 to 12.

```
Private Sub cmdDraw_Click()
  'Draw a circle with center (7, 6) and radius 3
  picOutput.Cls
  picOutput.Scale (-2, 12)-(12, -2) 'Specify viewing window
  picOutput.Line (-2, 0)-(12, 0)    'Draw x-axis
  picOutput.Line (0, -2)-(0, 12)    'Draw y-axis
  picOutput.PSet (7, 6)             'Draw center of circle
  picOutput.Circle (7, 6), 3        'Draw the circle
End Sub
```

[Run, and then click the command button. The contents of the picture box is shown in Figure 5.3.]

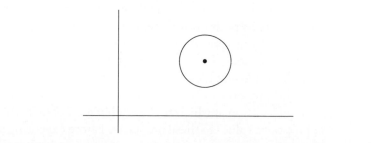

Figure 5.3 Graph for Example 1.

The numbers appearing in the Scale, Line, Pset, and Circle methods can be replaced by variables or expressions. The following example demonstrates this feature.

EXAMPLE 2

The following event procedure draws a graph of the square-root function for values of *x* from 0 to 100 (see Figure 5.4).

```
Private Sub cmdDraw_Click()
  Dim r As Single, h As Single, x As Single
  'Graph the Square-root function
  r = 100                          'Largest x-value used
  h = 10                           'Largest y-value used
  picOutput.Cls
  picOutput.Scale (-20, 12)-(120, -2) 'Specify coordinate system
  picOutput.Line (-5, 0)-(r, 0)       'Draw x-axis
  picOutput.Line (0, -1)-(0, h)       'Draw y-axis
  For x = 0 To r Step 0.2             'Plot about 500 points
    picOutput.PSet (x, Sqr(x))        'Plot point on graph
  Next x
End Sub
```

[Run, and then click the command button. The resulting graph is shown in Figure 5.4.]

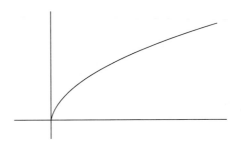

Figure 5.4 Graph of the square-root function.

Positioning Text

There are times when text is placed on the screen in conjunction with graphics. This would be the case if a graph were to be titled or a tick mark needed a label. The ability to position such text appropriately in the picture box is essential to good-looking graphs. A picture box has two properties, CurrentX and CurrentY, and two methods, TextHeight and TextWidth, that allow us to precisely position text alongside graphics.

The properties CurrentX and CurrentY record the precise horizontal and vertical location at which the next character of text will be printed. By assigning appropriate values to these properties before executing a Print method, text can be positioned very precisely in the picture box. In the following event procedure, the coordinates of the right end of the tick mark are $(x, y) = (.3, 3)$. As a first attempt at labeling a tick mark on the *y* axis, the CurrentX and CurrentY properties are set to these coordinates. The result is shown in Figure 5.5(a).

```
Private Sub cmdDraw_Click()
  picOutput.Cls
  picOutput.Scale (-4, 4)-(4, -4)
  picOutput.Line (-4, 0)-(4, 0)       'Draw x-axis
  picOutput.Line (0, -4)-(0, 4)       'Draw y-axis
  picOutput.Line (-.3, 3)-(.3, 3)     'Draw tick mark
  picOutput.CurrentX = .3             'Right end of tick mark
  picOutput.CurrentY = 3              'Same vertical position as tick mark
  picOutput.Print "y=3"               'Label for tick mark
End Sub
```

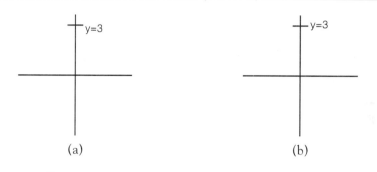

(a)   (b)

Figure 5.5 Placing labels: (a) first attempt and (b) second attempt.

Note that the top of the text is even with the tick mark. This reflects the fact that the value of the CurrentY property used by Visual Basic is the location for the **top** of the character cursor. Ideally, the text should be moved up so that the tick mark aligns with the middle of the text. To do this, the value of the CurrentY property needs to be increased by one-half the height of the text. The following statement assigns a corrected value to the CurrentY property by using the TextHeight method to obtain the height of the text being used as the tick mark label. (Since $c < d$ in the Scale method, TextHeight returns $(-1) \times$ [height of text].)

```
picOutput.CurrentY = 3 - picOutput.TextHeight("y=3") / 2
```

The result of using this corrected value for CurrentY is shown in Figure 5.5(b).

When the TextHeight method is used, all characters have the same height. Thus the height of a string can be obtained by asking for the height of any single character. The following procedure uses the TextHeight method with a space character to center the text cursor at the requested graphic point:

```
Private Sub PositionText(x As Single, y As Single)
  'Center text cursor at the point (x, y)
  picOutput.CurrentX = x
  picOutput.CurrentY = y - picOutput.TextHeight(" ") / 2
End Sub
```

Another useful picture box method is TextWidth. The Len function returns the number of characters in a string, whereas the TextWidth method considers the varying widths of characters and returns the physical width of the entire string in the units of the current scale for the picture box.

Line Charts

A line chart displays the change in a certain quantity in relation to another quantity (often time). The following steps produce a line chart:

1. Look over the data to be displayed. A typical line chart displays between 3 and 20 items of data corresponding to evenly spaced units of time: years, months, or days. The positions on the x axis will contain labels such as "Jan Feb Mar Apr . . ." or "1996 1997 1998 1999 . . .". These labels can be placed at the locations 1, 2, 3, . . . on the x axis.

2. Choose a coordinate system based on the number of data items and the size of the quantities. A convenient scale for the x axis is from –1 to one more than the number of data items. The scale for the y axis is determined by the largest quantity to be displayed.

3. Draw the line segments. It is a good idea to draw a small circle around the end points of the line segments.

4. Draw and label tick marks on the coordinate axes. The x axis should have a tick mark for each time period. The y axis should have at least one tick mark to indicate the magnitude of the quantities displayed.

5. Title the chart, and give the source of the data.

EXAMPLE 3

Table 5.1 gives enrollment data for 2-year colleges taken from the *Statistical Abstract of the United States*. (The data for 2000 is a projection.) The following program displays the enrollments for the given years in a line chart:

Year	1960	1970	1980	1990	2000
Enrollment	453	2320	4526	5240	5756

Table 5.1 Two-year college enrollments (in thousands).

Figure 5.6 shows the graph that results from executing the following program. The data from the table is contained in the file Enroll.txt. The first line of the file is "1960", 453.

```
Dim numYears As Integer, maxEnroll As Single

Private Sub cmdDraw_Click()
  'Line Chart of Total Two-Year College Enrollments
  numYears = 5
  ReDim label(1 To numYears) As String, total(1 To numYears) As Single
  Call ReadData(label(), total())
  Call DrawAxes
  Call DrawData(total())
  Call ShowTitle
  Call ShowLabels(label())
End Sub
```

```
Private Sub DrawAxes()
  'Draw axes
  picEnroll.Scale (-1, 1.2 * maxEnroll)-(numYears + 1, -0.2 * maxEnroll)
  picEnroll.Line (-1, 0)-(numYears + 1, 0)
  picEnroll.Line (0, -0.1 * maxEnroll)-(0, 1.1 * maxEnroll)
End Sub

Private Sub DrawData(total() As Single)
  Dim i As Integer
  'Draw lines connecting data and circle data points
  For i = 1 To numYears
    If i < numYears Then
        picEnroll.Line (i, total(i))-(i + 1, total(i + 1))
    End If
    picEnroll.Circle (i, total(i)), 0.01 * numYears
  Next i
End Sub

Private Sub Locate(x As Single, y As Single)
  picEnroll.CurrentX = x
  picEnroll.CurrentY = y
End Sub

Private Sub ReadData(label() As String, total() As Single)
  Dim i As Integer
  'Assume the data has been placed in the file "Enroll.txt"
  '(First line of the file is "1960",453)
  'Read data into arrays, find highest enrollment
  maxEnroll = 0
  Open "Enroll.txt" For Input As #1
  For i = 1 To numYears
    Input #1, label(i), total(i)
    If total(i) > maxEnroll Then
        maxEnroll = total(i)
    End If
  Next i
  Close #1
End Sub

Private Sub ShowLabels(label() As String)
  Dim i As Integer, lbl As String, lblWid As Single, lblHght As Single
  Dim tickFactor As Single
  'Draw tick marks and label them
  For i = 1 To numYears
    lblWid = picEnroll.TextWidth(label(i))
    tickFactor = 0.02 * maxEnroll
    picEnroll.Line (i, -tickFactor)-(i, tickFactor)
    Call Locate(i - lblWid / 2, -tickFactor)
    picEnroll.Print label(i)
  Next i
```

```
    lbl = Str(maxEnroll)
    lblWid = picEnroll.TextWidth(lbl)
    lblHght = picEnroll.TextHeight(lbl)
    tickFactor = 0.02 * numYears
    picEnroll.Line (-tickFactor, maxEnroll)-(tickFactor, maxEnroll)
    Call Locate(-tickFactor - lblWid, maxEnroll - lblHght / 2)
    picEnroll.Print lbl
End Sub

Private Sub ShowTitle()
  'Display source and title
  Call Locate(-0.5, -0.1 * maxEnroll)
  picEnroll.Print "Source: Statistical Abstract of the United States"
  Call Locate(0.5, 1.2 * maxEnroll)
  picEnroll.Print "Two-Year College Enrollments (in thousands)"
End Sub
```

[Run, and then click the command button. The resulting line chart is shown in Figure 5.6.]

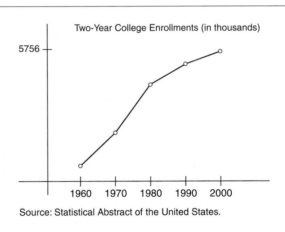

Figure 5.6 Line chart for Example 3

Bar Charts

Drawing bar charts requires a variation of the line statement. If $(x1, y1)$ and $(x2, y2)$ are two points in picBox, then the statement

```
    picBox.Line (x1, y1)-(x2, y2), , B
```

draws a rectangle with the two points as opposite corners. If B is replaced by BF, a solid rectangle will be drawn (see Figure 5.7).

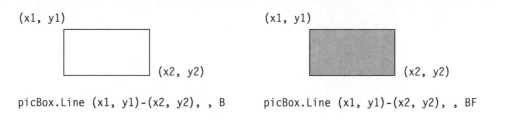

Figure 5.7 Line method with B and BF options.

EXAMPLE 4 The 1998 populations of California and New York are 32 and 18 million, respectively. The following program produces the chart shown in Figure 5.8. The first five lines are the same as those of a line chart with two pieces of data. The base of the rectangle for California is centered above the point $(1, 0)$ on the x axis and extends .3 unit to the left and right. (The number .3 was chosen arbitrarily; it had to be less than .5 so that the rectangles would not touch.) Therefore, the upper-left corner of the rectangle has coordinates $(.7, 32)$ and the lower-right corner has coordinates $(1.3, 0)$. Figure 5.9 shows the coordinates of the principal points of the rectangles.

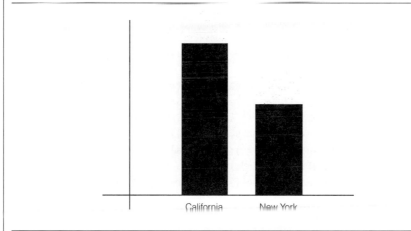

Figure 5.8 Bar chart for Example 4.

```
Private Sub cmdDisplayPop_Click()
   'Populations of California and New York
   picPop.Scale (-1, 40)-(3, -5)          'Specify coordinates
   picPop.Line (-1, 0)-(3, 0)             'Draw x-axis
   picPop.Line (0, -5)-(0, 40)            'Draw y-axis
   picPop.Line (0.7, 32)-(1.3, 0), , BF   'Draw solid rectangle for CA
   picPop.Line (1.7, 18)-(2.3, 0), , BF   'Draw solid rectangle for NY
   picPop.CurrentY = -1          'Vertical position for labels
   picPop.CurrentX = 0.7         'Beginning horizontal position of label for CA
   picPop.Print "California";
   picPop.CurrentX = 1.7         'Beginning horizontal position of label for NY
   picPop.Print "New York";
End Sub
```

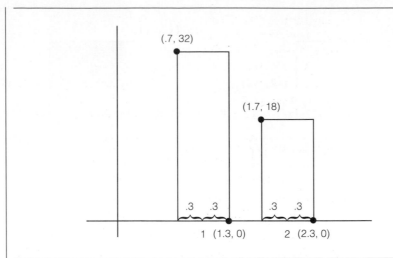

Figure 5.9 Coordinates of principal points of Example 4.

EXAMPLE 5 Any program that draws a line chart can be easily modified to produce a bar chart. The following program, which is a modification of the program in Example 3, displays 2-year college enrollments in a bar chart.

```
Private Sub cmdDraw_Click()
  Dim numYears As Integer, maxEnroll As Single
  'Bar Chart of Total Two-Year College Enrollments
  numYears = 5
  ReDim label(1 To numYears) As String
  ReDim enroll(1 To numYears) As Single
  Call ReadData(label(), enroll(), numYears, maxEnroll)
  Call DrawAxes(numYears, maxEnroll)
  Call DrawData(enroll(), numYears)
  Call ShowTitle(maxEnroll)
  Call ShowLabels(label(), numYears, maxEnroll)
End Sub

Private Sub DrawAxes(numYears As Integer, maxEnroll As Single)
  'Draw axes
  picEnroll.Scale (-1, 1.2 * maxEnroll)-(numYears + 1, -0.2 * maxEnroll)
  picEnroll.Line (-1, 0)-(numYears + 1, 0)
  picEnroll.Line (0, -0.1 * maxEnroll)-(0, 1.1 * maxEnroll)
End Sub

Private Sub DrawData(enroll() As Single, numYears As Integer)
  'Draw rectangles
  For i = 1 To numYears
    picEnroll.Line (i - 0.2, enroll(i))-(i + 0.2, 0), , BF
  Next i
End Sub
```

```
Private Sub Locate(x As Single, y As Single)
  picEnroll.CurrentX = x
  picEnroll.CurrentY = y
End Sub


Private Sub ReadData(label() As String, enroll() As Single, _
                     numYears As Integer, maxEnroll As Single)
  Dim i As Integer
  'Assume the data has been placed in the file Enroll.txt
  '(First line of file is "1960", 283, 170)
  'Read data into arrays, find highest enrollment
  Open "Enroll.txt" For Input As #1
  maxEnroll = 0
  For i = 1 To numYears
    Input #1, label(i), enroll(i)
    If enroll(i) > maxEnroll Then
        maxEnroll = enroll(i)
    End If
  Next i
  Close #1
End Sub


Private Sub ShowLabels(label() As String, numYears As Integer, _
                       maxEnroll As Single)
  Dim i As Integer, lbl As String, lblWid As Single
  Dim lblHght As Single, tickFactor As Single
  'Draw tick marks and label them
  For i = 1 To numYears
    lbl = label(i)
    lblWid = picEnroll.TextWidth(lbl)
    tickFactor = 0.02 * maxEnroll
    picEnroll.Line (i, -tickFactor)-(i, tickFactor)
    Call Locate(i - lblWid / 2, -tickFactor)
    picEnroll.Print lbl
  Next i
  lbl = Str(maxEnroll)
  lblWid = picEnroll.TextWidth(lbl)
  lblHght = picEnroll.TextHeight(lbl)
  tickFactor = 0.01 * numYears
  picEnroll.Line (-tickFactor, maxEnroll)-(tickFactor, maxEnroll)
  Call Locate(-tickFactor - lblWid, maxEnroll - lblHght / 2)
  picEnroll.Print lbl
End Sub


Private Sub ShowTitle(maxEnroll As Single)
  'Display source and title
  Call Locate(0.5, -0.1 * maxEnroll)
  picEnroll.Print "Source: Statistical Abstract of the United States"
  Call Locate(0.5, 1.2 * maxEnroll)
  picEnroll.Print "Two-Year College Enrollments (in thousands)"
End Sub
```

[Run, and then click the command button]

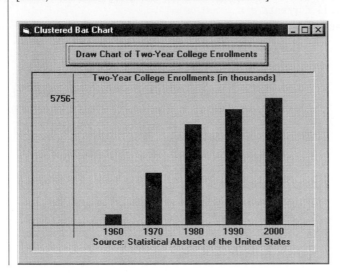

Comments

1. The following technique can be used to determine a good range of values for a Scale method when graphs with only positive values are to be drawn.

   (a) Let *r* be the *x* coordinate of the rightmost point that will be drawn by any Line, Pset, or Circle method.
   (b) Let *h* be the *y* coordinate of the highest point that will be drawn by any Line, Pset, or Circle method.
   (c) Let the numbers on the *x* axis range from about –[20% of *r*] to about *r* + [20% of *r*]. Let the numbers on the *y* axis range from about –[20% of *h*] to about *h* + [20% of *h*]. That is, use

   ```
   picOutput.Scale (-.2 * r, 1.2 * h)-(1.2 * r, -.2 * h)
   ```

2. The line and bar graphs drawn in Examples 3 and 5 can also be printed on the printer. Just replace each occurrence of picOutput with Printer, and add Printer.EndDoc as the last statement of the event procedure. Also, the graphs will look best in landscape orientation which is invoked with the statement Printer.Orientation = 2.

3. Lines, rectangles, and circles can be drawn in color. Some examples are

   ```
   picBox.Line (x1, y1)-(x2, y2), vbBlue       'Draw a blue line
   picBox.Line (x1, y1)-(x2, y2), vbGreen, BF  'Draw a green rectangle
   picBox.Circle (x1, y1)-(x2, y2), r, vbRed   'Draw a red circle
   ```

4. Usually one unit on the *x* axis is a different length than one unit on the *y* axis. The statement picBox.Circle (x, y), r draws a circle whose radius is *r* *x*-axis units.

5. If one or both of the points used in the Line method fall outside the picture box, Visual Basic draws only the portion of the line that lies in the picture box. This behavior is referred to as **clipping** and is used for the Circle method also.

6. You can use graphics methods in a Form_Load event procedure. If so, you must set the AutoRedraw property of the picture box to True. Otherwise the contents of the picture box will be erased when the event procedure terminates.

PRACTICE PROBLEMS 5.1

Suppose you want to write a program to draw a line from (3, 45) to (5, 80).

  1. Use the technique of Comment 1 to select appropriate values for the Scale method.

  2. Write an event procedure to draw the axes, the line, and a small circle around each end point of the line.

  3. Write the statements that draw a tick mark on the y axis at height 80 and label it with the number 80.

➤ **EXERCISES 5.1**

  1. Suppose the statement picBox.Scale (–1, 40)–(4, –8) has been executed. Write down the statements that draw the x axis and the y axis.

In Exercises 2 and 3, write an event procedure to draw a line between the given points. Select an appropriate Scale method, draw the axes, and draw a small circle around each end point of the line.

  2. (2, .5), (4, .3)   **3.** (3, 200), (10, 150)

In Exercises 4 to 8, write an event procedure to draw the given figures in a picture box. Draw the axes only when necessacy.

  4. Draw a tick mark on the x axis at a distance of 5 from the origin.

  5. Draw a circle whose center is located at the center of the picture box.

  6. Draw a rectangle inside a circle.

  7. Draw a graph of the function $y = x^2$ for x between 0 and 10.

  8. Draw a triangle with two sides of the same length.

In Exercises 9 to 12, write a program to display the given information in a line chart.

  9. Percentage of persons 25 years old and older who are college graduates

Year	1975	1985	1995
Percent	13.9	19.4	23.0

Source: U.S. Bureau of the Census.

  10. Cars in use (in millions)

Year	1980	1985	1990	1995
Cars	104.6	114.7	123.3	123.2

Source: Statistical Abstract of the United States, 1997.

  11. Percentage of college freshmen who smoke

Year	1987	1989	1991	1993	1995	1997
Percent	8.9	10.3	11.4	11.7	14.6	16.1

Source: Higher Education Research Institute.

12. The Consumer Price Index is a measure of living costs based on changes in retail prices. The following table uses 1968 as the base year and gives the value of the index in January for several years:

Year	1968	1973	1978	1983	1988	1993	1998
CPI	100.0	124.9	183.3	286.8	339.3	418.2	473.9

Source: Bureau of Labor Statistics.

In Exercises 13 to 16, write a program to display the given information in a bar chart.

13. Normal monthly precipitation in Portland, Oregon

Month	Jan	Apr	July	Oct
Inches	6.2	2.3	.5	3.0

14. United States minimum wage

Year	1958	1968	1978	1988	1998
Dollars	1.00	1.15	2.65	3.35	5.15

15. Most popular majors for college freshmen in Fall 1997 (**Hint:** Use two lines to display the fields).

Field	Percent
Elementary Education	5.1
Business Administration	4.5
Predent, Premed, Prevet	3.9
Psychology	3.8
Therapy (occup, phys, speech)	3.6

Source: "The American Freshman: National Norms for Fall 1997"; Higher Education Research Institute.

16. Principal languages of the world (in millions of speakers) (**Hint:** Display half the languages on one line and the other half on a second line; extend the tick marks for the languages on the second line).

Arabic	235	German	126	Mandarin	1025
Bengali	207	Hindi	476	Portuguese	187
English	497	Japanese	126	Russian	279
French	127	Malay	170	Spanish	409

Source: The World Almanac, 1998

✔✔ Solutions to Practice Problems 5.1

1. The largest value of any *x* coordinate is 5. Because 20% of 5 is 1, the numbers on the *x* axis should range from –1 to 6 (= 5 + 1). Similarly, the numbers on the *y* axis should range from –16 to 96 (= 80 + 16). Therefore, an appropriate scaling statement is

```
picOutput.Scale (-1, 96)-(6, -16)
```

2.
```
Private Sub cmdDraw_Click()
    picOutput.Scale (-1, 96)-(6, -16) 'Specify coordinate system
    picOutput.Line (-1, 0)-(6, 0)      'Draw x-axis
    picOutput.Line (0, -16)-(0, 96)    'Draw y-axis
    picOutput.Line (3, 45)-(5, 80)     'Draw the line
    picOutput.Circle (3, 45), .1       'Draw small circle about left end point
    picOutput.Circle (5, 80), .1       'Draw small circle about right end point
End Sub
```

The radius for the small circles about the end points was determined by trial and error. As a rule of thumb, it should be about 2 percent of the length of the *x* axis.

3. Add the following lines before the End Sub statement of the preceding event procedure. The length of the tick mark was taken to be the diameter of the circle.

```
picOutput.Line (-.1, 80)-(.1, 80)   'Draw tick mark
picOutput.CurrentX = -.5            'Prepare cursor position for label
picOutput.CurrentY = 80 - picOutput.TextHeight(" ") / 2
picOutput.Print "80"                'Display label
```

5.2   FOUR ADDITIONAL CONTROLS

In this section, we discuss the four controls indicated on the Toolbox in Figure 5.10.

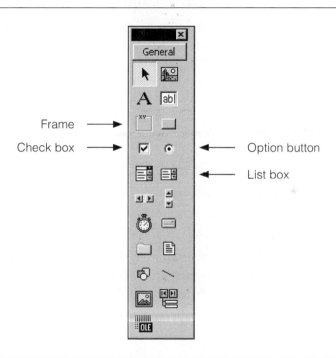

Figure 5.10

 The Frame Control

Frames are passive objects used to group related sets of controls for visual effect. You rarely write event procedures for frames. The frame above has a group of three text boxes attached to it. When you drag the frame, the attached controls follow as a unit. If you hide the frame, the attached controls will be hidden as well.

A control must be attached to a frame in a special way. You cannot just double-click to create the control and then drag it into a frame. To attach a control to a frame, first create the frame. Next, single-click on the control icon to activate it, then move the mouse pointer inside the frame to the point where you want to place the upper-left corner of the control. Finally, drag the mouse to the right and down, and then release the mouse button when you are satisfied with the size of the control. This is referred to as the **single-click-draw technique**.

A group of controls also can be attached to a picture box. The advantages of using frames are that they have a title sunk into their borders that can be set with the Caption property and that they cannot receive the focus. As shown later in this section, the frame control is particularly important when working with groups of option button controls. The standard prefix for the name of a frame is *fra*.

☑ The Check Box Control

A check box, which consists of a small square and a caption, presents the user with a yes/no choice. The form in Example 1 uses four check box controls. The Value property of a check box is 0 when the square is empty and is 1 when the square is checked. At run time, the user clicks on the square to toggle between the unchecked and checked states. So doing also triggers the Click event.

EXAMPLE 1

The following program allows an employee to compute the monthly cost of various benefit packages:

Object	Property	Setting
frmBenefits	Caption	Benefits Menu
chkDrugs	Caption	Prescription Drug Plan ($12.51)
	Value	0 – Unchecked
chkDental	Caption	Dental Plan ($9.68)
	Value	0 – Unchecked
chkVision	Caption	Vision Plan ($1.50)
	Value	0 – Unchecked
chkMedical	Caption	Medical Plan ($25.25)
	Value	0 – Unchecked
lblTotal	Caption	Total monthly payment:
lblAmount	Caption	$0.00

```
Private Sub chkDental_Click()
  Call Tally
End Sub

Private Sub chkDrugs_Click()
  Call Tally
End Sub

Private Sub chkMedical_Click()
  Call Tally
End Sub

Private Sub chkVision_Click()
  Call Tally
End Sub
```

```
Private Sub Tally()
  Dim sum As Single
  If chkDrugs.Value = 1 Then
      sum = sum + 12.51
  End If
  If chkDental.Value = 1 Then
      sum = sum + 9.68
  End If
  If chkVision.Value = 1 Then
      sum = sum + 1.5
  End If
  If chkMedical.Value = 1 Then
      sum = sum + 25.25
  End If
  lblAmount.Caption = FormatCurrency(sum)
End Sub
```

[Run, and then click on the desired options.]

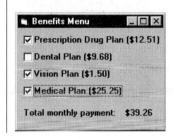

When a check box has the focus, the spacebar can be used to check (or uncheck) the box and invoke the Click event. In addition, the state of a check box can be toggled from the keyboard without first setting the focus to the check box if you create an access key for the check box by including an ampersand in the Caption property. (Access keys appear underlined.) For instance, if the Caption property for the Dental Plan in Example 1 is set as "&Dental Plan", then the user can check (or uncheck) the box by pressing Alt+D.

The Value property of a check box also can be set to "2-Grayed". When a grayed square is clicked, it becomes unchecked. When clicked again, it becomes checked.

The Option Button Control

Option buttons are used to give the user a single choice from several options. Normally, a group of several option buttons is attached to a frame or picture box with the single-click-draw technique. Each button consists of a small circle accompanied by text that is set with the Caption property. When a circle or its accompanying text is clicked, a solid dot appears in the circle and the button is said to be "on." At most one option button in a group can be on at the same time. Therefore, if one button is on and another button in the group is clicked, the first button will turn off. By convention, the names of option buttons have the prefix *opt*.

The Value property of an option button tells if the button is on or off. The condition

```
optButton.Value
```

is True when optButton is on and False when optButton is off. The statement

```
optButton.Value = True
```

turns on optButton and turns off all other buttons in its group. The statement

```
optButton.Value = False
```

turns off optButton and has no effect on the other buttons in its group.

The Click event for an option button is triggered only when an off button is turned on. It is not triggered when an on button is clicked.

EXAMPLE 2   The following program tells you if an option button is on.

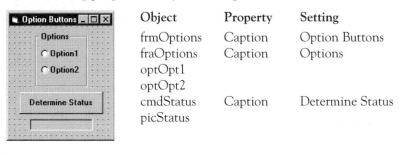

Object	Property	Setting
frmOptions	Caption	Option Buttons
fraOptions	Caption	Options
optOpt1		
optOpt2		
cmdStatus	Caption	Determine Status
picStatus		

```
Private Sub cmdStatus_Click()
  picStatus.Cls
  If optOpt1.Value = True Then
      picStatus.Print "Option1 is on."
  End If
  If optOpt2.Value = True Then
      picStatus.Print "Option2 is on."
  End If
End Sub

Private Sub Form_Load()
  optOpt1.Value = False    'Turn off optOpt1
  optOpt2.Value = False    'Turn off optOpt2
End Sub
```

[Run, click on one of the option buttons, and then click the command button.]

The text alongside an option button is specified with the Caption property. As with a command button and a check box, an ampersand can be used to create an access key for an option button.

EXAMPLE 3   The following program allows the user to select the text size in a text box. The three option buttons have been attached to the frame with the single-click-draw technique.

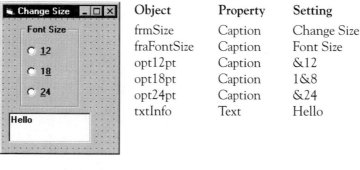

Object	Property	Setting
frmSize	Caption	Change Size
fraFontSize	Caption	Font Size
opt12pt	Caption	&12
opt18pt	Caption	1&8
opt24pt	Caption	&24
txtInfo	Text	Hello

```
Private Sub opt12pt_Click()
  txtInfo.Font.Size = 12
End Sub

Private Sub opt18pt_Click()
  txtInfo.Font.Size = 18
End Sub

Private Sub opt24pt_Click()
  txtInfo.Font.Size = 24
End Sub
```

[Run, and click on the last option button (or press Alt+2).]

A single form can have several groups of option buttons. However, each group must be attached to its own frame, picture box, or to the form itself.

The List Box Control

The fifth row of the standard toolbox (in most editions of Visual Basic) contains the list box icon on the right. The list boxes discussed in this text will display a single column of strings, referred to as **items**. The items to appear initially can either be specified at design time with the List property or set with code in a procedure. Then code is used to access, add, or delete items from the list. We will first carry out all tasks with code and then show how the initial items can be specified at design time. The standard prefix for the name of a list box is *lst*.

The Sorted property is perhaps the most interesting list box property. When it is set to True, the items will automatically be displayed in alphabetical (that is, ANSI) order. The default value of the Sorted property is False.

If *str* is a string, then the statement

```
lstBox.AddItem str
```

adds *str* to the list. The item is added at the proper sorted position if the Sorted property is True, and otherwise is added to the end of the list. If a list box is too short to display all the items that have been added to it, Visual Basic automatically places a vertical scroll bar on the right side of the list box. The user can then scroll to see the remaining items of the list. At any time, the value of

```
lstBox.ListCount
```

is the number of items in the list box.

Each item in lstBox is identified by an index number ranging from 0 through lstBox.ListCount − 1. The value of

```
lstBox.NewIndex
```

is the index number of the item most recently added to lstBox by the AddItem method. During run time you can highlight an item from a list by clicking on it with the mouse or by moving to it with the up- and down-arrow keys when the list box has the focus. (The second method triggers the Click event each time an arrow key causes the highlight to move.) The value of

```
lstBox.ListIndex
```

is the index number of the item currently highlighted in lstBox. (If no item is highlighted, the value of ListIndex is −1.)

The string array lstBox.List( ) holds the list of items stored in the list box. In particular, the value of

```
lstBox.List(n)
```

is the item of lstBox having index *n*. For instance, the statement `picBox.Print lstBox.List(0)` displays the first item of the list box. The value of

```
lstBox.List(lstBox.ListIndex)
```

is the item (string) currently highlighted in lstBox. Alternatively, the value of

```
lstBox.Text
```

is also the currently highlighted item. Unlike the Text property of a text box, you may not assign a value to lstBox.Text.

The statement

```
lstBox.RemoveItem n
```

deletes the item of index *n* from lstBox, the statement

```
lstBox.RemoveItem lstBox.ListIndex
```

deletes the item currently highlighted in lstBox, and the statement

```
lstBox.Clear
```

deletes every item of lstBox.

EXAMPLE 4 An oxymoron is a pairing of contradictory or incongruous words. The following program displays a sorted list of oxymorons. When you click an item (or highlight it with the up- and down-arrow keys), it is displayed in a picture box. A command button allows you to add an additional item with an Input box. You can delete an item by double-clicking on it with the mouse. (**Note:** When you double-click the mouse, two events are processed—the Click event and the DblClick event.) After running the program, click on different items, add an item or two (such as "same difference" or "liquid gas"), and delete an item.

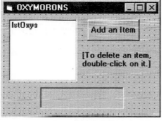

Object	Property	Setting
frmOxyMor	Caption	OXYMORONS
lstOxys	Sorted	True
cmdAdd	Caption	Add an Item
lblDelete	Caption	[To delete an item, double-click on it.]
picSelected		

```
Private Sub cmdAdd_Click()
  Dim item As String
  item = InputBox("Item to Add:")
  lstOxys.AddItem item
End Sub

Private Sub Form_Load()
  lstOxys.AddItem "jumbo shrimp"
  lstOxys.AddItem "definite maybe"
  lstOxys.AddItem "old news"
  lstOxys.AddItem "good grief"
End Sub

Private Sub lstOxys_Click()
  picSelected.Cls
  picSelected.Print "The selected item is"
  picSelected.Print Chr(34) & lstOxys.Text & Chr(34) & "."
End Sub

Private Sub lstOxys_DblClick()
  lstOxys.RemoveItem lstOxys.ListIndex
End Sub
```

[Run, and then click on the second item of the list box.]

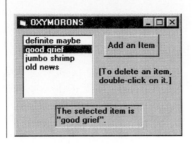

The following steps show how to fill a list box at design time.

1. Select the List property of the list box.

2. Click on the down arrow of the Settings box. (A small box will be displayed.)

3. Type in the first item and press Ctrl+Enter. (The cursor will move to the next line.)

4. Repeat Step 3 for each of the other items.

5. When you are finished entering items, press the Enter key.

When the Sorted property of a list box is True, the index associated with an item will change when a "lesser" item is added to or removed from the list. In many applications it is important to have a fixed number associated with each item in a list box. Visual Basic makes this possible using the ItemData property. The statement

```
List1.ItemData(n) = m
```

associates the number m with the item of index n, and the statement

```
List1.ItemData(List1.NewIndex) = m
```

associates the number m with the item most recently added to the list box. Thus, the List1 list box can be thought of as consisting of two arrays, List1.List( ) and List1.ItemData( ). The contents of List1.List( ) are displayed in the list box, allowing the user to make a selection while the hidden contents of List1.ItemData( ) can be used by the programmer to index records or, as illustrated in Example 5, to set up parallel arrays that hold other data associated with each item displayed in the list box.

EXAMPLE 5 The following program uses NewIndex and ItemData to provide data about inventions. When an item is highlighted, its ItemData value is used to locate the appropriate entries in the inventor( ) and date( ) arrays. Assume the file Inventor.txt contains the following three lines:

"Ball-point pen", "Lazlo and George Biro", 1938
"Frozen food", "Robert Birdseye", 1929
"Bifocal lenses", "Ben Franklin", 1784

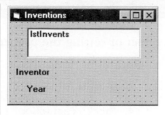

Object	Property	Setting
frmInvent	Caption	Inventions
lstInvents	Sorted	True
lblInventor	Caption	Inventor
lblWho	Caption	(none)
lblYear	Caption	Year
lblWhen	Caption	(none)

```
'In the (Declarations) section of (General)
Dim inventor(0 To 10) As String
Dim yr(0 To 10) As Integer

Private Sub Form_Load()
  Dim what As String, who As String, when As Integer, index As Integer
  Open "Inventor.txt" For Input As #1
  index = 0
  Do While (index < 10) And (Not EOF(1))
    Input #1, what, who, when
    index = index + 1
    lstInvents.AddItem what
    lstInvents.ItemData(lstInvents.NewIndex) = index
    inventor(index) = who
    yr(index) = when
  Loop
  Close #1
End Sub

Private Sub lstInvents_Click()
  lblWho.Caption = inventor(lstInvents.ItemData(lstInvents.ListIndex))
  lblWhen.Caption = Str(yr(lstInvents.ItemData(lstInvents.ListIndex)))
End Sub
```

[Run, and then highlight the second entry in the list.]

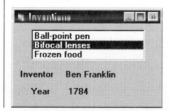

✔ **PRACTICE PROBLEMS 5.2**

1. Suppose you create a frame and then drag a preexisting text box into the frame. How will this text box differ from a text box that was attached to the frame by the single-click-draw method?

2. What is the difference between a group of check boxes attached to a frame and a group of option buttons attached to a frame?

3. Write code to copy the contents of a list box into a file.

➤ **EXERCISES 5.2**

In Exercises 1 to 6, determine the effect of setting the property to the value shown.

1. `Frame1.Caption = "Income"`

2. `Check1.Value = 1`

3. `Check1.Value = 0`

4. `Check1.Caption = "&Vanilla"`

5. `Option1.Value = False`

6. `Option1.Caption = "Punt"`

In Exercises 7 and 8, determine the state of the two option buttons after the command button is clicked.

7.
```
Private Sub Command1_Click()
    Option1.Value = True
    Option2.Value = True
End Sub
```

8.
```
Private Sub Command1_Click()
    Option1.Value = False
    Option2.Value = False
End Sub
```

9. Which of the controls presented in this section can receive the focus? Design a form containing all of the controls and repeatedly press the Tab key to confirm your answer.

10. Create a form with two frames, each having two option buttons attached to it. Run the program and confirm that the two pairs of option buttons operate independently of each other.

11. Suppose a frame has two option buttons attached to it. If the statement Frame1.Visible = False is executed, will the option buttons also vanish? Test your answer.

12. Why are option buttons also called "radio buttons"?

For Exercises 13 to 22, suppose that the list box lstBox is as shown and determine the effect of the code. (Assume the Sorted property is set to True.)

13. `picOutput.Print lstBox.Text`

14. `picOutput.Print lstBox.List(2)`

15. `picOutput.Print lstBox.List(lstBox.ListCount - 1)`

16. `lstBox.AddItem "Haydn"`

17. `lstBox.AddItem "Brahms"`
    `picOutput.Print lstBox.List(lstBox.NewIndex)`

18. `lstBox.RemoveItem 0`

19. `lstBox.RemoveItem lstBox.ListIndex`

20. lstBox.RemoveItem lstBox.ListCount - 1

21. lstBox.Clear

22. For n = 0 To lstBox.ListCount - 1
    If Len(lstBox.List(n)) = 6 Then
        lstBox.RemoveItem n
    End If
Next n

A form contains a command button, a small picture box, and a frame with three check boxes (Check1, Check2, and Check3) attached to it. In Exercises 23 and 24, write a Click event procedure for the command button that displays the stated information in the picture box when the command button is clicked.

23. The number of boxes checked.

24. The captions of the checked boxes.

In Exercises 25 to 30, suppose the form contains a list box containing positive numbers, a command button, and a picture box. Write a Click event procedure for the command button that displays the requested information in the picture box.

25. The average of the numbers in the list.

26. The largest number in the list.

27. Every other number in the list.

28. All numbers greater than the average.

29. The *spread* of the list, that is, the difference between the largest and smallest numbers in the list.

30. The median of the numbers in the list.

31. A computer dealer offers two basic computers, the Deluxe ($1500) and the Super ($1700). In addition, the customer can order any of the following additional options: multimedia kit ($300), internal modem ($100), 64MB of added memory ($150). Write a program that computes the cost of the computer system selected.

32. Item 34a of Form 1040 for the U.S. Individual Income Tax Return reads as follows:

    34a Check if: ☐ **You** were 65 or older, ☐ Blind; ☐ **Spouse** was 65 or older, ☐ Blind
       Add the number of boxes checked above and enter the total here   → **34a** ☐

Write a program that looks at the checked boxes and displays the value for the large square.

33. Write a program for the Font Style form in Figure 5.11. The style of the words in the text box should be determined by the settings in the two frames.

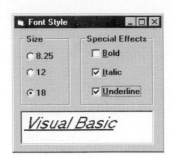

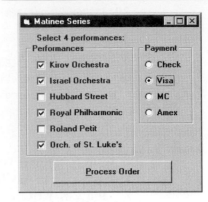

Figure 5.11 Form for Exercise 33.   **Figure 5.12** Form for Exercise 34.

34. Subscribers to the Matinee Series for a recent season at the Kennedy Center for the Performing Arts had to select four performances out of the six shown in the Matinee Series form in Figure 5.12 and had to indicate the method of payment. Write the Click event procedure for the command button. The procedure should first determine whether exactly four performances have been checked. If not, the user should be so informed with a message box. Then the method of payment should be examined. If no method has been indicated, the user must be reminded to select one. Depending on the method of payment, the user should be told with a message box to either mail in the check with the order form or to give the credit card number with an input box request. At the end of the process, the caption on the command box should change to "Thank You".

35. Assume the data in Table 5.2 are contained in the sequential file Stateinf.txt. Write a program that shows the states in a sorted list box and displays a state's nickname and motto when the state is double-clicked.

State	Nickname	Motto
Wisconsin	Badger State	Forward
Rhode Island	Ocean State	Hope
Texas	Lone Star State	Friendship
Utah	Beehive State	Industry

Table 5.2 State nicknames and mottos.

36. Table 5.3 contains the five U.S. presidents rated highest by history professors. Create a form with a list box and two command buttons captioned "Order by Year Inaugurated" and "Order by Age at Inaugural". Write a program that shows the presidents in the list box. When one of the command buttons is clicked, the list box should display the presidents in the requested order.

President	Year Inaugurated	Age at Inaugural
Abraham Lincoln	1861	52
Franklin Roosevelt	1933	51
George Washington	1789	57
Thomas Jefferson	1801	58
Theodore Roosevelt	1901	42

Table 5.3 Highest-rated U.S. presidents.

37. Suppose a form contains a list box (with Sorted = False), a label, and two command buttons captioned "Add an Item" and "Delete an Item". When the "Add an Item" button is clicked, the program should request an item with an input box and then insert the item above the currently highlighted item. When the "Delete an Item" button is clicked, the program should remove the highlighted item from the list. At all times, the label should display the number of items in the list.

38. Consider the Length Converter in Figure 5.13. Write a program to place the items in the list and carry out the conversion. (See the first programming project in Chapter 4 for a table of equivalent lengths.)

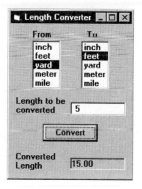

Figure 5.13 Form for Exercise 38.

✔✔ Solutions to Practice Problems 5.2

1. The text box attached by the single-click-draw method will move with the frame, whereas the other text box will not.

2. With option buttons, at most one button can be on at any given time, whereas several check boxes can be checked simultaneously.

3.
```
Private Sub SaveListBox()
    Dim i As Integer
    Open "Listdata.txt" For Output As #1
    For i = 0 to lstBox.ListCount - 1
      Write #1, lstBox.List(i)
    Next i
    Close #1
End Sub
```

5.3 AN INTRODUCTION TO DATABASES

The management of databases is the number one use of computers today. Airlines use databases to handle nearly 1.5 billion passenger reservations per year. The 6500 hospitals in the United States use databases to document the care of over 30 million patients per year. Banks in the United States use databases to monitor the use of 350 million credit cards. Although databases vary considerably in size and complexity, most of them adhere to the fundamental principles of design discussed in this chapter. That is, they are composed of a collection of inter-related tables.

A **table** is a rectangular array of data. Table 5.4 provides information about large cities. Each column of the table, called a **field**, contains the same type of information. (The third column gives the 1995 population in millions and the fourth column gives the projected 2015 population in millions.) The names of the fields are *city*, *country*, *pop1995*, and *pop2015*. Each row, called a **record**, contains the same type of information as every other row. Also, the pieces of information in each row are related; they all apply to a specific city. Table 5.5, Countries, has three fields and nine records.

city	country	pop1995	pop2015
Beijing	China	12.4	19.4
Bombay	India	15.1	27.4
Calcutta	India	11.7	17.6
Los Angeles	USA	12.4	14.3
Mexico City	Mexico	15.6	18.8
New York	USA	16.3	17.6
Sao Paulo	Brazil	16.4	20.8
Shanghai	China	15.1	23.4
Tianjin	China	10.7	17.0
Tokyo	Japan	26.8	28.7

Table 5.4 Cities

country	pop1995	currency
Brazil	155.8	real
China	1185.2	yuan
India	846.3	rupee
Indonesia	195.3	rupiah
Japan	125.0	yen
Mexico	85.6	peso
Nigeria	95.4	naira
Russia	148.2	ruble
USA	263.4	dollar

Table 5.5 Countries

Source: An Urbanized World—Global Report on Human Settlements 1996, a report presented at Habitat II, a UN conference on the world's cities held in Istanbul in June 1996.

A **database** (or **relational database**) is a collection of one or more (usually related) tables that has been created with **database management software**. The best known dedicated database management products are Access, Btrieve, dBase, FoxPro, and Paradox. Every version of Visual Basic 6.0 can manage, revise, and analyze a database that has been created with one of these products.

The databases used in this chapter can be found in the collection of files on the CD accompanying this text. The database files have the extension .mdb. For instance, the file Megacty1.mdb is a database file containing the two tables presented on the preceding page. (**Note:** mdb files should be copied from the CD onto a hard drive and accessed from the hard drive.)

The Data Control

Visual Basic communicates with databases through the data control. Data controls can read, modify, delete, and add records to databases. The following walkthrough uses a data control to connect Visual Basic to the database Megacty1.mdb.

A Data Control Walkthrough

1. Press Alt/File/New Project and double-click on Standard EXE.

2. Double-click on the data control icon. Set its Name property to datCities and its Caption property to Cities.

3. Stretch it horizontally to see the caption Cities.

4. Select the DatabaseName property and set it to the filespec for the file Megacty1.mdb.

   An Open File dialog box will help you locate the file.

5. Select the RecordSource property and click on the down-arrow button at the right of the Settings window.

   The names of the two tables in the database, Cities and Countries, are displayed.

6. Select Cities.

7. Place a text box, txtCity, on the form.

   Text boxes are said to be **data-aware** because they can be bound to a data control and access its data.

8. In the Properties window, select the DataSource property of txtCity.

9. Click on the down arrow to the right of the Settings box and select datCities.

10. Select the DataField property and click on the down arrow at the right of the Settings box.

    You will see the names of the different fields in the table.

11. Select the field *city*.

    The text box now is said to be **bound** to the data control. It can now display data from the *city* field of the Cities table.

12. Place another text box, txtPop1995, on the form.

13. Select txtPop1995's DataSource property.

14. Click on the down arrow to the right of the Settings box and select datCities.

15. Select the DataField property, click on the down arrow at the right of the Settings box, and select *pop1995*.

16. Run the program.

> The form will appear as in Figure 5.14. The arrows on the data control, called **navigation arrows**, look and act like VCR buttons. The arrows have been identified by the tasks they perform.

17. Click on the various navigation arrows on the data control to see the different cities and their populations in the Cities table displayed in the text boxes.

18. Change the name of a city or change its population and then move to another record.

> If you look back through the records, you will see that the data have been permanently changed.

First ———→   Cities   ←——— Last

Previous   Next

Figure 5.14 A Data control with two text boxes bound to it.

Using Code with a Data Control

Only one record can be accessed at a time; this record is called the **current record**. In this walkthrough, the text boxes bound to the data control showed the contents of the *city* and *pop1995* fields of the current record. The user clicked on the navigation arrows of the data control to select a new current record.

Code can be used to designate another record as the current record. The methods MoveNext, MovePrevious, MoveLast, and MoveFirst select a new current record as suggested by their names. For instance, the statement

```
Data1.Recordset.MoveLast
```

specifies the last record of the table to be the current record. (The word Recordset is inserted in most data-control statements that manipulate records for reasons that needn't concern us now.)

The entry of the field *fieldName* of the current record is

```
Data1.Recordset.Fields("fieldName").Value
```

For instance, with the status as in Figure 5.14, the statement

```
strVar = datCities.Recordset.Fields("city").Value
```

assigns "Beijing" to the variable *strVar* and the statements

```
datCities.Recordset.Edit
datCities.Recordset.Fields("city").Value = "Peking"
datCities.Recordset.Update
```

change the *city* field of the current record to "Peking". (The first statement makes a copy of the current record for editing. The second statement alters the copy, and the third statement sends the new copy of the record to the database.)

The number of previously accessed records in the table is given by the RecordCount property. The EOF (End Of File) and BOF (Beginning Of File) run-time properties indicate whether the end or beginning of the file has been reached. For instance, the following two sets of statements each place the cities into a list box.

```
datCities.Recordset.MoveLast     'Needed to set value of RecordCount
datCities.Recordset.MoveFirst
For i = 1 to datCities.Recordset.RecordCount
  lstBox.AddItem datCities.Recordset.Fields("city").Value
  datCities.Recordset.MoveNext
Next i

datCities.Recordset.MoveFirst
Do While Not datCities.Recordset.EOF
  lstBox.AddItem datCities.Recordset.Fields("city").Value
  datCities.Recordset.MoveNext
Loop
```

The current record can be marked for removal with the statement

```
Data1.Recordset.Delete
```

The record will be removed when a data control navigation arrow is clicked or a Move method is executed. A new record can be added to the end of the table with the statement

```
Data1.Recordset.AddNew
```

followed by

```
Data1.Recordset.Fields("fieldName").Value = entryForField
```

statements for each field and a

```
Data1.Recordset.Update
```

statement. Alternately, the AddNew method can be followed by the user typing the information into text boxes bound to the data control and then moving to another record. (**Note:** When you add a record and then click on the Move-Previous arrow, you will not see the next-to-last record, but rather will see the record preceding the record that was current when AddNew was executed.)

The following program is a general database manager for the Cities table in the Megacty1.mdb database. It allows the user to edit the Cities table as needed and to locate information based on the city name.

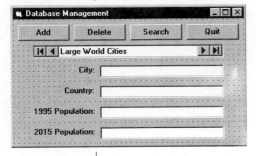

Object	Property	Setting
frmDBMan	Caption	Database Management
cmdAdd	Caption	Add
cmdDelete	Caption	Delete
cmdSearch	Caption	Search
cmdQuit	Caption	Quit
datCities	Caption	Large World Cities
	DatabaseName	Megacty1.mdb
	RecordSource	Cities
lblCity	Caption	City:
txtCity	Text	(blank)
	DataSource	datCities
	DataField	City
lblCountry	Caption	Country:
txtCountry	Text	(blank)
	DataSource	datCities
	DataField	Country
lblPop1995	Caption	1995 Population:
txtPop1995	Text	(blank)
	DataSource	datCities
	DataField	pop1995
lblPop2015	Caption	2015 Population:
txtPop2015	Text	(blank)
	DataSource	datCities
	DataField	pop2015

```
Private Sub cmdAdd_Click()
  'Add a new record
  datCities.Recordset.AddNew
  txtCity.SetFocus     'Data must be entered and a new record moved to
End Sub

Private Sub cmdDelete_Click ()
  'Delete the currently displayed record
  datCities.Recordset.Delete
  'Move so that user sees deleted record disappear
  datCities.Recordset.MoveNext
  If datCities.Recordset.EOF Then
      datCities.Recordset.MovePrevious
  End If
End Sub

Private Sub cmdSearch_Click()
  Dim strSearchFor As String, foundFlag As Boolean
  'Search for the city specified by the user
  strSearchFor = UCase(InputBox("Name of city to find:"))
  If Len(strSearchFor) > 0 Then
      datCities.Recordset.MoveFirst
      foundFlag = False
```

```
      Do While (Not foundFlag) And (Not datCities.Recordset.EOF)
        If UCase(datCities.Recordset.Fields("City").Value) = strSearchFor Then
            foundFlag = True
        Else
            datCities.Recordset.MoveNext
        End If
      Loop
      If Not foundFlag Then
          MsgBox "Unable to locate requested city.", , "Not Found"
          datCities.Recordset.MoveLast   'move so that EOF is no longer true
      End If
    Else
      MsgBox "Must enter a city.", , ""
  End If
End Sub

Private Sub cmdQuit_Click ()
  End
End Sub
```

[Run, click the Search button, and enter New York.]

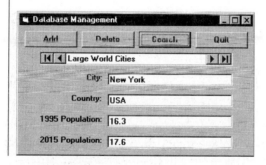

Comments

1. App.Path cannot be used when you set the DatabaseName property of a data control in the Properties window at design time. However, App.Path can be used in the Form_Load event procedure. For instance, if you add the lines

```
Private Sub Form_Load()
   datCities.DatabaseName = App.Path & "\Megacty1.mdb"
End Sub
```

to Example 1, the program will find the database when it is located in the same folder as the program. The assignment made in the Form_Load event procedure will override any setting made in the Properties window. (The setting in the Properties window even can be left blank.) The programs for Chapter 5 on the CD accompanying this textbook contain the above Form_Load event procedure.

2. You will most likely alter the file Megacty1.mdb while experimenting with the data control or running the program in Example 1. You can always obtain a fresh copy of Megacty1.mdb by recopying it from the CD.

3. You can prevent the user from altering the data in a table by setting the ReadOnly property of its data control to True.

4. The following controls can be bound to a data control: text box, check box, image, label, picture box, list box, combo box, data bound list box, data bound combo box, and FlexGrid.

5. A form can contain more than one data control.

6. Some entries in a table can be empty. For instance, in the Cities table, if the 2015 projected value is not known for a particular city, it can be omitted.

7. Field names can be up to 64 characters in length and can consist of letters, numbers, and spaces. If spaces are used in a name, then the name must be enclosed in brackets when used in Visual Basic.

8. Both tables in the database Megacty1.mdb have fields called *country*. If there is ever any question about which is being referred to, we can distinguish them by using the two (full) names Cities.country and Countries.country.

9. In the Megacty1.mdb database, the values in the field *city* are all of data type String and the values in the field *pop1995* are all of data type Single.

10. When a field is first created, a type must be specified. When that type is String, a maximum length must also be specified. In the Megacty1.mdb database, the fields *city* and *country* have maximum length 20 and the field *currency* has maximum length 10.

11. The database Megacty1.mdb was created with Visual Data Manager, which has the same format as Access. When the database to be used has been created with other software, such as FoxPro 3.0 or dBase 5.0, then the walkthrough requires an additional step. Namely, between Steps 3 and 4, the Connect property of the data control has to be set to the name of the software product. (This step was not necessary in our case because Access is the default software.) **Note:** Access database file names end with .mdb, which is an abbreviation for Microsoft Data Base. Btrieve, FoxPro, dBase, and Paradox database file names end with .dat, .dbf, .dbf, and .db, respectively.

✔ **PRACTICE PROBLEMS 5.3**

The Access database BIBLIO.MDB is supplied with Visual Basic 6.0 and is usually stored in the folder Program files\Microsoft Visual Studio\VB98. How might you determine each of the following quantities?

1. The number of tables in this database

2. The names of the fields in the table Titles

3. The number of records in the table Titles

➤ **EXERCISES 5.3**

Exercises 1 through 14 refer to the database Megacty1.mdb.

1. Write a program to place in a list box the names of the countries in the Countries table in the order they appear in the table.

2. Write a program to place in a list box the names of the countries in the Countries table in the reverse order that they appear in the table.

3. Write a program to place in a list box the names of the cities in the Cities table whose populations are projected to exceed 20 million in the year 2015.

4. Write a program to place in a list box the names of the cities in the Cities table whose 1995 populations are between 12 and 16 million.

5. Write a program to place in a list box the names of the countries in the Countries table, where each name is followed by a hyphen and the name of its currency.

6. Write a program to find and display the city in the Cities table that will experience the greatest percentage growth from 1995 to 2015. [**Note:** The percentage growth is 100 * (pop2015 − pop1995) / pop1995.]

7. Write a program to place the countries from the Countries table in a list box in descending order of their 1995 populations. (**Hint:** Place the countries and their 1995 populations in a pair of parallel arrays and sort the pair of arrays in descending order based on the populations.)

8. Write a program to place the cities from the Cities table in a list box in descending order of their percentage population growth from 1995 to 2015.

9. Write a program to display the name and currency of each city in the table Cities.

10. Write a program to display the names and 1995 populations of the countries in the table Country. The countries should be displayed in descending order of their populations.

11. Write a program to back up the contents of the Cities table in one sequential file and the Countries table in another sequential file. Run the program and compare the sizes of these two sequential files with the size of the file Megacty1.mdb.

12. Suppose the sequential file Addctry.txt contains several records for countries not in Megacty1.mdb, where each record consists of the name of a country, its 1995 population (in millions), and the name of its currency. Write a program to add the contents of this file into the Countries table.

13. Suppose the sequential file Update.txt contains several records, where each record consists of the name of a country, its 1995 population (in millions), and the name of its currency. Write a program to use the information in Update.txt to update the Countries table. If a record in Update.txt contains the same country as a record in the Countries table, then the population in 1995 and the name of the currency in the Countries table should be replaced with the corresponding values from Update.txt. If a record in Update.txt contains a country that does not appear in the Countries table, a new record should be added to the table.

14. Write a program that allows the user to specify a city and then displays the percentage of its country's population that lives in that city.

Exercises 15 through 18 refer to the Biblio.mdb database supplied with Visual Basic.

15. How many tables are in the database?

16. Give the names of the fields in the table Publishers.

17. How many records are in the table Publishers?

18. Write a program that requests the name of a publisher (such as Prentice Hall or Que Corp) and gives the publisher's address.

19. The database St_abbr.mdb contains one table, States, having two fields, *abbreviation* and *state*. Each record consists of a two-letter abbreviation and the name of a state. Some records are (AZ, Arizona) and (MD, Maryland). Write a program that allows the user to enter a two-letter abbreviation and obtain the name of the state. Of course, if the two-letter abbreviation does not correspond to any state, the user should be so informed.

Exercises 20 and 21 use the database EXCHANGE.MDB found on the CD accompanying this book. It gives the exchange rates (in terms of American dollars) for about 55 major currencies on October 1, 1998. Figure 5.15 shows the first eight records of the database in a FlexGrid control. The DollarRate column gives the number of units of the currency that can be purchased for one American dollar. For instance, one American dollar purchases 1.536 Canadian dollars.

Name	DollarRate
American Dollars	1
Argentine Pesos	0.9998
Australian Dollars	1.67424
Austrian Schillings	11.6127
Belgian Francs	34.0532
Brazilian Reals	1.18318
British Pounds	0.586615
Canadian Dollars	1.536

Figure 5.15 Exchange rates.

20. Write a program that displays the names of the currencies in a list box. As soon as the program is run, the user should click on SHOW LIST to fill the list box. When the user clicks on one of the names, the exchange rate should be displayed.

21. Write a program containing two list boxes as shown in Figure 5.16. As soon as the program is run, the user should click on SHOW LISTS to fill the list boxes. When the user selects two currencies and an amount of money, and clicks on CALCULATE, the program should convert the amount from one currency to the other.

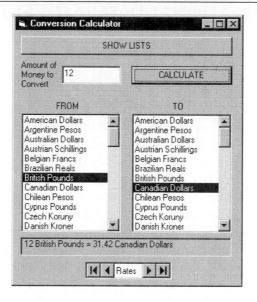

Figure 5.16 A possible output for Exercise 21.

22. A data control can also be connected to an Excel spreadsheet. (Set the Connect property of the data control to Excel 3.0 or Excel 4.0 or Excel 5.0 or Excel 8.0, . . . , and set the DatabaseName property to the name of the spreadsheet.) The Excel 5.0 spreadsheet Chkbook5.xls and the Excel spreadsheet Chkbook8.xls are on the CD accompanying this text. These spreadsheets have four columns labeled *date*, *checkNum*, *description*, and *amount*. Write a program that displays the rows of one of the speadsheets in text boxes. The program should allow you to search for checks and add checks to the spreadsheet. (**Note:** Set the RecordSource property to Checks$. The column names serve as field names and should be specified in the DataField property of the text boxes.)

✔✔ **Solutions to Practice Problems 5.3**

Place a data control, call it datBooks, on a form and set its DatabaseName property to the file Biblio.mdb.

1. Select the RecordSource property and click on the down-arrow button at the right of its settings box. Count the number of entries in the dropdown list of tables that appears.

2. Set the RecordSource property of datBooks to the table Titles. Place a text box, call it txtBook, on the form and bind it to the data control by setting its DataSource property to datBooks. Select the DataField property of txtBook and click on the down-arrow button at the right of its Settings box. Count the number of entries in the dropdown list of fields that appears.

3. Place a picture box and a command button on the screen. Place the statements

```
datBooks.Recordset.MoveLast
picBox.Print datBooks.Recordset.RecordCount
```

in the cmdDisplay_Click event procedure. Run the program and then click on the command button.

5.4 RELATIONAL DATABASES AND SQL

Primary and Foreign Keys

A well-designed table should have a field (or set of fields) that can be used to uniquely identify each record. Such a field (or set of fields) is called a **primary key**. For instance, in the Countries table of Section 5.3, the *country* field is a primary key. In the Cities table, because we are only considering very large cities (of over 1 million population), the *city* field is a primary key. Databases of student enrollments in a college usually use a field of social security numbers as the primary key. Names would not be a good choice because there could easily be two students having the same name.

When a database is created, a field can be specified as a primary key. If so, Visual Basic will insist that every record have an entry in the primary key field and that the same entry does not appear in two different records. If the user tries to enter a record with no data in the primary key, the error message "Index or primary key can't contain a null record." will be generated. If the user tries to enter a record with the same primary key data as another record, the error message "Duplicate value in index, primary key, or relationship. Changes were unsuccessful." will be displayed.

When a database contains two or more tables, the tables are usually related. For instance, the two tables Cities and Countries are related by their *country* field. Let's refer to these two fields as Cities.country and Countries.country. Notice that every entry in Cities.country appears uniquely in Countries.country and Countries.country is a primary key . We say that Cities.country is a **foreign key** of Countries.country. Foreign keys can be specified when a table is first created. If so, Visual Basic will insist on the **Rule of Referential Integrity**, namely, that each value in the foreign key must also appear in the primary key of the other table.

The CD accompanying this book contains a database named Megacty2. Mdb. It has the same information as Megacty1.mdb except that Cities.city and Countries.country have been specified as primary keys for their respective tables, and Cities.country has been specified as a foreign key of Countries.country. If the user tries to add a city to the Cities table whose country does not appear in the Countries table, then the error message "Can't add or change record. Referential integrity rules require a related record in table 'Countries'." will be displayed. The message will also be generated if the user tries to delete a country from the Countries.country field that appears in the Cities.country field. Due to the interdependence of the two tables in Megacty2.mdb, this database is called a **relational database**.

A foreign key allows Visual Basic to link (or **join**) together two tables from a relational database in a meaningful way. For instance, when the two tables Cities and Countries from Megacty2.mdb are joined based on the foreign key Cities.country, the result is Table 5.6. The record for each city is expanded to show its country's population and its currency. This joined table is very handy if, say, we wanted to click on navigation arrows and display a city's name and currency. We only have to create the original two tables; Visual Basic creates the joined table as needed. The request for a joined table is made in a language called SQL.

city	Cities. country	Cities. pop1995	pop2015	Countries. country	Country. pop1995	currency
Tokyo	Japan	26.8	28.7	Japan	125.0	yen
Sao Paulo	Brazil	16.4	20.8	Brazil	155.8	real
New York	USA	16.3	17.6	USA	263.4	dollar
Mexico City	Mexico	15.6	18.8	Mexico	85.6	peso
Bombay	India	15.1	27.4	India	846.3	rupee
Shanghai	China	15.1	23.4	China	1185.2	yuan
Los Angeles	USA	12.4	14.3	USA	263.4	dollar
Beijing	China	12.4	19.4	China	1185.2	yuan
Calcutta	India	11.7	17.6	India	846.3	rupee
Tianjin	China	10.7	17.0	China	1185.2	yuan

Table 5.6 A join of two tables.

SQL

Structured Query Language (SQL) was developed in the early 1970s at IBM for use with relational databases. The language was standardized in 1986 by ANSI (American National Standards Institute). Visual Basic uses a version of SQL that is compliant with ANSI-89 SQL. There are some minor variations that are of no concern in this book.

SQL is a very powerful language. One use of SQL is to request specialized information from an existing database and/or to have the information presented in a specified order.

Four SQL Requests

We will focus on four basic types of requests that can be made with SQL.

Request I: Show the records of a table in a specified order.

Some examples of orders with Megacty2.mdb are

(a) Alphabetical order based on the name of the city.
(b) Alphabetical order based on the name of the country, and within each country group, the name of the city.
(c) In descending order based on the projected 2015 population.

Request II: Show just the records that meet certain criteria.

Some examples of criteria with Megacty2.mdb are

(a) Cities that are in China.
(b) Cities whose 2015 population is projected to be at least 20 million.
(c) Cities whose name begins with the letter S.

Request III: Join the tables together, connected by a foreign key, and present the records as in Requests I and II.

Some examples with Megacty2.mdb are

(a) Show the cities in descending order of the populations of their countries.
(b) Show the cities whose currency has "u" as its second letter.

Request IV: Make available just *some* of the fields of either the basic tables or the joined table. (For now, this type of request just conserves space and effort by Visual Basic. However, it will be very useful when used with a FlexGrid control.)

Some examples with Megacty2.mdb are

(a) Make available just the city and country fields of the table Cities.
(b) Make available just the city and currency fields of the joined table.

Normally, we set the RecordSource property of a data control to an entire table. Also, the records of the table are normally presented in the order they are physically stored in the table. We make the requests discussed above by specifying the RecordSource property as one of the following kinds of settings.

Request I: SELECT * FROM *Table1* ORDER BY *field1* ASC
   or SELECT * FROM *Table1* ORDER BY *field1* DESC

Request II: SELECT * FROM *Table1* WHERE *criteria*

Request III: SELECT * FROM *Table1* INNER JOIN *Table2* ON *foreign field =
primary field* WHERE *criteria*

Request IV: SELECT *field1* , *field2* , . . . *fieldN* FROM *Table1* WHERE *criteria*

The words ASC and DESC specify ASCending and DESCending orders, respectively. A *criteria* clause is a string containing a condition of the type used with If blocks. In addition to the standard operators <, >, and =, *criteria* strings frequently contain the operator Like. Essentially, Like uses the wildcard characters ? and * to compare a string to a pattern. A question mark stands for a single character in the same position as the question mark. For instance, the pattern "B?d" is matched by "Bid", "Bud", and "Bad". An asterisk stands for any number of characters in the same position as the asterisk. For instance, the pattern "C*r" is matched by "Computer", "Chair", and "Car". See Comments 3 through 5 for further information about Like.

In the sentence

```
SELECT fields FROM clause
```

fields is either * (to indicate all fields) or a sequence of the fields to be available (separated by commas), and *clause* is either a single table or a join of two tables. A join of two tables is indicated by a *clause* of the form

```
table1 INNER JOIN table2 ON foreign key of table1=primary key of table2
```

Appending

```
WHERE criteria
```

to the end of the sentence restricts the records to those satisfying *criteria*. Appending

```
ORDER BY field(s) ASC (or DESC)
```

presents the records ordered by the specified *field* or *fields*.

In general, the SQL statements we consider will look like

```
SELECT www FROM xxx WHERE yyy ORDER BY zzz
```

where SELECT *www* FROM *xxx* is always present and accompanied by one or both of WHERE *yyy* and ORDER BY *zzz*. In addition, the *xxx* portion might contain an INNER JOIN phrase.

The settings for the examples mentioned earlier are as follows:

I (a) Show the records from Cities in alphabetical order based on the name of the city.

```
SELECT * FROM Cities ORDER BY city ASC
```

I (b) Show the records from Cities in alphabetical order based first on the name of the country and, within each country group, the name of the city.

```
SELECT * FROM Cities ORDER BY country, city ASC
```

I (c) Show the records from Cities in descending order based on the projected 2015 population.

```
SELECT * FROM Cities ORDER BY pop2015 DESC
```

II (a) Show the records for the Cities in China.

```
SELECT * FROM Cities WHERE country = 'China'
```

II (b) Show the records from Cities whose 2015 population is projected to be at least 20 million.

```
SELECT * FROM Cities WHERE pop2015 >= 20
```

II (c) Show the records from Cities whose name begins with the letter S.

```
SELECT * FROM Cities WHERE city Like 'S*'
```

III(a) Show the records from the joined table in descending order of the populations of their countries.

```
SELECT * FROM Cities INNER JOIN Countries ON Cities.country =
Countries.country ORDER BY Countries.pop1995 DESC
```

III(b) Show the records from the joined table whose currency has "u" as its second letter.

```
SELECT * FROM Cities INNER JOIN Countries ON Cities.country =
Countries.country WHERE currency Like '?u*'
```

IV(a) Make available just the city and country fields of the table Cities.

```
SELECT city, country FROM Cities
```

IV(b) Make available just the city and currency fields of the joined table.

```
SELECT city, currency FROM Cities INNER JOIN Countries ON
Cities.country = Countries.country
```

Note: In several of the statements, the single quote, rather than the normal double quote was used to surround strings. This is standard practice with SQL statements.

We can think of an SQL statement as creating in essence a new "virtual" table from existing tables. For instance, we might regard the statement

```
SELECT city, pop2015 FROM Cities WHERE pop2015>=20
```

as creating the "virtual" table

city	pop2015
Tokyo	28.7
Sao Paulo	20.8
Bombay	27.4
Shanghai	23.4

This table is a subtable of the original table Cities, that is, it consists of what is left after certain columns and rows are deleted.

As another example, the statement

```
SELECT Cities.city, Cities.Country, Country.currency FROM Cities INNER JOIN
Countries ON Cities.country = Countries.country WHERE Countries.country>'K'
```

creates in essence the "virtual" table

Cities.city	Cities.country	currency
New York	USA	dollar
Mexico City	Mexico	peso
Los Angeles	USA	dollar

which is a subtable of a join of the two tables Cities and Countries.

These "virtual" tables don't really exist physically. However, for all practical purposes, Visual Basic acts as if they did. In Visual Basic terminology, a "virtual" table is called a **recordset** and SQL statements are said to create a recordset. In standard relational database books, a "virtual" table is called a **view**.

SQL also can be used in code with a statement of the form

```
Data1.RecordSource = "SELECT ... FROM ..."
```

to alter the order and kinds of records presented from a database. However, such a statement must be followed by the statement

```
Data1.Refresh
```

to reset the information processed by the data control.

The Microsoft FlexGrid Control

When the FlexGrid control is bound to a data control, it can display an entire table or view in a rectangular array. The FlexGrid control does not initially appear in your Toolbox. To add the control, click on Components in the Project menu, click the Controls tab, and click on the check box to the left of "Microsoft FlexGrid Control 6.0." Then press the OK button. By convention, names of Microsoft FlexGrids have the prefix *msg*.

The FlexGrid in Figure 5.17 has 6 rows and 7 columns. Rows and columns are numbered beginning with 0. For instance, the columns in Figure 5.17 are numbered (from left to right) as 0, 1, 2, 3, 4, 5, and 6. The width, measured in twips (there are about 1440 twips to an inch), of each column can be specified only at run time with the ColWidth property. A typical statement is msgFlex. ColWidth(3) = 1200, which sets the width of column 3 to 1200 twips. (The default column width is 912 twips.)

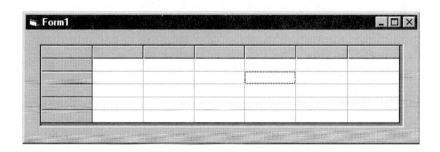

Figure 5.17 A FlexGrid control

The grayed row and column in Figure 5.17 are referred to as **fixed**. The number of fixed rows and columns is specified at design time by the FixedRows and FixedCols properties. The grid in Figure 5.17 has the default settings FixedRows = 1 and FixedCols = 1. When you bind a FlexGrid to a data control, you should set the FixedCols property to 0 and leave the FixedRows property set to 1. When the program is run, the size of the grid will automatically adjust to accommodate the table. The field names will be displayed in the fixed row and each nonfixed row will contain a record. If the width of the grid is too small to show all the columns, a horizontal scroll bar will automatically appear across the bottom of the grid. Then, during run time, the nonfixed columns can be scrolled to reveal the hidden columns. Similarly, a vertical scroll bar appears when the height of the grid is too small to show all the rows.

The individual small rectangles are called cells. Unfortunately, you can't just place text into a cell by clicking on the cell and typing, as you would with a text box. Although you can use code to alter the contents of the cells in a FlexGrid, changes in the cells of a FlexGrid will not alter the contents of the database to which it is bound.

You can use an SQL statement to specify the fields displayed in a FlexGrid control. For instance, if the control has datCities as its DataSource and the DatabaseName setting for datCities is Megacty2.mdb, then the statement

```
datCities.RecordSource = "SELECT city, country FROM Cities"
```

causes the FlexGrid to display only the first two columns of the Cities table. The same effect can be achieved at design time by setting the RecordSource property of datCities to

```
SELECT city, country FROM Cities
```

EXAMPLE I

The following program displays the contents of the Cities table of the Megacty2.mdb database. When you click on the command button, the FlexGrid displays the cities, their countries, and currency. Also, the caption of the command button changes to "Show City, Country, Populations". The next time you click the command button, the contents of the FlexGrid returns to its original state.

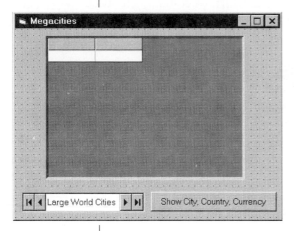

Object	Property	Setting
frm5_4_1	Caption	Megacities
datCities	Caption	Large World Cities
	DatabaseName	Megacty2.mdb
	RecordSource	Cities
msgCities	DataSource	datCities
	FixedCols	0
cmdShow	Caption	Show City, Country, Currency

```
Private Sub cmdShow_Click()
  If cmdShow.Caption = "Show City, Country, Currency" Then
      'Join the two tables and display cities, countries, and currency
      datCities.RecordSource = "SELECT city, Cities.country, currency FROM " & _
      "Cities INNER JOIN Countries ON Countries.country = Cities.country " & _
      "ORDER BY city"
      datCities.Refresh
      cmdShow.Caption = "Show City, Country, Populations"
    Else
      datCities.RecordSource = "Cities"
      datCities.Refresh
      cmdShow.Caption = "Show City, Country, Currency"
  End If
End Sub

Private Sub Form_Load()
  msgCities.ColWidth(0) = 1000   'Widen the first column slightly
End Sub
```

[Run]

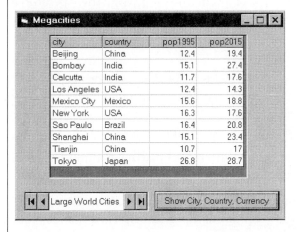

[Click on the command button.]

Comments

1. Each record of the Countries table is related to one or more records of the Cities table, but each record of the Cities table is related to only one record of the Countries table. Therefore, we say that there is a **one-to-many relationship** from the Countries table to the Cities table.

2. SQL statements are insensitive to case. For instance, the following choices for *criteria* have the same effect: City='China', city='china', CITY='china', CiTy='CHINA'.

3. When the Like operator is used, the "pattern" must appear on the right of the operator. For instance, the SQL statement

```
SELECT * FROM Cities WHERE city Like 'S*'
```

cannot be replaced by

```
SELECT * FROM Cities WHERE 'S*' Like city
```

4. The operator Like permits a refinement of the wildcard character "?". Whereas "?" is a placeholder for any letter, an expression such as "[*letter1-letter2*]" is a placeholder for any letter from *letter1* to *letter2*. For instance, the pattern "[A-F]ad" is matched by Bad and Dad, but not Sad.

5. The Like operator can be used in If blocks in much the same way as the operators >, =, and <. In this situation, the operator is case-sensitive. For instance, the condition ("bad" Like "[A-F]ad") is False. However, when Like is used in SQL statements, it is case-insensitive. That is, ("bad" Like "[A-F]ad") is True.

6. Sometimes a pair of fields is specified as a primary key. For instance, in a table of college courses, a single course might have several sections—a course might be identified as CMSC 102, Section 3. In this case, the pair of fields *course, section* would serve as a primary key for the table.

7. The requirement that no record may have a null primary key is called the **Rule of Entity Integrity**.

8. If there is no field with unique entries, database designers usually add a "counter field" containing the numbers 1, 2, 3, and so on. This field then can serve as a primary key.

✔ **PRACTICE PROBLEM 5.4**

1. Consider the procedure cmdSearch_Click( ) of Example 1 in Section 5.3. Rewrite the procedure using an SQL statement to display the requested record.

➤ **EXERCISES 5.4**

Exercises 1 and 4 refer to the database Megacty2.mdb, where the primary keys of Cities and Countries are *city* and *country*, respectively, and *Cities. country* is a foreign key to *Countries.country*. Determine whether the stated action could ever cause a problem. Explain.

1. Add a new record to the Cities table.

2. Delete a record from the Countries table.

3. Delete a record from the Cities table.

4. Add a new record to the Countries table.

In Exercises 5 through 10, use the database Biblio.mdb that is provided with Visual Basic. By experimentation, determine the primary keys for each of the tables in Exercises 5 through 8.

5. Authors   6. Publishers

7. Titles   8. Title Author

Determine the foreign keys for the pairs of tables in Exercises 9 and 10.

9. Authors, Titles   10. Publishers, Titles

The following tables are "virtual" tables derived from the Megacty2.mdb database. In Exercises 11 through 14, identify the "virtual" table associated with the SQL statement.

(A)

country	pop1995	currency
Russia	148.2	ruble
Indonesia	195.3	rupiah
India	846.3	rupee
Brazil	155.8	real

(B)

country	pop1995	currency
China	1185.2	yuan

(C)

country	pop1995	currency
China	1185.2	yuan
India	846.3	rupee

(D)

country	pop1995	currency
China	1185.2	yuan
Brazil	155.8	real

11. SELECT * FROM Countries WHERE pop1995>1000 ORDER BY pop1995 ASC

12. SELECT * FROM Countries WHERE country<'E' ORDER BY pop1995 DESC

13. SELECT * FROM Countries WHERE currency Like 'r*' ORDER BY country DESC

14. SELECT * FROM Countries WHERE pop1995>700 ORDER BY country ASC

The following tables are "virtual" tables derived from the Megacty2.mdb database. In Exercises 15 through 18, identify the "virtual" table associated with the SQL statement.

(A)

city	currency
Sao Paulo	real
Shanghai	yuan

(B)

city	currency
Tokyo	yen
Bombay	rupee
Shanghai	yuan

(C)

city	currency
Bombay	rupee
Calcutta	rupee

(D)

city	currency
Tokyo	yen

15. SELECT city, currency FROM Cities INNER JOIN Countries ON Cities.country = Countries.country WHERE city='Tokyo'

16. SELECT city, currency FROM Cities INNER JOIN Countries ON Cities.country= Countries.country WHERE pop2015>22 ORDER BY pop2015 DESC

17. SELECT city, currency FROM Cities INNER JOIN Countries ON Cities.country = Countries.country WHERE Cities.country='India' ORDER BY Cities.pop1995 DESC

18. SELECT city, currency FROM Cities INNER JOIN Countries ON Cities.country = Countries.country WHERE city Like 'S*' ORDER BY Countries.pop1995 ASC

For each grid in Exercises 19 through 28, give an SQL statement that can be used to create the grid from the Megacty2.mdb database. Then test your answer with a FlexGrid attached to a data control having the SQL statement as its RecordSource. (*Note*: Several of the exercises have more than one correct answer.)

19.

country	pop1995	currency
Indonesia	195.3	rupiah
India	846.3	rupee

20.

country
Mexico
Brazil

21.

country	currency
Japan	yen
Russia	ruble
Brazil	real
Indonesia	rupiah

22.

country	pop1995	currency
India	846.3	rupee
Indonesia	195.3	rupiah
Brazil	155.8	real
Russia	148.2	ruble

23.

city	country	pop1995	pop2015
Shanghai	China	15.1	23.4
Beijing	China	12.4	19.4
Tianjin	China	10.7	17

24.

city	country	pop1995	pop2015
Sao Paulo	Brazil	16.4	20.8
Shanghai	China	15.1	23.4
Bombay	India	15.1	27.4
Tokyo	Japan	26.8	28.7

25.

city	country	pop1995	pop2015
Shanghai	China	15.1	23.4
Bombay	India	15.1	27.4
Mexico City	Mexico	15.6	18.8

26.

city	country	pop1995	pop2015
Sao Paulo	Brazil	16.4	20.8
Mexico City	Mexico	15.6	18.8

27.

city	pop2015	currency
Bombay	27.4	rupee
Calcutta	17.6	rupee

28.

city	Cities.pop1995	Countries.pop1995
Tokyo	26.8	125
Sao Paulo	16.4	155.8
New York	16.3	263.4

Exercises 29 and 30 refer to the database Phonebk.mdb, which holds all the information for the residence listings of a telephone book for a city. Assume the database consists of one table, Names, with six fields; lastName, firstName, middleInitial, streetNumber, street, and phoneNumber.

29. Write a program that displays the contents of the phone book in the standard form shown in Figure 5.18(a).

30. Write a program that displays a "criss-cross" directory that gives phone numbers with the entries organized by street as in Figure 5.18(b).

AAKER Larry	3 Main St	874-2345	APPLE ST	3 Carl Aaron	405-2345
AARON Alex	23 Park Ave	924-3456	5	John Smith	862-1934
Bob R	17 Elm St	347-3456	7	Ted T Jones	405-1843
Carl	3 Apple St	405-2345	ARROW RD	1 Ben Rob	865-2345
	(a)			(b)	

Figure 5.18 **(a)** Standard phone directory and **(b)** criss-cross directory.

✔✔ **Solution to Practice Problem 5.4**

```
1. Private Sub cmdSearch_Click ()
      Dim strSearchFor As String, strSQL As String
      'Search for the city specified by the user
      strSearchFor = InputBox("Name of city to find:")
      If Len(strSearchFor) > 0 Then
          strSQL = "SELECT * FROM Cities " & _
                  "WHERE city=" & "'" & strSearchFor & "'"
          datCities.RecordSource = strSQL
          datCities.Refresh
          If txtCity.Text = "" Then
              MsgBox "Unable to locate requested city.",,"Not Found"
              datCities.RecordSource = "SELECT * FROM Cities"
              datCities.Refresh
          End If
      Else
          Msgbox "Must enter a city.", , ""
      End If
   End Sub
```

CHAPTER 5 SUMMARY

1. Data can be vividly displayed in line and bar charts.

2. The programmer specifies a coordinate system (viewing window) with the Scale method.

3. The Line method draws lines, rectangles, and solid rectangles.

4. The PSet method turns on a single point and is useful in graphing functions.

5. The Circle method is used to draw circles.

6. *Frames* are used to group controls, especially option buttons, as a unit.

7. Selections are made with *check boxes* (allow several) and *option buttons* (allow at most one). The state of the control (*checked* vs. *unchecked* or *on* vs. *off*) is stored in the Value property. Clicking on a check box toggles its state. Clicking on an option button gives it the *on* state and turns *off* the other option buttons in its group.

8. *List boxes* provide easy access to lists of strings. The lists can be automatically sorted (Sorted property = True), altered (AddItem, RemoveItem, and Clear

methods), the currently highlighted item identified (Text property), and the number of items determined (ListCount property). The array List( ) holds the items stored in the list. Each item is identified by an index number (0, 1, 2, . . .). The most recently inserted item can be determined with the NewIndex property. The ItemData property associates a number with each item of text.

9. A *table* is a group of data items arranged in a rectangular array, each containing the same categories of information. Each data item (row) is called a *record*. Each category (column) is called a *field*. Two tables with a common field are said to be *related*. A *database* is a collection of one or more, usually related, tables.

10. The *data control* is used to access a database. When a text box is bound to a data control through its DataSource and DataField properties, the user can read and edit a field of the database. At any time, one record is specified as the *current record*. The user can change the current record with the data control's *navigator arrows* or with *Move* statements. The properties *Record-Count*, *BOF*, and *EOF* count records and indicate whether the ends of a recordset have been reached. The *Value* property of Fields("*fieldName*") reads the contents of a field of the current record.

11. A *primary key* is a field or set of fields that uniquely identifies each row of a table. The *rule of entity integrity* states that no record can have a null entry in a primary key. A *foreign key* is a field or set of fields in one table that refers to a primary key in another table. The *rule of referential integrity* states that each value in the foreign key must also appear in the primary key.

12. Structured Query Language (SQL) is used to create a "virtual" table consisting of a subtable of a table or of a join of two tables and imposes an order on the records. The subtable is specified with the reserved words SELECT, FROM, WHERE, ORDER BY, and INNER JOIN . . . ON. The WHERE clause of an SQL statement commonly uses the Like operator in addition to the standard operators. SQL statements are either employed at design time or run time as the setting of the RecordSource property. During run time, the Refresh method for the data control should be executed after the Record-Source property is set.

13. The *FlexGrid control* can show an entire "virtual" table in a spreadsheet-like display.

CHAPTER 5   PROGRAMMING PROJECTS

1. Figure 5.19 Is called a *range chart*. Using the data in Table 5.7, write a program to produce this chart. The program should use Sub procedures with names such as ReadData, DrawAxis, DrawData, ShowTitle, and ShowLabels.

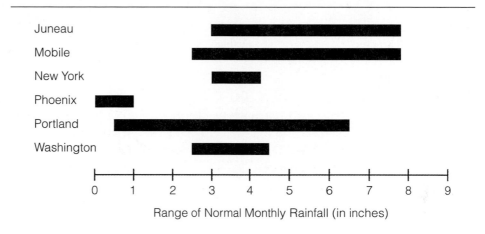

Figure 5.19 Range chart.

	Lowest NMR	Highest NMR
Mobile	2.6	7.7
Portland	.5	6.4
Phoenix	.1	1.0
Washington	2.6	4.4
Juneau	2.9	7.7
New York	3.1	4.2

Table 5.7 Range of normal monthly rainfall for selected cities (in inches).

2. *Voting Machine.* The members of the local Gilligan's Island fan club bring a computer to their annual meeting to use in the election of a new president. Write a program to handle the election. The program should add each candidate to a list box as he or she is nominated. After the nomination process is complete, club members should be able to approach the computer one at a time and double-click on the candidate of their choice. When a "Tally Votes" command button is clicked, a second list box, showing the number of votes received by each candidate, should appear alongside the first list box. Also, the name(s) of the candidate(s) with the highest number of votes should be displayed in a picture box.

APPENDIX A ANSI Values

ANSI Value	Character	ANSI Value	Character	ANSI Value	Character
000	(null)	040	(	080	P
001	□	041	)	081	Q
002	□	042	*	082	R
003	□	043	+	083	S
004	□	044	,	084	T
005	□	045	–	085	U
006	□	046	.	086	V
007	□	047	/	087	W
008	□	048	0	088	X
009	(tab)	049	1	089	Y
010	(line feed)	050	2	090	Z
011	□	051	3	091	[
012	□	052	4	092	\
013	(carriage return)	053	5	093	]
014	□	054	6	094	^
015	□	055	7	095	_
016	□	056	8	096	'
017	□	057	9	097	a
018	□	058	:	098	b
019	□	059	;	099	c
020	□	060	<	100	d
021	□	061	=	101	e
022	□	062	>	102	f
023	□	063	?	103	g
024	□	064	@	104	h
025	□	065	A	105	i
026	□	066	B	106	j
027	□	067	C	107	k
028	□	068	D	108	l
029	□	069	E	109	m
030	□	070	F	110	n
031	□	071	G	111	o
032		072	H	112	p
033	!	073	I	113	q
034	"	074	J	114	r
035	#	075	K	115	s
036	$	076	L	116	t
037	%	077	M	117	u
038	&	078	N	118	v
039	'	079	O	119	w

ANSI Value	Character	ANSI Value	Character	ANSI Value	Character
120	x	166	¦	212	Ô
121	y	167	§	213	Õ
122	z	168	¨	214	Ö
123	{	169	©	215	×
124	|	170	ª	216	Ø
125	}	171	«	217	Ù
126	~	172	¬	218	Ú
127	□	173	-	219	Û
128	□	174	®	220	Ü
129	□	175	¯	221	Ý
130	‚	176	°	222	þ
131	ƒ	177	±	223	ß
132	„	178	²	224	à
133	…	179	³	225	á
134	†	180	´	226	â
135	‡	181	µ	227	ã
136	^	182	¶	228	ä
137	‰	183	·	229	å
138	Š	184	‚	230	æ
139	‹	185	¹	231	ç
140	Œ	186	º	232	è
141	□	187	»	233	é
142	□	188	¼	234	ê
143	□	189	½	235	ë
144	□	190	¾	236	ì
145	'	191	¿	237	í
146	'	192	À	238	î
147	"	193	Á	239	ï
148	"	194	Â	240	õ
149	•	195	Ã	241	ñ
150	–	196	Ä	242	ò
151	—	197	Å	243	ń
152	▪	198	Æ	244	ô
153	™	199	Ç	245	õ
154	š	200	È	246	ö
155	›	201	É	247	÷
156	œ	202	Ê	248	ø
157	□	203	Ë	249	ù
158	□	204	Ì	250	ú
159	Ÿ	205	Í	251	û
160		206	Î	252	ü
161	¡	207	Ï	253	ý
162	¢	208	Ð	254	þ
163	£	209	Ñ	255	ÿ
164	¤	210	Ò		
165	¥	211	Ó		

APPENDIX B　How To

HOW TO: Install, Invoke, and Exit Visual Basic

A. Install the Working Model Edition of Visual Basic

1. Place the CD accompanying this book into your CD drive. In about five seconds you will most likely hear a whirring sound from the CD drive.
2. Double-click on My Computer in the Windows Desktop. A window showing the different disk drives will appear.
3. Double-click on the icon containing a picture of a CD (along with a drive) and having the word "Schneider" and the drive letter below the icon. A list of folders and files will appear.
4. Double-click on the icon labeled "Setup.exe". (The icon is a colorful sideways 8.) A large window with the words "Visual Basic 6.0 Working Model" will appear.
5. The title bar of the large window says "Installation Wizard for Visual Basic 6.0 Working Model." The installation wizard will guide you through the installation process. Click on Next to continue.
6. An End User License Agreement will appear. After reading the agreement, click on the the circle to the left of the sentence "I accept the agreement." and then click on Next.
7. The next window to appear has spaces for an ID number, your name, and your company's name. Ignore the ID number. Just type in your name and, optionally, a company name, and then click Next.
8. Visual Basic 6.0 requires that you have Internet Explorer 4.0 or later version on your computer. If a recent version is not present, the Installation Wizard will install it for you. If so, successive windows will guide you through the installation. At some point you will be required to restart your computer. We recommend doing the standard installation and using the recommended destination folder.
9. You will next be guided through the installation of DCOM98, which is also needed to Visual Basic 6.0. After installing DCOM98, the installation wizard will automatically restart your computer and then continue with the installation of VB 6.0. **Note:** If another widow is covering the Installation Wizard window, then click on the Installation Wizard window. If you can't find the Installation Wizard window, repeat Steps 1–5.

You will now be guided through the installation of the Working Model Edition VB 6.0. At the end of the installation, Visual Basic will be invoked.

10. The next window requests the name of the Common Install Folder. We recommend that you simply click on Next, which will accept the default folder and copy some files into it.
11. The next window to appear is the Visual Basic 6.0 Working Model Setup. Click on Continue.

12. The next screen shows your Product ID number. Enter your name and then click on OK.
13. The next window asks you to choose between Typical and Custom installations. We recommend that you click on the Typical icon.
14. About one minute is required for the VB6.0 Working Model to be installed. On the next screen to appear, click on Restart Windows.
15. The next window to appear gives you the opportunity to register your copy of VB6.0 over the web. Uncheck the Register Now box and click on Finish.

B. Invoke Visual Basic after installation.

1. Click the Start button.
2. Point to Programs.
3. Point to Microsoft Visual Basic 6.0. (A new panel will open on the right.)
4. In the new panel, click on Microsoft Visual Basic 6.0.

C. Exit Visual Basic.

1. Press the Esc key.
2. Press Alt/F/X.
3. If an unsaved program is present, Visual Basic will prompt you about saving it.

Note: In many situations, Step 1 is not needed.

HOW TO: Manage Programs

A. Run a program from Visual Basic.

1. Click on the Start icon (right arrowhead) in the Toolbar.

or

1. Press F5.

or

1. Press Alt/R and make a selection from the Run menu.

B. Save the current program on a disk.

1. Press Alt/F/V [or click the Save Project icon (shows a diskette) on the Toolbar].
2. Fill in the requested information. Do not give an extension as part of the project name or the file name. Two files will be created —one with extension .VBP and the other with extension .FRM. The .VBP file holds a list of files related to the project. The .FRM file actually holds the program.

Note: After a program has been saved once, updated versions can be saved with the same filenames by pressing Alt/F/V. Alt/F/E and Alt/F/A are used to save the program with new file names.

C. Begin a new program.

1. Press Alt/F/N.
2. If an unsaved program is present, Visual Basic will prompt you about saving it.

D. Open a program stored on a disk.

1. Press Alt/F/O [or click the Open Project icon (shows an open folder) on the Toolbar].
2. Click on one of the two tabs, Existing or Recent.
3. If you selected Existing, choose a folder for the "Look in:" box, type a filename into the "File name:" box, and press the Enter key. Alternatively, double-click on one of the filenames displayed in the large box in the middle of the dialog box.
4. If you selected Recent, double-click on one of the files in the list.

Note 1: (In Steps 3 and 4, if an unsaved program is present, Visual Basic will prompt you about saving it.)

Note 2: The form or code for the program may not appear, but can be accessed through the Project Explorer window. Another way to obtain the Code and Form windows is to run and then terminate the program.

E. Use the Project Explorer.

Note: Just below the Project Explorer title bar are three icons (View Code, View Object, and Toggle Folders), and below them is the List window. At any time, one item in the List window is selected.

1. Click on View Code to see the code associated with the selected item.
2. Click on View Object to see the Object (usually the form) associated with the selected item.

F. Display the form associated with a program.

1. Press Alt/V/B. (If the selection Object is grayed, first run and then terminate the program.)

   or

1. Press Shift+F7.

   or

1. Press Alt/V/P to activate the Project Explorer window.
2. Select the name of the form.
3. Click on the View Object button.

HOW TO: Use the Editor

A. Mark a section of text as a block.

1. Move the cursor to the beginning or end of the block.
2. Hold down a Shift key and use the direction keys to highlight a block of text.
3. Release the Shift key.

   or

1. Move the mouse to the beginning or end of the block.
2. Hold down the left mouse button and move the mouse to the other end of the block.
3. Release the left mouse button.

Note 1: To unblock text, press a direction key or click outside the block.

Note 2: To select a word, double-click on it. To select a line, move the mouse pointer just far enough into the left margin so that the pointer changes to an arrow, and then single-click there.

B. Delete a line of a program.

1. Move the cursor to the line.
2. Press Ctrl+Y.

   or

1. Mark the line as a block. (See item A of this section.)
2. Press Alt/E/T or press Ctrl+X.

Note: In the preceding maneuvers, the line is placed in the clipboard and can be retrieved by pressing Ctrl+V. To delete the line without placing it in the clipboard, mark it as a block and press Del.

C. Move a line within the Code window.

1. Move the cursor to the line and press Ctrl+Y.
2. Move the cursor to the target location.
3. Press Ctrl+V.

D. Use the clipboard to move or duplicate statements.

1. Mark the statements as a block.
2. Press Ctrl+X to delete the block and place it into the clipboard. Or press Ctrl+C to place a copy of the block into the clipboard.
3. Move the cursor to the location where you desire to place the block.
4. Press Ctrl+V to place a copy of the text from the clipboard at the cursor.

E. Search for specific text in the program.

1. Press Alt/E/F or Ctrl+F.
2. Type sought-after text into the rectangle.
3. Select desired options if different from the defaults.
4. Press the Enter key.
5. To repeat the search, press Find Next or press Cancel and then F3.

F. Find and Replace.

1. Press Alt/E/E or Ctrl+H.
2. Type sought-after text into first rectangle.
3. Press Tab.
4. Type replacement text into second rectangle.
5. Select desired options if different from the defaults.
6. Press the Enter key.
7. Press Replace to make the change or press Replace All to make all such changes.

G. Cancel a change.

1. Press Alt/E/U or Ctrl+Z to undo the last change made to a line.

HOW TO: Get Help

(Available only with Learning, Professional, and Enterprise Editions.)

A. Obtain information about a Visual Basic topic.

1. Press Alt/H/M.
2. Click on the Index tab and follow the instructions.
3. To display a topic, double-click on it.
4. If a second list pops up, double-click on an item from it.

B. View the syntax and purpose of a Visual Basic keyword.

1. Type the word into a Code window.
2. Place the cursor on, or just following, the keyword.
3. Press F1.

C. Display an ANSI table.

1. Press Alt/H/M and click on the Index tab.
2. Type ANSI and press the Enter key.
3. To move between the displays for ANSI characters 0-127 and 128-255, click on "See Also," and then click on the Display button.

D. Obtain a list of Visual Basic's reserved words.

1. Press Alt/H/M.
2. Type "keywords", press the down-arrow key, and double-click on a category of keywords from the list below the blue bar.

E. Obtain a list of shortcut keys.

1. Press Alt/H/M and click on the Contents tab.
2. Double-click on the Additional Information book.
3. Double-click on the Keyboard Guide book.
4. Double-click on one of the collections of shortcut keys.

F. Obtain information about a control.

1. Click on the control at design time.
2. Press F1.

G. Exit Help.

1. Press Esc.

HOW TO: Manipulate a Dialog Box

A. Use a dialog box.

A dialog box contains three types of items: rectangles (text or list boxes), option lists, and command buttons. An option list is a sequence of option buttons or check boxes of the form $\bigcirc$ *option* or $\square$ *option*.

1. Move from item to item with the Tab key. (The movement is from left to right and top to bottom. Use Shift+Tab to reverse the direction.)
2. Inside a rectangle, either type in the requested information or use the direction keys to make a selection.

3. In an option list, an option button of the form ○ *option* can be selected with the direction keys. A dot inside the circle indicates that the option has been selected.
4. In an option list, a check box of the form ☐ *option* can be checked or unchecked by pressing the space bar. An X or ✓ inside the square indicates that the option has been checked.
5. A highlighted command button is invoked by pressing the Enter key.

B. Cancel a dialog box

1. Press the Esc key.

or

1. Press the Tab key until the command button captioned "Cancel" is highlighted and then press the Enter key.

HOW TO: Manage Menus

A. Open a drop-down menu.

1. Click on the menu name.

or

1. Press Alt.
2. Press the underlined letter in the name of the menu. Alternatively, use the Right Arrow key to move the highlighted cursor bar to the menu name, and then press the Down Arrow key.

B. Make a selection from a drop-down menu.

1. Open the drop-down menu.
2. Click on the desired item.

or

1. Open the drop-down menu. One letter in each item that is eligible to be used will be underlined.
2. Press the underlined letter. Alternatively, use the Down Arrow key to move the cursor bar to the desired item and then press the Enter key.

C. Obtain information about the selections in a drop-down menu.

1. Press Alt/H/M and click on the Contents tab.
2. Double-click on the Interface Reference book
3. Double-click on the Menu book
4. Double-click on the name of the menu of interest.
5. Double-click on the selection of interest.

D. Look at all the menus in the menu bar.

1. Press Alt/F.
2. Press the Right Arrow key each time you want to see a new menu.

E. Close a drop-down menu.

1. Press the Esc key or click anywhere outside the menu.

HOW TO: Utilize the Windows Environment

A. Place a section of code in the Windows clipboard.

1. Mark the section of code as a block as described in the How to Use the Editor section.
2. Press Ctrl+C.

B. Access Windows' Notepad.

1. Click the Start button.
2. Point to Programs.
3. Point to Accessories.
4. Click Notepad.

C. Display all characters in a font.

1. Click the Start button.
2. Point to Programs.
3. Point to Accessories.
4. Click Character Map.
5. Click on the underlined down arrow at the right end of the Font box.
6. Highlight the desired font and press the Enter key or click on the desired font.

D. Display an ANSI or ASCII code for a character with a code above 128.

1. Proceed as described in item C above to display the font containing the character of interest.
2. Click on the character of interest. Displayed at the right end of the bottom line of the font table is Alt+0xxx, where xxx is the code for the character.

HOW TO: Design a Form

A. Display the ToolBox.

1. Press Alt/V/X.

B. Place a new control on the form.

Option I: (new control with default size and position)

1. Double-click on the control's icon in the ToolBox. The new control appears at the center of the form.
2. Size and position the control as described in items G and H, which follow.

Option II: (a single new control sized and positioned as it is created)

1. Click on the control's icon in the ToolBox.
2. Move the mouse to the approximate position on the form desired for the upper-left corner of the control.
3. Press and hold the left mouse button.
4. Move the mouse to the position on the form desired for the lower-right corner of the control. A dashed box will indicate the overall shape of the new control.

    5. Release the left mouse button.

    6. The control can be resized and repositioned as described in items G and H.

Option III: (create multiple instances of the same control)

    1. Click on the control's icon in the ToolBox while holding down the Ctrl key.

    2. Repeatedly use Steps 2 to 5 of Option II to create instances of the control.

    3. When finished creating instances of this control, click on the arrow icon in the ToolBox.

C. Create a related group of controls.

    1. To hold the related group of controls, place a picture box or frame control on the form.

    2. Use Option II or III in item B of this section to place controls in the picture box or frame.

D. Select a particular control.

    1. Click on the control.

       or

    1. Press the Tab key until the control is selected.

E. Delete a control.

    1. Select the control to be deleted.

    2. Press the Del key.

F. Delete a related group of controls.

    1. Select the picture box or frame holding the related group of controls.

    2. Press the Del key.

G. Move a control, related group of controls, or form to a new location.

    1. Move the mouse onto the control, the picture box or frame containing the related group of controls, or the title bar of the form

    2. Drag the object to the new location.

H. Change the size of a control.

    1. Select the desired control.

    2. Move the mouse to one of the eight sizing handles located around the edge of the control. The mouse pointer will change to a double-arrow which points in the direction that resizing can occur.

    3. Drag to the desired size.

I. Change the size of a Project Container window.

    1. Move the mouse to the edge or corner of the window that is to be stretched or shrunk. The mouse pointer will change to a double-arrow which points in the direction that resizing can occur.

    2. Drag to the desired size.

J. Use the Color palette to set foreground and background colors.

1. Select the desired control or the form.
2. Press Alt/V/L to activate the Color palette.
3. If the Color palette obscures the object you are working with, you may wish to use the mouse to grab the Color palette by its title bar and move it so that at least some of the object shows.
4. To set the foreground color, click on the square within a square at the far left in the Color palette and click on the desired color from the palette.
5. To set the background color, click on the region within the outer square but outside the inner square and click on the desired color from the palette.

   or

1. Select the desired control or the form.
2. Press Alt/V/W or F4 to activate the Properties window.
3. To set the foreground color, click on the down-arrow to the right of the ForeColor settings box, click on the Palette tab, and click on the desired color.
4. To set the background color, click on the down-arrow to the right of the BackColor settings box, click on the Palette tab, and click on the desired color.

HOW TO: Work with the Properties of an Object

A. Activate the Properties window.

1. Press Alt/V/W.

   or

1. Press F4.

   or

1. Click on an object on the form with the right mouse button.
2. In the shortcut menu, click on Properties.

B. Highlight a property in the Properties window.

1. Activate the Properties window and press the Enter key.
2. Use the Up or Down Arrow keys to move the highlight bar to the desired property.

   or

1. Activate the Properties window.
2. Click on the up or down arrow located at the ends of the vertical scroll bar at the right side of the Properties window until the desired property is visible.
3. Click on the desired property.

C. Select or specify a setting for a property.

1. Highlight the property whose setting is to be changed.
2. Click on the settings box or press Tab to place the cursor in the settings box.

    a. If a black down-arrow appears at the right end of the settings box, click on the down-arrow to display a list of all allowed settings, and then click on the desired setting.

    b. If an ellipsis (three periods: …) appears at the right end of the settings box, press F4 or click on the ellipsis to display a dialog box. Answer the questions in the dialog box and click on OK or Open, as appropriate.

    c. If the cursor moves to the settings box, type in the new setting for the property.

D. Change a property setting of an object.

1. Select the desired object.
2. Activate the Properties window.
3. Highlight the property whose setting is to be changed.
4. Select or specify the new setting for the property.

E. Let a label change size to accommodate its caption.

1. Set the label's AutoSize property to True. (The label will shrink to the smallest size needed to hold the current caption. If the caption is changed, the label will automatically grow or shrink horizontally to accommodate the new caption. If the WordWrap property is set to True as well, the label will grow and shrink vertically, keeping the same width.)

F. Let a label caption use more than one line.

1. Set the label's WordWrap property to True. [If the label is not wide enough to accommodate the entire caption on one line, part of the caption will wrap to additional lines. If the label height is too small, then part or all of these wrapped lines will not be visible (unless the AutoSize property is set to True).]

G. Let a text box display more than one line.

1. Set the text box's MultiLine property to True. (If the text box is not wide enough to accommodate the text entered by the user, the text will scroll down to new lines. If the text box is not tall enough, lines will scroll up out of view, but can be redisplayed by moving the cursor up.)

H. Assign an access key to a label or command button.

1. When assigning a value to the Caption property, precede the desired access key character with an ampersand (&).

I. Allow a particular command button to be activated by a press of the Enter key.

1. Set the command button's Default property to True.

Note: Setting the Default property True for one command button automatically sets the property to False for all the other command buttons on the form.

J. Adjust the order in which the Tab key moves the focus.

1. Select the first control in the tabbing sequence.
2. Change the setting of the TabIndex property for this control to 0.
3. Select the next control in the tabbing sequence.

4. Change the setting of the TabIndex property for this control to 1.
5. Repeat Steps 3 and 4 (adding 1 to the Tab Index property) until all controls on the form have been assigned a new TabIndex setting.

Note: In Steps 2 and 4, if an object is moved to another position in the sequence, then the TabIndex property for the other objects will be renumbered accordingly.

K. Allow the pressing of Esc to activate a particular command button.

1. Set the command button's Cancel property to True. (Setting the Cancel property to True for one command button automatically sets it to False for all other command buttons.)

L. Keep the contents of a picture box from being erased accidentally.

1. Set the picture box's AutoRedraw property to True. (The default is False. Unless the property is set to True, the contents will be erased when the picture box is obscured by another window.)

HOW TO: Manage Procedures

A. Access the Code window.

1. Press Alt/V/C or F7. (If the Code window does not appear, run and then terminate the program.)

or

1. Press Alt/V/P to activate the Project Explorer window.
2. Select the name of the form.
3. Click on the "View Code" button.

B. Look at an existing procedure.

1. Access the Code window.
2. Press Ctrl+Down Arrow or Ctrl+Up Arrow to see all the procedures.

or

1. Access the Code window.
2. Click on the down arrow at the right of the Object box and then select an object. [For general procedures select (General) as the Object.]
3. Click on the down arrow at the right of the Procedure box and then select a procedure.

C. Create a general procedure.

1. Access the Code window.
2. Move to a blank line that is not inside a procedure.
3. Type Private Sub (for a Sub procedure) or Private Function (for a Function procedure) followed by the name of the procedure and any parameters.
4. Press the Enter key. (The Code window will now display the new procedure heading and an End Sub or End Function statement.)
5. Type the procedure into the Code Window.

or

1. Access the Code window.

2. Press Alt/T/P. (A dialog box will appear.)
3. Type the name of the procedure into the Name rectangle.
4. Select the type of procedure.
5. Select the Scope by clicking on Public or Private. (In this book, we always use Private.)
6. Press the Enter key. (The Code window will now display the new procedure heading and an End Sub or End Function statement.)
7. Type the procedure into the Code Window.

D. Alter a procedure.

1. View the procedure in the Code Window as described in item B of this section.
2. Make changes as needed.

E. Remove a procedure.

1. Bring the procedure into the Code Window as described in item B of this section.
2. Mark the entire procedure as a block. That is,
   a. Press Ctrl+PgUp to move the cursor to the beginning of the procedure.
   b. Hold down the Shift key and press Ctrl+PgDn to move the cursor to the start of the next procedure.
   c. Press the Up Arrow key until just after the end of the procedure to be deleted.
3. Press the Del key.

F. Insert an existing procedure into a program.

1. Open the program containing the procedure.
2. View the procedure in the Code Window as described in item B of this section.
3. Mark the entire procedure as a block, as described in step 2 of item E of this section.
4. Press Ctrl+C to place the procedure into the clipboard.
5. Open the program in which the procedure is to be inserted and access the Code Window.
6. Move the cursor to a blank line.
7. Press Ctrl+V to place the contents of the clipboard into the program.

HOW TO: Manage Windows

A. Enlarge the active window to fill the entire screen.

1. Click on the Maximize button (page icon; second icon from the right) on the Title bar of the window.
2. To return the window to its original size, click on the Restore (double-page) button that has replaced the Maximize button.

B. Move a window.

1. Move the mouse to the title bar of the window.
2. Drag the window to the desired location.

C. Change the size of a window.

1. Move the mouse to the edge of the window which is to be adjusted or to the corner joining the two edges to be adjusted.
2. When the mouse becomes a double arrow, drag the edge or corner until the window has the desired size.

D. Close a window.

1. Click on the X button on the far right corner of the title bar.

HOW TO: Use the Printer

A. Obtain a printout of a program.

1. Press Alt/F/P.
2. Press the Enter key.

Note: To print just the text selected as a block or the active (current) window, use the direction keys to select the desired option.

B. Obtain a printout of the form during run time.

1. Place the statement PrintForm in the Form_Click( ) or other appropriate procedure of the program which will be executed at the point when the desired output will be on the form.

HOW TO: Use the Debugger

A. Stop a program at a specified line.

1. Place the cursor on the desired line.
2. Press F9 or Alt/D/T to highlight the line in red. (This highlighted line is called a *breakpoint*. When the program is run it will stop at the breakpoint before executing the statement.)

Note: To remove this breakpoint, repeat Steps 1 and 2.

B. Remove all breakpoints.

1. Press Alt/D/C or Ctrl+Shift+F9.

C. Run a program one statement at a time.

1. Press F8. The first executable statement will be highlighted. (An event must first occur for which an event procedure has been written.)
2. Press F8 each time you want to execute the currently highlighted statement.

Note: You will probably need to press Alt+Tab to switch back and forth between the form and the VB environment. Also, to guarantee that output is retained while stepping through the program, the AutoRedraw property of the form and any picture boxes may need to be set to True.

D. Run the program one statement at a time, but execute each general procedure call without stepping through the statements in the procedure one at a time.

   1. Press Shift+F8. The first executable statement will be highlighted.
   2. Press Shift+F8 each time you want to execute the currently highlighted statement.

E. Continue execution of a program that has been suspended.

   1. Press F5.

   Note: Each time an attempt is made to change a suspended program in a way that would prevent the program from continuing, Visual Basic displays a dialog box warning that the program will have to be restarted from the beginning and gives the option to cancel the attempted change.

F. Have further stepping begin at the line containing the cursor (no variables are cleared).

   1. Press Alt/D/R or Ctrl+F8.

G. Set the next statement to be run in the current procedure.

   1. Place the cursor anywhere in the desired statement.
   2. Press Alt/D/N or Ctrl+F9.

H. Determine the value of an expression during run time.

   1. Press Alt/D/A (Add Watch)
   2. Type the expression into the Expression text box, adjust other entries in dialog box (if necessary), and click on OK.

   Note: The value of the expression will appear in the Watches window during break mode.

   or

   1. In Break mode, hover the cursor over the variable to have its value displayed.

APPENDIX C — Visual Basic Debugging Tools

Errors in programs are called *bugs* and the process of finding and correcting them is called *debugging*. Since Visual Basic does not discover errors due to faulty logic, they present the most difficulties in debugging. One method of discovering a logical error is by **desk checking**, that is, tracing the values of variables on paper by writing down their expected value after "mentally executing" each line in the program. Desk checking is rudimentary and highly impractical except for small programs.

Another method of debugging involves placing Print methods at strategic points in the program and displaying the values of selected variables or expressions until the error is detected. After correcting the error, the Print methods are removed. For many programming environments, desk checking and Print methods are the only debugging methods available to the programmer.

The Visual Basic debugger offers an alternative to desk checking and Print methods. It allows you to pause during the execution of your program in order to view and alter values of variables. These values can be accessed through the Immediate, Watch, and Locals windows, known collectively as the three Debug windows.

The Three Program Modes

At any time, a program is in one of three modes—design mode, run mode, or break mode. The current mode is displayed in the Visual Basic title bar.

Title bar during design time.

Title bar during run time.

Title bar during break mode.

At design time you place controls on a form, set their initial properties, and write code. Run time is initiated by pressing the Start button. Break mode is invoked automatically when a run-time error occurs. While a program is running, you can manually invoke Break mode by pressing Ctrl+Break, clicking on Break in the Run menu, or clicking on the Break icon ▮ (located between the Start and Stop icons). While the program is in break mode, you can use the Immediate window to examine and change values of variables and object settings. When you enter Break mode, the Start button on the Toolbar changes to a Continue button. You can click on it to proceed with the execution of the program.

The Immediate Window

You can set the focus to the Immediate window by clicking on it (if visible), by pressing Ctrl+G, or by choosing "Immediate Window" from the View menu. Although the Immediate window can be used during design time, it is primarily used in Break mode. When you type a statement into the Immediate window and press the Enter key, the statement is executed at once. A statement of the form

```
Print expression
```

displays the value of the expression on the next line of the Immediate window. In Figure 1, three statements have been executed. (When the program was interrupted, the variable *numVar* had the value 10.) In addition to displaying values of expressions, the Immediate window also is commonly used to change the value of a variable with an assignment statement before continuing to run the program. **Note 1:** Any statement in the Immediate window can be executed again by placing the cursor anywhere on the statement and pressing the Enter key. **Note 2:** In earlier versions of Visual Basic, the Immediate window was called the Debug window.

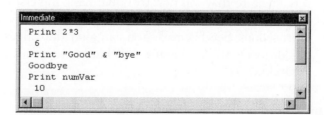

Figure C.1 Three Print statements executed in the Immediate window.

The Watch Window

You can designate an expression as a watch expression or a break expression. Break expressions are of two varieties: those that cause a break when they become true and those that cause a break when they change value. At any time, the Watch window shows the current values of all watch and break expressions. In the Watch window of Figure 2, the type of each expression is specified by an icon as shown in Table 1.

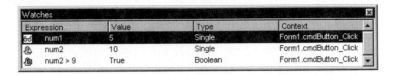

Figure C.2 The Watch window.

Icon	Type of expression
👓	Watch expression
🖐	Break when expression is true
🖐	Break when expression has changed

Table C.1 Watch type icons.

The easiest way to add an expression to the Watch window is to right-click on a variable in the code window and then click on "Add Watch" to call up an Add Watch dialog box. You can then alter the expression in the Expression text box and select one of the three Watch types. To delete an expression from the Watch window, right-click on the expression and then click on "Delete Watch." To alter an expression in the Watch window, right-click on the expression and click on "Edit Watch."

The Locals Window

The Locals window, invoked by clicking on "Locals Window" in the View menu, is a feature that was new to Visual Basic in version 5.0. This window automatically displays the names, values, and types of all variables in the current procedure. See Figure 3. You can alter the values of variables at any time. In addition, you can examine and change properties of controls through the Locals window.

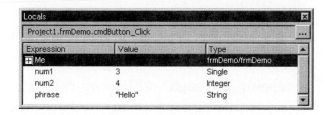

Figure C.3 The Locals window.

Stepping Through a Program

The program can be executed one statement at a time, with each press of an appropriate function key executing a statement. This process is called **stepping** (or **stepping into**). After each step, values of variables, expressions, and conditions can be displayed from the debugging windows, and the values of variables can be changed.

When a procedure is called, the lines of the procedure can be executed one at a time, referred to as "stepping through the procedure," or the entire procedure can be executed at once, referred to as "stepping over a procedure." A step over a procedure is called a **procedure step**. In addition, you can execute the remainder of the current procedure at once, referred to as "stepping out of the procedure."

Stepping begins with the first line of the first event procedure invoked by the user. Program execution normally proceeds in order through the statements in the event procedure. However, at any time the programmer can specify the next statement to be executed.

As another debugging tool, Visual Basic allows the programmer to specify certain lines as **breakpoints**. Then, when the program is run, execution will stop at the first breakpoint reached. The programmer can then either step through the program or continue execution to the next breakpoint.

The tasks discussed previously are summarized below, along with a means to carry out each task. The tasks invoked with function keys can also be produced from the menu bar.

Step Into:	Press F8
Step Over:	Press Shift+F8
Step Out:	Press Ctrl+Shift+F8
Set a breakpoint:	Move cursor to line, press F9
Remove a breakpoint:	Move cursor to line containing breakpoint, press F9
Clear all breakpoints:	Press Ctrl+Shift+F9
Set next statement:	Press Ctrl+F9
Continue execution to next breakpoint or the end of the program:	Press F5
Run to cursor:	Press Ctrl+F8

Six Walkthroughs

The following walkthroughs use the debugging tools with programming structures covered in Chapters 2, 3, and 5.

Stepping Through an Elementary Program: Chapter 2

The following walkthrough demonstrates several capabilities of the debugger.

1. Create a form with a command button (cmdButton) and a picture box (picBox). Set the AutoRedraw property of the picture box to True. (During the debugging process, the entire form will be covered. The True setting for AutoRedraw prevents the contents of the picture box from being erased.)

2. Double-click on the command button and enter the following event procedure:

```
Private Sub cmdButton_Click()
    Dim num As Single
    picBox.Cls
    num = Val(InputBox("Enter a number:"))
    num = num + 1
    num = num + 2
    picBox.Print num
End Sub
```

3. Press F8, click the command button, and press F8 again. A yellow arrow points to the picBox.Cls statement and the statement is highlighted in yellow. This indicates that the picBox.Cls statement is the next statement to be executed. (Pressing F8 is referred to as stepping. You can also step to the next statement of a program with the Step Into option from the Debug menu.)

4. Press F8. The picBox.Cls statement is executed and the statement involving InputBox is designated as the next statement to be executed.

5. Press F8 to execute the statement containing InputBox. Respond to the request by typing 5 and clicking the OK button.

6. Press F8 again to execute the statement num = num + 1.

7. Let the mouse sit over any occurrence of the word "num" for a second or so. The current value of the variable will be displayed in a small box. See Figure 4.

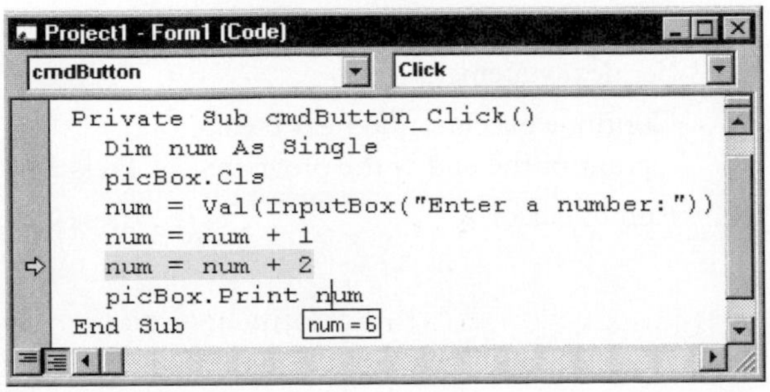

Figure C.4 Obtaining the value of a variable.

8. Click on the End icon to end the program.

9. Move the cursor to the line

```
num = num + 2
```

and then press F9. A red dot appears to the left of the line and the line is displayed in white text on a red background. This indicates that the line is a breakpoint. (Pressing F9 is referred to as toggling a breakpoint. You also can toggle a breakpoint with the Toggle Breakpoint option from the Debug menu.)

10. Press F5 and click on the command button. Respond to the request by entering 5. The program executes the first three lines and stops at the breakpoint. The breakpoint line is not executed.

11. Open the Immediate window by pressing Ctrl+G. If necessary, clear the contents of the window. Type the statement

```
Print "num ="; num
```

into the Immediate window and then press Enter to execute the statement. The appearance of "num = 6" on the next line of the Immediate window confirms that the breakpoint line was not executed.

12. Press F7 to return to the Code window.

13. Move the cursor to the line num = num + 1 and then press Ctrl+F9 to specify that line as the next line to be executed. (You can also use the Set Next Statement option from the Debug menu.)

14. Press F8 to execute the selected line.

15. Press Ctrl+G to return to the Immediate window. Move the cursor to the line containing the Print method and press Enter to confirm that the value of *num* is now 7, and then return to the Code window.

16. Move the cursor to the breakpoint line and press F9 to deselect the line as a breakpoint.

17. Press F5 to execute the remaining lines of the program. Observe that the value displayed in the picture box is 9.

General Comment: As you step through a program, the form will become hidden from view. However, the form will be represented by a button on the Windows taskbar at the bottom of the screen. The button will contain the name of the form. You can see the form at any time by clicking on its button.

Stepping Through a Program Containing a General Procedure: Chapter 2

The following walkthrough uses the single-stepping feature of the debugger to trace the flow through a program and a Sub procedure.

1. Create a form with a command button (cmdButton) and a picture box (picBox). Set the AutoRedraw property of the picture box to True. Then enter the following two procedures:

```
Private Sub cmdButton_Click()
  Dim p As Single, b As Single
  picBox.Cls
  p = 1000      'Principal
  Call GetBalance(p, b)
  picBox.Print "The balance is"; b
End Sub

Private Sub GetBalance(prin As Single, bal As Single)
  'Calculate the balance at 5% interest rate
  Dim interest As Single
  interest = .05 * prin
  bal = prin + interest
End Sub
```

2. Press F8, click the command button, and press F8 again. The picBox.Cls statement is highlighted to indicate that it is the next statement to be executed.

3. Press F8 two more times. The Call statement is highlighted.

4. Press F8 once, and observe that the heading of the Sub procedure Get-Balance is now highlighted in yellow.

5. Press F8 three times to execute the assignment statements and to highlight the End Sub statement. (Notice that the Dim and comment statements were skipped.)

6. Press F8, and notice that the yellow highlight has moved back to the cmdButton_Click event procedure and is on the statement immediately following the Call statement.

7. Click on the End icon to end the program.

8. Repeat Steps 2 and 3, and then press Shift+F8 to step over the procedure GetBalance. The procedure has been executed in its entirety.

9. Click on the End icon to end the program.

Communication Between Arguments and Parameters

The following walkthrough uses the Locals window to monitor the values of arguments and parameters during the execution of a program.

1. If you have not already done so, type the preceding program into the Code window.

2. Press F8, and click on the command button.

3. Select "Locals Window" from the View window. Notice that the variables from the cmdButton_Click event procedure appear in the Locals window.

4. Press F8 three more times to highlight the Call statement. Notice that the value of the variable *p* has changed.

5. Press F8 to call the Sub procedure. Notice that the variables displayed in the Locals window are now those of the procedure GetBalance.

6. Press F8 three times to execute the procedure.

7. Press F8 to return to cmdButton_Click event procedure. Notice that the value of the variable *b* has inherited the value of the variable *bal*.

8. Click on the End icon to end the program.

Stepping Through Programs Containing Decision Structures: Chapter 3

If Blocks

The following walkthrough demonstrates how an If statement evaluates a condition to determine whether to take an action.

1. Create a form with a command button (cmdButton) and a picture box (picBox). Set the AutoRedraw property of the picture box to True. Then open the Code window and enter the following procedure:

```
Private Sub cmdButton_Click()
  Dim wage As Single
  picBox.Cls
  wage = Val(InputBox("wage:"))
  If wage < 5.15 Then
      picBox.Print "Below minimum wage."
    Else
      picBox.Print "Wage Ok."
  End If
End Sub
```

2. Press F8, click the command button, and press F8 twice. The picBox.Cls statement will be highlighted and executed, and then the statement containing InputBox will be highlighted.

3. Press F8 once to execute the statement containing InputBox. Type a wage of 3.25 and press the Enter key. The If statement is highlighted, but has not been executed.

4. Press F8 once and notice that the highlight for the current statement has jumped to the statement picBox.Print "Below minimum wage." Because the condition "wage < 5.15" is true, the action associated with Then was selected.

5. Press F8 to execute the picBox.Print statement. Notice that Else is skipped and End If is highlighted.

6. Press F8 again. We are through with the If block and the statement following the If block, End Sub, is highlighted.

7. Click on the End icon to end the program.

8. If desired, try stepping through the program again with 5.75 entered as the wage. Since the condition "wage < 5.15" will be false, the Else action will be executed instead of the Then action.

Select Case Blocks

The following walkthrough illustrates how a Select Case block uses the selector to choose from among several actions.

1. Create a form with a command button (cmdButton) and a picture box (picBox). Set the AutoRedraw property of the picture box to True. Then open the Code window and enter the following procedure:

```
Private Sub cmdButton_Click()
  Dim age As Single, price As Single
  picBox.Cls
  age = Val(InputBox("age:"))
  Select Case age
    Case Is < 12
      price = 0
    Case Is < 18
      price = 3.5
    Case Is >= 65
      price = 4
    Case Else
      price = 5.5
  End Select
  picBox.Print "Your ticket price is "; FormatCurrency(price)
End Sub
```

2. Press F8, click on the command button, and press F8 twice. The picBox.Cls statement will be highlighted and executed, and then the statement containing InputBox will be highlighted.

3. Press F8 once to execute the statement containing InputBox. Type an age of 8 and press the Enter key. The Select Case statement is highlighted, but has not been executed.

4. Press F8 twice and observe that the action associated with Case Is < 12 is highlighted.

5. Press F8 once to execute the assignment statement. Notice that End Select is highlighted. This demonstrates that when more than one Case clause is true, only the first is acted upon.

6. Click on the End icon to end the program.

7. If desired, step through the program again, entering a different age and predicting which Case clause will be acted upon. (Some possible ages to try are 12, 14, 18, 33, and 67.)

Stepping Through a Program Containing a Do Loop: Chapter 3

Do Loops

The following walkthrough demonstrates use of the Immediate window to monitor the value of a condition in a Do loop that searches for a name.

1. Access Windows' Notepad, enter the following line of data, and save the file on the A drive with the name Data.txt.

```
Bert, Ernie, Grover, Oscar
```

2. Return to Visual Basic. Create a form with a command button (cmdButton) and a picture box (picBox). Set the AutoRedraw property of the picture box to True. Then double-click on the command button and enter the following procedure:

```
Private Sub cmdButton_Click()
  'Look for a specific name
  Dim searchName As String, nom As String
  picBox.Cls
  searchName = InputBox("Name:")  'Name to search for in list
  Open "Data.txt" For Input As #1
  nom = ""
  Do While (nom <> searchName) And Not EOF(1)
    Input #1, nom
  Loop
  Close #1
  If nom = searchName Then
      picBox.Print nom
    Else
      picBox.Print "Name not found"
  End If
End Sub
```

3. Press F8, and click on the command button. The heading of the event procedure is highlighted in yellow.

4. Double-click on the variable *searchName*, click the right mouse button, click on "Add Watch," and click on OK. The variable *searchName* has been added to the Watch window.

5. Repeat Step 4 for the variable *nom*.

6. Drag the mouse across the words

```
(nom <> searchName) And Not EOF(1)
```

to highlight them. Then click the right mouse button, click on "Add Watch," and click on OK. Widen the Watch window as much as possible in order to see the entire expression.

7. Press F8 three more times to execute the picBox.Cls statement and the statement containing InputBox. Enter the name "Ernie" at the prompt.

8. Press F8 repeatedly until the entire event procedure has been executed. Pause after each keypress and notice how the values of the expressions in the Watch window change.

9. Click on the End icon to end the program.

ANSWERS To Selected Odd-Numbered Exercises

CHAPTER I

Exercises 1.2

1. The program is busy carrying out a task; please wait.
3. Double-clicking means clicking the left mouse button twice in quick succession.
5. Cursor
7. Starting with an uppercase W, Windows refers to Microsoft's Windows program. Starting with a lowercase w, windows refers to the rectangular regions of the screen in which different programs are displayed.
9. Double-click on the Notepad icon.
11. A toggle is a key like the Ins, NumLock, and CapsLock keys that changes keyboard operations back and forth between two different typing modes.
13. PgDn

15. Backspace
17. NumLock
19. CapsLock
21. End
23. Shift
25. Alt/F/P
27. Ctrl+Home
29. Alt
31. Alt
33. Alt/F/A
35. End/Enter

Exercises 1.3

1. A file name cannot contain a question mark.
3. Forward slashes (/) are not allowed in filespecs. Use a backslash (\ ) to separate folders in a filespec.
5. 4
7. 4 (Answers may vary)
9. Files are sorted by size.

11. Files are sorted by the date they were last modified.
13. Create a new directory called TEMP on your hard drive and then copy the file from the first diskette to TEMP. Place the second diskette in the diskette drive and then copy the file from TEMP to the second diskette. Delete the file and TEMP from the hard drive.

CHAPTER 2

Exercises 2.1

1. Command buttons appear to be pushed down and then let up when they are clicked.

3. When a command button is clicked, it appears to be pressed and then released. The left and top borders are temporarily darkened.

(In Exercises 7 to 27, begin by pressing Alt/F/N to create a new form.)

7. Click on the Properties window or Press F4 to activate the Properties window.
   Press Shift+Ctrl+C to highlight the Caption property.
   Type in "CHECKING ACCOUNT".
9. Double-click the text box icon in the Toolbox.
   Activate the Properties window and highlight the BackColor property.

   Click on the down-arrow to the right of the Settings box.
   Click on the Palette tab.
   Click on the desired yellow in the palette.
   Press Shift+Ctrl+T followed by three down arrows to highlight the Text property.
   Click on the Settings box and delete "Text1".
   Click on the form to see the empty, yellow text box.

11. Double-click on the text box icon in the Toolbox.

    Activate the Properties window and highlight the Text property.

    Type the requested sentence.

    Highlight the MultiLine property.

    Double-click on the highlighted MultiLine property to change its value to True.

    Highlight the Alignment property.

    Double-click twice on the highlighted Alignment property to change its value to 2-Center.

    Click on the form.

    Use the mouse to resize the text box so that the sentence occupies three lines.

13. Double-click on the text box icon in the Toolbox.

    Activate the Properties window and highlight the Text property.

    Type "VISUAL BASIC".

    Highlight the Font property.

    Click on the ellipsis to the right of the Settings box.

    Click on "Courier" in the Font box, and click OK.

    Resize the text box to accommodate its text.

    Click on the form to see the resulting text box.

15. Double-click on the command button icon in the Toolbox.

    Activate the Properties window and highlight the Caption property.

    Type "PUSH".

    Highlight the Font property and click on the ellipsis.

    Click on Italic in the Font Style box.

    Click on 24 in the Size box.

    Click OK.

    Click on the form to see the resulting command button.

    Resize the command button to accommodate its caption.

17. Double-click on the command button icon in the Toolbox.

    Activate the Properties window and highlight the Caption property.

    Type "PUS&H".

    Click on the form to see the resulting command button.

19. Double-click on the label icon in the Toolbox.

    Activate the Properties window and highlight the Caption property.

    Type "ALIAS".

    Click on the form to see the resulting label.

21. Double-click on the label icon in the Toolbox.

    Activate the Properties window and highlight the Alignment property.

    Double-click twice on the highlighted Alignment property to change its value to "2-Center".

    Highlight the Caption property.

    Type "ALIAS".

    Double-click on the BorderStyle property to change its value to "1–Fixed Single".

    Highlight the Font property and click on the ellipsis.

    Click on Italic in the Font Style box and click OK.

    Click on the form to see the resulting label.

23. Double-click on the label icon in the Toolbox.

    Activate the Properties window and highlight the Font property.

    Click on the ellipsis to the right of the Settings box.

    Click on Wingdings in the Font box.

    Click on the largest size available (72) in the Size list box.

    Click OK.

    As one means of determining which keystroke in the Wingdings font corresponds to a diskette, follow steps a–g.

    (a) Click the Start button.
    (b) Point to Programs and then point to Accessories.
    (c) Click Character Map.
    (d) Click on the down arrow in the Font box and click on Wingdings.
    (e) Click on the diskette character (fourth from the right end of the first row).
    (f) Note in the Status bar at the bottom of the Character map window that the keystroke for the diskette character is a less than sign.
    (g) Close the Character Map and return to Visual Basic.

    Highlight the Caption property.

    Change the caption setting to a less than sign by pressing <.

    Click on the label, and enlarge it.

25. Double-click on the picture box icon in the Toolbox.

    Activate the Properties window and highlight the BackColor property.

    Click on the down-arrow to the right of the Settings box.

    Click on the Palette tab.

    Click on the desired yellow in the palette.

    Click on the form to see the yellow picture box.

27. Double-click on the picture box icon in the Toolbox.

    Increase the size of the picture box so that it can easily hold two standard size command buttons.

    Click (do NOT double-click) on the command button icon in the Toolbox.

    Move the mouse to the desired location in the picture box where you want the upper-left corner of the first command button to be.

    Press and hold the left mouse button and drag the mouse down and to the right until the rectangle attains the size desired for the first command button

    Release the left mouse button.

    Repeat the preceding four steps (starting with clicking on the command button icon in the Toolbox) to place the second command button on the picture box.

29. Create a new project. Change the form's caption to "Dynamic Duo". Place two command buttons on the form. Enter as the caption of the first "&Batman" and of the second "&Robin". Increase the font size for both command buttons to 14.

31. Create a new project. Change the form's caption to "Fill in the Blank". Place a label, a text box, and another label on the form at appropriate locations. Change the caption of the first label to "Toto, I don't think we're in" and of the second label to "A Quote from the Wizard of Oz". Delete "Text1" from the Text property of the text box. Resize and position the labels as needed.

33. Create a new project. Change the form's caption to "An Uncle's Advice". Place a picture box on the form and increase its size to provide plenty of space. Place on the picture box five labels and three command buttons. Change the captions of each label to the appropriate text. Change the BorderStyle property of the last label to "1–Fixed Single". Change the captions of the command buttons to "1", "2", and "3". Resize and position the labels and command buttons as is appropriate. Finally, the size of the picture box and form can be adjusted down as appropriate.

Exercises 2.2

1. The word Hello.

3. The word Hello in italic letters.

5. The text box vanishes; nothing is visible.

7. The word Hello in green letters.

9. The word Hello in big, fixed-width letters.

11. The name of the control has been given but not the property being assigned. The line frmHi ="Hello" must be changed to frmHi.Caption = "Hello".

13. Text boxes do not have a Caption property. Information to be displayed in a text box must be assigned to the Text property.

15. Only 0 and 1 are valid values for the BorderStyle property of a label.

17. `lblTwo.Caption = "E.T. phone home."`

19. `txtBox.ForeColor = vbRed`
`txtBox.Text = "The stuff that dreams are made of."`

21. `txtBox.Text = ""`

23. `lblTwo.Visible = False`

25. `picBox.BackColor = vbBlue`

27. `txtBox.Font.Bold = True`
`txtBox.Font.Italic = True`
`txtBox.Text = "Hello"`

29. `cmdButton.SetFocus`

31. `lblTwo.BorderStyle = 1`
`lblTwo.Alignment = 2`

37.
```
Private Sub cmdLeft_Click()
    lblShow.Alignment = 0
    lblShow.Caption = "Left Justify"
End Sub

Private Sub cmdCenter_Click()
    lblShow.Alignment = 2
    lblShow.Caption = "Center"
End Sub

Private Sub cmdRight_Click()
    lblShow.Alignment = 1
    lblShow.Caption = "Right Justify"
End Sub
```

35. Create a new project. Change the form's caption to "Picture Box." Place a picture box and a label on the form. Change the label's Caption property to the sentence shown. Change the label's BackColor property to white, and its Font Size property to 14. Access the picture box's Picture property and select the picture file Picbox.bmp from the Pictures folder on the CD accompanying this textbook.

39.
```
Private Sub cmdRed_Click()
    txtShow.BackColor = vbRed
End Sub

Private Sub cmdBlue_Click()
    txtShow.BackColor = vbBlue
End Sub

Private Sub cmdWhite_Click()
    txtShow.ForeColor = vbWhite
End Sub

Private Sub cmdYellow_Click()
    txtShow.ForeColor = vbYellow
End Sub
```

41.
```
Private Sub txtLife.GotFocus()
    txtQuote.Text = "I like life, it's something to do."
End Sub

Private Sub txtFuture.GotFocus()
    txtQuote.Text = "The future isn't what it used to be."
End Sub

Private Sub txtTruth.GotFocus()
    txtQuote.Text = "Tell the truth and run."
End Sub
```

43.

Object	Property	Setting
cmdLarge	Caption	Large
cmdSmall	Caption	Small
cmdBold	Caption	Bold
cmdItalics	Caption	Italic
txtShow	Text	(blank)

```
Private Sub cmdLarge_Click()
    txtShow.Font.Size = 18
End Sub

Private Sub cmdSmall_Click()
    txtShow.Font.Size = 8
End Sub

Private Sub cmdBold_Click()
    txtShow.Font.Bold = True
    txtShow.Font.Italic = False
End Sub

Private Sub cmdItalics_Click()
    txtShow.Font.Italic = True
    txtShow.Font.Bold = False
End Sub
```

45.

Object	Property	Setting
frmEx45	Caption	Face
lblFace	Font.Name	Wingdings
	Caption	K
	Font.Size	24
cmdVanish	Caption	Vanish
cmdReappear	Caption	Reappear

```
Private Sub cmdVanish_Click()
  lblFace.Visible = False
End Sub

Private Sub cmdReappear_Click()
  lblFace.Visible = True
End Sub
```

47.

Object	Property	Setting
cmdPush1	Caption	Push Me
cmdPush2	Caption	Push Me
cmdPush3	Caption	Push Me
cmdPush4	Caption	Push Me

```
Private Sub cmdPush1_Click()
  cmdPush1.Visible = False
  cmdPush2.Visible = True
  cmdPush3.Visible = True
  cmdPush4.Visible = True
End Sub

Private Sub cmdPush2_Click()
  cmdPush1.Visible = True
  cmdPush2.Visible = False
  cmdPush3.Visible = True
  cmdPush4.Visible = True
End Sub

Private Sub cmdPush3_Click()
  cmdPush1.Visible = True
  cmdPush2.Visible = True
  cmdPush3.Visible = False
  cmdPush4.Visible = True
End Sub

Private Sub cmdPush4_Click()
  cmdPush1.Visible = True
  cmdPush2.Visible = True
  cmdPush3.Visible = True
  cmdPush4.Visible = False
End Sub
```

Exercises 2.3

1. 12

3. .03125

5. 8

7. 3E+09

9. 4E–08

11. Valid

13. Valid

15. Not valid

17. 10

19. 16

21. 9

23.
```
Private Sub cmdCompute_Click()
  picOutput.Cls
  picOutput.Print 7 * 8 + 5
End Sub
```

25.
```
Private Sub cmdCompute_Click()
  picOutput.Cls
  picOutput.Print .055 * 20
End Sub
```

27.
```
Private Sub cmdCompute_Click()
  picOutput.Cls
  picOutput.Print 17 * (3 + 162)
End Sub
```

29. True

31. True

33. True

35. 8

37. 1.28

39. 7

41.

x	y
2	0
2	6
11	6
11	6
11	6
11	7

43. 6

45. 1 2 3 4
11

47. 1
64

49. 27   12

51. The third line should read c = a + b

53. The first line should not contain a comma. The second line should not contain a dollar sign.

55. picOutput.Print 1; 2; 1 + 2

57.
```
Private Sub cmdCompute_Click()
  picOutput.Cls
  revenue = 98456
  costs = 45000
  profit = revenue - costs
  picOutput.Print profit
End Sub
```

59.
```
Private Sub cmdCompute_Click()
    picOutput.Cls
    price = 19.95
    discountPercent = 30
    markDown = (discountPercent / 100) * price
    price = price - markDown
    picOutput.Print price
End Sub
```

61.
```
Private Sub cmdCompute_Click()
    picOutput.Cls
    balance = 100
    balance = balance + balance * .05
    balance = balance + balance * .05
    balance = balance + balance * .05
    picOutput.Print balance
End Sub
```

63.
```
Private Sub cmdCompute_Click()
    picOutput.Cls
    balance = 100
    balance = balance * (1.05 ^ 10)
    picOutput.Print balance
End Sub
```

65.
```
Private Sub cmdCompute_Click()
    picOutput.Cls
    acres = 30
    yieldPerAcre = 18
    corn = yieldPerAcre * acres
    picOutput.Print corn
End Sub
```

67.
```
Private Sub cmdCompute_Click()
    picOutput.Cls
    distance = 233
    elapsedTime = 7 - 2
    averageSpeed = distance / elapsedTime
    picOutput.Print averageSpeed
End Sub
```

69.
```
Private Sub cmdCompute_Click()
    picOutput.Cls
    waterPerPersonPerDay = 1600
    people = 270000000
    days = 365
    waterUsed = waterPerPersonPerDay * people * days
    picOutput.Print waterUsed
End Sub
```

Exercises 2.4

1.
```
Hello
1234
```

3. 12 12 TWELVE

5. A ROSE IS A ROSE IS A ROSE

7. 1234 Main Street

9. "We're all in this alone." Lily Tomlin

11.
```
12345678
   3 1 3
```

13. The variable phone should be declared as type String, not Single.

15. End is a keyword and cannot be used as a variable name.

17. True

19. True

21. ha

23. 2

25. $2 BILL

27. e

29. 3

31. 12,345.00

33. $12,346

35. Tomorrow's date

37. Friday, December 31, 1999

39. The current year

41. The interest rate is 4.50%

43. The minimum wage is $5.15

45.
```
12345678
  2,000
```

47.
```
1234567890
    abcd
```

49.
```
Yada

Yada Yada
```

51.
```
Private Sub cmdDisplay_Click()
    Dim firstName As String, middleName As String
    Dim lastName As String, yearOfBirth As Integer
    picOutput.Cls
    firstName = "Thomas"
    middleName = "Alva"
    lastName = "Edison"
    yearOfBirth = 1847
    picOutput.Print firstName; " "; middleName; " "; lastName; ","; yearOfBirth
End Sub
```

53.
```
Private Sub cmdDisplay_Click()
    Dim publisher As String
    picOutput.Cls
    publisher = "Prentice Hall, Inc."
    picOutput.Print Chr(169); " "; publisher
End Sub
```

55.
```
Private Sub cmdCompute_Click()
    picSum.Print Val(txtNum1.Text) + Val(txtNum2.Text)
End Sub
```

57.
```
Private Sub cmdCompute_Click()
    lblNumMiles.Caption = Str(Val(txtNumSec.Text) / 5)
End Sub
```

59.
```
Private Sub cmdCompute_Click()
    Dim cycling As Single, running As Single, swimming As Single, pounds As Single
    picWtLoss.Cls
    cycling = Val(txtCycle.Text)
    running = Val(txtRun.Text)
    swimming = Val(txtSwim.Text)
    pounds = (200 * cycling + 475 * running + 275 * swimming) / 3500
    picWtLoss.Print pounds; "pounds were lost."
End Sub
```

61.

Object	Property	Setting
frmEx61	Caption	Net Income
lblRevenue	Caption	Revenue
txtRevenue	Text	(blank)
lblExpenses	Caption	Expenses
txtExpenses	Text	(blank)
cmdCompute	Caption	Display Net Income
picOutput		

```
Private Sub cmdCompute_Click()
    Dim income As Single
    picOutput.Cls
    income = Val(txtRevenue.Text) - Val(txtExpenses.Text)
    picOutput.Print "The company's net income is"; income
End Sub
```

63.

Object	Property	Setting
frmCompoundInterest	Caption	Compound Interest
lblPrincipal	Caption	Principal
txtPrincipal	Text	(blank)
lblInterestRate	Caption	Interest Rate
txtInterestRate	Text	(blank)
cmdCompute	Caption	Compute Balance
lblBalance	Caption	Balance after 10 years
lblOutput	Caption	(blank)

```
Private Sub cmdCompute_Click()
    Dim principal As Single, intRate As Single, balance As Single
    principal = Val(txtPrincipal.Text)
    txtPrincipal.Text = FormatCurrency(principal)
    intRate = Val(txtInterestRate.Text)
    txtInterestRate.Text = FormatPercent(intRate)
    balance = principal * (1 + intRate) ^ 10
    lblOutput.Caption = FormatCurrency(balance)
End Sub

Private Sub txtPrincipal_GotFocus()
    txtPrincipal.Text = ""
End Sub

Private Sub txtInterestRate_GotFocus()
    txtInterestRate.Text = ""
End Sub
```

65.

Object	Property	Setting
frmEx65	Caption	Tipping
lblAmount	Caption	Amount of bill:
txtAmount	Text	(blank)
lblPercentTip	Caption	Percentage Tip
txtPercentTip	Text	(blank)
cmdComputeTip	Caption	Compute Tip
picOutput		

```
Private Sub cmdComputeTip_Click()
    picOutput.Cls
    picOutput.Print "The tip is"; FormatCurrency(Val(txtAmount.Text) * Val(txtPercentTip.Text) / 100)
End Sub
```

Exercises 2.5

1. 16

3. baseball

5. Age: 20

7. setup

9. The White House has 132 rooms.

11. 1 OneTwo 2

2

1

13. Harvard University is 363 years old.

15. You might win 180 dollars.

17. Hello John Jones

19. 1 one   won

21. one   two

23. 1234567890

5

25. 1234567890

one two

27. 12345678901234

one

two

29. The Input #1 statement will assign "John Smith" to *str1*, leaving nothing left to assign to *str2*. An "Input past end of file" error will occur.

31. Each line in the file consists of three items, but the Input #1 statements are reading just two. As a result, the second Input #1 statement will assign the numeric data 110 to the string variable *building* and 0 to *ht*. This is not what was intended.

33. The response is to be used as a number, so the input from the user should not contain commas. With the given user response, the value in the variable *statePop* will be 8.

35. Should be Printer.Font.Name = "Courier".

37. Commas can not be used to format the caption of a label. Also, the value of the caption must be surrounded by quotation marks. The programmer might have intended

lblTwo.Caption = " 1   2"

39. When assigning properties of the form, the correct object name is Form1 (or whatever the form is named), not Form. Also, Tab(5) and semicolons can only be used with a Print method.

41.

category	amount	total
(undefined)	(undefined)	(undefined)
""	(undefined)	(undefined)
""	0	(undefined)
""	0	0
""	0	0
"phone"	35.25	0
"phone"	35.25	35.25
"postage"	14.75	35.25
"postage"	14.75	50
"postage"	14.75	50
"postage	14.75	50
(undefined)	(undefined)	(undefined)

43.
```
Private Sub cmdDisplay_Click()
    Dim activity As String, percent96 As Single, percent97 As Single
    'Compute change in political activity
    picOutput.Cls
    Open "Politics.txt" For Input As #1
    Input #1, activity, percent96, percent97
    picOutput.Print "The change in the percentage of college freshmen who ";
    picOutput.Print activity; " was "; percent97 - percent96
    Input #1, activity, percent96, percent97
    picOutput.Print "The change in the percentage of college freshmen who ";
    picOutput.Print activity; " was "; percent97 - percent96
    Close #1
End Sub
```

45.
```
Private Sub cmdDisplay_Click()
    Dim begOfYearPrice As Single, endOfYearPrice As Single, percentIncrease As Single
    'Report percent increase for a basket of goods
    picOutput.Cls
    begOfYearPrice = 200
    endOfYearPrice = Val(InputBox("Enter price at the end of the year:"))
    percentIncrease = 100 * (endOfYearPrice - begOfYearPrice) / begOfYearPrice
    picOutput.Print "The percent increase for the year is"; percentIncrease
End Sub
```

47. MsgBox "The future isn't what it used to be."

49.
```
Private Sub cmdSummarize_Click()
    Dim account As String, beginningBalance As Single
    Dim deposits As Single, withdrawals As Single
    Dim endOfMonth As Single, total As Single
    'Report checking account activity
    picReport.Cls
    Open "2-5-e49.txt" For Input As #1
    '1st account
    Input #1, account, beginningBalance, deposits, withdrawals
    endOfMonth = beginningBalance + deposits - withdrawals
    total = endOfMonth
    picReport.Print "Monthly balance for account "; account; " is "; FormatCurrency(endOfMonth)
    '2nd account
    Input #1, account, beginningBalance, deposits, withdrawals
    endOfMonth = beginningBalance + deposits - withdrawals
    total = total + endOfMonth
    picReport.Print "Monthly balance for account "; account; " is "; FormatCurrency(endOfMonth)
    '3rd account
    Input #1, account, beginningBalance, deposits, withdrawals
    endOfMonth = beginningBalance + deposits - withdrawals
    total = total + endOfMonth
    picReport.Print "Monthly balance for account "; account; " is "; FormatCurrency(endOfMonth)
    picReport.Print "Total for all accounts = "; FormatCurrency(total)
    Close #1
End Sub
```

51.
```
Private Sub cmdComputeAvg_Click()
    Dim socNmb As String, exam1 As Single, exam2 As Single, exam3 As Single
    Dim final As Single, average As Single, total As Single
    'Compute semester averages
    picOutput.Cls
    Open "2-5-e51.txt" For Input As #1
    '1st student
    Input #1, socNmb, exam1, exam2, exam3, final
    average = (exam1 + exam2 + exam3 + final * 2) / 5
    total = average
    picOutput.Print "Semester average for "; socNmb; " is"; average
    '2nd student
    Input #1, socNmb, exam1, exam2, exam3, final
    average = (exam1 + exam2 + exam3 + final * 2) / 5
    total = total + average
    picOutput.Print "Semester average for "; socNmb; " is"; average
    '3rd student
    Input #1, socNmb, exam1, exam2, exam3, final
    average = (exam1 + exam2 + exam3 + final * 2) / 5
    total = total + average
    picOutput.Print "Semester average for "; socNmb; " is"; average
    picOutput.Print "Class average is"; total / 3
    Close #1
End Sub
```

53.
```
Private Sub cmdCompute_Click()
    Dim athlete As String, sport As String
    Dim winnings As Single, endorsements As Single
    'Display a table of sports salaries
    picOutput.Cls
    picOutput.Print , , "Salary or"
    picOutput.Print "Athlete", "Sport", "Winnings", "Endorsements", "Total"
    Open "2-5-e53.txt" For Input As #1
    Input #1, athlete, sport, winnings, endorsements
    picOutput.Print athlete, sport, winnings, endorsements, winnings + endorsements
    Input #1, athlete, sport, winnings, endorsements
    picOutput.Print athlete, sport, winnings, endorsements, winnings + endorsements
    Input #1, athlete, sport, winnings, endorsements
    picOutput.Print athlete, sport, winnings, endorsements, winnings + endorsements
    Input #1, athlete, sport, winnings, endorsements
    picOutput.Print athlete, sport, winnings, endorsements, winnings + endorsements
    Close #1
End Sub
```

55.
```
Private Sub txtPhoneNum_GotFocus()
    MsgBox "Be sure to include the area code!"
End Sub
```

57.
```
Private Sub cmdCompute_Click()
    Dim price As Single, quantity As Single, revenue As Single
    picOutput.Cls
    Open "2-5-e57.txt" For Input As #1
    Input #1, price
    Input #1, quantity
    revenue = price * quantity
    picOutput.Print "The revenue is "; FormatCurrency(revenue)
    Close #1
End Sub
```

Exercises 2.6

1. Why do clocks run clockwise?
Because they were invented in the northern hemisphere where sundials move clockwise.

3. Keep cool, but don't freeze.
Source: A jar of mayonnaise.

5. 168 hourse in a week
76 trombones in the big parade

7. 24 blackbirds baked in a pie

9. 9

11. 25

13. Less is more

15. Buckeyes

33.
```
Private Sub cmdDisplay_Click()
    Dim price As Single, tax As Single, cost As Single
    'Calculate sales tax
    picOutput.Cls
    Call InputPrice(price)
    Call Compute(price, tax, cost)
    Call ShowData(price, tax, cost)
End Sub

Private Sub Compute(price As Single, tax As Single, cost As Single)
    'Calculate the cost
    tax = .05 * price
    cost = price + tax
End Sub

Private Sub InputPrice(price As Single)
    'Get the price of the item
    price = Val(InputBox("Enter the price of the item:"))
End Sub

Private Sub ShowData(price As Single, tax As Single, cost As Single)
    'Display bill
    picOutput.Print "Price: "; price
    picOutput.Print "Tax: "; tax
    picOutput.Print "--------------"
    picOutput.Print "Cost: "; cost
End Sub
```

17. 1 1

19. 203

21. The population will double in 24 years.

23. train

25. moral has the negative amoral
political has the negative apolitical

27. There is a parameter in the Sub procedure, but no argument in the statement calling the Sub procedure.

29. The Private Sub Tea() declaration has no parameter to match the argument in the Call Tea(num) statement.

31. The first line of the function definition should end with As String, not As Single.

```
35. Private Sub cmdDisplay_Click()
       Dim animal As String, sound As String
       'Old McDonald Had a Farm
       picOldMcDonald.Cls
       Open "Farm.txt" For Input As #1
       Input #1, animal, sound
       Call ShowVerse(animal, sound)
       picOldMcDonald.Print
       Input #1, animal, sound
       Call ShowVerse(animal, sound)
       picOldMcDonald.Print
       Input #1, animal, sound
       Call ShowVerse(animal, sound)
       picOldMcDonald.Print
       Input #1, animal, sound
       Call ShowVerse(animal, sound)
       Close #1
     End Sub

     Private Sub ShowVerse(animal As String, sound As String)
       'Display a verse from Old McDonald Had a Farm
       picOldMcDonald.Print "Old McDonald had a farm. Eyi eyi oh."
       picOldMcDonald.Print "And on his farm he had a "; animal; ".  Eyi eyi oh."
       picOldMcDonald.Print "With a "; sound; " "; sound; " here, ";
       picOldMcDonald.Print "and a "; sound; " "; sound; " there."
       picOldMcDonald.Print "Here a "; sound; ", there a "; sound;
       picOldMcDonald.Print ", everywhere a "; sound; " "; sound; "."
       picOldMcDonald.Print "Old McDonald had a farm. Eyi eyi oh."
     End Sub

37. Private Sub cmdDisplay_Click()
       'Display Hat Rack mall comparison table
       picTable.Cls
       picTable.Print Tab(15); "Rent per"
       picTable.Print Tab(15); "Square"; Tab(25); "Total"; Tab(35); "Monthly"
       picTable.Print "Mall Name"; Tab(15); "Foot"; Tab(25); "Feet"; Tab(35); "Rent"
       picTable.Print
       Open "Malls.txt" For Input As #1
       Call DisplayInfo
       Call DisplayInfo
       Call DisplayInfo
       Close #1
     End Sub

     Private Function Rent(rentPerFoot As Single, squareFeet As Single) As Single
       'Compute monthly rent given rent/foot and number of feet
       Rent = rentPerFoot * SquareFeet
     End Sub

     Private Sub DisplayInfo()
       Dim mall As String, rentPerFoot As Single, squareFeet As Single
       'Display the information for a single mall
       Input #1, mall, rentPerFoot, squareFeet
       picTable.Print mall; Tab(15); FormatCurrency(rentPerFoot); Tab(25); squareFeet; Tab(35); _
                    FormatCurrency(Rent(rentPerFoot, squareFeet))
     End Sub

39. Private Sub cmdCalculate_Click()
       picResult.Cls
       picResult.Print "Your BMI is"; BMI(Val(txtWeight), Val(txtHeight))
     End Sub

     Private Function BMI(w As Single, h As Single) As Single
       'Calculate body mass index
       BMI = Round(703 * w / h ^ 2)
     End Function
```

41.
```
Private Sub cmdGreetSenator_Click()
    Dim nom As String
    'Display a greeting for a senator
    picGreeting.Cls
    nom = InputBox("Enter the senator's name:")
    picGreeting.Print
    picGreeting.Print "The Honorable "; nom
    picGreeting.Print "United States Senate"
    picGreeting.Print "Washington, DC 20001"
    picGreeting.Print
    picGreeting.Print "Dear Senator "; LastName(nom); ","
End Sub

Private Function LastName(nom As String) As String
    Dim spaceNmb As Integer
    'Determine the last name of a two part name
    spaceNmb = InStr(nom, " ")
    LastName = Mid(nom, spaceNmb + 1, Len(nom) - spaceNmb)
End Function
```

CHAPTER 3

Exercises 3.1

1. Less than ten

3. 10

5. Cost of call: $11.26

7. Nope.
He worked with the developer, von Neumann, on the ENIAC.
Correct

9. The less things change, the more they remain the same.
Less is more.
Time keeps everything from happening at once.

11. Incorrect conditional. Should be If (1 < num) And (num < 3) Then

13. no Then in second line

15. Incorrect conditional. Should be If (j = 4) Or (k = 4) Then

17. Should have a Case clause.

19. Error in second Case clause.

21. a = 5

23.
```
If j = 7 Then
    b = 1
Else
    b = 2
End If
```

31.
```
Private Sub cmdComputeBalance_Click()
    Dim balance As Single, amount As Single
    'Savings account withdrawal
    picBalance.Cls
    balance = Val(InputBox("Current balance:"))
    amount = Val(InputBox("Amount of withdrawal:"))
    If (balance >= amount) Then
        balance = balance - amount
        picBalance.Print "New balance is "; FormatCurrency(balance)
        If balance < 150 Then
            picBalance.Print "Balance below $150"
        End If
    Else
        picBalance.Print "Withdrawal denied."
    End If
End Sub
```

25.
```
Select Case a
    Case 1
        picOutput.Print "one"
    Case Is > 5
        picOutput.Print "two"
End Select
```

27.
```
Select Case a
    Case 2
        picOutput.Print "yes"
    Case Is < 5
        picOutput.Print "no"
End Select
```

29.
```
Private Sub cmdComputeTip_Click()
    Dim cost As Single, tip As Single
    'Give waiter a tip
    picTip.Cls
    cost = Val(InputBox("Enter cost of meal:"))
    tip = cost * .15
    If tip < 1 Then
        tip = 1
    End If
    picTip.Print "Leave "; FormatCurrency(tip); " for the tip."
End Sub
```

```
33.  Private Sub cmdConvert_Click()
         Dim word As String, first As String
         'Convert to Pig Latin
         picPigLatin.Cls
         word = InputBox("Enter a word (use all lowercase):")
         first = Left(word, 1)
         If Instr("aeiou", first) <> 0 Then
             word = word & "way"
           Else
             word = Mid(word, 2, Len(word) - 1) & first & "ay"
         End If
         picPigLatin.Print "The word in pig latin is "; word
     End Sub

35.  Private Sub cmdCompute_Click()
         Dim percent As Single
         'Determine degree of cloudiness
         picCloudCover.Cls
         percent = Val(InputBox("Percentage of cloud cover:"))
         Select Case percent
           Case 0 To 30
             picCloudCover.Print "Clear"
           Case 31 To 70
             picCloudCover.Print "Partly cloudy"
           Case 71 To 99
             picCloudCover.Print "Cloudy"
           Case 100
             picCloudCover.Print "Overcast"
           Case Else
             picCloudCover.Print "Percentage must be between 0 And 100."
         End Select
     End Sub

37.  Private Sub cmdFindNumDays_Click()
         Dim monthName As String, days As Integer
         'Give number of days in month
         picNumDays.Cls
         Call InputMonth(monthName)
         Call GetDays(monthName, days)
         Call ShowDays(days, monthName)
     End Sub

     Private Sub GetDays(monthName As String, days As Integer)
         Dim answer As String
         'Compute number of days in the month
         Select Case UCase(monthName)
           Case "FEBRUARY"
             answer = InputBox("Is it a leap year?")
             If UCase(Left(answer, 1)) = "Y" Then
                 days = 29
               Else
                 days = 28
             End If
           Case "APRIL", "JUNE", "SEPTEMBER", "NOVEMBER"
             days = 30
           Case "JANUARY","MARCH","MAY","JULY","AUGUST","OCTOBER","DECEMBER"
             days = 31
         End Select
     End Sub

     Private Sub InputMonth(monthName As String)
         'Input a month of the year
         monthName = InputBox("Enter a month (do not abbreviate):")
     End Sub

     Private Sub ShowDays(days As Integer, monthName As String)
         'Report number of days in month
         picNumDays.Print monthName; " has"; days; "days."
     End Sub
```

39.

Object	Property	Setting
frmEx39	Caption	Presidential Trivia
lblQuestion	Caption	Last name of one of the four most recent Presidents
txtName	Text	(blank)
cmdGetFacts	Caption	OK
picTrivia		

```
Private Sub cmdGetFacts_Click()
  Dim pres As String, state As String, trivia As String
  pres = txtName.Text
  Select Case UCase(pres)
    Case "CARTER"
      state = "Georgia"
      trivia = "The only soft drink served in the Carter "
      trivia = trivia & "White House was Coca-Cola."
    Case "REAGAN"
      state = "California"
      trivia = "His secret service code name was Rawhide."
    Case "BUSH"
      state = "Texas"
      trivia = "He was the third left-handed president."
    Case "CLINTON"
      state = "Arkansas"
      trivia = "In college he did a good imitation of Elvis Presley."
    Case Else
      state = ""
      trivia = ""
  End Select
  If state <> "" Then
      picTrivia.Cls
      picTrivia.Print "President "; pres; "'s ";
      picTrivia.Print "home state was "; state; "."
      picTrivia.Print trivia
  End If
  txtName.Text = ""
  txtName.SetFocus
End Sub
```

Exercises 3.2

1. 17

3. 13

5. pie
   cake
   melon

7. Program never stops.

9. Loop statement missing. Also, loop cannot be entered because the value of num is 0.

11. `While num >= 7`

13. `Until response <> "Y"`

15. `Until nom = ""`

17.
```
Private Sub cmdDisplay_Click()
    Dim nom As String, num As Integer
    'Request and display three names
    picOutput.Cls
    num = 0
    Do While num < 3
      nom = InputBox("Enter a name:")
      picOutput.Print nom
      num = num + 1
    Loop
End Sub
```

19.
```
Private Sub cmdDisplayConvTable_Click()
    Dim celsius As Single
    picTempTable.Cls
    picTempTable.Print "Celsius"; Tab(10); "Fahrenheit"
    celsius = -40
    Do While celsius <= 40
      picTempTable.Print celsius; Tab(10); (9 / 5) * celsius + 32
      celsius = celsius + 5
    Loop
End Sub
```

```
21. Private Sub cmdDisplay_Click()
      Dim money As Single, liquid As String, price As Single
      'Display liquids available given an amount of money
      picOutput.Cls
      money = Val(txtAmount.Text)
      picOutput.Print "You can purchase one gallon of any of the following liquids."
      Open "Liquids.txt" For Input As #1
      Do While Not EOF(1)
        Input #1, liquid, price
        If price <= money Then
            picOutput.Print liquid
        End If
      Loop
      Close #1
    End Sub

23. Private Sub cmdDisplay_Click()
      Dim largest As Single, num as Single
      'Find largest of a collection of numbers
      picOutput.Cls
      largest = 0
      Open "3-2-e23.txt" For Input As #1
      Do While Not EOF(1)
        Input #1, num
        If num > largest Then
            largest = num
        End If
      Loop
      picOutput.Print "The largest number is"; largest
    End Sub

25. Private Sub cmdDisplay_Click()
      Dim total As Single, numGrades As Integer, grade As Single
      Dim average As Single, aaCount As Integer
      'Display percentage of grades that are above average
      Open "Final.txt" For Input As #1
      total = 0
      numGrades = 0
      Do While Not EOF(1)
        Input #1, grade
        total = total + grade
        numGrades = numGrades + 1
      Loop
      Close #1
      If numGrades > 0 Then
          average = total / numGrades
          aaCount = 0
          Open "Grades.txt" For Input As #1
          Do While Not EOF(1)
            Input #1, grade
            If grade > average Then
                aaCount = aaCount + 1
            End If
          Loop
          Close #1
          picOutput.Cls
          picOutput.Print FormatPercent(aaCount / numGrades); " of grades are above the average of ";
          picOutput.Print FormatNumber(average)
      End If
    End Sub
```

```
27. Private Sub cmdShowPresident_Click()
        Dim n As Integer, num As Integer, nom As String
        'Display the name of the nth president
        n = Val(txtPresNum.Text)
        If (1 <= n) And (n <= 42) Then
            picPresident.Cls
            Open "Uspres.txt" For Input As #1
            num = 0
            Do
              Input #1, nom
              num = num + 1
            Loop Until num = n
            picPresident.Print nom; " was President number"; n
            Close #1
        End If
    End Sub
```

Exercises 3.3

1. Pass # 1
Pass # 2
Pass # 3
Pass # 4

3. 2 4 6 8 Who do we appreciate?

5. 5 6 7 8 9 10 11 12 13

7. Steve Cram   3:46.31
Steve Scott   3:51.6
Mary Slaney   4:20.5

9.
```
1    4    7    10
2    5    8    11
3    6    9    12
```

11. Loop is never executed because 1 is less than 25.5 and the step is negative.

13. A For statement can only have one Next statement.

15.
```
For num = 1 To 10 Step 2
    picOutput.Print num
Next num
```

17.
```
Private Sub cmdDisplay_Click()
    Dim i As Integer
    'Display a row of 10 stars
    picOutput.Cls
    For i = 1 To 10
      picOutput.Print "*";
    Next i
End Sub
```

19.
```
Private Sub cmdDisplay_Click()
    Dim i As Integer, j As Integer
    'Display 10 x 10 array of stars
    picOutput.Cls
    For i = 1 To 10
      For j = 1 To 10
        picOutput.Print "*";
      Next j
      picOutput.Print
    Next i
End Sub
```

21.
```
Private Sub cmdComputeSum_Click()
    Dim sum As Single, denominator As Integer
    'Compute the sum 1 + 1/2 + 1/3 + 1/4 + ... + 1/100
    picOutput.Cls
    sum = 0
    For denominator = 1 To 100
      sum = sum + 1 / denominator
    Next denominator
    picOutput.Print "The sum is"; sum
End Sub
```

23.
```
Private Sub cmdAnalyzeOptions_Click()
    Dim result1 As Single, result2 As Single
    'Compare salaries
    picResults.Cls
    Call Option1(result1)
    Call Option2(result2)
    If result1 > result2 Then
        picResults.Print "Option 1";
      Else
        picResults.Print "Option 2";
    End If
    picResults.Print " pays better"
End Sub

Private Sub Option1(result As Single)
    Dim i As Integer
    'Compute the total salary for 10 days,
    'with a flat salary of $100 / day
    result = 0
    For i = 1 To 10
      result = result + 100
    Next i
    picResults.Print "Option 1 = "; FormatCurrency(result)
End Sub

Private Sub Option2(result As Single)
    Dim i As Integer, daySalary As Single
    'Compute the total salary for 10 days,
    'starting at $1 and then doubling each day
    result = 0
    daySalary = 1
    For i = 1 To 10
      result = result + daySalary
      daySalary = daySalary * 2
    Next i
    picResults.Print "Option 2 = "; FormatCurrency(result)
End Sub
```

25.
```
Private Sub cmdCompIdealWeights_Click()
    Dim lower As Integer, upper As Integer, height As Integer,
    Dim prompt as string
    'Ideal weights for men and women
    picWeightTable.Cls
    'Input the lower and upper bounds on height
    prompt = "Give lower bound on height in inches:"
    lower = Val(InputBox(prompt, "Weight Table"))
    prompt = "Give upper bound on height in inches:"
    upper = Val(InputBox(prompt, "Weight Table"))
    'Display table of weights
    picWeightTable.Print
    picWeightTable.Print "Height", "Wt - Women", "Wt - Men"
    picWeightTable.Print
    For height = lower To upper
        picWeightTable.Print height, 3.5 * height - 108, 4 * height - 128
    Next height
End Sub
```

27.
```
Private Sub cmdAnalyze_Click()
    Dim numSibs As Integer, i As Integer, letter As String
    'Count the number of sibilants (i.e., the letters S and Z)
    picOutput.Cls
    numSibs = 0
    For i = 1 To Len(txtSentence)
      letter = UCase(Mid(txtSentence, i, 1))
      If (letter = "S") Or (letter = "Z") Then
          numSibs = numSibs + 1
      End If
    Next i
    picOutput.Print "There are"; numSibs; "sibilants in the sentence."
End Sub
```

29.
```
Private Sub cmdCalcBalance_Click()
    Dim amt As Single, yearNum As Integer
    'Bank interest for ten years
    picBalance.Cls
    amt = 800
    For yearNum = 1 To 10
      amt = amt * 1.04 + 100
    Next yearNum
    picBalance.Print "The final amount is "; FormatCurrency(amt)
End Sub
```

31.
```
Private Sub cmdDecay_Click()
    Dim grams As Single, yearNum As Integer
    'Cobalt-60 decays at a rate of about 12% per year
    picOutput.Cls
    grams = 10
    For yearNum = 1 To 5
      grams = 0.88 * grams
    Next yearNum
    picOutput.Print "Of 10 grams of cobalt-60,"
    picOutput.Print grams; "grams remain after 5 years."
End Sub
```

33.
```
Private Sub cmdDraw_Click()
    Dim stars As Integer, i As Integer, j As Integer
    'Draw a hollow box
    picOutput.Cls
    picOutput.Font.Name = "Courier"
    stars = Val(InputBox("Number of stars?"))
    'Draw the top of the rectangle
    For i = 1 To stars
      picOutput.Print "*";
    Next i
    picOutput.Print
    For i = 1 To stars - 2
      'Draw a row (put spaces between the two stars)
      picOutput.Print "*";
      For j = 1 To stars - 2
        picOutput.Print " ";
      Next j
      picOutput.Print "*"
    Next i
    'Draw the bottom of the rectangle
    For i = 1 To stars
      picOutput.Print "*";
    Next i
    picOutput.Print
End Sub
```

35.
```
Private Sub cmdDisplay_Click()
    Dim title1 As String, title2 As String
    Dim yr As Integer, percentGrowth As Integer, i As Integer
    'Create a histogram
    picData.Cls
    picData.Font.Name = "Courier"
    Open "Pcsales.txt" For Input As #1
    Input #1, title1, title2
    Do While Not EOF(1)
      Input #1, yr, percentGrowth
      picData.Print yr;
      'Display a row of stars
      For i = 1 To percentGrowth
        picData.Print "*";
      Next i
      picData.Print percentGrowth
    Loop
    Close #1
    picData.Print
    picData.Print title1
    picData.Print title2
End Sub
```

CHAPTER 4

Exercises 4.1

1. 3 7 0

3. Stuhldreher
Crowley

5. 6 2 9 11 3 4

7. The Dim statement in the (Declarations) section of
(General) dimensions *companies()* with subscripts from 1 to
100 and makes *companies()* available to all procedures.
Therefore, the ReDim statement in the Form_Load event
procedure produces the error message "Array already
dimensioned." First line should be `Dim companies()`
`As String`.

9. Array subscript out of range (when $k > 4$).

11. Improper syntax in first Dim statement.

13.

river(1)	river(2)	river(3)	river(4)	river(5)
Thames	Ohio	Amazon	Volga	Nile

river(1)	river(2)	river(3)	river(4)	river(5)
Ohio	Amazon	Volga	Nile	Thames

15. (a) 2
(b) 7
(c) 10
(d) 9

17. Replace lines 18 to 24 with
```
'Display all names and difference from average
picTopStudents.Cls
For student = 1 To 8
  picTopStudents.Print nom(student), score(student) - average
Next student
```

19. `Dim bestPicture(1975 To 1995) As String`

21.
```
Dim marx(1 To 4) As String  'In (Declarations) section
                            'of (General)
Private Sub Form_Load()
  marx(1) = "Chico"
  marx(2) = "Harpo"
  marx(3) = "Groucho"
  marx(4) = "Zeppo"
End Sub
```

23.
```
Dim i As Integer
'Reverse array a() and store in b()
For i = 1 To 4
  b(i) = a(5 - i)
Next i
```

25.
```
Dim i As Integer, k As Integer
'Display the elements of the array a()
For i = 1 To 26 Step 5
  For k = 0 To 4
    picArray.Print Tab(10 * k + 1); a(i + k);
  Next k
  picArray.Print
Next i
```

27.
```
Dim i As Integer, differFlag As Boolean
'Compare arrays a() and b() for same values
differFlag = False
For i = 1 To 10
  If a(i) <> b(i) Then
      differFlag = True
  End If
Next i
If differFlag Then
    picOutput.Print "The arrays are not identical."
  Else
    picOutput.Print "The arrays have identical values."
End If
```

29.
```
Dim i As Integer
'Curve grades by adding 7
For i = 1 To 12
  grades(i) = grades(i) + 7
Next i
```

31.
```
Private Sub cmdDisplay_Click()
    Dim range As Integer, dataElement As Integer, score As Integer, interval As Integer
    'Create and display the frequency of scores
    Dim frequency(1 To 5) As Integer
    'Set array elements to 0
    For range = 1 To 5
      frequency(range) = 0
    Next range
    'Read scores, count scores in each of five intervals
    Open "4-1-e31.txt" For Input As #1
    For dataElement = 1 To 30
      Input #1, score
      range = Int(score / 10) + 1    'Number in the range of 1-5
      frequency(range) = frequency(range) + 1
    Next dataElement
    Close #1
    'Display frequency in each interval
    picTable.Cls
    picTable.Print "Interval"; Tab(12); "Frequency"
    picTable.Print
    For interval = 1 To 5
      picTable.Print 10 * (interval - 1); "to"; 10 * interval - 1;
      picTable.Print Tab(14); frequency(interval)
    Next interval
End Sub
```

33.
```
Private Sub cmdDisplay_Click()
    Dim i As Integer, total As Single
    'Display names, percentage of total units for top ten pizza chains
    Dim nom(1 To 10) As String, units(1 To 10) As Single
    'Read from data file and record names and number of units
    'Compute total units
    Open "4-1-e33.txt" For Input As #1
    total = 0                     'Total units
    For i = 1 To 10
      Input #1, nom(i), units(i)
      total = total + units(i)
    Next i
    Close #1
    'Display names and percentage of total units
    picOutput.Cls
    picOutput.Print "Name"; Tab(30); "Percentage of units"
    For i = 1 To 10
      picOutput.Print nom(i); Tab(30); FormatPercent(units(i) / total)
    Next i
End Sub
```

35.
```
Dim monthNames(1 To 12) As Single  'In (Declarations) section of (General)

Private Sub Form_Load()
  monthNames(1) = "January"
  monthNames(2) = "February"
  monthNames(3) = "March"
  monthNames(4) = "April"
  monthNames(5) = "May"
  monthNames(6) = "June"
  monthNames(7) = "July"
  monthNames(8) = "August"
  monthNames(9) = "September"
  monthNames(10) = "October"
  monthNames(11) = "November"
  monthNames(12) = "December"
End Sub
```

```
Private Sub cmdDisplay_Click()
  Dim monthNum As Integer
  'Display month name
  picOutput.Cls
  Do
    monthNum = Val(InputBox("Enter month number:"))
    If (monthNum < 1) Or (monthNum > 12) Then
      MsgBox "Number must be between 1 and 12"
    End If
  Loop Until (monthNum >= 1) And (monthNum <= 12)
  picOutput.Print "Month name is "; monthNames(monthNum)
End Sub
```

Exercises 4.2

1. No

3. 200 100

5. 11 7 Numbers interchanged.

7. Items not properly swapped.

9. Sequential, since the array is not ordered

11. 4 swaps

13. $(n-1) + (n-2) + \ldots + 1$ or $n(n-1)/2$

15. Go through the list once, and count the number of times that each of the four integers occurs. Then list the determined number of 1s, followed by the determined number of 2s, etc.

17.
```
Private Sub TripleSwap(x As Single, y As Single, z As Single)
  Dim temp As Single
  'Interchange the values of x, y, and z
  temp = x
  x = y
  y = z
  z = temp
End Sub
```

23.
```
Private Sub cmdCalcAvg_Click()
  Dim nom As String, i As Integer
  Dim score(1 To 7) As Integer, sum As Integer
  Dim passNum As Integer, temp As Integer
  'Input student's name and seven test scores
  nom = InputBox("Student's name:")
  For i = 1 To 7
    score(i) = Val(InputBox("Test score " & Str(i) & ":", ""))
  Next i
  For passNum = 1 To 6
    For i = 1 To 7 - passnum
      If score(i) < score(i + 1) Then
          temp = score(i)
          score(i) = score(i + 1)
          score(i + 1) = temp
      End If
    Next i
  Next passNum
  picAvg.Cls
  sum = 0
  For passNum = 1 To 5
    sum = sum + score(passNum)
  Next passNum
  PicAvg.Print nom & ":   "; "Average ="; sum / 5
End Sub
```

Exercises 4.3

1. Hello

3. Hello
Aloha
Bon Jour

5. No quotes surrounding file name.

7.
```
Private Sub cmdCreateFile_Click()
  'Create file of names and prices of items bought by cowboys
  Open "Cowboy.txt" For Output As #1
  Write #1, "Colt Peacemaker", 12.2
  Write #1, "Holster", 2
  Write #1, "Levi Strauss Jeans", 1.35
  Write #1, "Saddle", 40
  Write #1, "Stetson", 10
  Close #1
End Sub
```

9.
```
Private Sub cmdAddItem_Click()
    'Add Winchester rifle to end of file Cowboy.txt
    Open "Cowboy.txt" For Append As #1
    Write #1, "Winchester rifle", 20.5
    Close #1
End Sub
```

13.
```
Private Sub cmdRemoveItem_Click()
    Dim item As String, price As Single
    'Produce Cowboy4.txt with Holster removed
    Open "Cowboy.txt" For Input As #1
    Open "Cowboy4.txt" For Output As #2
    Do While Not EOF(1)
      Input #1, item, price
      If item <> "Holster" Then
          Write #2, item, price
      End If
    Loop
    Close #1
    Close #2
End Sub
```

15.
```
Private Sub cmdFind_Click()
    Dim search As String, nom As String, yob As Integer
    'Search for a name in Yob.txt
    picOutput.Cls
    search = txtName.Text
    Open "Yob.txt" For Input As #1
    nom = ""
    Do While (search > nom) And (Not EOF(1))
      Input #1, nom, yob
    Loop
    Close #1
    If (nom = search) And (search <> "") Then
        picOutput.Print nom; "'s age is"; 1999 - yob
      Else
        picOutput.Print search; " is not in Yob.txt"
    End If
End Sub
```

17.
```
Private Sub cmdCreateFile_Click()
    'Add initial batting average record to Average.txt
    Write #1, txtPlayer.Text, 0, 0      'Initialize counters
    txtPlayer.Text = ""
    txtPlayer.SetFocus
End Sub

Private Sub cmdQuit_Click()
    Close #1
    End
End Sub

Private Sub Form_Load()
    Open "Average.txt" For Output As #1
End Sub
```

19.
```
Private Sub cmdAddPlayer_Click()
    'Add a player to the end of the file Average.txt
    Write #1, txtPlayer.Text, 0, 0
    txtPlayer.Text = ""
    txt Player.SetFocus
End Sub

Private Sub cmdQuit_Click()
    Close #1
    End
End Sub

Private Sub Form_Load()
    Open "Average.txt" For Append As #1
End Sub
```

CHAPTER 5

Exercises 5.1

1.
```
picBox.Line (-1, 0)-(4, 0)      'x-axis
picBox.Line (0, -8)-(0, 40)     'y-axis
```

3.
```
Private Sub cmdDraw_Click()
    'Draw axes and line
    picOutput.Scale (-2, 240)-(12, -40)
    picOutput.Line (-2, 0)-(12, 0)        'Draw x-axis
    picOutput.Line (0, -40)-(0, 240)      'Draw y-axis
    picOutput.Line (3, 200)-(10, 150)     'Draw line
    picOutput.Circle (3, 200), .05
    picOutput.Circle (10, 150), .05
End Sub
```

5.
```
Private Sub cmdDraw_Click()
    'Draw a circle in the center of the picture box
    picOutput.Scale (-10, 10)-(10, -10)
    picOutput.Circle (0, 0), 4
End Sub
```

7.
```
Private Sub cmdDraw_Click()
    Dim maxX As Single, maxY As Single, x As Single
    'Graph the Square Function
    maxX = 10
    maxY = maxX * maxX
    picOutput.Cls
    picOutput.Scale (-0.2 * maxX, 1.2 * maxY)-(1.2 * maxX, -0.2 * maxY)
    picOutput.Line (-0.2 * maxX, 0)-(1.2 * maxX, 0) 'Draw x-axis
    picOutput.Line (0, -0.2 * maxY)-(0, 1.2 * maxY) 'Draw y-axis
    For x = 0 To maxX Step 0.01
      picOutput.PSet (x, x * x)
    Next x
End Sub
```

Exercises 5.2

1. The word "Income" becomes the caption embedded in the top of Frame1.

3. The Check1 check box becomes unchecked.

5. The Option1 option button becomes unselected.

7. Option2 is selected (True) and Option1 is unselected (False).

9. Check boxes, list boxes, and option buttons can receive the focus.

11. Yes, the option buttons attached to a frame will become invisible if the frame is made invisible.

13. The currently selected item, Mozart, in lstBox is displayed in picOutput.

15. The last item, Tchaikovsky, from lstBox is displayed in picOutput.

17. Brahms is added to the list (after Beethoven) and is displayed in picOutput.

19. The currently selected item in lstBox is deleted.

21. All items are removed from lstBox.

23.
```
Private Sub cmdDisplay_Click()
    Dim numChecked As Integer
    numChecked = 0
    If Check1.Value = 1 Then
        numChecked = numChecked + 1
    End If
    If Check2.Value = 1 Then
        numChecked = numChecked + 1
    End If
    If Check3.Value = 1 Then
        numChecked = numChecked + 1
    End If
    picOutput.Cls
    picOutput.Print "You have checked"; numChecked; "check box";
    If numChecked <> 1 Then
        picOutput.Print "es."
      Else
        picOutput.Print "."
    End If
End Sub
```

25.
```
Private Sub cmdDisplay_Click ()
    Dim i As Integer, total As Single
    total = 0
    For i = 0 to lstNumbers.ListCount - 1
      total = total + Val(lstNumbers.List(i))
    Next i
    picOutput.Print "The average of the numbers is";
    picOutput.Print total / lstNumbers.ListCount
End Sub
```

27.
```
Private Sub cmdDisplay_Click ()
    Dim i As Integer
    For i = 0 to lstNumbers.ListCount - 1 Step 2
      picOutput.Print lstNumbers.List(i)
    Next i
End Sub
```

29.
```
Private Sub cmdDisplay_Click ()
    Dim i As Integer, largest As Single, smallest As Single
    largest = Val(lstNumbers.List(0))
    smallest = largest
    For i = 1 to lstNumbers.ListCount - 1
      If Val(lstNumbers.List(i)) < smallest Then
          smallest = Val(lstNumbers.List(i))
      End If
      If Val(lstNumbers.List(i)) > largest Then
          largest = Val(lstNumbers.List(i))
      End If
    Next i
    picOutput.Print "The spread of the numbers is"; largest - smallest
End Sub
```

35.

Object	Property	Setting
frmStates	Caption	State Facts
lstStates	Sorted	True
picStates		

```
'In (Declarations) section of (General)
Dim nickName(1 to 4) As String, motto(1 to 4) As String

Private Sub Form_Load()
  Dim i As Integer, state As String
  Open "Stateinf.txt" For Input As #1
  For i = 1 To 4
    Input #1, state, nickName(i), motto(i)
    lstStates.AddItem state
    lstStates.ItemData(lstStates.NewIndex) = i
  Next i
  Close #1
End Sub


Private Sub lstStates_DblClick()
  picStates.Cls
  picStates.Print "Nickname: "; nickName(lstStates.ItemData(lstStates.ListIndex))
  picStates.Print "Motto: "; motto(lstStates.ItemData(lstStates.ListIndex))
End Sub
```

37.
```
Private Sub cmdAdd_Click()
  Dim item As String, tmp As String
  Dim index As Integer, numItems As Integer
  'Insert an item into the list above the current selection.
  'If there is no selection, add to the top
  item = InputBox("Item to Add:")
  index = lstBox.ListIndex
  If index < 0 Then
      index = 0
  End If
  numItems = lstBox.ListCount
  lstBox.AddItem item, index
  lblNumItems.Caption = Trim(Str(lstBox.ListCount))
  lstBox.SetFocus
End Sub


Private Sub cmdDelete_Click()
  'Delete an item from the list
  If (lstBox.ListCount > 0) And (lstBox.ListIndex >= 0) Then
      lstBox.RemoveItem lstBox.ListIndex
  End If
  lblNumItems.Caption = Trim(Str(lstBox.ListCount))
  lstBox.SetFocus
End Sub
```

Exercises 5.3

1.

Object	Property	Setting
datCountries	DatabaseName	Megacty1.mdb
	RecordSource	Countries
lstCountries		
cmdList	Caption	List Countries

```
Private Sub cmdList_Click()
  datCountries.Recordset.MoveFirst
  Do While Not datCountries.Recordset.EOF
    lstCountries.AddItem _
    datCountries.Recordset.Fields("country").Value
    datCountries.Recordset.MoveNext
  Loop
End Sub
```

3.

Object	Property	Setting
datCities	DatabaseName	Megacty1.mdb
	RecordSource	Cities
lstCities		
cmdList	Caption	List Megacities

```
Private Sub cmdList_Click()
  datCities.Recordset.MoveFirst
  Do While Not datCities.Recordset.EOF
    If datCities.Recordset.Fields("pop2015").Value > 20 Then
      lstCities.AddItem _
              datCities.Recordset.Fields("city").Value
    End If
    datCities.Recordset.MoveNext
  Loop
End Sub
```

15. 5

17. 727

29.

Object	Property	Setting
frmConversion	Caption	Conversion Calculator
datRates	Caption	Rates
	DatabaseName	Exchrate.mdb
	RecordSource	Rates
lblAmount	Caption	Amount of Money to Convert
txtAmount	Text	1
cmdCalculate	Caption	Calculate
lstFrom		
lstTO		
lblFROM	Caption	FROM:
lblTO	Caption	TO:
picResult		

```
Dim fromRates(0 To 54) As Single
Dim toRates(0 To 54) As Single

Private Sub cmdCalculate_Click()
  Dim fromRate As Single, toRate As Single
  picResult.Cls
  fromRate = fromRates(lstFROM.ItemData(lstFROM.ListIndex))
  toRate = toRates(lstTO.ItemData(lstTO.ListIndex))
  picResult.Print Val(txtAmount); lstFROM.Text; " = "; _
    FormatNumber(txtAmount * (toRate / fromRate)); " " & lstTO.Text
End Sub

Private Sub cmdShow_Click()
  Dim index As Integer
  datRates.Recordset.MoveFirst
  index = 0
  Do While Not datRates.Recordset.EOF
    lstFROM.AddItem datRates.Recordset.Fields("Name").Value
    lstFROM.ItemData(lstFROM.NewIndex) = index
    fromRates(index) = datRates.Recordset.Fields("DollarRate").Value
    lstTO.AddItem datRates.Recordset.Fields("Name").Value
    lstTO.ItemData(lstFROM.NewIndex) = index
    toRates(index) = datRates.Recordset.Fields("DollarRate").Value
    datRates.Recordset.MoveNext
    index = index + 1
  Loop
End Sub
```

Exercises 5.4

1. Could cause a problem if the country added is not one of the countries in the Countries table

3. No problem

5. Au_ID

7. ISBN

9. None

11. (B)

13. (A)

15. (D)

17. (C)

19. `SELECT * FROM Countries WHERE country Like 'I*' ORDER BY pop1995 ASC`

21. `SELECT country, currency FROM Countries WHERE pop1995>100 AND pop1995<200 ORDER BY pop1995 ASC`

23. `SELECT * FROM Cities WHERE country='China' ORDER BY pop2015 DESC`

25. `SELECT * FROM Cities WHERE pop1995>15 AND pop1995<16 ORDER BY pop1995 ASC, pop2015 ASC`

27.
```
SELECT city, Cities.pop2015, currency
FROM Cities INNER JOIN Countries
ON Countries.country=Cities.country
WHERE Countries.country='India'
ORDER BY pop2015 DESC
```

INDEX

ACCOMPANYING CD

The CD in this book contains the files needed to install the Working Model Edition of Visual Basic 6.0. To install the software, follow the steps in the first part of Appendix B.

In addition, the CD contains all the programs from the examples and case studies of this textbook, most of the txt files needed for the exercises, and several bmp (picture) files. The programs (and txt files) are contained in the folder Programs, in subfolders called CH2, CH3, CH4, and CH5. The picture files are contained in the folder Pictures. We recommend that you copy the entire contents of the folder Programs onto your hard drive or a diskette.

Each program has a name of the form chapter-section-number.vbp For instance, the program in Chapter 3, Section 2, Example 4 has the name 3-2-4.vbp. Many of the programs make use of txt files that are also in the subfolder. When one of these programs accesses a text file, the filespec for the text file is preceded with App.Path. This tells Visual Basic to look for the program in the folder from which the program has been opened.

END-USER LICENSE AGREEMENT FOR MICROSOFT SOFTWARE

IMPORTANT—READ CAREFULLY: This Microsoft End-User License Agreement ("EULA") is a legal agreement between you (either an individual or a single entity) and Microsoft Corporation for the Microsoft software product identified above, which includes computer software and may include associated media, printed materials, and "online" or electronic documentation ("SOFTWARE PRODUCT"). The SOFTWARE PRODUCT also includes any updates and supplements to the original SOFTWARE PRODUCT provided to you by Microsoft. Any software provided along with the SOFTWARE PRODUCT that is associated with a separate end-user license agreement is licensed to you under the terms of that license agreement. By installing, copying, downloading, accessing or otherwise using the SOFTWARE PRODUCT, you agree to be bound by the terms of this EULA. If you do not agree to the terms of this EULA, do not install , copy , or otherwise use the SOFTWARE PRODUCT.

Software PRODUCT LICENSE

The SOFTWARE PRODUCT is protected by copyright laws and international copyright treaties, as well as other intellectual property laws and treaties. The SOFTWARE PRODUCT is licensed, not sold.

1. GRANT OF LICENSE. This EULA grants you the following rights:

1.1 **License Grant.** You may install and use one copy of the SOFTWARE PRODUCT on a single computer. You may also store or install a copy of the SOFTWARE PRODUCT on a storage device, such as a network server, used only to install or run the SOFTWARE PRODUCT over an internal network; however, you must acquire and dedicate a license for each separate computer on or from which the SOFTWARE PRODUCT is installed, used, accessed, displayed or run.

1.2 **Academic Use.** You must be a "Qualified Educational User" to use the SOFTWARE PRODUCT in the manner described in this section. To determine whether you are a Qualified Educational User, please contact the Microsoft Sales Information Center/One Microsoft Way/Redmond, WA 98052-6399 or the Microsoft subsidiary serving your country. If you are a Qualified Educational User, you may either:

(i) exercise the rights granted in Section 1.1, OR

(ii) if you intend to use the SOFTWARE PRODUCT solely for instructional purposes in connection with a class or other educational program, this EULA grants you the following alternative license models:

(A) Per Computer Model. For every valid license you have acquired for the SOFTWARE PRODUCT, you may install a single copy of the SOFTWARE PRODUCT on a single computer for access and use by an unlimited number of student end users at your educational institution, provided that all such end users comply with all other terms of this EULA, OR

(B) Per License Model. If you have multiple licenses for the SOFTWARE PRODUCT, then at any time you may have as many copies of the SOFTWARE PRODUCT in use as you have licenses, provided that such use is limited to student or faculty end users at your educational institution and provided that all such end users comply with all other terms of this EULA. For purposes of this subsection, the SOFTWARE PRODUCT is "in use" on a computer when it is loaded into the temporary memory (i.e., RAM) or installed into the permanent memory (e.g., hard disk, CD ROM, or other storage device) of that computer, except that a copy installed on a network server for the sole purpose of distribution to other computers is not "in use". If the anticipated number of users of the SOFTWARE PRODUCT will exceed the number of applicable licenses, then you must have a reasonable mechanism or process in place to ensure that the number of persons using the SOFTWARE PRODUCT concurrently does not exceed the number of licenses.

2. DESCRIPTION OF OTHER RIGHTS AND LIMITATIONS.

- **Limitations on Reverse Engineering, Decompilation, and Disassembly.** You may not reverse engineer, decompile, or disassemble the SOFTWARE PRODUCT, except and only to the extent that such activity is expressly permitted by applicable law notwithstanding this limitation.

- **Separation of Components.** The SOFTWARE PRODUCT is licensed as a single product. Its component parts may not be separated for use on more than one computer.

- **Rental.** You may not rent, lease or lend the SOFTWARE PRODUCT.
- **Trademarks.** This EULA does not grant you any rights in connection with any trademarks or service marks of Mirosoft
- **Software Transfer.** The initial user of the SOFTWARE PRODUCT may make a one-time permanent transfer of this EULA and SOFTWARE PRODUCT only directly to an end user. This transfer must include all of the SOFTWARE PRODUCT (including all component parts, the media and printed materials, any upgrades, this EULA, and, if applicable, the Certificate of Authenticity). Such transfer may not be by way of consignment or any other indirect transfer. The transferee of such one-time transfer must agree to comply with the terms of this EULA, including the obligation not to further transfer this EULA and SOFTWARE PRODUCT.
- **Termination.** Without prejudice to any other rights, Microsoft may terminate this EULA if you fail to comply with the terms and conditions of this EULA. In such event, you must destroy all copies of the SOFTWARE PRODUCT and all of its component parts.

4. **COPYRIGHT.** All title and intellectual property rights in and to the SOFTWARE PRODUCT (including but not limited to any images, photographs, animations, video, audio, music, text, and "applets" incorporated into the SOFTWARE PRODUCT), the accompanying printed materials, and any copies of the SOFTWARE PRODUCT are owned by Microsoft or its suppliers. All title and intellectual property rights in and to the content which may be accessed through use of the SOFTWARE PRODUCT is the property of the respective content owner and may be protected by applicable copyright or other intellectual property laws and treaties. This EULA grants you no rights to use such content. All rights not expressly granted are reserved by Microsoft.

5. **BACKUP COPY.** After installation of one copy of the SOFTWARE PRODUCT pursuant to this EULA, you may keep the original media on which the SOFTWARE PRODUCT was provided by Microsoft solely for backup or archival purposes. If the original media is required to use the SOFTWARE PRODUCT on the COMPUTER, you may make one copy of the SOFTWARE PRODUCT solely for backup or archival purposes. Except as expressly provided in this EULA, you may not otherwise make copies of the SOFTWARE PRODUCT or the printed materials accompanying the SOFTWARE PRODUCT.

6. **U.S. GOVERNMENT RESTRICTED RIGHTS.** The SOFTWARE PRODUCT and documentation are provided with RESTRICTED RIGHTS. Use, duplication, or disclosure by the Government is subject to restrictions as set forth in subparagraph (c)(1)(ii) of the Rights in Technical Data and Computer Software clause at DFARS 252.227-7013 or subparagraphs (c)(1) and (2) of the Commercial Computer Software—Restricted Rights at 48 CFR 52.227-19, as applicable. Manufacturer is Microsoft Corporation/One Microsoft Way/Redmond, WA 98052-6399.

7. **EXPORT RESTRICTIONS.** You agree that you will not export or re-export the SOFTWARE PRODUCT, any part thereof, or any process or service that is the direct product of the SOFTWARE PRODUCT (the foregoing collectively referred to as the "Restricted Components"), to any country, person, entity or end user subject to U.S. export restrictions. You specifically agree not to export or re-export any of the Restricted Components (i) to any country to which the U.S. has embargoed or restricted the export of goods or services, which currently include, but are not necessarily limited to Cuba, Iran, Iraq, Libya, North Korea, Sudan and Syria, or to any national of any such country, wherever located, who intends to transmit or transport the Restricted Components back to such country; (ii) to any end-user who you know or have reason to know will utilize the Restricted Components in the design, development or production of nuclear, chemical or biological weapons; or (iii) to any end-user who has been prohibited from participating in U.S. export transactions by any federal agency of the U.S. government. You warrant and represent that neither the BXA nor any other U.S. federal agency has suspended, revoked, or denied your export privileges.

8. **NOTE ON JAVA SUPPORT.** THE SOFTWARE PRODUCT MAY CONTAIN SUPPORT FOR PROGRAMS WRITTEN IN JAVA. JAVA TECHNOLOGY IS NOT FAULT TOLERANT AND IS NOT DESIGNED, MANUFACTURED, OR INTENDED FOR USE OR RESALE AS ON-LINE CONTROL EQUIPMENT IN HAZARDOUS ENVIRONMENTS REQUIRING FAIL-SAFE PERFORMANCE, SUCH AS IN THE OPERATION OF NUCLEAR FACILITIES, AIRCRAFT NAVIGATION OR COMMUNICATION SYSTEMS, AIR TRAFFIC CONTROL, DIRECT LIFE SUPPORT MACHINES, OR WEAPONS SYSTEMS, IN WHICH THE FAILURE OF JAVA TECHNOLOGY COULD LEAD DIRECTLY TO DEATH, PERSONAL INJURY, OR SEVERE PHYSICAL OR ENVIRONMENTAL DAMAGE.

MISCELLANEOUS

If you acquired this product in the United States, this EULA is governed by the laws of the State of Washington.

If you acquired this product in Canada, this EULA is governed by the laws of the Province of Ontario, Canada. Each of the parties hereto irrevocably attorns to the jurisdiction of the courts of the Province of Ontario and further agrees to commence any litigation which may arise hereunder in the courts located in the Judicial District of York, Province of Ontario.

If this product was acquired outside the United States, then local law may apply.

Should you have any questions concerning this EULA, or if you desire to contact Microsoft for any reason, please contact Microsoft, or write: Microsoft Sales Information Center/One Microsoft Way/ Redmond, WA 98052-6399.

LIMITED WARRANTY

LIMITED WARRANTY. Microsoft warrants that (a) the SOFTWARE PRODUCT will perform substantially in accordance with the accompanying written materials for a period of ninety (90) days from the date of receipt, and (b) any Support Services provided by Microsoft shall be substantially as described in applicable written materials provided to you by Microsoft, and Microsoft support engineers will make commercially reasonable efforts to solve any problem. To the extent allowed by applicable law, implied warranties on the SOFTWARE PRODUCT, if any, are limited to ninety (90) days. Some states/jurisdictions do not allow limitations on duration of an implied warranty, so the above limitation may not apply to you.

CUSTOMER REMEDIES. Microsoft's and its suppliers' entire liability and your exclusive remedy shall be, at Microsoft's option, either (a) return of the price paid, if any, or (b) repair or replacement of the SOFTWARE PRODUCT that does not meet Microsoft's Limited Warranty and that is returned to Microsoft with a copy of your receipt. This Limited Warranty is void if failure of the SOFTWARE PRODUCT has resulted from accident, abuse, or misapplication. Any replacement SOFTWARE PRODUCT will be warranted for the remainder of the original warranty period or thirty (30) days, whichever is longer. Outside the United States, neither these remedies nor any product support services offered by Microsoft are available without proof of purchase from an authorized international source.

NO OTHER WARRANTIES. To the maximum extent permitted by applicable law, Microsoft and its suppliers disclaim all other warranties and conditions, either express or implied, including, but not limited to, implied warranties OR CONDITIONS of merchantability, fitness for a particular purpose, title and non-infringement, with regard to the SOFTWARE PRODUCT, and the provision of or failure to provide Support Services. This limited warranty gives you specific legal rights. You may have others, which vary from state/jurisdiction to state/jurisdiction.

LIMITATION OF LIABILITY. TO THE MAXIMUM EXTENT PERMITTED BY APPLICA- BLE LAW, IN NO EVENT SHALL MICROSOFT OR ITS SUPPLIERS BE LIABLE FOR ANY SPECIAL, INCIDENTAL, INDIRECT, OR CONSEQUENTIAL DAMAGES WHATSOEVER (INCLUDING, WITHOUT LIMITATION, DAMAGES FOR LOSS OF BUSINESS PROFITS, BUSINESS INTERRUPTION, LOSS OF BUSINESS INFORMATION, OR ANY OTHER PECUNIARY LOSS) ARISING OUT OF THE USE OF OR INABILITY TO USE THE SOFT- WARE PRODUCT OR THE FAILURE TO PROVIDE SUPPORT SERVICES, EVEN IF MICROSOFT HAS BEEN ADVISED OF THE POSSIBILITY OF SUCH DAMAGES. IN ANY CASE, MICROSOFT'S ENTIRE LIABILITY UNDER ANY PROVISION OF THIS EULA SHALL BE LIMITED TO THE GREATER OF THE AMOUNT ACTUALLY PAID BY YOU FOR THE SOFTWARE PRODUCT OR U.S.$5.00; PROVIDED, HOWEVER, IF YOU HAVE ENTERED INTO A MICROSOFT SUPPORT SERVICES AGREEMENT, MICROSOFT'S ENTIRE LIABILITY REGARDING SUPPORT SERVICES SHALL BE GOVERNED BY THE TERMS OF THAT AGREEMENT. BECAUSE SOME STATES/JURISDICTIONS DO NOT ALLOW THE EXCLUSION OR LIMITATION OF LIABILITY, THE ABOVE LIMITATION MAY NOT APPLY TO YOU.